Library of Congress Control Number: 2011904553
ISBN: 978-0-9835820-2-1

Copies of this book are available on Amazon.com

OUR HADELAND ANCESTORS
VOLUME ONE

Editor
Anne Sladky

Book Committee
Evonne Anderson
Sharon Arends
Barb Schmitt
Joy Sundrum

Dedicated to Peder H. Nelson
Editor of the *Brua* 1931-1951

In the 1937 issue of the *Brua*, page 33, Peder wrote:

"The pioneer history of Hadeland immigrants in *Vesterheim* (Home in the West) is so valuable that it ought to be published in the *Brua* so that it does not go into the *glemmeboken* (literally: the forgotten book or the oblivion book). In our *Brua*, your stories will be preserved so that future generations – on both sides of the ocean – will be able to read them in the future. Send in your reminiscences now, before they are forgotten."

Brua Editor Verlyn Anderson took this wise counsel to heart and introduced the "Our Hadeland Ancestors" column in 1997. Since that time, dozens of our members have shared the stories of their immigrant ancestors in our newsletter's pages. These stories have now been brought together in two special volumes. We trust that Peder Nelson would be pleased with all of our efforts to preserve the stories of "Our Hadeland Ancestors."

Peder Nelson's biography can be found on page 215 of this volume.

Table of Contents

VOLUME TWO

Acknowledgements

Contributors

The following lag members, their family members, and friends of the lag wrote or submitted the immigrant ancestor stories found in volume one: Harland Anderson, Paul Anderson, Verlyn Anderson, Etta Hokenstad Berge, Jane Brosius, Kari-Mette Stavhaug Avtjern, Norman Brynsaas, Delores Cleveland, Esther Grianger Embrey, Dorothy Evens, Frank Evenson, J. H. Fonkert, Ann Urness Gesme, Mary Margaret Rekstad Gibson, Shaun Gibson, John Gilbertson, Marie Gleason, Myron A. Gnadt, Eddie Goplin, Larry Grinaker, Paul Grinaker, Lynne Hogan, David Halbakken, Jan Heusinkveld, Ruth Holtan, Harald Hvattum, Dean Johnson, Shirley Kanten, Maren Koller, George R. and Nila Anderson Krenos, Jan McKeown, Doris Stark Morland, Terje Nilsen, Howard Bernett Norland, Lawrence Onsager, Cindy Ostlie, Laurel and Barry Peterson, David Pfeffer, Bruce Plomasen, Alton Quanbeck, Diane Resvick, Leslie Rogne, Frances Lynne Ronning, Georgia Rosendahl, Robert Rosendahl, Richard Rowe, Tanya Rylee, Karen Schau-Stein, Anne Sladky, Dean Sorum, Helge Stenersen, Pauline Stowman, Oliver Thingelstad, Diane Teigen, Donald Thompson, Beverly Jean-Ohe Tolle, Andy Tweito, Denise Wallack, Luann Ward, and Beverly Webster.

Special Thanks

The committee wishes to express its gratitude to

> ➢ Kari-Mette Avtjern and the staff of the Hadeland Folkemuseum for permission to include their articles about Hadeland emigrants in this book.
> ➢ Dr. Verlyn Anderson, *Brua* editor since 1992, who introduced the "Our Hadeland Ancestors" column in February 1997 and has championed the efforts to collect these valuable stories for almost 20 years.
> ➢ Ole Gamme for his tireless work on the Kontaktforum Emigrant Identification Project and for compiling the lists of veterans of the Civil War and World War I.

About the Cover

In 1921, the Hadeland Lag met in Northwood, North Dakota. The book cover uses a portrion of the panoramic picture taken of those in attendance. The original framed picture is now held by the Norwegian-American Historical Association at St. Olaf College, Northfield, Minnesota. A complete high-resolution digital copy can be viewed on-line at

http://www.naha.stolaf.edu/archivesdata/images/panorama/Hadeland1924.htm

Introduction

"Our Hadeland Ancestors" has since its inception been a favorite feature of the *Brua*. It has flourished because of the willingness of our members to share not just dates and places but also the photographs and remembrances of generations past.

For their descendants, the profiles of *Hadelanding* foreparents help explain and put into context family traditions, experiences, and relationships. On another level, the stories come together to create a great saga of the Hadeland emigrant experience. In writing down, sharing, and reading their stories, we bear witness to the dreams, determination, courage, family, and faith that allowed our Hadeland ancestors to put down the roots of our American families in this new land.

One of the primary missions of the Hadeland Lag is to preserve the history of Hadelanders in America. We all owe a debt of thanks to our members' continuing commitment to writing down oral history, carefully researching historical records and, most importantly, sharing the results. Kontaktforum Hadeland-America's Emigrant Identification Project has identified over 11,000 Hadeland emigrants, so there are many more stories left to tell!

In these two volumes, the biographical articles have been roughly ordered by date of publication, with some attempt made to group stories about members of the same family together. As a result, most – but not all - of the many stories submitted specifically for this project can be found in Volume Two. As well as being included in this collection, all of the new submissions will eventually find their way into the pages of the *Brua*.

A reference to the Kontaktforum Hadeland-America Emigrant Identification Project family record (form#) is included in the header or body of each story. These forms may provide additional biographical information. The Kontaktforum Hadeland-Amerika Emigrant Identification Project database and associated forms are available to lag members in the Limited Access Archive on the Hadeland Lag website, www.hadelandlag.org.

Anne Sladky, Editor

Peder Anders Pedersen Lynne

published November 1988   *Form 51*   *Frances Lynne Ronning*

My father, Peder Anders Pederson (Lynne) was born on January 14, 1871 at Gran in Hadeland, Norway. He was baptized and confirmed in the same Sister Church where his father, sisters and brother are buried. Local Norwegians tell the tale of how the second of the Sister Churches was built within fifty feet of the other, when the two sisters could no longer agree.

Peder came to America in 1887 at the age of 16, under the sponsorship of Peder Cornelius, a farmer living near Clarkfield in Lisbon Township, Minnesota. As I remember my father telling me, Mr. Cornelius had sent $50 to him in Norway, to get help on his farm in Minnesota. My father worked for Mr. Cornelius for two years.

My father was a very quiet man, who was content just to sit and listen. He never wrote to his family (perhaps because he had very little schooling) or ever went back to Norway. We children would often ask him if he didn't want to go back to see his folks, but all we could get from him was a "NO." He did, however, talk about his sick brother and his Dad, but he never mentioned any of the other family members.

At family reunions, my mother Florence (nee Kirkeby Grinager) always had brothers, uncles, aunts and cousins attending. This must have been a very lonesome time for him, as all he had were us six children, his immediate family in America, consisting of four boys and two girls, myself being the youngest of the family. The six included one step-son from my mother's first marriage. Her first husband died in 1900.

My father and mother were married in Madison, Lac qui Parle County, Minnesota, on December 13, 1908, and they farmed in that area for several years.

Our oldest daughter, Barbara, was compiling a family tree, but was unsuccessful in obtaining any information about the Pederson (Lynne) side here in the U.S.A. She wrote to Lillehammer in Norway and received an answer stating that Peder Anders Pederson (Lynne) had two sisters and two brothers. This was the first time that I had any knowledge that my father had sisters or more than one brother in Norway.

We, my husband Jim and I, had several times talked about going to Norway, but we never did. However, in 1978, our youngest daughter, Susan, came home and said "I'm going to Norway. Are you coming with?" We both said, "YES, WE ARE GOING TO NORWAY."

After some sightseeing, including a fjord trip, we headed to Gran, Hadeland. After arriving by train, we asked the depot agent at Gran if there was a restaurant close by. "Yes," he said, "there is a cafeteria up on the hill and there you can get some coffee." Our waitress asked us if we were looking for relatives. We told her that my father had come from Gran and she suggested that we meet her sister and her husband, as they loved helping people find their relatives. Ten minutes later her sister, Beret Skiaker, walked in.

I asked Mrs. Skiaker if she knew Jan Olsen, the father of a foreign exchange student at Rochester, Minnesota, who had been a dinner guest at our home only two days before. She said, "Yes, he is our neighbor."

Jan and Gudrun Olsen, of whom we knew only their daughter, opened their home to us, and we stayed with them for three days and nights, as they and the Skiakers tried to help us find my ancestors. Paul would be so excited when he came over to the Olsen's each evening to tell us what he had found. Gudrun Olsen would drive us over the countryside during the day.

We went to the Sister Churches and found the graves of my relatives. The church caretaker said he thought we were probably relatives. It turned out that his father and I were third cousins.

It was a great feeling to walk upon the homestead trails where my father had walked some 90 years before. As I picked up a few stones to keep, I thought that he, too, might have stepped on these very stones. Gudrun informed us that if we had come one year earlier, her mother could have told us everything about my father and his family.

The Skiakers had a big gathering for us and for as many of my relatives as could be found. I now had two first cousins and many second cousins in Norway. It was like opening a door to a new world.

Kari Bakken, my cousin, and her son, Karsten, visited us at Easter in 1979, and my second cousin, Eva Eriksen and her husband, Sven, and their family visited us during the summer of 1987, having celebrated their 25th wedding anniversary at that time.

Finding my father's relatives in Norway has been a great and wonderful experience, not only for myself but for my family as well. Along with our youngest daughter, Susan, who accompanied us to Norway in 1978, our oldest daughter, Barbara and her daughter, Tamara, visited Norway in 1986. Our youngest son, Steven, and his wife Jean, will be going to Norway next May for a high school graduation of one of our relatives.

Tracing and finding your ancestors in Norway is extremely rewarding. Don't miss the opportunity.

The Schiager Family

A project in American History at St. Olaf College, Northfield, Minnesota
published May 1993 Form 271 *Howard Bernett Norland*
Written January 16, 1952

Paul Schiager was born March 18, 1835, in Hadeland, Norway. His parents, Gunder and Mari, operated a small farm. There has always been a controversy as to whether Gunder or his father came from Germany, for SCHIAGER is certainly a German name. Paul, as a young man, helped his father on the farm and attended a nearby common school. But, because he was an adventurous youth, he left the farm and went to Christiania to work. I do not know what kind of work he pursued there. When he returned, he found that his brother Simen was engaged to a very attractive girl whose name was Goro Gamme. More experienced and polished, Paul won his brother's girl away from him and married her in 1863.

Goro Gamme was the daughter of Iver and Rangdi Gamme, wealthy landowners in Hadeland. She, as a girl, was not used to the hard work and toil of the farm and household since her parents had servants to take care of the household and hired hands to work the farm. She later, however, proved that she was capable of hard labor.

Goro and Paul, after they were married, began farming land her parents had given them. But Paul, eager to try something new and craving adventure, persuaded Goro to go to America. They sailed with Simen and two tiny children to America in 1866 on one of the first steamships to cross the Atlantic. They arrived in New York, a bit amazed, but anxious to travel on to the frontier. One of their neighbors, who had gone to America a few years earlier, lived in Winneshiek County, Iowa, so they went there. They got jobs as hired hands on a farm so that Paul could learn the techniques that were employed in America. They lived in the same house as the family they worked for.

Goro was to work along with the men in order for them to live there. She soon learned to do farm chores and proved to be a very good worker. They had lived there about two years when one early spring morning, while Goro was out milking, her baby woke up and began to cry. The lady of the house had company and so, not to disturb her guests, she put the baby out on the front steps. When Goro returned to the house after milking, she took her baby into the house and asked the lady why she had done such a foolish thing. When Goro heard her reply, she wrapped the baby up, went out and called Paul and Simen, and told them she refused to stay with such an inconsiderate woman. They had been receiving letters from their parents, and Goro's family wanted them to return. Goro's father promised them that he would set Paul up in business if he so desired. After much discussion and after Paul had emphatically stated that

3

he would not return to Norway, they decided to go out to Dakota Territory where they had heard there was good land.

They then went into the house, packed their few belongings, bundled up their children, and crawled into the covered wagon they had bought from a neighboring farmer. They traveled across the treeless prairie to the Dakota Territory, stopping at farm houses at night. They arrived in the latter part of June, 1868, in Canton, South Dakota, which then consisted of only seven sod shanties, and they were taken in by an old Norwegian farmer. Paul and Simen secured land, one mile north and one and one-half miles east of Canton, and set to work making a dugout home in a side hill. After the house was completed, neighboring farm families gave them enough food and necessary equipment to get along. The family moved in, and the men began farming their newly acquired land.

After a time they built a one-room shanty from wood they hauled from the Sioux River Valley. Paul and Simen drove oxen to Sioux City twice a year to get their wheat ground and get the necessary supplies. At that time there were many Indians living near and, when any of them came, it was essential to feed them as much as they wanted.

While Paul and Simen were gone on one of their bi-yearly trips, seven Indians came and ate almost all the food in the house. Fearing that more would come expecting hospitality, which she had none to give, Goro took her children – Gunder was born a year after they had come to Canton – and walked to the nearest farm house which was two miles away. When Paul and Simen returned after their 7-day trip – it took three days to go down, one day to transact their business, and three days to make the trip back – finding no one home, they rushed immediately to their neighbors and, much to their relief, found the family safe.

They were so hard-pressed for good food that oftentimes the family made a meal out of cooked potatoes and milk. On Sundays they always attempted to have a decent meal including meat. In those days it was customary that the people living near the church feed those who had a long way to go. Since the Schiagers lived only two and one-half miles from Canton, every Sunday they had guests – sometimes numbering up in the twenties.

Goro continued helping the men with the farm work when she could. When the older children were big enough to take care of the younger, she spent most of her time outside. When she was nursing a baby, the oldest child, Rangdi, would carry the baby out to the field. Goro would stop her work and nurse it, and Rangdi would carry the baby back to the house.

In spite of the hardship and setbacks, Goro and Paul raised six children. One child died when only seven months old. Clara was the third to the youngest child and was born August 5, 1873. Clara, my grandmother, married E.J. Canton and moved to Watson, Minnesota, in 1895.

Paul Schiager died in 1900 and Simen, Paul's brother, in 1905 married his old girl Goro. They lived together for 13 years. Goro died in 1918 and Simen on December 21, 1932 at the age of 94 years and 4 months.

Birch Bark Bread – The Brynsaas Family

published November 1995   *Form 431*   *Luann Ward & Norman Brynsaas*

This is a story about the emigration of the Brynsaas family to Iowa as written by the granddaughter of Norman and Mae Brynsaas, Luann Ward. The family helped with the founding of the Glenwood Church in rural Decorah, Iowa.

My great-great-grandfather was a *husmann* which was a disadvantaged class of people who paid rent to the large landowner in work rather than money. Another disadvantaged situation for some Norwegians dealt with titles residing in the heads of families, under a system called *odelsrett*. Upon the owner's death there was no subdivision of land. The eldest son inherited the property, leaving younger sons without the means of income. Situations like these brought poverty to many Norwegian families. From the destitution came "Birch Bark Bread." My grandfather told me about "Birth Bark Bread" with teary eyes. He said that his father's mother would grind the bark of a birch tree until it was fine enough to use as flour to make bread to help feed the family.

The hardship conditions during the 19th century in Norway persuaded many of the Norwegian people to leave their home soils for the cities and prairies of America. My grandfather said those family members who were settled in America would send money back to Norway to help feed the family members left behind. Favorable reports from America were bound to emphasize the shortcomings or the snail-like progress of Norway and make America look very attractive.

The Brynsaas family also wanted the American Dream, for in 1874 they departed from their small farming community located in Hadeland, Norway, to travel to America, the land of opportunity.

John Brynsaas, the head of the family, was a tall slender man who was very quiet but very hardworking and strong in his faith. John's wife, Pernille, was a strong woman with a large body frame who oddly enough smoked a clay pipe. John, Pernille and their three children, the oldest being Hans, age 6, who was my Grandpa (Norman) Brynsaas's father, boarded the steamship *S.S. Dagmar* at the Port of Kristiania, now Oslo.

In preparation for the long voyage Pernille packed a trunk of needed supplies and cherished belongings for the Brynsaas family. The trunk was rather old but very strong and had a rounded lid known as a camel back trunk. The reason for the camel back trunk was so that other trunks could not be piled on top of theirs, enabling them to get at much-needed supplies. Inside the trunk that Pernille packed we might find cheese, flatbread, lefse and dried fruit for the family to eat, as well as clothing, yarn, quilts, a washboard, candle holder and candle for reading by night, family Bible, school books for the children and cherished pictures of family left behind in Norway.

On the *S.S. Dagmar* they traveled by way of Liverpool, England, on to Quebec, Canada, where their voyage ended. The ocean journey experience was not a major ordeal but a thrilling adventure, because by mid-century the voyage had become safer and speedier. We believe that the Brynsaas family was met by family members and traveled by covered wagon west to the Mississippi River, perhaps crossed on the ferry at Lansing and then on to Decorah.

John and Pernille Brynsaas purchased a small farm among the hills and valleys east of Decorah known as Glenwood. Many families from Hadeland had already settled in this area. I am sure that this must have helped the Brynsaas family feel more comfortable in their new land, never letting each other forget about their native land of rock and fjords that they left behind.

The Brynsaas family, along with the other Norwegian immigrants, had many hardships to endure. They now had to build their own homes, farm the land and feed their families. They also had to learn about the United States, its history, its language, its schools and churches, its governmental mechanics and the role of politics. Most settlers could not deal with matters of state and national concern until their immediate problems as pioneers had been solved.

A change that the Norwegian immigrants had to adapt to was in their churches. The Norwegians were from the Lutheran faith and in Norway, the government paid for the church expenses as well as hiring the pastor. The settlers now had the opportunity to build their own church, elect their own church officials, and hire a pastor of their choice. It would all sound very exciting, but would take much time, work and money from the settlers.

At the age of 12, Hans helped by hauling stones from the quarry to the building site of the Glenwood Lutheran Church.

As Hans grew older he took on a job as a butter maker at the Johnson Creamery and Mill located on the Gus Johnson farm in Glenwood Township, seven miles from Decorah. He often told of high water and floods on the Trout Creek while he worked there.

He earned money to send back to Norway to help the poverty-stricken Brynsaas family members still in Norway. There do not seem to be any other Brynsaas families in America nor in Norway with this name. Others emigrated from the same area in Norway with the Brynsaas family name, but changed it. Some settled in Wisconsin. One family used the name Gilbert Brynsaas-Gilbertson, another Peter Brynsaas-Peterson.

Hans was the first generation of the Brynsaas family to become Americanized, but most importantly he never forgot the Old Norway he left behind as a young boy. John and Pernille raised their family including two more children, Anton and Pauline, on their small farm outside Decorah and lived their until their deaths. Their five children all grew to adulthood in this area. Nils and Anton did not marry. Ingeborg married Theodor Bolson. Pauline married John

Tangen, also of this area. Only Hans, the oldest of this family, carried on the family name, and he did it well. He married Karen Erickson, daughter of Erick and Hanna Erickson. Hans and Karen had seven children: three daughters, Pearl, Emma and Nina; and four sons, Arthur, Henry, Edwin and Norman.

Norman Brynsaas adds this to the story written by his granddaughter:
 In 1874, John Brynsaas, with his wife Pernille and three small children, Hans, Nils and Ingeborg came to America and managed to buy a small farm among the hills and deep valleys east of Decorah. Many families from the Hadeland area had already settled in this area. This must have made them feel much at home.

   Hans often told of his experience as a young teenager helping haul stones from the quarry to the building site of the Glenwood Lutheran Church, perhaps using his father's team and wagon.

Olaf Nelson

published August 1996　　　　　　*Form 763*　　　　　　*Jane McKeown*

This article and photo appeared in the Montevideo American News, April 4, 1996

When the snow melts, uncovering the fields after the long winter, and there's a smell of newness from the black earth, Olaf Nelson makes his morning coffee stop downtown shorter than usual and heads north on Highway 29.

"I miss the farm terribly," he says. "There's no better place. The quietness, the birds singing, freedom."

Nick Hofstad, his nephew, runs the farm in a different way than Olaf used to, using a computer. "The plow is a thing you can cut up for scrap iron. The way you do it now is to leave trash on top of the field. If I'd known that years ago, it would have saved me a lot of time." But he and Nick get along well, he says.

Olaf was born on the farm across the road from his place, north and east of Montevideo. He was one of 12 children. "Dad rented his farm from Eliason Trust for 35 years, until 1947," Olaf said. "It was sold then for $55 an acre to E.H. Mogck, and I rented from him after I got married in 1948. Mother and Dad moved across the field to another place and lived there 38 years. I could have bought the farm for $50 (an acre) in 1945, but couldn't make it. I paid $250 in 1970, and now it's probably worth about $1,200."

"I remember very well the depression in '33 and '34. We haven't really seen the likes of it since. There's no comparison. I hauled oats to the Milan elevator and got 8 cents a bushel. I had to haul 1,200 bushels to get enough money to pay a note and interest to Theo. Rodeberg for building a truck box for Dad's 1931 Studebaker truck. Corn was 14 cents."

"We had livestock, and Rhoda had 400 chickens. That was the bread and butter for the table. We had cattle and hogs -- 60 stock cows at one time. Made good money some years, not so much other years. But we were always grateful because we had something to fall back on in case the crops failed. Had our own eggs, made our own bacon, baked our own bread and had a big garden. We bought milk from the neighbors across the road.

"When we started out, the land was really wet, then the ditch was dug. It's a lot different now."

"One of the things I miss most is the neighbors' banty roosters crowing. So still you could hear a needle drop there, but they put up a real musical concert. I tell you, I miss that. Especially this time of year."

Olaf also misses the sound of the church bells. "The janitor would get up early and ring in Sunday. You could hear the church bells six, seven miles away. And we knew we had two hours to get ready. A lot of older people walked to church. We'd see our neighbor, John Christianson, walking by – 3½ miles to Jevnaker. Said he got a chance on the long walk to prepare himself for taking communion."

After church – theirs at Mandt was at 2 p.m. – kids would get together in the cow pasture to play ball and the folks would sit around and visit. And we'd make waffles with thick cream – I still like them."

"Seemed like every day, someone would drive in to talk to us about farming, politics, family talk, fishing. It was very enjoyable. We had quite a few stop by." Rhoda served them coffee, sandwiches and cake around the kitchen table. "If there'd been rain the night before so we couldn't get into the fields, there'd be quite a few at our house."

Sunday afternoons Rhoda and Olaf went for a ride. "It was exciting driving by fields and seeing the corn just popping out of the fields and the beans, how they grow, to know we had planted them," Rhoda said.

Olaf sold seedcorn, too, so he wanted to see how his corn compared to competitors. "We had a slogan: 'There is no crop like corn, and no corn like Pioneer.' I had to believe that. It was the best for my fields at that time."

Nowadays, the couple keeps busy in town. "We still drive Sundays to Mandt (13 miles) for church. We wanted to build a new consolidated church on the 17-mile corner. I still think it would be a good idea," said Olaf.

But, instead, Olaf and Rhoda still attend the church where he was baptized, confirmed and married. "I'll make one more – my final trip," he says. "My folks and seven of us kids are buried there."

Retirement is good, but the pull to the farm is strong, Olaf says. "When the weather gets nice, I get spring fever. I'm carrying as much black dirt from Mandt Township under my fingernails as any farmer who lived out there. I like to get back to that dirt."

Ole Olsen Hovland & Jøran Olsdtr Haugen

published February 1997   *Form 481*   *Verlyn Anderson*

All of my mother's, Cora Hovland Anderson (1 January 1908 – 10 February 1992), ancestors immigrated from Hadeland. My great-great-grandparents, Ole Olsen and Jøran Olsdatter Haugen and their six sons all immigrated to America between 1867 and 1883. Ole and Jøran's son Nils was my mother's paternal grandfather.

Ole Olsen (b. 24 Jun 1814) and Jøran Olsdatter (b. 16 Oct 1810) were among Hadeland's poorest of the poor. They were *husmenn* who moved from farm to farm as they were able to find employment in order to make a scant livelihood. Much about Ole's birth, his parents and his youth remains shrouded in mystery. At the time of their marriage on 1 December 1835, the Gran parish records state that the marriage was between "unmarried

Ole and Joran Hovland
photo from Hadeland Ärbok

man Ole <u>Hansen</u> born in Harestuskogen, in Lunner, and living at Falangs(eie),* in Gran, son of Hans Olsen of Falangs(eie)* and unmarried Jøran Olsdatter Haugen, daughter of Ola Tufto, born in Ål, Hol parish, Hallingdal, age 25.* But research in both the Jevnaker/Lunner Parish records and in the Gran/Brandbu parish records do not reveal an Ole <u>Hansen</u>, son of a Hans Olsen, born about 1814. According to both the census of 1865 and the census of 1875, Ole <u>Hansen</u> was born in the Jevnaker/Lunner parish. Therefore, as verified by Randi Bjørkvik, well-known Hadeland genealogist, Ole must be the illegitimate son of Ole Tosen Røsterud of Gjerdrum (in Romerike) and Guri Nilsdatter Kloppa, Lunner parish. There was an Ole <u>Olsen</u> born at Kloppa on 24 June 1814 to unmarried Guri Nilsdatter Kloppa. Kloppa is in Lunner, in or near Harestuskogen. 24 June 1814 is the date that Ole consistently gives as his birthday. Guri died when Ole was only six months old. I am confident that this is my great-great-grandfather Ole because of the exact date and the location of the birth.

Who raised Ole after his mother died? Most likely it was not his father who was probably a "hired man" or servant on the Kloppa or a neighboring farm. Did his father leave and return to Romerike when he found out that Guri was pregnant? Maybe Hans Olsen Falangs(eie)* raised

*(ier) or (eie) at the end of a farm name means that the person lived on the farm, but was not a member of the owner's family. The suffix –eie or –ier means possession or owned.

him. Ole uses the name Hansen at the time of his confirmation, his marriage and at his immigration. Probably Hans Olsen was the man who acted as Ole's father, but was not his biological father. Ole must have lived somewhere after his mother died and maybe Hans was that man who provided him a home in which to grow up. More research is needed to solve that mystery!

Jøran was apparently among the many young women who walked over the mountains from Hallingdal to Hadeland in search of work. Hadeland was a rich dairy-raising area so there were job opportunities for young women working as milk maidens on large Hadeland farms. She was working as a milkmaid on the Falang farm when she married Ole. At that time Ole was working as a hired man or servant on the Øvre Helmen farm, less than a mile from the Falang farm. Both farms are in the Gran parish.

The six Hovland brothers and their wives are pictured. Left to right: Otto and Thea, Nels and Mari, Syver and Guri, Ole and Anne, Gudbrand and Guro. Hans and Marie are standing upper right. The brothers emigrated to America between 1867 and 1883. Their parents, Ole and Jøran, accompanied Otto, the last brother to emigrate to America in 1883. Ole was 69 and Jøran was 72 years old at that time. This photograph was probably taken at the time of Jøran's funeral in 1893. Hans and Gulbrand lived in Iowa; the other four brothers lived in Trondhjem Township, Otter Tail County, Minnesota.

Between 1835 and 1856, Ole and Jøran had nine children, eight sons and one daughter. Only six sons survived to adulthood. Their children were:

1) Gudbrand (b. 1 July 1835, d. 26 March 1923)
2) Ole (b. 23 December 1837, d. 24 December 1914)
3) Hans (b. 27 August 1841, d. 7 February 1915)
4) Siri (b. 1844, d. 1847)
5) Lars (b. 1847, died at 2 months of age)
6) Lars (b. 1848, died when only 6 days old)
7) Syver (b. 1 October 1849, d. 1936)
8) Nils (b. 12 March 1852, d. 14 April 1939)
9) Otto (b. 2 April 1856, d. 18 September 1918)

Gudbrand was born on 1 July 1835 on the farm Falang where his mother was a servant. His birth took place exactly five months before Ole and Jøran were married on 1 December 1835. This was not unusual among poor people in Norway at this time. Often the couple did not marry until after the first child was born. This ensured both partners that they would be able to have children who could help care for them in their old age. In other words, it was the parents' assurance of a kind of "social security."

Ole and all of the rest of his siblings, except Otto, were born on the *husmann's* place, Ulverud, which was owned by the farm Hvinden in Gran. Otto, their youngest son, was born at a *husmann's* place on the Rud farm. At the time of the 1865 and the 1875 census, Ole and Jøran and their family were living on the *husmann's* place Vestbråten which was owned by the Hovland farm, located near Roa.

The second and third sons, Ole and Hans, were the first to immigrate to America. Ole and his wife, Anna Arnesdatter Blekene(ier) and their two daughters, and his brother, Hans, left for America on 25 April 1867 on the sailing ship, *Dagmar*. They arrived in Quebec on June 7. Syver was next to leave for America. He left on 24 April 1868 on the ship *Oder*, giving the information that he was going to Lansing, Iowa. The *Oder* was a sailing ship that took him to Hull, England. From there he took a train to Liverpool where he boarded an English steamship that took him to New York. Gudbrand, his wife, Berte Halvorsdatter Prestbråten from the Jevnaker parish, and their four children left for America on 17 September 1869, also on the ship *Oder*, traveling the same route as his brother Syver had done a year earlier. Their tickets were also paid to Lansing, Iowa.

Nils, my great-grandfather, did not wait long before also deciding to migrate to America. Eight months later, in May, 1870, having just turned 18 years of age, Nils left on the ship *Hero*, bound for New York, with one *spesiedaler* (worth about one dollar or a month's salary) in his pocket. His ticket, including the food on the ship, had been paid for and sent from America.

The youngest son, Otto, was only 14 years old when his last brother left for America. He remained in Norway with his parents. In 1881 he married Margrete Hansdatter Bråstad(eie). They had a son, Hans Martin, born on 6 September 1881. Margrete died in 1882.

On 12 October 1883 Otto, together with his parents, Ole and Jøran, emigrated to Northwood, Iowa, leaving on the ship *Rollo*. Otto left his 2-year-old son, Hans Martin, with his in-laws in Hadeland. The boy died at his grandparents' home in 1892 at the age of 11. He never saw his father again.

Hovland was the family name that the first immigrants from this family adopted soon after they arrived in the United States in 1867. As the rest of the family arrived they apparently all accepted Hovland (sometimes spelled Haavland) as their family name in America. Where did they get this name? We can only guess. Most likely it was because the parents, Ole and Jøran, were living on a *husmann* place called Vestbråten when their first two sons, Ole and Hans, went to America in 1867. They did not own Vestbråten. They were *husmenn* (cotters in English) living on this small plot. They paid their "rent" on this cottage and an acre or two of land by working for the farmer who owned Vestbråten. Vestbråten was owned by the Hovland farm which is located on the east side of the valley. Another reason for choosing Hovland might be that Ole or Hans may have worked on the Hovland farm before they emigrated and thus decided to adopt the name when they got to America. It is not unusual that they did not select Vestbråten as their name. Vestbråten was just a couple of steep hillside acres and a tiny, poor cottage in a small grove of trees. It did not have the prestige of the Hovland name. Also, Vestbråten is quite difficult for Americans to pronounce correctly and cannot be properly written in English because of the Norwegian vowel *å*. Nonetheless, Hovland was the name they took when they got to America and it has stuck now for over 140 years.

During the first several years in America Ole and his family, Hans, and later Gudbrand and his family settled in Fillmore County, Minnesota, but about 1870 Gudbrand and Hans moved south and west to Winnebago County, Iowa, in the rural area between Fertile, Lake Mills and Forest City. Many of their descendants still live there. Ruth Tweeten Holtan, a great-granddaughter of Gudbrand, is a member of our Hadeland Lag. She and her husband, Stanford, live in Forest City, Iowa. She is an excellent genealogist and has been of great assistance in my research of the Hovlands. Sometime after arriving in America, Gudbrand changed the spelling of his first name to Gulbrand.

When Gulbrand and Hans moved to Iowa, the remaining three, now Hovland, brothers moved north to Otter Tail County where they took homesteads in Trondheim Township in rural Rothsay, Minnesota.

When Otto and his parents arrived in Minnesota in 1883 they also settled in Otter Tail County with Ole, Syver and Nils. A small second house was built for them on Syver's farm. This became the parents' new home where 73-year-old Jøran and 69-year-old Ole lived with Otto.

Ole died on 5 August 1890 at the age of 76; Jøran lived another three years, dying on 4 April 1893 at the age of 82. Both are buried in the North Friberg Cemetery, rural Rothsay, Minnesota.

My great-grandfather Nils (or Nels as it became spelled in America) married Marie Brørby in 1880. She had immigrated from Jevnaker in 1867 with her parents when she was five years old. Her parents were Anders Jorgenson Brørby and Anna Hansdatter. My grandfather, also named Ole (28 August 1880 – 23 September 1980) was their oldest son.

Ole Olsen (Hovland) and Jøran Olsdatter Haugen have many descendants in America. Their six sons had a total of 61 surviving children at their deaths. Our grandchildren are members of the seventh generation of Hovland descendants in America. No one has yet taken a census of Ole and Jøran's descendants, but I can confidently estimate that there are now more than 2,000 who can claim them as their Hadeland Ancestors.

Additional information about these Hovland families

A more complete history of the Ole and Jøran Hovland immigrant family that I wrote was published with the title "*De Tok navnet Hovland i Amerika*" in the following

Årbøker for Hadeland:	*2002*, pages 109-115
	2003, pages 110-117
	2004, pages 116-118.

These articles are written in Norwegian.

English-language copies are available from the author or from other family members.

Gulbrand Hovland

published May 2000   *Form 73*   *Ruth Holtan*

Gulbrand Hovland Family - Photo taken before 1923

Back row: Carl Hovland, Hans Madeson, Bendick Tweeten, Oscar Hovland, Halvor Hovland, Tobias Harris, Gunder Gunderson

Second row from back: Thea Hovland (Carl), Thea Madeson (Hans), Olava Tweeten (Bendick), Carrie Hovland (Halvor), Mlla Harris (Tobias), Helen Gunderson (Gunder)

Seated: Christopher Gunderson, Sever Hovland, Gulbrand Hovland and wife Guro Hovland, Bertha Nelson.

Seated on the floor: Tune Anderson, Tom Gunderson.

Gulbrand was the first-born of Ole and Hjoren who had met in Hadeland while working on neighboring farms. Edna Rude helped me identify Hjoren as the child of an unmarried mother from Hol, Hallingdal. After her confirmation rite of passage, Hjoren joined other desperate young Hallings who left their homes to find a place to work on the bigger farms of Hadeland so they could eat! After Hjoren met Ole they experienced the difficulty of having a home of sorts in their poverty.

Their first baby was born at Fålang where she was a servant. When this baby was baptized Gudbrand on July 12, 1835, his father still lived as a servant on the farm Helman in Gran.

Ole and Hjoran were married Dec. 1, 1835, and were able to live together on the same farm Hvinden(eie). The farm lies high above and a very long way from the fjord. Its name in the

15

record (eie at the end of a farm name) is the clue that they were *husmenn*, i.e., hired workers. Besides Gudbrand, they had four other sons who reached adulthood as well as a daughter Siri and two sons, Lars, and Lars who died young. The last place they lived in Gran was a *husmans* place called Vestbråten, under the farm Hovland in Lunner.

In a story written by Halvor Hovland "Next to the Sweetest Name" which appeared in the *Morning Glory, Genie Bug* and other Hovland information, they lived on the Hovland farm and had a good life, but this is not very accurate.

The census record shows they lived on a different cotters' place each time a child was born, which made them the poorest of the poor in the overpopulated area of Gran.

Gudbrand married Bertha Halvorsdatter from Prestegårds(eie), Jevnaker, and they had four children: Julia, Miklsa, Halvor and Olava. Baby Olava was almost two years old when they arrived in the U.S.A. She is my paternal grandmother. Tickets prepaid for them came from Lansing, Iowa, for the ship *Oder* and they arrived September 17, 1869. They spent several years in Fillmore County, Minnesota. Two more babies, Oscar and Albert, were born in Minnesota and Iowa.

Gulbrand (Americanized spelling) was a big man and hard worker but one summer he became ill and Bertha had to take his place in the harvest field. She experienced a sunstroke and was never strong after that.

In 1870 they came to the Ferile, Iowa, area where they lived in a dugout with two other families. On this site across the field northeast from Jim Petersburg's house site, on a steep hillside sloping to the southeast, they used timbers to make a wall for the face of their home.

Research shows no relationship between the Hovlands, Oswalds and Levangs who shared the dugout. In 1874 the wife and mother died so the desperate circumstances forced Gulbrand to give the baby, Albert, to the Murkve family who were childless and on their way to North Dakota. Olava stayed with the kind Hans Hovland family.

Gulbrand was a carpenter by trade and had to be gone a lot. By now he had his own home on the west edge of Goose Lake – a beautiful site with an oak grove and hills where later Hovlands also lived.

A widow in Mt. Valley, Guro Kristoffersdatter Gunderson, hired Gulbrand to add a log addition to her home. When it was time to pay him, she married him instead and they joined their families of six and five and eventually added three more children. Gulbrand also kindly took Hannah Maasestad's father to raise, replacing the baby Albert that he had given away.

Gulbrand was a good singer and served as *klokker* (song leader) at Winnebago Lutheran Church many years. Olava helped him learn the tunes, using a simple one-stringed instrument with a bow called a Psalmodikon. Imagine our minor Lutheran chorales taught in this simple way! This instrument was acceptable in lieu of a dance instrument – the violin.

I find much evidence of piety in these families. On Ole and Hjoren's grave marker are the words, "God's Son's blood cleanses us from all sins" (translation from Norwegian). What a rich heritage from a life of the least of this world's goods!

Gulbrand and Hans raised their families in Iowa and the evidence of their piety is in their descendants also. Hans gave his leadership in the Elim Lutheran Free Church of rural Fertile, Iowa, where many of his descendants are buried. These families lived in a rural area where the "Little Synod" was adding members and building their own church building. These Norwegian immigrants took their worship experience seriously.

Several sources name Ole Olesson Hovland as the first-born son, which would be the Norwegian naming system. Leslie Rogne helped me understand that perhaps a Gulbrand was a key benefactor to Hjoren and Ole and Hjoren used "Gulbrandsdatter" in the 1865 census, even though Ola Hermosson, N. Tufto, was recorded as her illegitimate father. This may explain their first-born naming choice. My father was named for Gulbrand with the American name of Gilbert and his sisters said he was most like his grandfather who lived until he was 88 years old in 1923.

Ole O. and Anne Hovland

published November 2009/February 2010   *Form 480*   *David Pfeffer*

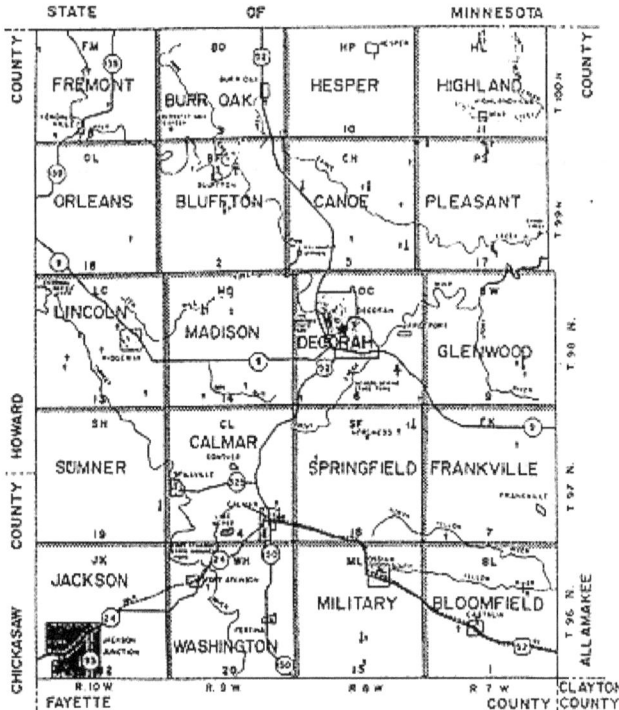

Township Map for Winnishiek County, Iowa

The year was 1870 and the ninth United States decennial census was under way in Winneshiek County, Iowa. The 2nd day of June found census Taker Cyrus Wellington visiting the farm family of "Ole Olson, his wife Anna and their four children, Julia, Maria, Olaus, and Anton."[1] Mr. Wellington recorded that Highlandville was the post office for this area of Highland Township. Highlandville is located about 15 miles northeast of Decorah. A real estate value of $600 and personal estate of $125 was recorded for their dwelling place. Whether the $600 was land and/or buildings is unknown. However this real estate value was smaller than most other values in Highland Township. The Highland Township census covered 24 pages and 149 dwelling places. There were only seven dwelling places with smaller real estate values. It can be surmised that the Olson family was living in very modest quarters. It is likely that the Olsons were tenants, not owners.

Their sons Olaus and Anton were recorded by the census taker as having been born in Iowa. Olaus had been born in 1868 and Anton was nearly three months old at the time of the census.

18

The rest of the family had been born in Norway. Ole and Anne were married before Rev. Halbo on 14 November 1863 at the Lunner Church, Hadeland, Norway.[2] Ole was 25 years old and Anne was 23 years of age. Ole was from a family of nine children, eight sons and one daughter. Three of those children died as infants and six sons grew to adulthood. Very likely Ole and Anne were *husmenn* (cottagers, tenant farmers) much like their parents who moved from farm to farm to find employment. Their daughter Julia was born 1 January 1865 at Vestbråten in Lunner, Norway and Anne Marie was born 2 February 1867 at Håkenstadeist, Lunner, Norway.[3]

Ole and his family left for America in the spring of 1867. Their daughter Julia was two years old and her sister Maria had been born that February. Ole's next youngest brother Hans accompanied the family on their sailing ship journey across the Atlantic. Their journey took about seven weeks. They found their way to northeastern Iowa to an area called Big Canoe.

Immigration by Norwegians to the Big Canoe area began in 1851 and increased rapidly in succeeding years. Big Canoe was a Native American Chief, also known as One-Eyed Decorah. The region bearing his name was not closely defined, but was a general name for what is now northeastern Winneshiek County, a part of the adjoining northwestern Allamakee county to the east and a part of adjoining Fillmore County across the state line in Minnesota.[4]

The following spring in 1868 Ole's brother Syver, the fourth son in the Olsen family, left Norway for America. He was only 18 years old and continued the migration of the Olsens to America. His journey on steamships and railroads took about a month. The 1870 census records him as a farm laborer working for Arne Arneson in Black Hammer Township, Houston county, Minnesota.[5]

The fall of 1869 brought Ole's older brother Gudbrand, his wife Bertha and their four children to America. Ruth Holtan wrote about her great-grandparents in "The Story of Gulbrand Hovland."[6] That same year Ole's brother Hans would marry Marie Walhus. She had been born in Iowa and her parents were immigrants from Telemark, Norway.

Ole's younger brother Nils was 18 years old when he immigrated to Iowa in the census year of 1870. He left for America on May 20th. It appears that he had arrived and found work by July 15th in Allamakee County, Iowa. The census taker for Unity City Township recorded a "Nels Oleson" age 20 as a farm laborer living with an immigrant family of seven from England.[7] The discrepancy in Nils' age may be that Nils wanted to appear older or probably that the person who gave the information to the census taker guessed at the hired man's age.

About this time Ole's brothers Hans and Gudbrand would move their families about 90 miles (45 kilometers) further west of Decorah to the area surrounding Fertile, Iowa. They would remain Iowans the rest of their lives and become farmers and landowners.

At some time during those early years in America all the brothers changed their surname to Hovland. They had used Hanson and Olsen as their patronymic or surnames in Norway. What led them to change their surname? Possibly it was that the Olsen name was a very common name in Iowa. In the 1870 census for Winneshiek County there were over 300 families with the Olson, Oleson, and Olsen names. What led the brothers to choose Hovland? In "They took the name Hovland in America," Verlyn Anderson theorized that "most likely it was because their parents Ole and Jøren were living on a *husman* place called Vestbråten ... They did not own Vestbråten ... Vestbråten was owned by the Hovlandvestre Farm ... Vestbråten was surely only a couple of acres with a tiny, poor set of buildings ... The name did not have the prestige of the Hovland name."[8] The brothers Gudbrand and Nils would eventually Americanize their first names to Gulbrand and Nels.

It seems likely that Ole was scouting out desirable land in western Minnesota that was being opened up for homesteading. It would be the next spring before Ole would return with his family to Otter Tail County to settle and homestead.One of the first recorded uses of the Hovland name appears in the book *Nordmændene i Amerika* by Martin Ulvestad:

> "Christian O. Bye from Rørass [Norway] ... left from Wilmington [Township, Houston County] in the southeast corner of Minnesota with his wife and children and his household goods in a wagon drawn by 4 oxen. A man by the name of Ole Hovland accompanied him as far as Otter Tail County (Minn.) where he got off, while the aforementioned continued the trip to the Red River Valley ... in the spring of 1870."[9]

One spring day in 1871 found the Ole and Syver Hovland families in a small group of covered wagons pulled by oxen. They were making their way north toward St. Paul out of southeastern Minnesota. Already several days had passed since Ole, his wife Anne and their 4 children had left their home in Highland Township in far northeastern Iowa. They had lived in the Highlandville area near Decorah for four years. Ole and Anne had said their good-byes to their next-door neighbors, the Nels and Ragnhild Torstenson family. The Torstenson family, like the Hovlands, had come from Norway. They lived at Sandbæklokken, Brandbu, Hadeland and immigrated to America in 1862. Nels and Rachel's oldest son Torsten and his wife Gjori had moved to Otter Tail County the previous year in 1870 and settled in Trondhjem Township.[10]

On the first day of their journey Ole and Anne had made their way about 10 miles (16 kilometers) into Minnesota to the Spring Grove area. Here they had joined up with Ole's brother Syver and his wife Guri. Syver had come to America three years earlier in 1868. Then in 1870, Syver and Guri Torgersdatter Flatin were married in Spring Grove. Guri and her parents were immigrants from Buskerud County (*fylke*), Norway.

We do not know if the Ole and Syver Hovland families traveled by themselves or possibly with others as they made their way toward Otter Tail County. They were part of a small chain of immigrants from southeastern Minnesota and northeastern Iowa seeking land of their own. Their destination in western Minnesota had been recently surveyed and opened up for European settlement. Land for homesteading was available there. Land in southeastern

Minnesota and northeastern Iowa was only available for purchase. That migration chain was made up of people like Ole and Syver who had emigrated to America and envisioned land of their own. Others in that migration chain were adult children of earlier settlers who were also seeking and of their own.

During those first few years in America Ole and Syver very likely worked as hired men on farms settled by earlier immigrants. During that time they would have added to their Norwegian farming skills by learning information about farming practices in frontier America, Upper Midwest climate and geography and land acquisition. A smattering of English would have been acquired even though they were living in predominately Norwegian settlements. These purposeful families would have earned and saved money and prepared to live their vision of acquiring their own farms. Verlyn Anderson wrote of this in "They took the name Hovland in America:"

> "This included buying or building a covered wagon, acquiring a pair of oxen and purchasing the many essential household items, supplies and small farm equipment that every homestead needed. In addition, they needed to have extra money to purchase food and pay unforeseen expenses that they knew they would encounter along their travel route and during their first critical year on their homestead until their crops were harvested the following year."[11]

Ole and Syver would have planned and prepared carefully for the long trek to Otter Tail County. This would have meant packing all their earthly possessions into their covered wagons. They likely used lightweight covered wagons sometimes called prairie wagons.

These wagons were small, about 9 feet (2.75 meters) long and about 4 feet (1.25 meters) wide. A cover of water-proof canvas would have been attached over curved wood bows.[12] Despite the Hovland's modest means there possibly was "downsizing" of their possessions to fit into the limited space. They likely shared a space as Syver's family of two was much smaller than Ole's family of six.

Typical immigrant prairie wagon

Somewhere in their possessions Ole and Anne would have carefully tucked away Ole's "Intent" document. Ole had completed one of the necessary steps in homesteading land earlier that year. He had appeared in the Winneshiek District Court in Decorah, Iowa on February 14 and declared his "Intention to become a Citizen of the United States." On that document he chose to spell Hovland as "Haavland." He would continue this spelling in the future on legal documents.

What route did they follow? No known written or oral accounts of their journey exist anymore. Current highway mileage between Spring Grove and Trondhjem Township is over 300 miles (500 kilometers). Maps of Minnesota at that time are few and limited. A "Rice & Reed's Township Map of Minnesota 1870" is on file at the Minnesota History Center. It only shows existing railroads, county (*fylke*) borders and outlines of townships *(kommunes)* for those counties surveyed.

In Rhoda R. Gilman's *The Red River Trails* there are several maps[13] and descriptions of the various trails used by the Red River Oxcarts for hauling furs and freight for the Hudson Bay Company between St. Paul and the Red River Settlement at Fort Garry near present-day Winnipeg, Canada. It seems likely that the Hovlands followed the *Military Road* north from St. Paul and St. Anthony to the St. Cloud area. The *Military Road* was built to connect St. Paul with Fort Ripley north of Little Falls. It was on the east side of the Mississippi because the terrain was relatively level there compared to the hilly west side of the river. Nowadays U.S. Highway 10 follows that corridor. After crossing the Mississippi River in St. Cloud or Sauk Rapids they would have had their choice of following the *Old Middle Trail* or the *Stage Road* westward into Stearns County. The *Old Middle Trail* let southwest from St. Cloud to Cold Spring and Richmond, then west toward Glenwood.   After Glenwood it led northwest toward Elbow Lake approximately along the route of modern day state Highway 55. Interstate Highway 94 approximates the route followed by the *Stage Road*.

Ole had visited Otter Tail County and returned to Iowa the prior year so he likely had a good sense of trail routes and experience with life on the trails. At that time the trails west from St. Cloud had frequent bogs and low ground stretches that were prone to the narrow wagon wheels becoming mired in the mud or muck. These low-lying areas were also home to the ever present mosquitoes. Maybe they followed the *Old Middle Trail* to Cold Spring and Richmond and then the *Stage Road* to Sauk Centre and Alexandria. A firsthand account of a trip from southeastern Minnesota by a Norwegian family to the Red River Valley over this route in 1870 is related by Levi Thortvedt in "To the Northwestern Frontier."[14]

Possibly they visited the United States Land Office in Alexandria for information about vacant, surveyed and unsurveyed lands. At that time Alexandria was also the last chance to purchase needed tools, utensils and supplies.

It was early June. A few weeks had passed since they had left Spring Grove. They likely were approaching the Otter Tail River crossing near Dayton Hollow. Dayton Hollow was downriver a few miles from Fergus Falls. At that time Fergus Falls consisted of a few houses. Otter Tail County had been formally organized in 1868 and the county seat at that time was in Otter Tail

City on the northeast shore of Otter Tail Lake. An older established settlement was located at Clitherall.

Perhaps Ole assured the group upon approaching the river that this would be their last major river to cross. There had been several rivers to ford or pay a toll to use bridges on their journey. The first sizable river was the Root River near Rochester which was followed by the Zumbro and Cannon Rivers before reaching St. Paul. After crossing the Mississippi in St. Paul, they would have crossed the Rum and the Elk Rivers before reaching St. Cloud. Here they would have crossed to the west bank of the Mississippi. After leaving St. Cloud, the Sauk, Cottonwood and Pomme de Terre Rivers needed to be crossed before reaching the Otter Tail River.

Leaving the Otter Tail River crossing behind them they quite possibly followed the *Woods-Middle Link Trail* north to Trondhjem Township. There were 20 miles (32 kilometers) left to go. One or two more days would complete their journey. It is hard to picture the trail-weary group at this point. There were at least two covered wagons pulled by oxen. Possibly there were cows tied to the wagon's tailgates and maybe a crate of chickens also fastened somewhere. Most likely Ole and Syver were leading the oxen. Both wives were pregnant so they may well have been riding, at least part of the time. Anne was six months pregnant and Guri would give birth a month after their arrival. Ole and Anne's children were likely impatient wondering how much longer and further. Julie, Anne Marie, Olaus, and Anton were ages six, four, two and one.

Both Hovland families would homestead on adjoining farms in Section 26 of Trondheim Township. Their former Iowa neighbors Torsten and Gjori (Thorsten Nelson) lived about a half mile west. When Ole "proved up" his homestead he stated that he settled on the land "on or about June 13th, 1871."[15]

"Golden Wedding in Trondhjem" from Rothsay Enterprise, November 20, 1913

A very happy event took place here last Friday when Mr. and Mrs. Ole Hovland celebrated their golden wedding. All of their children and a large number of other relatives and friends were present to congratulate the couple on this particular day. Rev. Austvold held short services and at its conclusion on behalf of their friends presented them with a beautiful couch. From their children they received $75 in gold. Mr. and Mrs. Hovland were both born in Norway. They came to America in 1867, living four years in Iowa. In 1871 they came west and have lived here ever since. Fourteen children were born to them of which ten still live. They have 43 grandchildren and three great grandchildren. Their youngest daughter, Mrs. A. Sommerness and her husband celebrated the 10th anniversary of their wedding on the same day. They were also presented with a nice purse. The occasion was a happy one and will long be remembered by those who were present.

Ole and Anne Hovland (seated) surrounded by their children.
From left to right: Carl Edwin b. 1882, John Frederick b. 1875, Sophie (m. Kittelson) b. 1874, Anne Marie (m. Stoen) b. 1867, Thea Mathilde (m. Osten) b. 1871, Minna Telise (m. Ulsrud) b. 1881, Ida Caroline (m. Sommerness) b. 1884, Lewis b. 1872, Olaus b. 1878, and Anton b. 1870. Sophie is David's grandmother.

....

Sources:
[1] 1870 U.S. Census, Iowa, Winneshiek County, Highland Township, page 6, dwelling 36, family 36; *Heritage Quest Online* (accessed through participating library 28 March 2006).
[2] [Selma (Osten) Bullis], "*The Ole O. Hovland Family Tree 1953.*"
[3] Verlyn D. Anderson, "They took the name Hovland in America," 2002, page 11; also in *Arbok for Hadeland 2002*, page 113

[4] *Centennial History of the Big Canoe Lutheran Church* (Decorah, Iowa, 1953, page 4.

[5] 1870 U.S. Census, Minnesota, Houston County, Blackhammer Township, p. 5, dwelling 39, family 39, line 15; *Heritage Quest Online* (accessed through participating library 30 March 2006).

[6] Ruth Holtan, "The Story of Gulbrand Hovland:, *Brua,* November, 1999, page 4.

[7] 1870 U.S. Census, Iowa, Allamakee County, Union City Township, page 14, dwelling 93, family 95, line 14; *Heritage Quest Online* (accessed through participating library 1 April 2006).

[8] Verlyn D. Anderson, "They took the name Hovland in America," 2002, pages 5-6.

[9] Martin Ulvestad, *Nordmændene i Amerika,* (Minneapolis, Minnesota: History Book Company's Forlag, 1907) page 158.

[10] Torstenson family information provided by Mark Hekiner (Sacklin), 26 December 2009 email to author. Mary is a great-granddaughter of Torsten and Gjori.

[11] Verlyn D. Anderson, "They took the name Hovland in America," p. 9: also in *Årbok for Hadeland, 2003, "De tok navnet Hovland i Amerika,"* pp. 111-112.

[12] Covered wagon descriptions from "Recollections of Pioneer Times, Travels by Covered Wagon" by Verlyn Anderson, *Brua*, May 2003, p. 10.

[13] Rhoda R. Gilman, Carolyn Gilman, and Deborah M. Stultz, *The Red River Trails* (St. Paul: Minnesota Historical Society, 1979), maps of the mentioned trails are located on pp. 72, 76-77, and 84-85.

[14] Anne Sladky, editor, *Celebrating our Norwegian-Minnesota Heritage* (LaPorte, Minnesota: The Norwegian Statehood Pioneer Project, 2009), pp. 203-213.

[15] Ole O. Haavland, "Testimony of Claimant," homestead certificate 2178, Fergus Falls Land Office, Land Entry Papers 1800-1908, National Archives, Washington D.C.

Martin Andreas Østen & Thea Hovland

published May 2003   *Forms 263,480*   *Tanya Rylee*

*Andrew and Thea on their wedding day,
24 November 1891
and on their 50th wedding anniversary.*

Martin Andreas S. (Andrew) Østen was born 15 July 1867 in Gran, Hadeland, Norway. He was the second of three children born to Simen Larson Boren Østen and Kjersti Pedersdatter Stadum. Simen was a bricklayer/mason while living in Norway. The first child born to Simen and Kjersti was Lars Simensen (born 21 June 1859). Both Andrew and Lars were born on the "Østen" farm in Hadeland. The last couple born to the couple was Pauline (born 1 April 1873). She was born in Norwegian Grove Township, Otter Tail County, Minnesota, America.

The Østen farm was/is located in the *fylke* (Norwegian county) of Oppland in Hadeland, Gran *Kommune* (municipality or community), Norway, part of the parish church of Tingelstad, farm number 134. The Østen farm, by 1950, was with the Sværtbeck farm, still farm number 134 and in the Brandbu Kommune.

The family left their homestead 16 April 1869 from the port of Oslo on the ship *Øder* and emigrated to America in May 1869. At the time, Andrew was two years old and his brother Lars was 10. After landing in America (conflicting reports of the actual arrival destination exist) – Ellis Island, New York or Quebec, Canada), they made their way to Rushford, Fillmore County, Minnesota, where they stayed for three years. During their time in Fillmore County, the Østens lived in a little shack on the corner of a farm while Simen worked on a nearby farm and also performed mason work as needed.

In 1872, the Østen family gathered all their belongings, loaded them into a covered wagon and began their journey to Norwegian Grove Township in Otter Tail County, Minnesota. Their livestock consisted of a team of oxen and a few head of cattle.

Upon arriving in Norwegian Grove, Simen decided not to homestead property but instead chose to buy the homestead rights to the present-day Østen farm located approximately eight miles west of Pelican Rapids. He mortgaged the property 28 July 1872. Initially he purchased 160 acres but a few years later 90 acres were purchased from a neighbor, making a farm of 250 acres. As of today, there have been four generations of Østens who have lived and worked on the farm.

26

At first the Østens lived in a log cabin where the floor was nothing but soil. The countryside apparently was almost barren of trees, so each farmer planted trees around the buildings. Østens built the first frame house in Norwegian Grove Township.

Life in Norwegian Grove did not start out well for the family. According to family history, locusts were had for the first two years. Reports note that the locusts were so thick that the sun could not be seen through them. The first year that the Østens planted crops, the crops were stripped by the locusts, but the second year they were a little more fortunate because only part of the grain was taken. The family's diet consisted mostly of whole grain cooked in milk. They had four or five milk cows.

Not only did the Østens have to deal with locusts those first few years, there were also threats of Native American attacks to contend with. Shortly after Andrew and his parents arrived in Norwegian Grove Township (1872) he witnessed Native Americans walking and on horseback, single file in a line about one mile long, making their way past the farm on their way from White Earth Reservation to Breckenridge, Minn. Apparently the Native Americans were wearing war paint. At that time that this group of Native Americans was passing through, Andrew was six years old and home alone with his sister. Years later he recalled becoming frightened and taking his sister to the cellar where they stayed to be safe. At one time, all of the Norwegian Grove Township neighbors gathered south of the Østen farm with axes and other implements for protection against the Native Americans. They even discussed building a fort on a lofty hill located west of the Østen farm. One can only imagine the fear associated with living in a new land and dealing with unknown cultures.

Family history indicates that the prairie chickens were plentiful in the earlier days of the family's settlement in Norwegian Grove Township. Andrew could recall an occurrence when he stood in one place and shot eight times at the same covey of prairie chickens. They would fly up every time he shot, but come right back to the same place.

As with most families living in rural America in the 1870's, the Østen family had a long journey to obtain groceries. Alexandria, Minnesota, was the nearest place to travel to secure provisions. Apparently it took one week to make the trip there to sell their goods and stock up on more supplies. It was recounted that they received 50 cents for a bushel for wheat, three cents per dozen for eggs, and six cents per pound for butter.

Eventually the town of Pelican Rapids began to form, which was a relief to the family. Being "only" eight miles away, they apparently felt it was at their back door. Usually Kjersti would walk to Pelican Rapids carrying butter, eggs, and produce to sell in order to receive further provisions for her clan. Barnesville, Minn., was not as far away as Pelican Rapids but the journey was much more difficult. The land was covered with swamp water. Barnesville at the time was located two miles north of present-day Barnesville. Kjersti also spun and made all the clothes for the family, using the linen thread she had created.

The family's beef cattle were sold most often to the butcher in Moorhead, Minnesota. Family histories relay that the family members involved in selling the cattle would start out at 3:00 in the morning and make it as far as the Buffalo River the first day. They would camp at the river overnight and finish out the journey the next day. At that time, they received $20 for a large, fat steer.

Andrew Østen was educated in the common school of District No. 48, Norwegian Grove Township. As an adult, he was a regular reader of the Norwegian newspaper entitled *Decorah-Posten* and its literary supplement, *Ved Arnen*. No doubt he enjoyed staying current with the news of his Norwegian homeland. He may have been looking for information regarding his family members. In addition to reading, writing and speaking Norwegian, Andrew could read, write and speak English.

Andrew's father, Simen Larsen Østen, passed away 15 February 1896 at the age of 68. Andrew's mother Kjersti passed away 6 September 1911 at the age of 78. Kjersti dies of complications from a stroke she suffered five months prior to her death.

On November 29, 1891, Andrew Østen was united in marriage with Thea Mathilde Hovland. They were married at South Immanuel Lutheran Church, Otter Tail County, Minnesota. Reverend T. Rosholt performed the ceremony.

Thea was born 27 Sept 1871 in Trondhjem Township, Otter Tail County, Minnesota. She was the daughter of Ole Hovland and Anna (Teslo) Hovland. Her parents came to America in 1868 and settled in Winnisheik County, Iowa, where they stayed for three years. In 1871 they moved to Trondhjem Township, Otter Tail County, Minnesota, where her father took a farmstead. She was confirmed 16 May 1887 in the South Immanuel Lutheran Church in Otter Tail County, Minnesota. Thea attended school in District No. 89 in Trondhjem Township.

The couple welcomed their first child, a daughter named Clara Alice, on 20 July 1893.

They had nine more children during their marriage. The other children included Ole Sigvart Andrew born 14 July 1894, Salem Luella born 31 January 1900, Mable Theoline born 12 March 1902, Olga Josephine born 22 December, Pearl Gilma born 3 November 1908, Elmer Garnet born 3 November 1910, and my grandfather, Victor Allen, born 4 December 1914.

Sadly, the couple experienced the death of two of their children. Their son Elmer died 3 November 1910, when he was less than two months of age. He died as an infant of a disease similar to a cold (exact cause of death unknown). The family believed that sickness was brought on by baptismal water that was too cold for the tiny baby.

The author's grandfather, Victor Allen Osten, at 6 months old

28

Their daughter Pearl was 20 years of age at the time of her death. She was murdered 2 October 1927 in Minneapolis, Minnesota, two weeks after her arrival in the city. She had moved to Minneapolis to pursue her dreams in the musical talent. She was a student at the Minnesota College and was studying to obtain a musical degree. Despite numerous investigative leads, her murderer was never identified and therefore has not been brought to justice.

There were three huge windstorms (possibly tornadoes) to hit the Østen farm. The first storm hit in 1924 and the windmill, barn, machine shed and some smaller buildings were all destroyed. In 1928 another storm blew down the barn, windmill, much of the planted windbreak and some smaller buildings. Unfortunately another storm came through in 1944 and again blew down the barn and smaller buildings. The family lost almost all of their crops that year. Family members say that after the third storm, the family did not want to rebuild the roof on the barn because they were superstitious about another storm appearing.

Andrew Østen was very musical. He played the harmonica and the organ. His son Victor recalls that he had a beautiful voice. He was the organist and choir director at North Immanuel Lutheran Church in Norwegian Grove Township. Thea, along with her husband, was also an active member of North Immanuel Lutheran Church. She was a lifetime member of the Ladies Aide organization. In addition to Andrew's activity in church life, he was a member of the school board for several years.

Andrew's father Simen was instrumental in the incorporation of the North Immanuel Lutheran Church and was elected one of the first trustees of the church. Andrew's mother Kjersti organized the first Ladies Aid meeting at the church. For the Ladies Aid meetings, the women always served a full dinner at noon and coffee and lunch in the afternoon. Later Kjersti organized the first Luther League meeting and held it at the Østen farm.

Andrew was naturalized as a U.S. citizen 25 November 1898 in the 7th Judicial District Court in Otter Tail County by Judge D. B. Searle. The sheriff and clerk served as official witnesses. In addition, he had two personal witnesses present (Oscar Sillerud and Mr. Christianson). He signed his name on the official naturalization document as Andreas S. Østen, an alien of Norway. At the time he was naturalized he had been in the States 29 years.

Andrew retired from farming in 1952 because of failing health. At Andrew's retirement, Andrew and Thea had resided on the farm for more than 60 years. Andrew and Thea moved to Pelican Rapids, Minnesota, to reside at the Good Samaritan Nursing Home. An interesting tidbit of information is the fact that Andrew did not sell his car until he was 86 years of age. It is quite remarkable that he maintained his independence until this point in time. Andrew was eventually transported to the Battle Lake Memorial Home (the country home) because he required special medical care.

On 15 February 1956 Andrew passed away at the Battle Lake Memorial Home. He was 88 years of age at the time. He suffered from a stroke which precipitated his death but otherwise, according to family members, he was healthy his entire life. Funeral services were held 21 February 1956 at North Immanuel Lutheran Church with Pastor N.K. Estrem officiating. At the time of his death, his wife Thea was still living as well as three sons and five daughters, 26 grandchildren and 43 great-grandchildren.

Thea passed away 27 April 1957 at the Good Samaritan Nursing Home in Pelican Rapids. She was 85 years of age at the time. When Thea passed away, three of her sons and five of her daughters were living. In addition, she was survived by 26 grandchildren and 45 great-grandchildren. Her funeral was held 3 May 1957 at the North Immanuel Lutheran Church with Reverends Arthur Grimstad and Jacob Rosholt officiating. She is buried in the west North Immanuel Cemetery beside Andrew.

My grandfather Victor Østen and his wife Alma (Johnson) Østen currently reside on the Østen farm.

Anders Ingebretson & Kari Olerud Trana

published May 1997 *Form 398* *Leslie Rogne*

Anders Ingebretsen boarded a boat in 1877 with three other persons from Hadeland, Norway, destined for America. Anders was 20 years old and the first of his family to emigrate to America.

Anders, using the name Andrew, homesteaded on land near the town Norman, North Dakota territory. The family lived last on a place called Olerud and that would be their surname in America. Olerud is the name of a *gaard* (farm) in Gran, Hadeland, near the town of Brandbu.

The first family found to be certain ancestors of our Oleruds is seen in the census record of the *gård* Molstad: 1801.

Jorgen Hansen Molstad	man	36	cotter with land and Betler
Ragnild Oldsdtr.	wife	29	
Hans Jorgensen	son	9	
Ole Jorgensen	son	7	
Anne Jorgensdtr.	daughter	5	
Kari Jorgensdtr.	daughter	3	

Jorgen Hansen was married in 1792 to Ragnild Oldstr. Rosendal.

The following children were born later: another Kari born in 1808 on Olerud; Amund, born 1803 on Molstad; and Joen, born on Rossum in 1812.

Amund Jorgensen Molstad was married in 1824 to Marthe Engebretsdtr. Hilden. Marthe was born in 1800 to Engebret Olsen and Anne Pedersdtr. Helmij. The following children were born to Amund and Marthe: Jorgen Amundsen Hilden, born 1824; Engebret Amundsen Hilden, born 1826; Ragnvie Amundsdtr., born 1828 (died at age 10); Olle Amundsen Hilden, born 1830; and Anne Amundsdtr. Hilden, born 1830; and Anne Anundsdtr. Hilden, born 1831.

Ingebret Amundsen, born Hilden, living on Hvinden 26, was married in 1849 to Kari Agrimsdtr., born on Almsengen, living on Hougtvedt. Kari Agrimsdtr.'s parents were Agrim Pedersen, born on Wenaasen, Hamsedal, Hallingdal, and widow Kari Larsdtr. Almsengen.

Six children were born to Ingebret and Kari. Marthe was born on Hougtvedt in 1850; Kari (my grandmother) was born in 1852 on Dahlen; Amund was born in Olerud in 1855; Anders was born in 1857 on Dahlen; Jorgen was born in 1854 on Olerud; Karen was born in 1858 on Olerud.

On Oct. 20, 1868, Kari Agrimsdtr. Alm Olerud died at the age of 41.

The family is shown in the 1865 census of Olerud living on a part of Olerud called "Auken."

31

Kari Ingebretsdtr., age 27, and brother, Jorgen Ingebretsen, age 18, in 1880 were sent tickets by their brother Andrew. They sailed from Oslo, Norway on March 12, 1980 destined for Fargo, Dakota Territory.

In 1882 Kari Ingebretsdtr. Olerud married Peder Andreas Thoresen, 35, who had come from Sparbu in Nord Trondelag in 1871 and who lived on the Sheyenne River near Norman, Dakota Territory. The next year Kari's sisters, Marthe and Karen, and their father, Ingebret Amundsen Olerud, came to Norman where they lived in a log house on Peder Trana's land and which he had purchased from the Northern Pacific Railroad.

A Lutheran congregation had been organized in 1871. All the marriages of Ingebret Amundsen's children except Marthe were consummated in this congregation "The Norwegian Evangelical Church at the Sheyenne River, Dakota Territory." Later the name was changed to "Norman Lutheran Church."

Marthe Ingebretsdtr. married Paul Aalberg of Nord Trondelag; Jorgen Ingebretsen, great-grandfather of John Olerud, now playing with the New York Mets baseball team, married Marie Andersdtr. Dvertgsteen of Gran, Hadeland. Andrew Ingebretsen married Berthe Gulbrandsdtr. Oppen of Jevnaker, Hadeland; and Karen Ingebretsdtr married Bernt Nelsen Sandbeck, immigrant fron Gran, Hadeland.

My mother was Emma, second daughter of Peder and Kari Olerud Trana. She married Bryjulv Johannes Rogne from Rogne on Vossevangen, Voss, Norway. I have a brother, Johannes, now deceased and my sister, Charlotte Marick, lives in Kindred, N.D. Three nephews Duane, Robert and Erik, and a niece Kay Lindblad, live in Fargo and West Fargo – children of Johannes.

I married Katherine Kazmark of Decator, Ill., in 1943 and we have three children. Peder Trana Rogne lives near Coarsegold, Calif., Seward Rogne lives in Miami, Fla., and Lea lives at Gheen near Orr, Minn.

Addendum:

Research looking for birth of Jorgan Hansen has not been finished.

A Jorgen Hansen born in 1765 would be 36 in the 1801 census:

1. A Jorgen Hansen Augedal, born 1765. Parents – Hans Bentsen and Anna Jorgensdtr. Augedal. Wit – Hans Jorgensen Bilden, Jon Fredriksen Augedal, Birthe Bilden, Marta – dater Augedal.

2. A Jorgen Hansen, born 1755 (age would be wrong): Jorgen Hansen Eichen. Hans Jorgensen and Lisbet Nielsdtr. Ellfsrue. Wit – Hans Knudsen Augedals, Anders Andersen Eliefrue, Jon Jorgensen Bilden, Mari Juumsdtr. Askiem, Anna Andersdtr. Askim.

(Note the Augedals in both entries.)

32

The following is from a WPA interview with Kari Olerud Trana in about 1936. Kari's daughter Julia added to the interview.

Pioneer Biography Files 1936-1940 by North Dakota WPA. Interviewer – M. Naomi Wuflestad

Kari Olerud Trana was born Oct. 11, 1852 at Hadeland, Norway. She was the daughter of Ingebrit and Kari Olerud. There were two brothers and two sisters, viz: Anders – born 1857, lives in Kindred, N.D.; Jorgen – born in 1863, died in 1894 and is buried near Colfax, N.D.; Marta (Mrs. Aalberg), born in 1860, died in 1934 and is buried near Abercrombie; and Karen (Mrs. Bernt Sandbeck), born in 1867, died in 1921 and is buried near Davenport. Mrs. Olerud died in 1868 in Norway. Mr. Olerud came to America in the '80s.

In 1880 Anders, the brother who was already living in Dakota, sent tickets to Norway in order that Kari, 27, and Jorgen, 18, might come to America. On about March 12, 1880, the brother and sister sailed from Oslo, Norway. After crossing the North Sea, they landed at Hull, England, where they stayed at a rooming and boarding establishment for three or four days. All their clothing, etc., was sacked in one chest. Among other things in this chest Kari Trana had seven yards of plaid, black and white, woolen material which she had woven herself in Norway. After coming to Dakota she made a dress for herself out of part of it. She also had in this chest a black woolen knit shawl, the yarn of which she had first spun from wool and then knit. Another chest was filled with food consisting of flat bread, lefse, dried leg of mutton which was for the journey from Quebec to Dakota.

Peder and Kari (Olerud) Trana Family
Top row: Ana Trana Hertsgaard and Emma Trana Rogne;
Second row: Peder Trana and Kari Olerud Trana;
Third row: Julia Trana, Palmer Trana and Alvilde Trana Tryhus;
Bottom row: Thonette Trana and Thora Trana Simmons.

From Hull they crossed England by train and sailed from Liverpool on a steamboat of the Inman Line with a passenger capacity of 800. Mrs. Trana and her brother disliked the food served them on the boat. They held a special grievance once against the fresh biscuits, not being used to fresh breads in Norway. In Norway the housewife either called someone in or she herself baked up to six months or a years supply of flat bread. These round sheets of flat bread were stacked up in a storeroom and their baking was done for months to come.

Because of their dislike of the ship's food they opened their food chest and ate most of their food. After 12 days on the Atlantic they neared Quebec but because of icebergs they could not enter the St. Lawrence River. The ship therefore landed at Halifax, Nova Scotia. From there they took a train to Dakota Territory. The train trip took about a week during which time Mrs. Trana and her brother almost starved because they had already eaten most of their food. The whole trip, boat and train, cost $62 for each of them.

On April 12, 1880 the train pulled into Fargo with Kari and Jorgen Olerud as the only passengers coming this far west. Their brother, Andrus, who lived in Norman Township, was not in Fargo to meet them that afternoon. Fortunately there was a neighbor who was going back to Kindred that day, so they put their chests in the station. The depot was so small that it was all they could do to find room to store the two chests for a few days. Mrs. Trana and Jorgen drove with the neighbor in a lumber wagon and stayed at Peter Trana's house until the next day. In the morning they walked along the Sheyenne River and reached their brother's home about 10:00 that morning.

Anders Olerud, the brother, had just moved to this farm three days before. He had been working for several years on farms in the neighborhood. During that time he managed to build a house on his homestead from logs cut along the Sheyenne River. This house was one large room. The inside was plastered and the outside was covered with sod. The roof was also sod. The barn had not yet been built when the immigrants arrived. The cow was kept in an improvised stall made out of poles with a manger at one end. This was an open affair.

The traveling agents, who entered Dakota at Fort Ambercrombie, often spent the night at the Trana home. From there they continued on their way north.

The first church in Norman was built in 1889. It burned in 1893 and was rebuilt the same year. The Norman congregation is the oldest Norwegian church in North Dakota. The first Norwegian settlers came in the spring of 1871. On December 27, 1871, they gathered at Peder A.Bordenrud's house and agreed to organize a Norwegian congregation and to call Rev. T. Wetlesen, Otter Tail County, as pastor. He came on May 8, 1872. At a church business meeting on May 18, 1872, the following officers were elected: Ole E. Wie, chairman; Ole J. Hertsgaard, secretary; Peder A. Borderud, trustee; Hans Trangsrud and Soren J. Ottis, deacons. The church was organized under the name "The Norwegian Evangelical Lutheran on the Sheyenne River, Dakota Territory." The first resident pastor was Johannes Hellestvedt, who served them from 1873-78. He was succeeded by Rev. Jens Bale, who was their pastor for 22 years, 1878-96.

Some of the first members were Jakob Bjerke, Halvor Olsen, Erick Lee, Erik Tune, Ole Olsgaard, O. Brekke, Petter Trana, Peder Dahlen and Sven Ulsaker.

During the years that Rev. Hellestvedt served the congregation, 1873-78, the services were held in this house. This was a log house which he had built on his homestead and was located about a quarter of a mile from Mr. Trana's home. A wash basin served as the baptismal font. Whenever an infant was to be baptized, a jar of water was brought into the house. The jar of water and the basin were set on the floor underneath the heating stove where they remained until the ceremony was to be performed. The wash basin was then placed on the chair on which the pastor had been sitting – there being no other place to put it – and the child was christened. One of the ladies did not think it the proper thing that the Rev. Hellestvedt should have to sit on the chair after the wash basin had been standing on it. So she brought a new chair, a little better than the ordinary chair, which was used exclusively by the pastor and the other chair was used for baptisms.

After the departure of the Rev. Hellestvedt in 1878, the house in which he had lived was moved out on the sand hills. There it stood until 1930. At that time it was purchased by the Sons of Norway and moved to the old site in the Norman village – near the church and the school, about four miles east of Kindred on the Sheyenne River. The Sons of Norway fixed it up as a museum for pioneer relics and implements and as such Hellestvedt's log house now stands.

The schoolhouse was built about 1876. Karl Steneger was the first school teacher and church song director with a salary of $10 and offerings. After the school was erected religious services were held there until the church was built in 1889. The original school building is still standing on its original location and is being used for school purposes. It has been somewhat remodeled. A new heating system has been installed.

When Kari Trana's father came to America from Norway in 1883, he brought three spinning wheels. Petter Trana had given his oldest daughter a lamb. The wool was shorn off the lamb, corded, and then spun into yarn on the spinning wheel by Mrs. Trana. She knitted the yarn into clothing for the family.

To Mr. and Mrs. Petter Trana were born the following children, all born near Kindred and all living: Anna (Mrs. J. K. Hertsgaard), born Oct. 18. 1883; Emma (Mrs. B. J. Rogne), born Oct. 2, 1886; Thora (Mrs. M. T. Simmons), born Jan 9, 1887; Thonette Trana, born Feb. 7, 1888; Palmer Thrane, born March 17, 1889; Julia Trana, born April 5, 1890; Alvilde (Mrs. A. Tryhus), born Aug. 22,1892.

The village of Norman was located about half mile north of the Trana home. It was a small town consisting of a general store, post office, church and schoolhouse. In about 1900 the Great Northern Railroad cut across the prairie from Wahpeton but failed to pass through Norman. As a result the town of Kindred sprang up about four miles east of Norman and Norman went off the map. Now all that's left of Norman is a church, school and the museum.

(*Editor's note*: These WPA interviews were done about 1935-39 by people who were given employment through F. D. Roosevelt's Works Progress Administration. The North Dakota WPA interviews are on file at the North Dakota Heritage Center in Bismark, N.D. Other states often have kept these on file in the county museums.)

Eric Olson and Christiane Andersdatter

published August 1997   *Form 312*   *George R. and Nila Anderson Krenos*

Eric and Christiane are Nila's great-grandparents.

The Jevnaker *prestegjeld kirke rekord* of 5 April 1852 shows the following people *udflyttede til Amerika* (leaving the parish for America)*:*

      Erick Olson Bratvalseje, 27 years, born 25 August 1823

      Christiane Andersdatter, 27 years

      Christine, 2 ½ years

Eric was born on the *husmansplass* Bratvalsgrinda under the farm Bratval in Jevnaker. Christiane Andersdatter was born 9 October 1825 on the *husmansplass* Næsset under the Mo farm in Jevnaker. They were married 6 October 1849. Christine was born 15 November 1849 on the *husmansplass* Dalen under the farm Olum (also spelled Olim or Olimb). Birth and death records show Eric spelled with a "K" in place of the "C" and Christiane with a "K" instead of a "C." Eric Olsen used Bratvalseje (his place of birth) as part of his name on the Jevnaker *kirke rekord* when he left Norway.

On the same page of the *kirke rekord* but dated 10 April 1852 is found "Maren Andersdatter Olumeje, 7 *aar*." Maren was a younger sister of Christiane Andersdatter and had been living with Christiane since their parents emigrated in the spring of 1851. Maren's twin brother Halvor had died in his first year (1843). Maren Andersdatter used Olumeje, just as her father Anders had done when he left in 1851. The significance is that this was their last residence in Jevnaker which was the *husmansplass* Dalen under *gård* Olum (Olumeje=Dalen). We know that Anders and Anne had been living there since 1839 when a son Gudbjør was born. Five

37

additional children would be born on Dalen through the year 1850. We do not know how long

Olson's Log Cabin

Eric and Christiane were on Dalen, but Christine was born there.

When Eric, Christiane and Christine arrived in America in 1852 they entered via the Port of Quebec, Canada, then went to Milwaukee and overland to Lafayette County, Wisconsin where a few other Hadelanders had settled. The first year they lived in a dugout or cave in the side of a hill. In 1855 they homesteaded land in the Town of Moscow, Iowa County, which is just south of the village of Hollandale, Wisconsin. They built a log house and this would be the only home Eric would live in. His youngest son, Caspar, would build a new home on the homestead in 1906 and his children would use the old log building as a playhouse as youngsters. Over 156 years later, this homestead is still owned by descendants of Eric Olson.

In February 1865 Erick Oleson (as spelled on his military record) enlisted at Argyle, Lafayette County, Wisconsin for a period of one year as a volunteer in the Union Army. He mustered in at Camp Randall, Madison, Wisconsin, on March 9, 1865 and served as a private in Company "C," 50th Wisconsin Volunteer Infantry Regiment. His records show "age 42, born in Norway, farmer, blue eyes, hair light, complexion florid, height 5'7" and he signed his name with an "X." His age of 42 years wa more than 20 years older than the average age of a Civil War soldier. We asked his granddaughters about this and they said their father told them "that he needed the money." On 9 March 1865 Eric was paid a bounty of $33.33 with $66.67 due him.

Private Oleson

The 50th Wisconsin Volunteer Infantry Regiment went first to Fort Leavenworth, Kansas. They were then assigned a destination of Dakota Territory to help hold the Sioux Indians "in check" as they were causing considerable trouble. The regiment went up the Missouri River by steamboat and reached Yankton, Dakota Territory (now South Dakota) on 8 September 1865. They had to walk the last 700 miles to Fort Rice, Dakota Territory (now North Dakota) because of the lateness of the season. The water was so low on the Missouri that a steamboat could not continue any farther up river without danger of running aground.

At the expiration of the one year term, the Regiment was not relieved owing to its isolated location; hence, many cases of desertion were reported of men who had faithfully fulfilled their duties for the term of one year but who were tempted by the prospect of an indefinite sojourn to take "French leave."

On 31 May 1866, Company "C" set out for Madison and Eric was mustered out at Camp Randall on 12 June 1866. His records show he had drawn $85.45 on his clothing account and $35.42 was due him; bounty paid $33.33, due him $66.67. Eric then returned to his home in the Town of Moscow, Iowa County, Wisconsin.

Like the spelling of so many Norwegian names, Eric Olsen's changed with the occasion. He used Eric Olsen, Erik Olsen, Eric Olson, Eric Olson Dalen, Erick Olesen and Eric Dalen. His youngest son Casper in his early years in Wisconsin used the gård name Dalen. Casper's sisters used Eriksdatter. Both of these Norwegian naming practices would change in later years.

Both Eric and Christiane are buried in the Yellowstone Lutheran Church Cemetery in rural Blanchardville, Wisconsin. The cemetery is actually in Argyle Township which is about 4 miles north of the village of Argyle and about 4 miles south of the village of Blanchardville; both villages are in Lafayette County. The cemetery is the resting place of many, many other Norwegian immigrants. Dane, Iowa, Lafayette, Green, Rock and other southwestern Wisconsin counties were very popular stopping places for newly arrived Norwegian immigrants. Many stayed in Wisconsin but many also left to homestead land further west in Iowa, Minnesota, and Dakota Territory.

The children of Erick and Christiane Olson were:

- Christine Eriksdatter (born Nov 15, 1849 on Olumseie-Dalen in Jevnaker; died April 26, 1904 in Hudson SD. On April 18, 1874 she married Peder Andersen in Argyle. He emigrated from Sorum in Gran, Hadeland. These are Nila's grandparents.
- Oline Eriksdatter (born May 4, 1855, Town of Moscow, Iowa County; died December 5, 1921) married Halvor Halversen.
- Andrew Olson (born 1856, Town of Moscow)
- Martha Eriksdatter (born October 10, 1858, Town of Moscow; died February 19, 1923) married Peter Hans Wang
- Casper Edward Olson (born October 8, 1865, Town of Moscow; died January 28, 1948) married Inger Disrud.

The daughters' names are recorded in early Wisconsin records as Ericsdatter and Eriksdatter rather than Olson. All of the children of Eric and Christiane with the exception of Christine lived their lives in the area of Hollandale, Iowa County and Wiota, Lafayette County, Wisconsin. Upon her marriage, Christine and her husband Peder left to homestead land in Sioux County, Iowa just across the Sioux River from Eden, Dakota Territory (now Hudson, South Dakota).

Christiane's parents and family: Anders Kristoffersen and Anne Svensdatter

Maren and Christiane's parents were Anders Kristoffersen (name changed to Christophersen in America) and Anne Svensdatter. He was born 6 October 1804 on Halvorsrud in Jevnaker. She was also born in 1804 on the *husmansplass* Næsset under the farm Mo. They were married in Jevnaker on 31 March 1834 and *udflytted til Amerika* in 1851. They must have left Maren with her older sister in Norway because they had four other children to handle on their ocean voyage and Eric and Christiane had already planned to follow her parents to America in 1852.

Anders served as a soldier in the Norwegian army in 1829. His parents were Kristoffer Houereje (Hauger), born in 1763 in Jevnaker, and Gjertrud Olsdatter Toso, who was born 17 September 1775. They were married 22 October 1795 at Vangseie-Toso in Jevnaker. Gjertrud died on 12 September 1836 and Kristoffer passed 12 November 1846. Both were *begraven* the Jevnaker church cemetery. Anders was the fifth-born child of Kristoffer and Gjertrud. He had a younger brother, Lars, who came to America in 1853 and died in 1884 at Dell Rapids, Dakota Territory (now South Dakota). Lars changed his name from Kristoffersen to Larson in America.

Anders and Anne signed out of the Jevnaker *kirke rekord* on 9 April 1851 with the notation *"Udflyttede til Amerika."* Records list the family as follows:

Anders Christoffersen Olumeje 45
Anne   46
Anne   17
Gulbrand, born 9 October 1841
  His name changed to Gilbert Anderson in America and he died in October 1915 in Hollandale, Wisconsin
Otter, born 29 June 1850
Halvor, born 16 November 1847.

It is believed that both Halvor and Otto died aboard ship and were buried at sea.

Anders and Anne settled in Iowa County, Wisconsin. Anne died in 1872 and Anders in 1885. Both are buried in the Perry Lutheran Church Cemetery in Daleyville, Dane County, Wisconsin. The cemetery is located just across the Iowa County line from where they homesteaded The church records show "Anders Christopherson Dalen, born 6-10-1804, Hadeland, *Norge*, died 3-10-1885, wife Anne Swendson, born 1804, died 1872."

The 1880 census shows that Anders was living with his son Gilbert Anderson (Gudbrand Christopherson). In 1885 Anders made his mark (an "X") on a document transferring his homestead in Iowa County, Wisconsin, to Gilbert for the sum of $100. This document carried the stipulation that it could not be mortgaged or sold during Anders' lifetime, thus assuring him a place to live as long as he was still alive. Anders died less than 30 days after signing this document.

Eric's father and family: Ole Knutsen

Eric Olsen was the oldest of five children of Ole Knutsen (born *Prestbråten* in Jevnaker) and died in 1840 on Bjellumseie. He never left Norway. His wife died in 1839. Soon after the death of their parents the children had to leave Bjellumseie. The five orphans must have had a difficult time; the times were hard enough for *husmannfolk*.

Eric's sister Kristi Olsdatter (born 2 August 1836 on Bjellumseie; died 1897 at Prestlia in Jevnaker) married Borger Olson Prestlia but never left Norway.

Kari Olsdatter (born 16 February 1828 on Bjellumseie) married Mons Olson Enga and later Peder Hansen in Norway. Peder and Kari came to America in 1871 with their two children and two children from her first marriage. She died on 23 May 1917 in Blanchardville, Wisconsin and is buried at Yellowstone Lutheran Cemetery in Lafayette County, Wisconsin.

Kari Olsdatter Hansen is the great-great-grandmother of fellow Hadeland Lag member John Monson of Green River, Wyoming. We located John by chance when he put an article in an old issue of the *Brua* seeking information on names we immediately recognized as our family members. As a result, a new cousin was found and we were able to exchange a considerable amount of family genealogy.

Another brother, Hans Olson (born February 2, 1823 on Bjellumseie) came to America *ugift* (unmarried). He was living in Blanchardville, Wisconsin, in 1917 and attended his sister Kari's funeral there. Nothing more is known about him.

While there is considerable more history concerning the above people, space dictates that we will end this here with just some ancestors and first generatioin immigrants. Our genealogy research over the past 27 years has yielded information on more than 7500 ancestors and descendants. With all of this information it gives us great satisfaction that we have been able to share our research and give guidance to others searching for their Norwegian roots.

Lars Olson Oe Family

published February 1998   *Form 479*   *Beverly Jean-Ohe Toelle*

Lars Olsen Oe was born December 23, 1814, in Vestre Gran, Hadeland, Norway. He was one of six children born to Ole Amundsen O and Karen Larsdatter Gjovik. Two children died as infants.

In 1835, Lars purchased the O farm for 400 specie dollars. At 21, he was the eldest son and by law entitled to the family farm; certain inheritance laws in Norway precluded younger sons from entering the trade. Sale of the farm occurred after his father's death in 1834.

Lars' surviving siblings were: Maren, 23; Amund, 17; and Gudbrand, 12. Maren's history is unknown. Amund married Maren Hansdatter Grymyr in 1844 and later emigrated to America. Gudbrand's history is less complete. His marriage date to Maren Torgersdatter Lynneeie is unknown as well as any information about possible descendants.

Lars Olsen Oe

Lars' mother remained a widow and lived out her life on the O farm. She was the daughter of Lars Torgersen Gløvik and Gubjør Gudbrandsdatter Rua. She died April 19, 1857, at the age of 74.

On November 19, 1840, Lars married Ingeborg Torgersdatter Vaterud from the Jevnaker parish. They were the parents of five children: Karen, born January 3, 1843; Randi, born October 7, 1846; Oline, born November 19, 1851; and Torger, born March 28, 1854. One daughter, Oline, born September 2, 1849, died in infancy.

As a land owner, Lars was better off than the emigrants who belonged to the cotter or laboring classes. So, it's difficult to speculate why he chose to emigrate. At the time, conditions in Norway were hard, even for small farmers. The population had nearly doubled in the last century, agricultural prices were stagnant and food was scarce. Many people from Hadeland emigrated to America in hopes of finding a better life for themselves and their children.

In order to escape the worsening conditions in Norway, Lars sold the O farm to Lars Hansen Scheslien on April 2, 1869. This was just two weeks before the family sailed for North America. According to the Certificate of Testimony from the pastor at Gran parish, the family received their emigration papers on April 8, 1869.

Just one month earlier Lars' brother, Amund, had sailed for North America. He and his wife, Maren, left eight children behind. Their destination was Manston, Minnesota. Why the children did not leave Norway is unknown. Amund and Maren are buried in Our Savior's Lutheran Church Cemetery at Rothsay, Minnesota.

The family's written history includes no details of the transatlantic voyage. Oslo passport cards from 1869 list Lars as 54, married and a farmer from Gran. The entire family is listed as leaving the port city of Christiania on April 16, 1869, on the sailing ship *Johan*. Traveling as a family group, the children were listed as: Karen, 26; Randi, 23; Oline 19; and Torger, 15. Their tickets were paid through as far as McGregor, Iowa.

The *Johan* carried 364 passengers to North America and over one-third of them were children under the age of 12 years. Captain of the ship was H. Thorsen. After nearly 10 weeks at sea the *Johan* arrived in Quebec, Canada, on June 24, 1869. All 364 passengers survived.

From Quebec, they took various steamboats up through the Welland Canal and across the Great Lakes, and then traveled by rail to Detroit. A freight car from Detroit probably brought them to their final destination – the Mississippi River town of McGregor, Iowa. Why they went to this town is unknown, but it's likely that immigrant friends or relatives were there.

In 1869, McGregor, Iowa, was a Norwegian settlement and a safe haven for immigrant travelers. While no homestead land was available in northern Iowa in 1869, work could be found for 50 cents a day – a large sum to a poor Norwegian. The Oe family stayed two years, long enough to save a little money and equip themselves with provisions.

In 1871, they were ready to travel north to the Pelican River Valley in Otter Tail County, Minnesota. Free homestead land, 450 miles northwest of McGregor would soon be theirs. The journey north would also reunite the Oe brothers, Lars and Amund, who left Norway aboard separate sailing ships in 1869.

In 1949, Martin L. Pearson and Edward Thompson recorded a short story about the Ohe family in A History of the Township of Erhards Grove. Their brief but factual account chronicles the family's journey north and their claim of homestead land in Otter Tail County, Minnesota. An edited version states:

> In the spring of 1871, they traveled to Otter Tail County with the Amundson, Stadum, Toso and Ulven families, all of them Hadelandingers. The 450-mile trip to Minnesota was a long, slow and difficult journey. Three wagons or prairie schooners were in the caravan. A couple of the families had horses, the others had oxen. They traveled with their cows, sheep, chickens, farm seeds, provisions and at least one breaking plow.
>
> After several days they came upon the Abercrombie Trail near St. Cloud. They crossed the river on a ferry at a place near the present site of Dayton Hollow Dam. This took almost two days. After crossing the river they turned north on a less beaten trail, the Pembina Trail, and arrived in Otter Tail County after four weeks of adventure.

The Lars Olsen Oe family filed a homestead claim on the east half of the southwest quarter of Section 18 in Erhards Grove Township. This was not a full 80 acres because of the township line. Eight other Norwegian families were already there.

A sod cellar dugout was probably their first home because the building of a log cabin took some time. Logs had to be cut and hauled from east of the Pelican River, near Erhard. A stable was built for the animals.

Very little land was broken during the first year, but a garden was raised. The first crops of wheat were cut by cradle or scythe, tied into sheaves with straw and thrashed with a flail, and the kernels winnowed out in the breeze. Meat for the table was provided by hunting deer and fishing in the lakes and rivers.

Alexandria was the nearest post office – a walk of almost 70 miles. Soon Elizabeth had a store and a post office. Grain was hauled to Campbell, Manston, Hawley and Frazee.

Obstacles were many, including blizzards, prairie fires, grasshoppers and poverty. Indian scares were also frequent. At night, the sound of barking dogs often prompted settlers to prepare for an Indian raid. But hostile Indians never came.

Next to a home and livelihood they wanted a church. Area settlers came together in the summer of 1870 to organize a church. In 1871 Immanuel Norwegian Evangelical Lutheran congregation was established with Pastor Tollef Rosholdt as the first pastor. The first church service was conducted at the home of Lars and Ingeborg Oe on November 27, 1871.

Tuberculosis was widespread in the early Norwegian settlements of America. Karen, the eldest daughter, died from TB in 1875. She was 32. On November 11, 1880, Ingeborg also succumbed to the disease.

According to the 1880 Agricultural Census Lars owned his farm. He had 60 acres of tillable land, 40 acres in permanent pasture and another 140 acres of unimproved land. He also owned 4 horses, 5 milk cows, 5 calves, 2 sheep, 2 lambs, 10 swine, 17 poultry, and 2 working oxen. The total value of his farm including land and buildings was $2000.

In 1880, Torger was 26 and living with Lars and Ingeborg along with his wife, Helena Kittilson, and their 1-year old daughter, Ida. By 1885, the Minnesota census revealed that Torger was head of the household. He and his wife, Helena, now had five children: Ida, 6; Karen, 5; Lea, 4; Ole, 2; and Sophie, 9 months. Lars was 70 years old and living with them.

Lars Olsen Ohe was a widower for 18 years and died October 22, 1898, at the age of 83. A brief obituary from the Rothsay Regional Report said:

Lars Ohe, an old and respected citizen of the town of Erhard's Grove died at his home, October 22. The funeral took place last Wednesday and was largely attended. Interment took place at the Sondre Immanuel Cemetery, Rev. Rosholdt officiating.

Lars and Ingeborg's daughters, Randi and Oline, also married. Randi married Iver Brorby and Oline married Iver Grina. Today the descendants of Randi, Oline, and Torger number over 1,000.

History of the O Farm

The O farm is located in Gran, Norway, about 65 miles northwest of Oslo. It's a half-mile east of the small village of Grymyr and about one and one-half miles from the Randsfjorden shoreline.

A summary of the O farm history includes the following facts. Lars Olsen Oe purchased the farm in 1835 for 400 specie dollars. Sale of the farm followed his father's death in 1834. Lars labored on the 25-acre farm for almost 34 years before emigrating to America.

Lars and Ingeborg sold the farm to Lars Hansen Scheslien on April 2, 1869, for an unknown sum. This was just two weeks before the Oe family sailed for North America. Without sale of the farm it's unlikely passage money would have been available for Ingeborg and the four children: Karen, Randi, Oline, and Torger.

In 1902, the farm was sold to Thorvald and Randi Haugtvedt for 6,000 kroner. At that time, the farm buildings were in poor condition and beyond repair. Over a period of time the buildings were replaced and the house rebuilt.

Thorvald and Randi's oldest daughter, Martha, married Arne Bernard Velsand. They lived on the farm for a number of years before selling it to their son, Halvor.

Halvor Vesland married Kirsten Bergsrud and together they operated the farm until their son, Arne, began farming. Today, the O farm at 2754 Gran is a pig farm owned by Arne and Astrid Velsand, son and daughter-in-law of Halvor and Kirsten Velsand.

Origin of the Ohe Name

The Ohe name has been spelled three different ways in public documents: O, Oe, and finally Ohe. Why the name evolved as it did is unknown.

Ohe Family Tree

O is probably the shortest farm name in Norway. Like all Norwegians, Lars used the farm name as a third name. In the Oslo passport records for 1869 he is listed as Lars Olsen Oe. South Immanuel Lutheran Church records show the letter "h" was added to the name around 1891. Why did the name change to Ohe? Lar's son, Torger, considered the Oe name too short and added the letter "h" or so the story goes.

Brua Editor's Note: Beverly Ohe Toelle grew up near Pelican Rapids, Minn. Her grandfather was Torger and Helena's oldest son. Beverly is a relative of mine, so this story is also a part of my family history. Karen, Torger and Helena's second daughter, is my maternal grandmother.

Torger Larsen & Helena Kittelsen Ohe

published May 2008   *Form 479*   *Verlyn Anderson*

This is a continuation of the history of the Ohe family in America. Torger was the son of Lars and Ingeborg Vaterud Oe (Ohe). Torger was 15 years old when he immigrated to America in 1869, together with his parents and three sisters.

Torger and Helena Ohe family – 1905
Front center – Clarence.
Seated – Karen, Torger, Oscar, Helena, Lena.
Standing – Lars, Sophie, Hilda, Theodore, Ole. Ingard is standing in front of Theodore.

Torger Larsen Oe (Ohe) was born 28 March 1854 in Vestre Gran, Hadeland. The Ohe family left Christiania (Oslo) on 20 April 1869 on the sailing ship *Johan*. This 660-ton vessel was built in Warren, Maine in 1844. There were 360 passengers in steerage, 4 cabin passengers and a crew of 18 on this voyage! After a 10-week trans-Atlantic voyage, they finally arrived in Quebec, Canada on 20 June. They continued by steamboat through the Great Lakes to Detroit and from there most likely traveled by rail to their destination, McGregor, Iowa. After living there for two years, the family traveled north and west by prairie wagon, together with the Amundon, Stadum, Toso and Ulven families --- all immigrants from Hadeland – to claim homestead land in Erhard Grove and Trondhjem Townships, Otter Tail County, Minnesota. The trip took about four weeks.

Lars and Ingeborg's daughter Randi, who was born 3 January 1843, married Iver Jørgensen Brørby in 1872. Another daughter, Olina, married Iver Olsen Grina 17 July 1873. He had also emigrated from Jevnaker. The third daughter born, Karen, died of tuberculosis 18 March 1875.

Torger married Helena Kittelson on 28 October 1878. She had emigrated from Kongsberg, Buskerud, Norway in 1876. Thirteen children were born to Helena and Torger:

- Ida, born 7 April 1879, died of tuberculosis at the age of 15 on 9 May 1894.
- Karen, born 14 July 1880, married Ole Hovland and homesteaded in western North Dakota before returning to Minnesota upon retirement in 1951. She died 1 September 1960.
- Lena, born 30 November 1881, married Helmer Hjermstad and also homesteaded in western North Dakota before moving back to Minnesota in 1950. She died 26 May 1954.
- Ole, born 14 September 1883, married Olga Ouren and farmed the Ole and Haaken Ouren farms in Trondhjem Township before taking over the Ohe farm in Trondhjem Township when his father retired. He died 21 Feb. 1952.
- Lars, born 25 September 1886, died one month later on 28 October 1886.
- Lars, born 12 September 1887, died of a brain hemorrhage on 1 September 1912, at the age of 24.
- Hilda, born 4 November 1889, married Gilbert Haga of Rothsay, where they operated a general store/gas station and later farmed north of Rothsay. She died 29 October 1956.
- Theodore, born 27 September 1891, married Jeanette Mellum and farmed near Rothsay. He died 15 February 1965.
- Oscar, born 1 September 1893, married Minnie Ostlund and farmed in Trondhjem Township; they moved to Fergus Falls. He died 14 July 1973.
- Ingard, born 28 January 1896, married Gertie Halbakken and farmed in Trondhjem Township. He died 29 June 1980.
- Clarence, born 25 July 1898 and died at 9½ months on 3 May 1899.
- Clarence, born 3 February 1901, married Bertha Velo and farmed on the Lars Ohe homestead in Erhard Grove Township. They later moved to another farm nearby. He died 7 August 1983.

The 1885 Minnesota Census confirms that Torger was at that time the head of the household. He and his wife, Helena, had five children: Ida, 6; Karen, 5; Lena, 4; Ole, 2; and Sophie, 9 months. Torger's father, Lars, was 70 years old and living with them. His mother, Ingeborg, had died 11 November 1880. Lars died 22 October 1898.

In 1895 the farmers of Otter Tail County raised the largest crops of wheat, considering acreage, that had ever been raised. Many granaries bulged and broke out under the weight of that bumper crop! That year's wheat crop made it possible for Torger to purchase the 160-acre A.P. Boe farm, located in the southeast quarter of section 14 of Trondhjem Township.

In 1898 the family purchased and moved into the Iver Johnson farmstead. This was located next to the Boe farm. Torger was a lover of fine horses. The raising of them was his hobby. To work all those 500 acres meant that he had to increase the number of horses that he owned to 20 plus, of course, a number of young growing colts. He built the largest barn ever erected in the township in 1903.

To the right is a 1950 aerial view of the Iver Johnson farmstead that Torger bought in 1898. This was a 120-acre farm. It was located directly north of the Boe farm that Torger had purchased three years earlier. Here in 1903 he built the then-largest barn in Trondhjem Township. He also enlarged the house. This became his residence until his death in 1910.

Shortly after 1900 the St. Paul, Minneapolis and Manitoba Railway Company sold their land in Section 13. This land had been deeded to the Railway Company in partial payment for building

Photo courtesy of Gerald Ohe, Moorhead, Minnesota

the railroad from Fergus Falls to Pelican Rapids. Torger bought one-half of that section – 360 acres (1,440 *mål*). Thus, during the last years of his life, Torger owned and farmed more than 700 acres (2,800 *mål*!). He was a wealthy man – a very successful farmer!

Torger Ohe was not a tall man, but stout and blocky. He was a genius in many endeavors. The Ladies Aid and Basket Social planners enjoyed having Torger as their auctioneer. He was an excellent blacksmith and did all his own work. He also did blacksmithing for his neighbors as his time permitted. He became a thresher and a steam engineer early in his life.

Torger Ohe did not live to be an old man. In 1909 he became the victim of the dreaded disease – cancer. He was sick for about a year. He was the *klokker* (sexton/song leader) at the Bagstevold Lutheran congregation, Erhard, Minnesota, for more than 20 years. Rev. E.J. Ovri, his pastor, wrote the following: "The Sunday before he died, Torger sang at Bagstevold and bade the congregation farewell because he wondered if the operation would be his death. Torger died in St. Paul after the stomach cancer operation and the funeral was at South Immanuel Church on October 15, 1910. I spoke at the home and preached at the church on Matthew 17:1-9. There was an unusually large crowd, 105 teams of horses followed the hearse from the home. When they arrived at the church there were 37 teams and three autos already there."

Torger did not live long enough to own an automobile. Helena, his wife, was the victim of a car accident on the farm and passed away from the effects of the accident on October 24, 1924. She was a faithful wife and loving mother, an active woman in all circles of church and community activities.

Elie Moger Thingelstad

published May 1998   *Form 478*   *Oliver Thingelstad*

Oliver Thingelstad, grandson of Elie Moger, grew up in Northwood and became a teacher in various places in North Dakota. He lived in Northwood when he retired and died in the early 1990s.

Elie Moger was born in Hadeland, Norway, on the 19th day of February, 1826. Her home was in the fir-topped mountains of lower Hadeland, where she lived with her parents, Ole and Marie Moger, and her brothers and sisters. Their playground was the cone-strewn foothills of the fir and pine covered mountain side. Their playmates were the goats and cows that had to be tended, fed and milked every day. When Elie was a young and beautiful girl of 21, she met a dapper, young man of age 30, full of health and vigor, who lived on the Thingelstad *gård* farther down the valley, and his name was Ole. Soon they were married and she became Mrs. Ole Hanson Thingelstad, and moved to the groom's parental home. In 1848 a son was born and they named him Hans.

Rumors of free land in America spread all over Norway, and Ole and Elie were tempted with the bright prospects of land and a home of their own in this far away country of opportunity. The temptation blossomed into reality, and in the year 1849 they sailed into the land of fortune, leaving brothers and sisters behind, and saying farewell to their parents whom they would never see again in this world. During the overland journey their son died. This was the first misfortune in their married life.

They arrived in Clayton County, Iowa, in 1849, where Ole filed on 80 acres of land, and built a one-room frame house with an attic and a lean-to. Earlier emigrants from Hadeland had settled here, and it was like coming home. Their second son was born here in 1850, and they named him Hans Olaus in honor of the first-born. Iver Martinus was born in 1852 and Marie Sophia, named after her grandmother, was born two years later. The second disappointment came when their young daughter died. In 1855 a second daughter was born, and she was named Ingeborg (she later married Anton N. Ostmo). In 1857 Siri was born (she later married Peter N. Korsmo). Ole and Elie had now lived in America 10 years, and prosperity seemed their lot, when misfortune again came to Elie. Ole passed away this year and left her with a family of 5 children (the oldest 9) to look after and a small farm to operate. In the community was a

50

young man by the name of Peder Aslakson Fyllesvold who offered his hand in marriage, and was not daunted by the prospect of becoming the head of a full-fledged family. They were married within the year. As was the custom from Norway of adopting the name of the farm on which they lived, he became known as Peder (or Per) Thingelstad, which was convenient for the widow and all the children. The farm prospered and so did the size of the family. The first child of this union was a daughter, born in 1860, and she was named Berthe Marie. The first name was given in honor of the Fyllesvold relation and the second from Elie's mother. (Berthe later married Andrew J. Haga.) In 1862 a son was born and they named him Andrew (Andreas in Norway). Joseph was born in 1868 and was only 8 years old when the family moved to Dakota. In 1872 their last child was born, and he was named Ole to carry on the name of Elie's first husband.

In 1875 Peder had heard of larger tracts of land available in the territory of Dakota. Since his family was growing up and there were few opportunities for finding work, with no more land available to file on in Iowa, he set off alone for the Dakota territory. He arrived in an area where a year ago the Tragetons and the Bakkens had settled. From there he walked along the banks of the Goose River, a river flourishing with growths of sturdy oak, tall straight elm, unyielding ash and soft pliable basswood. As he walked he thought of the unending use these different woods could serve him in building his log cabin, as well as for firewood. Checking every flat area for a prospective building spot, he came upon one that suited him, and was moved at once in filing for a claim. Then he set about cutting trees, measuring them for length, squaring them off, and soon had his log cabin built for the family to move into next year.

When he came back to Clermont, Iowa, to make the report, it was received with enthusiasm and excitement. Now there was a lot of work to be done and planning for the exodus that would take place next spring. A buyer for the land had not been secured, three covered wagons were needed, and if the land was not sold they would have to seed it in for another year.

The plans were to set out in May, and in the early spring activities had started. Hans, now 26, and Iver, 24, were left with the spring seeding. Marie had passed away. Siri, 19, and Ingeborg, 21, were great helpers both out in the field and around the house. Berthe, 16, helped mama and was responsible for looking after Ole who was only 4. Joseph, 8, and Andrew, 14, were ordered around by everyone. When the time came for the caravan to leave, Peder put Hans in charge of the covered wagons, and Ingeborg went along to drive one of the wagons and cook. Berthe and Andrew would herd the 15 head of cattle, 10 head of horses and 25 head of sheep that had been selected to be taken along. At their age they thought of the trip as a lark, and a pleasant experience, but later, when they found out they had to walk nearly all the way it became a chore. The caravan set off in the morning of an early May day, and set its route along the railroad track following it parallel to the tracks nearly all the way to Fargo. Peder and Elie took the two younger boys along on the train which they boarded at noon on the same day. Berthe and Andrew would look back at every train that came hoping to see the folks. They were rewarded as finally one train came by with one window open and smiling faces crammed into the small space, waving arms and shouting with their cheers and gladness, as they left the slow-moving caravan behind.

When they came to Fargo, which was as far as the railroad had advanced, Peder made arrangements with a settler from Caledonia to transport them as far as his settlement on the Red River in an oxcart, where Paul C. Johnson met them with a team of horses and drove them to his home on the Goose River. They waited seven weeks for the caravan to arrive, but the hospitality of Paul Johnson and the good neighbors to the south helped them with many problems and social activities.

When the covered wagons arrived and stopped to unload in front of the cabin, Berthe bounded off in a hurry and disappeared inside, but she came out again in a bigger hurry. When asked what was wrong, she answered in a sobbing voice, "How can we live in that place with only a dirt floor?" Well, they did! Most of Peder's land that was tillable was on the north and east side of the river, so the stock and what little machinery there was, was transported to that side. In the following weeks a pole barn was erected, and covered with long poles sealed from rain with sod and bark. A 'lean-to' was added for the cattle, and consisted of two rows of upright poles a foot apart and filled with slue hay. The roof was built the same as the structure of the horse barn. The first winter was spent in the log cabin, and every day the boys or young men had to walk across the wooded area and across the river to feed and water the stock. This was not too bad in fine weather, but when the North Dakota blizzards raged it became a problem. The big problem came, however, in the spring when the swollen river from the spring thaw made the crossing a hazard, even with a raft.

When the flood subsided, Peder set about cutting logs and prepared to build another dwelling on the other side of the river, close to the pole barn. The two-story log house was erected during the summer, with wood rafters, wood shingles, wooden window frames and glass, and flooring transported from Fargo. Here the family lived together until one by one the older ones established their own homes. Hans had his claim west of the homestead cabin, and Iver one-half mile farther southwest. Siri's claim was next to Hans on the south. Ingeborg had her claim on the east side of the river, south of the family's new home. When Berthe became 21 she filed on the land just east of Ingeborg's. Now there were only the three younger boys, Andrew, 23, Joseph, 17, and Ole, 13, who were left at home with the parents. Sometime during the period that followed Peder built a two-story, frame house next to the log house that was connected by a common stairway leading to the second floor. In 1892 Peder passed away leaving Elie a widow for the second time. The next year when Andrew got married, Elie moved into the new addition with Joseph and Ole, while Andrew and his bride, Caroline Korsmo, lived in the log house. Iver, his wife Thilda, and daughter Marie had moved back to Iowa, and while there Iver passed away, in the year 1896. The widow Thilda and her daughter came back to Dakota and lived for a year with Grandma Elie. The next year Joseph married the widow and established his home on the claim left by Iver which was located about 1 ½ miles due north. Here they built up one of the most modern farms in the community. The present owner is Canfield Sheggerud, a son of Marie (Malla), who married Mads Sheggerud. In 1903 Andrew's family had grown to the number of six boys, and he decided to build a modern 2 ½-story building and abandon the log house. Andrew had bought title to the farm, so Elie, in a generous mood, offered her home to the city of Northwood to be used as a much needed hospital. It later was converted into an Old Peoples Home. Not many years ago it was demolished and replaced by a three-story modern nursing home. When Elie donated her home for a hospital, she moved in with her daughter Berthe (Mrs. Andrew Haga) and lived there until the time of her death in 1907.

Harriet Foss, Northwood, N.D., great-granddaughter of Elie Moger, wrote about the photo above:

> This is the house that Great-Grandma gave to our city in October 1902 and was used until the middle of the '60s as Northwood's first hospital and later as an old people's home. It had been "rolled" into town with horses and logs (less than two miles). In this photo a group of Ladies Aid women gathered at the place and held a meeting on August 5, 1905. There are at least four Norwegian flags visible on the picture

Mons Grinager

"Mons Grinager..." published February 2006   *Form 401*   *Harald Hvattum*

It was just after the New Year that an immigrant from Hadeland was on his way from Minnesota to Madison, Wisconsin to enlist as a soldier in this New Land. It happened that just a few years after he had arrived in America, a civil war broke out between the Northern and Southern states in that land. Mons Grinager, the name of the man on this journey, would join and fight on the side of the Northern states.

This is the farm on which Mons Grinager was born. When he was growing up, the Old Grinaker Stave Church was still being used. The church was located on the hill, just north of the farm where Mons lived. That hill is to the left on the picture.   *Photo by Harald Hvattum*

It is just by chance that some people are remembered more than others. Mons wrote many letters about various Civil War battles to his relatives in Norway and those letters were also carefully preserved after the war. Much that we know about Mons comes from those letters. The letters have, naturally, aroused interest and have been published in several publications, including the *Årbok for Hadeland*.

In addition, Mons Grinager carefully preserved much of the original source material that he had used in the publicity campaign that he headed to recruit soldiers for the "Scandinavian Regiment." In this endeavor he was pictured on many publicity posters in the Midwest.

Mons was from one of the Grinaker farms in Tingelstad. Grinåker was the way his farm name was pronounced in the district, but the man who recorded the Census of 1865 spelled the name of that farm Grindager. When Mons came to America in 1853, he dropped the "d" from his name. As did many emigrants, Mons Grinager at first worked for an American farmer so that he could learn to understand and speak English. In 1854 we know that he was living in Decorah, Iowa. Here he worked in a local business establishment for three years. In 1859 he moved to Freeborn County in Minnesota where he and his wife, Anne, began farming.

Mons Grinager was 28 years old when the Civil War broke out and thus was a man who was physically in his "best years." He lived then, as mentioned above, in Freeborn County,

54

Minnesota and enlisted as many others in the Midwest into the military service for the North. Then, a short time after the war began, he was selected to recruit and organize a regiment primarily made up of immigrants from Scandinavia. The resulting regiment was the 15th Wisconsin Volunteer Infantry Regiment or The Scandinavian Regiment which it was also called. Mons Grinager was enrolled in the Regiment in January, 1862, and was promoted to the rank of captain and leader of Company K. He held this position until the Regiment was formally discharged in February, 1865.

The 15th Wisconsin Volunteer Infantry Regiment took part in many bloody battles, and in the Battle of Stone's River, Tennessee in late December, 1852, Grinager was wounded in the leg. He continued to stay on his feet, but within a short time he lost so much blood that he lost consciousness. A medic managed to transport him to a hospital in nearby Murfeesboro. The next day the hospital was captured by the Southern forces and Mons was then taken as a prisoner of war. Five days later, the hospital was recaptured by the forces of the North and Grinager was freed. His wounds were so serious that he was given a 3-month furlough back at home in Minnesota before he was able to return to the military, again as a captain.

After the war Mons Grinager returned to the farm and his family in Minnesota. It was perhaps a pretty quiet place for "an old warrior" with no one except his family around him. After a short time he decided to enter the political arena as a Republican and thus created another career in his home district. He lived only a short 25 years after the war and died in 1889 in Hennepin County, whose county seat is Minneapolis.

There is a considerable amount of historic research material available about Mons Grinager. The easiest way to find out more about him and other Norwegian-American immigrants who fought in the American Civil War is to access the homepage of the Vesterheim Norwegian-American Museum in Decorah, Iowa. The web address of the museum is http://www.vesterheim.org. On that website there is a link to a database, named *Civil War*

Database, that contains information about Norwegian-American immigrants who participated in the Civil War. In it you will find information about many other immigrants who came from Oppland County in Norway. I did just a little browsing in this database and looked under the letter "e" in the index. There I discovered the names Andrew A. Egge and Andrew Eggebraaten, both of whom were born in Hadeland! (Translator's note: Jerry Rosholt is the person who has headed this important research about Norwegian-Americans who participated in the Civil War. He wrote the book *Ole Goes to War* which was published by Vesterheim and is available for purchase from the museum for $14.95.)

It was the brother of Mons, Peder Hansen Grinager, who took over the Grinaker farm in Tingelstad. But in 1880, he decided to emigrate to America with his family. The farm was sold to someone outside the family. Some family members were supposed to return and take over the farm a few years later. In 1883, an uncle of Mons, Lars Pedersen Grinager, returned to Norway and bought the farm back again. He wasn't just anyone. This man had received excellent training as a violinmaker and, in fact, in 1886 was awarded a Gold Medal for violin making at the World's Fair in Paris, France!

Master Violinmaker Lars Grinager

published November 1998, February & May 1999   Form 402
An article from Brandu'stikka by Helge Stenersen, translated by Esther Grinager Embrey, submitted by Paul Grinaker

Hadeland has had just one violinmaker who attained world renown: LARS PEDERSEN GRINAGER. It is nearly a hundred years since he died, but his life and work have never been written about before now – here in *Brandbu'stikka*.

Lars P. Grinager was no prophet in his own land – in his own home parish of Brandbu. But out in the wide world he gained great recognition for his violin making. Moreover, like so many other capable artists and experts, he died a poor man.

Lars had the Grinager name from the farm SOUTH GRINAGER, gnr. 110, bnr. 1. That farm was owned by his parents, Peder Hansen and Lise Larsdatter, when Lars came into the world the 17th of March, 1848. The boy was baptized in Grinager Church on the 8th of April.

It is uncertain how early his ancestors came here. But Lars' grandfather, Hans Pedersen, had Grinager until his death in 1836. He was then 56 years old. The widow, Marthe Hansdatter, sold the farm to the son Peder for 2,000 *speciedaler* in a deed of conveyance on the 11th of November, 1839. Peder was at that time 21 years old and had six younger living siblings.

Drawing of Lars Grinager, reproduced in 'Verdens Gang' in 1887

Ancestors from 1700

It is time-consuming, but not especially difficult, to follow Lars Pedersen Grinager's lineage backwards in time. However, here we shall be satisfied to take as a starting point Thorsten Alm, who died in 1700.

Thorsten's son Steffen married Sigrid Eriksdatter. The couple's oldest son, Thorsten (1725-1807) was first married to Rangdi Haakenstad, then to Anne Hansdatter. Through inheritance and marriage Thorsten Steffensen became the owner of Alm, Svinning, Nordgar'n Raasum and Raasumshagen.

Anne and Thorsten had several children – among them, Hans (1755-1820). He was also married two times, first to Marthe Pedersdatter Hvattum, then to Maria Monsdatter Gjervigen. One of the children in the last marriage was Marthe Svinning, who in 1816, 27 years old, married the 35-year-old Hans Pedersen on Grinager. This was the couple who, two years later, had the son Peder, who was the father of the violinmaker Lars Pedersen.

Hans Pedersen, on his side, was a descendant of Hans Paulsen Bindeneje and his wife, Johanne Nilsdatter. They had a son Peder (1741-1812) who in 1774 married Thore Pedersdatter Hvattum. These were parents of Hans Pedersen and, in other words, also grandfather and grandmother to Peder Hansen, Lars' father.

We can add that Peder Hansen had eight siblings. Among them was Thorsten Grinager, who settled on Egge, and Mons Grinager, a well-known Civil War captain in the U.S.

Related to Many

About Lars' mother's family, it can shortly be said that it originated, among others, from Hvaleby in Gran. But Jacob Olsen, who in his time was owner of Hvaleby, sold the farm in 1751 and acquired Noklebye in Jevnaker instead. Jacob's son Lars was the father of Jacob Larsen Noklebye (1761-1828) who married Elizabeth Olsdatter.

Elizabeth and Jacob had seven children; one of them was Lars Noklebye (1799-1862) who married Anne Pedersdatter Nordby, who was two years younger than he was. Lars bought Hvinden in Gran and from there were the children scattered; Jacob to Lower Naes, Ingeborg to Daehlen, Peder to Stabo and Naess – and Lise Kirstine* to Grinager as wife of Peder Hansen.

Whoever wishes to go further into the subject can quickly establish that Lars Pedersen's family had – and has – branched off to nearly all the farms in Hadeland, a large part of Ringerike, Land and Toten; and do not forget the U.S., where many, many, emigrated.

>*Usually her second given name was written Kristine. But her father used Kirstine, and we have retained that here.*

Schooling and Work

Lise and Peder on Grinager had 14 children, born in the years 1846 to 1866. The oldest in the flock was Hans, two years older than Lars. Hans had alodial rights so Lars, at an early point in time, looked for training in order to have an occupation outside the farm.

In 1857 the parish's first higher public school was established, and was housed right at Grinager. Lars became a pupil, and was there for several years.

His report card has been preserved and the teacher, Svend P. Staavi, wrote in it on Oct. 6, 1864, the following:

"In some subjects Lars does quite well; but in others, where the capability is related to philosophy, it is not so good. A steady progress can nevertheless be shown. His conduct is very good."

In the review examination in December of the same year, Lars obtained the grade "Good" in religion, Bible reading, geography, Norwegian language and spelling. He got "Very Good" in Bible history, reading, arithmetic and geometry, and "Excellent" in writing.

In a corresponding examination one year later he obtained "Very Good" in all subjects except geography and Norwegian history, which were "Good." But in writing, plus the new subject of drawing, he got "Excellent."

Lars was confirmed in Grinager Church. That stave church was almost a neighbor to the farm, and his father – Peder Hansen – was the church warden for many years.*

At the same time he attended school, he also took part in doing the chores on the farm.

It soon became apparent that he had extra good skill when it concerned woodworking. As a small boy he made simple toys out of wood, and he was not very old when he did repair work in the barns.

Already, as a 15-year-old he began gradually to repair old violins and he tried also to build one. That didn't go too badly. But he had not pursued the fiddle work very long before he felt that he needed more knowledge and more education in that field. Therefore, as soon as he could be freed from the farm work, he applied for a job at Edmund Neupert's pianoforte factory in Kristiania. He was hired and was there for almost two years. He said later that that had been a very useful time, which had given him learning about the use of different kinds of wood, about resonance and tonal effect, about modern tools and about music. Besides, he also used the time in the city to go through a course at the public drawing school. This subject was very useful for anyone who wished to construct and build musical instruments. After the end of his training at the drawing school he got the best recommendations.

To get some further experience, he took a job with the master joiner Bonsnes, also in Kristiania. But he was not here long.

> *Peder was also active in community politics at one time; among other things, he was the vice-chairman of the parish in 1862-1865. In Grinager Church the last service was held in 1866, the same year as the new Tingelstad Church was dedicated. The old stave church was torn down after that.

The First Recognition

At home on Grinager the farm business was not going very well. The reason was not only that the family was large with many mouths to feed. There were also generally difficult economic conditions in the country at that time, not the least within agriculture. Lars chose to go home to help.

But violin work lay now nearest his heart. He used every free moment to be busy with the repair and building of instruments. He experimented with different kinds of wood and tried to develop a steadily better form and a steadily better tone. It is said that, among other things, he used the wood material from the Grinager Church which had been torn down. Whether it was the origin of the wood, its age and quality, or that it was "holy," which was the reason, is uncertain.

Lars became steadily more proficient as a violinmaker, and in 1877 he got recognition, which others than those nearest to him took notice of.

In September there was held a large exhibition of folk arts and crafts in connection with a country-wide agricultural meeting in Kristiania. Lars sent in one of the violins he had made, together with the case, and went to the exhibition. He obtained a bronze medal* and an official document, and the *Morgenblad* relates:

"We have sought the assistance of a couple of experts to evaluate the instrument's excellence. In their opinion, the violin is considered to be better than one usually finds in this category, and therefore we find a special talent in the exhibitor."

> *Editor's note: This medal was presented to the Hadeland Folkemuseum by Robert Means, Edina, Minnesota (now deceased), during the June 1990 visit of the Hadeland Lag. Lars Grinager was the brother of Robert's grandfather.

Strained Economy

Both the jury and the experts in the capital gave Lars Pedersen much commendatory mention for his work, and the medal and the recognition were a strong appeal for Lars to continue as he had begun. But the family's economic problems increased rather than diminished, and Lars must partly be satisfied witih a very low price when he sold a violin – it was more important to have a quick settlement than a high price.

Conditions had become so bad by the spring of 1879 that Peder Hansen began to talk seriously about emigrating to America. It was no joke for a man of his age, over 50 years, to break off abruptly. He also had a large family.

But thousands of Norwegians had long ago crossed the Atlantic Ocean and it was reported that many of them had done well in America, in "Possibility Land." Peder's brother Mons had gone over already in 1853. He had written many letters home, and had made his relatives very familiar with conditions in the new country. Peder and his wife and children knew, therefore, what to expect.

Money, and Again Money

But it was not just to decide to go. The trip was expensive. All resources must be sought to obtain traveling money and the necessary starting capital which would be needed in America.

Lars made his contribution in this way: He got the tax collector's permission to "raffle off one of my violins with case and bow." And it was not just any old violin; it was the same one which had won the bronze medal in Kristiania.

Two appraisers estimated its value. The one, Pastor C.P. Monrad, stated, "I consider the violin to be worth at least 200 *kroner*." The other, who signed himself A. Daehlen, Musician, wrote that he could testify "that the violin with case was the one which was awarded the medal in Christiania in 1877, and that among the musicians in Christiania it was discussed and praised as an especially good and well-made instrument, and can be estimated to be worth at least 200 *kroner.*"

The lottery brought in about the violin's worth. At the drawing on Aug. 7, 1879, the instrument was won by Lieutenant B. Dybwad in Kristiania.

But there was quite a bit more money needed than a lottery could bring in. The farm must be sold – and all that went with it. That was usual in such cases. The sheriff held an auction, and the bid on the farm went to Andreas Nilsen Berger. The purchase price was 36,000 *kroner*, an amount of money which was greatly reduced when Peder had paid all his debts.

To the New World

On the 14th of May 1880 the family left Kristiania on the emigrant steamship *S/S Angelo.*

There were Peder Hansen and his wife Lise, respectively 62 and 56 years of age, and five of the children. Edvard, 15, and Mons, 13, were unmarried. The family paid in all 798.70 *kroner* for the boat trip from Kristiania to New York.

Also, Lise and Peder's oldest son Hans left the homeland at the same time. Hans was 34 years old and with him was his wife, Ingeborg Andersdatter Haug, who was 28 years old. They had their three children with them – Peder, Adolf and Lars, ages 3, 1¼ and ½, respectively – also the 68-year-old Berthe Hansdatter. For these six the boat trip cost 465.52 *kroner.*

There were many reasons why Lars came with them to America. As the oldest unmarried son living at home, he probably felt an extra responsibility to help his parents in their new life. At the same time, his possibility as a violin maker in Norway was very small; perhaps it would be easier in America. Besides, he thought, as an experienced carpenter, he would have a chance to earn good money in better circumstances than in the homeland.

In America the family went westward from New York – to North Dakota – the new territory which had been opened up for settling. They settled down in Lisbon on the Cheyenne River, 8 to 10 miles southwest of Fargo.

But as they began here with farming, gradually the oldest children moved to other places. For example, a year after that, son Thorvald, 19 years old, was already working as a storekeeper in Albert Lea, Minnesota.*

> *Thorvald settled down later in Lisbon as a merchant. His brother Hans got a government job in Ransom County (County Treasurer and Clerk of Court), the county Lisbon belongs to.*

Health Problems

We have very little information about the time in America. However, Lars soon had a chance to prove himself as a carpenter. He managed to become employed in a furniture factory, something which suited well that precise and dexterous fellow. He was a first-rate carpenter, and it wasn't very long before he advanced to foreman in the factory.

For three years he took part in furniture production. He earned money and learned quite a bit, he thought, the first year. But now, as before, the violin work took all his free time. He began, at first, to repair old fiddles and other stringed instruments, and soon got a good reputation for his precision and ability. Little by little, he used more and more time to build new instruments, and often he worked at night.

Everything went well as long as he was healthy. But gradually he got health problems. He found out that the climate was unhealthy for him. He had never had such problems at home in Norway, and the result was that he decided to turn back to the old country.

The summer of 1883 he said farewell to America. His destination was Brandbu.

On Home Ground

In the home parish the circumstances had not changed worth mentioning, except that perhaps it had become still a little more difficult to run a farm. In any case, Lars had no great problem to buy back the family farm, Søndre Grinaker.

His father had thought that he had got about the least amount for the farm at the auction in 1880. Andreas N. Berger, who had had it since then must now let it go to Lars for 32,400 *kroner*. Berger lost three and a half thousand *kroner* in that affair. But probably he had sold timber and other things for that and more.

October 14, 1884, Lars got the deed to the farm. (Berger had had the formal title to it only from September 15, 1882.) The following spring Berger held an auction at Grinaker and sold the livestock, crop, equipment, household goods and personal property. Lars got hold of much of that – among other things – stoves for many rooms, windows, horse-drawn vehicles and other things.

Even if Lars could be happy to be back again on the family farm, his birthplace, life was far from rosy. He had not had capital worth mentioning with him from America. Andreas N. Berger now had a considerable bond on the farm, and at the same time Lars had to borrow money from other sources. In other words, he was quite weak economically. Much indicates that he was not such a great businessman; in any case, his work with the violins brought in far less than his efforts promised.

Fiddles in Focus

But just in these very years – after coming back from America – Lars pursued violin building and repairing full time.

He gradually made a considerable number of violins. Some he sold in his home parish, some he got orders for from America, and some he sold in Kristiania, among others, through

Neupert's piano factory business. Some were also sold in a lottery – by him or by acquaintances who bought them reasonably.

The repair work was probably the most profitable. He was handy both with fiddles and with other kinds of musical instruments. Some were really fine and good violins, others were almost a bunch of slivers in a bag. Lars managed to repair them reasonably well, and there exist today many violins around Hadeland with a label which showed that they have been repaired by Lars P.Grinager. Illustrating and interesting in this respect is a letter which the thankful customer, O. Miklebust, a Norwegian-American in Carthage, South Dakota, sent to *Hadelands Tidende*,

A Proficient Instrumentmaker

A translation of the letter from O. Miklebust:

> "Last summer I sent an old and completely damaged violin to the instrument maker, L.P. Grinager, at Hadeland, Norway, for repair. I had heard that Mr. Grinager was the most capable violin maker in his trade. I was not disappointed in my expectation when some time later I got my violin back here in America in excellent condition, so I surely can say that its excellence can be set beside the best violins.

> "I have recently seen that Mr. Grinager has obtained the gold medal in Paris, France, for three of the violins he has made. That is, I believe, an absolute guarantee that he is proficient in his trade, and I can with certainty recommend him to anyone who wishes either a good new instrument or the repair of old instruments, since I am certain that reasonable requirements will be satisfied."

O. Miklebust, Carthage, P.O. Miner Co., Dakota, North America. From *Hadelands Tidende*, March 4, 1887.

Paris and Barcelona

The greatest and best thing which happened to violin maker Lars P. Grinager was, without doubt, the success which his violins had at a world-wide exposition in Paris, France, in 1886. He had sent to it three of the violins he had made, and they aroused justified attention. For his first-class work he was awarded the exposition's gold medal.

Two years later he took one of his violins to a corresponding exposition in Barcelona, Spain. Here also the violin and its maker obtained a very flattering and honorable report from the jury.

Dark Clouds

But it was not easy for a violin builder to get along here in the country in the 1880s. The market was too small. There were also very few newspapers, so that what is understood today in marketing was a practically unknown concept. It was difficult for an expert like Lars Grinager to become known and to offer his services. Therefore, he could not live exclusively as a fiddle maker or fiddle repair man.

But Lars was more interested in violins than in agriculture. As before mentioned, the economy in agriculture was weak, and at the same time, Lars had quite a lot of indebtedness. In 1880 his father had been so bad off that he had had to sell the farm and emigrate. Now Lars was in about the same situation, and he was not completely over his health problems which he had contracted in America.

However, Lars was no longer living alone at Grinager. His mother, father and sister Lisa had also come back, probably in the summer of 1884. Lars, therefore, had help with the farm work, so that he could with good conscience use most of his time on violins. But the poor economy hung over him the whole time like a malicious shadow.

New Lotteries

People who struggled with difficult times in these years often suggested lotteries to help them. That did not apply only to poor people; also, merchants and craftsmen were engaged in lotteries.

Now also Lars. He usually allied himself with a country storekeeper who applied for permission and arranged for the lottery sale. For example, April 20, 1886:

Then the merchant, Edvard M. Daehlen, Brandbu, applied for – and received – permission to auction off a new violin made by Lars P. Grinager. It was appraised by the musician Anders O. Daehlen from Egge for 75 *kroner*. There were tickets sold for 25 *øre* Lars Grinager himself took 10 *kroner*'s worth. At the drawing on October 6 the violin was won by John Wien, who at that time operated a country store in Østgar'n på Skirstad.*

> *On May 8, 1890, Anne Marie Wien at Moe in Gran (John Wien's wife) applied for permission for a lottery for, among other things, "One violin from L. Grinager's factory." It was appraised by Lars Glorud and J. Hvattum for 50 kroner. The winner of the drawing on August 18 was Peder J. Lomsdalen, Elvetangen. Everything indicated that that was a different violin than the one that John Wien won in 1886.*

A Bad Agreement

February 2, 1888, Edward M. Daehlen, in agreement with Lars Grinager, obtained a new permission to raffle off a new Grinager violin that was appraised by Brødrene Hals for 100 *kroner*. Kristine P. Bjørnstuen, Brandbu, was the winner at the drawing on April 7, 1888.

P. Nøklebye in Jevnaker had a Grinager violin which he wished to sell to the dentist Ole P. Berger in Brandbu in the summer of 1888. But first he delivered it to Grinager for repairs. That work was to be paid for by Berger – the price was 10 *kroner*.

However, Grinager wanted the violin sent to the before-mentioned exposition in Barcelona at his expense and risk. Nøklebye gave permission for that. The parties agreed (together with Nøklebye) that if the violin was sold at the exposition for the stated price, 400 *kroner*, Grinager should have 50 *kroner* and Nøklebye the rest. If the sale should not come about, the violin should be assigned to Berger for the price which Berger and Nøklebye had agreed upon, but also Berger should pay for the repairs.

The violin was sold. However, Grinager was not in agreement with Nøklebye's interpretation of the contracted agreement. Later, in 1888, it was found that Nøklebye had to write a sharp letter to Grinager. Here Nøklebye cited witnesses who were willing to take an oath that his interpretation of the agreement was correct.

Grinager gave up. He accepted 50 *kroner* as the full and final settlement, repairs included.

Foreclosure

In spite of the Exposition and the lottery, Lars Pedersen did not manage to obtain enough profit to pay his debts.

Thursday, the 6th of March 1888, it came about as many had expected, and Lars himself had been afraid of: there was held a forced sale on Grinaker of horses, cattle, crops and farm implements of all kinds, together with some personal property. The auction was demanded by the attorney A. Støp, Gran, and the basis was the large debt to Akers Savings Bank, 15,000 *kroner*, plus rents and expenses.

The profits from the auction gave Lars a little breathing room, but not much more. Later in the year he found he also had to sell a part of his own farm, and the following parcels were therefore separated out (on October 24): Bnr. 2, Marka Vestre, bnr. 3, Marka Nordre, and bnr. 4, Hallingdal.

It ended as badly as it could, for also the main dwelling place – gnr. 110, bnr. 1 – had to be disposed of. The farm was sold at auction. Carl Grindvold got his bid accepted, with an offer of 21,675 *kroner* (deed of May 22, 1889).*

> *Three years later Grindvold sold the farm to Gunerius G. Elken for 25,000 kroner (deed of October 8, 1892). In 1896 it was taken over by Johs. Hornslien, A. Struksnæs, and P. Lomsdalen in joint ownership. On February 2, 1897, they sold it to the grocer, C. Gunnestad.*
>
> *On December 4, 1899, the towns of Brandbu and Gran obtained the deed to the property. They operated it as a common "poor farm" until 1916; then Brandbu municipality took it over alone.*
>
> *Grinaker old people's home was in operation totally until the newly built Marka aldershjem was put into use in 1950, after an exchange of real estate between the village and Marcus Sterud, father of the present owner of Grinaker Søndre.*

A Short Life

All that adversity naturally had an effect on Lars' health. And soon his hourglass had run out. He died at Grinaker the 18th of January, 1889, not yet 41 years old. The cause of death was stated to be "Hemmhorage."

He was buried at Tingelstad Church on January 25. There was not an official probate, since both of his parents were alive. But his father, now 71 years old, died later the same year.

On the 18th of January, 1890, there was a settlement of the estate after the death of Peder Hansen Grinager, whose wife, Lise Larsdatter, was still living. That was not especially lucrative for the creditors. For example, Lise's brother, Lars Hvinden, got a dividend of only 33.40 *kroner* for a total claim of 1,559.73 *kroner*.

A Fruitless Attempt

The merchant, Hjalmer Daehlen, Brandbu, had got permission to raffle off on March 22, 1888, a new violin which Lars had made. Anders O. Daehlen and K. Lyseng evaluated it at 65 *kroner*. The drawing was held on April 25, 1890, and the winner was Ole H. Sørum.

It was about two years from the sale of the first ticket until the drawing took place.

86 numbers were sold by Lars P. Grinager up to December 12, 1888, and 6 sold by the storekeeper Ive Lutken up to December 17. Later, 27 more numbers were sold by storekeeper H.A. Skattum, and 54 by storekeeper Tron Horn. Thereafter, the lottery book remained at Lutken's place until all 650 tickets were sold at 10 *øre*.

April 25, 1890, Hjalmer Daehlen then sent the list of names of those who had bought tickets to the sheriff for drawing. The drawing should naturally have happened before. Wrote Daehlen: "The reason there was so much time elapsed is this: that I did not know where the violin and lists have been, before Iver Lutken came with it here today."

The real reason that all this was forgotten was something else, namely, that the one who actually sponsored the lottery, Lars P. Grinager, had died in the meantime.

Lars' mother, the widow Lise Kirstine, moved away from Grinager after her son and husband had died. She lived for a time with her daughter Anna, who was married to Hans Andersen Haug in Drammen.

But the daughter Lise, who now had passed 30 years and still was unmarried, wanted to go back to America and her brothers there. She persuaded her mother to go with her, and June 3, 1892, the two Lises left Norway for good. Both died in America; the mother in 1904, and the daughter probably in 1919.

Today's Grinager Violins

What has become of the violins which Lars P. Grinager made? *Brandbu'stikka* has been searching for them for two years and has found seven, all of which have been photographed. Four of these are said with certainty to be genuinely Grinager-made, the rest are also in the greatest probability genuine (to the degree the layperson can judge such things).

Here are the present owners of these seven instruments, according to the year they were built:

- Guttorm P. Hoff, Brandbu. That violin carries Lars P. Grinager's trademark and the date, 20 November, 1879. Guttorm obtained it from his uncle (mother's brother) Paul Daehlen.

66

- Lars Jacob Hvinden Castberg, Vestre Gran. The violin has inserted 1885 as the year it was built. It originally belonged to the great-great-grandmother, Anna Marie Haug, who was very musical, and also played the violin. It has been at the Hvinden farm all these years.
- Olaf Wien, Gran. The violin is an heirloom from his father, Ansgar Wien, whose parents were Anne Marie and Ole Wien, winner of the lottery in 1888.
- Jane Grinager Brown, Milford, Michigan. The violin was inherited from their father, Robert (Bob) Grinager, who died last year. Bob was the son of Peder Hansen, Lars P. Grinager's nephew. Within the Grinager relatives in the U.S. it has been said that this is "the violin which got the gold medal in Paris in 1886."
- Yolanda Grinager Hager, Denver, Colorado. Lars' father, Peder, was Yolanda and Robert's great-grandfather. The violin was probably made in 1887.
- Ole Toverud, Vestre Brandbu. He obtained the violin from his father, Gudbrand, who inherited it from his father, Ole. His brother Bent bought Grinaker Nordre, and possibly acquired the instrument in the same deal. It is presumed to have been made in 1888.
- Lars Christen Bjone, Bjoneroa. That violin had earlier belonged to his grandfather, Martinius Bjone, who valued it very highly. It was never called anything except "Grinager-fiddle."

Those Which Have Vanished

The violins which are known to have been made by Lars P. Grinager, but which cannot be tracked down are as follows:

- Løytnant B. Dybwad, Incognito-gaten 7, Kristiania (1879).
- Grocerer Emil Tandberg, Drammen (1885).
- John Wien, Skirstad, Gran (1886).
- Lars Andersen Blegen, Brandbu (1887).
- Kristine P. Bjørnstuen, Brandbu (1888).
- Peder J. Lomsdalen, Elvetangen, Gran (1890).
- Ole H. Sørum (1890).
- Kristian Chr. Røkenbro, Røykfnvik (1894).

A Grinager violin was some years ago stolen from a relative who lived in South Dakota. Additionally, one instrument earlier had gone astray in the U.S. Moreover, there is much which suggests that Neupert's piano factory sold two or three violins for Grinager in 1886-87; in addition, *Brødrene Hals*, Kristiania, had one for sale. Finally, we have the violin which was sold for 400 *kroner* after the Barcelona exposition in 1888 (that was evidently sold right in Spain; plus one which the same year was sent to a customer in the U.S. (it was ordered in 1887).

Altogether 30 Violins?

We have now mentioned 23 violins in all which we believe Lars P. Grinager built.

Robert Grinager in Michigan was told by older relatives that Lars had made 19 violins. But that number presumably must date from a point in time several years before Lars died. The probability indicates that *Brandbu'stikka* has not managed to track down all, and that the production count, therefore, must lie well over 25. And that is terribly many, taking into consideration the facilities and working conditions of the day.

There were also many violins which Lars in his day had for repairs. They were all furnished with a label with Lars P. Grinager's name and address, together with the year of repair. Usually a picture of the medal he received was on the label.

Grinager violins have often been praised for their fine sound – a sound "which was mainly due to one of his own inventions" (*Ny Illustreret Tidende*) – and "which has cost him a lot of problems" (*Verdens Gang*). What that invention actually consisted of has never been more explicitly explained.

First-Class Quality

Brandbu'stikka has not been able to engage any specialist to analyze the existing Grinager violins to evaluate their quality or to estimate their worth. But the available source material indicates that the quality both of the violins and of his work must have been first-class. Here are some quotations:

"What has served to call attention to Grinager's violins is, in the judgment of experts, the excellent tone. May your parish produce many so persevering, competent and intelligent men as Grinager. (*Verdens Gang*, 1889)

A Loss for the Country

"It was an equally great honor for the artist and for his parish that Lars P. Grinager obtained the gold medal at the Paris Exposition in 1886," said the *Hadelands Tidende* afterwards. The newspaper continues:

"L. Grinager is of the kind of people who are called self-taught, since self-instruction would be the most important part of the training in his craft. But the violin cannot be created with definite dimensions and labels. There are so many things to take into consideration to get a clean, clear and loud tone. But it is the nature of genius that they, with patience, perseverance and constantly thorough thoughts, in a definite direction, care about what they are doing. No genius is finished immediately – it must be developed; and it doesn't surrender to unsuccessful attempts, but sets to work anew, until it reaches the goal. L. Grinager has reached that goal before others."

Ny Illustreret Tidende wrote in the obituary about Lars P. Grinager, among other things, this:

"Everywhere where his work became known was there testimony to his gift, and it was, therefore, a great loss both for the country and for the difficult trade in which he worked, when death so quickly ended his talented activity."

In Lars Grinager's home parish there is no memorial which tells about Hadeland's foremost violin maker – no gravestone, no mention in the parish record book, no instrument collection – nothing other than some few violins in private ownership and this account of him here in *Brandbu'stikka*.

Lars Grinager

published February 2000   *Dorothy Evans*

Photos, left to right: Lars Grinager, Edward Grinager, Hans Grinager & wife, Mons Grinager, Jacob Grinager

The series of articles about Lars Grinager was interesting to read again. I was glad Paul Grinager sent it in to be published. Esther Embrey (deceased 1995) sent me a copy when she finished translating it in 1987 as she did Paul and others. We had met Paul at a Hadeland Lag *stevne* after corresponding with him. He found a connection between our families further back.

Esther was very proud of her Norwegian heritage to the point she mastered the language so she could translate it. Lars P Grinager was her great uncle. She had a beautiful solo voice and could sing the Norwegian National Anthem along with the best of them.

There were a few errors in the article compared to the information I have gathered over the years. Peder Hansen Grinager and Lise Kristine Hvinden had only 13 children. I have copies of the births of their children from the microfilm of church records courtesy of the Latter Day Saints Library loan service. After reading the article years ago I searched the records for another child but found none. The eldest son was Hans, born 1844, not 1846 as the article indicates. Hans and his wife Ingeborg Haug had 8 children. Their eldest was Peder Hansen Grinager who in turn was the father of Robert (Bob) Grinager who owned one of the violins and passed it on to his daughter Jane Grinager Brown. Their second child was Lars Jacob Hansen Grinager who was the father of Esther Grinager Embrey, she being the first of six children and Yolanda Grinager Hager being the second and owner of one of the violins.

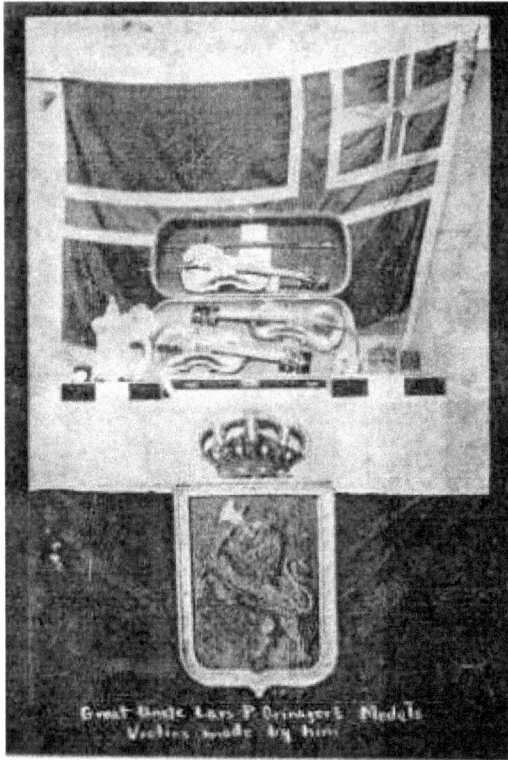

Dorothy's photo of violins made by, and medals awarded to, Lars P. Grinager

Lars was not two years younger than his brother Hans since Hans was born in 1844. A girl, Anne Maria, was born in 1846, then Lars P. Grinager in 1848 as stated in the article. Following Lars came another girl, Marthe (1850), then my grandfather Jacob Pedersen Grinager (1852) with eight more to follow. Except for two babies, the rest of the children lived to maturity and many emigrated to the U.S. Several of the Grinagers were in the mercantile business and Esther's father worked in my grandfather's store and lived with them for 10 years. He later became a lawyer and county judge in Canton SD.

Jacob P. Grinager had four daughters and two grandchildren, Robert Means and myself. Robert at one time owned one of the violins as well as the medals. He and his family gave the violin to Yolanda Grinager Hager, our second cousin, since she was very talented musically. If I'm not mistaken she played violin in the Denver Symphony Orchestra. In 1990, Robert presented the gold (not the bronze) medal to the Hadeland Folk Museum in Norway.

Dorothy was born in Lakeland, Florida, so says she was 'far removed' from Norwegian culture, but attended some of our stevner and enjoyed them immensely. She became acquainted with Esther Embrey when her son was at Stanford. She was introduced to the Hadeland Lag by her third cousin on the Larson/Wang side, Bonnie Wang.

Lars Halvorsen

published August 1999   *Form 500*   *Marie Gleason*

Family Statistics

Lars Halvorsen, b. Oct 24, 1812, at Molden, Gran (son of Halvor Gulbrandsen and Ingeborg Larsdatter; m. Jan. 3, 1805).

Confirmed Oct. 18, 1826, Gran.

Siblings: Gulbrand, b. April 23, 1810; Berthe, b. April 12, 1807; Kari, b. June 18, 1815.

On Nov. 28, 1840, Lars Halvorsen m. Christiane Engebretsdatter (daughter of Engebret Pedersen and Anne Marie Annefossen, m. Feb. 20, 1812).

Born to Lars and Christiane in Norway:
- Ingebret, Dec. 31, 1840. Lars was a *gaardmand* at Finstead, Gran.
- Halvor, b. May 12, 1844, died at 2 1/2 years of age, Dec. 20, 1846, Finstead.
- Second son named Halvor, b. March 15, 1847, Morstad, Gran, change of farms, father still a *gaardmand.*
- Anne Dorothea, b. Hvalfliet, Gran, April 3, 1849. Father's status: *husmann.*

Udflyttede, notice to leave the parish: destination, America, June 14, 1850; *Husmann* Lars Halvorsen *med husfru.*

St. John's, Newfoundland, Canada, 1995
I remove the dark sepia Xerox from a manila envelope provided by the Copy Center.   "It's

enlarged 400 percent," the student operator tells me, "that's the most I can do." He's made a 4" x 7" enlargement! To me, it's a miracle this miniscule tintype, 1" x 1 1/2", of indeterminate age, tin flaking from its metallic sides, should finally reveal its secrets to me. And that through a digital color copier in a university student centre.

I fasten him to the plastic arm of my computer's copy holder and study him, that enigmatic man, looking unhappily into a mid-1880s camera which captured his image.

Who is he and why should I be so obsessed with how he looks?

He is my grandmother's grandfather and the longer I peer at that 19th-century face, the larger Lars looms in the 19th-century play I'm writing. Great-great-grandfather Lars Halvorson.

Sinus swellings lie under his eyes (allergies, illness?) but he is a handsome man, clean-shaven, with well-spaced eyes, a high forehead and a "good" nose. The heavy, full-lipped mouth is drawn down in either suggering or bad temper; deep lines run from nose to mouth; his healthy head of hair has been hastily brushed into place.

Great-great-grandmother Christiane, at least, never forgot him. She told the offspring of her second marriage that she and Lars had the cultivated accents of Christiania (today's Oslo), far better accents than that of her second husband, from county Telemark.

Well into this fourth play I've written on my Norwegian homesteader ancestors, I realize all are based on photographs as well as written research. What primitive tribe fretted: "Take my photo, you steal my soul?" Do journalists miss something in all those photos commissioned, captioned, laid out on pages for printing? Do souls rise, like smoke or fog, from those printed pages? Stranger things have happened in the Age of Aquarius.

So I print the play's first dozen pages and carry the hard copy away to a neutral place to read, away from those pale, focused eyes. When I return to the keyboard, he'll still be there, pinned by plastic pin to the computer's arm, magnified four times, this man who lived 150 years ago, who contributed unwittingly to the DNA my sisters and I house.

Today's technology (via the Church of Jesus Christ of Latter Day Saints and its Salt Lake City cave of registrations from around the world) provides the story of Lars' hegira across Hadeland farms and ultimately to the United States. Leslie Rogne, genealogist for the Hadeland Lag in America, contributed the story to my sister, Lorraine Weiler.

Born a *gaardman's* son, Lars married as a *gaardmand*; four children were born on different *gaards* that he owned; but before he left Norway, he was a *husmann*, a cotter, a man who rented his land and owned little or nothing. Did he sell his land because of illness? Was it sold to provide money for the journey to America? Over a century later we have only statistics to study.

I found local help in my genealogical detective work. A photographer friend assured me the photo was a tintype and suggested I ask archivist Bert Riggs to determine the era in which the photo was taken. Itinerant photographers criss-crossed rural U.S.A. both during the pre- and post-Civil War periods, said Bert, adding they not only took photographs, but developed them in their horse-drawn wagons and provided paper envelopes like the one in which my tintype was found.

Lars was only 43 when he died in America, sometime after that last, that 43rd birthday. Had he been ill? It would explain the *ad hoc* photo, his look of exhaustion, of suffering; no tie, but an ascot hastily stuffed into his suit jacket. It also explains the hastily brushed-up hair.

An itinerant photographer's wagon had turned into their pioneer Wisconsin settlement; Christiane read the signs on Lars' face; she WOULD have a picture of him while he was still with her.

That's my interpretation of the tintype.

* * * * * *

A turn-of-the-century photograph album triggered this genealogical search. In rather poor condition, two pink celluloid albums were the property of my maternal grandmother, Lottie Peterson Tovson, Mayville, N.D.

In 1909, Lottie died at 29, probably from puerperal fever. Over the years, family members had extracted a number of my grandmother's photos from the albums. But, tucked insided one of the rifled folders, was this early tintype of HER grandfather.

A treasure within a treasure!

Dispatched to the Wisconsin Dells to track down family births and deaths, my son Tom found records of Lars' death in the 1850s, only a few years after the man's emigration to the U.S.

With the help of maps from the Vesterheim Library and Rogne's detailed internet records, a few years later, Tom and I headquartered at *Granavolden Gjestgiveri* and found several of the farms listed in the 19th-century Hadeland records.

Brede Olsen & Gudbjørg Andersdatter

published February 2001   *Form 407*   *Karen Schau-Stein*

Gudbjørg Andersdatter and Brede Olson

Brede Olsen, a tailor, was born on the Råssum farm December 17, 1831 and died 1899; Gudbjørg was born at Eidsand on June 23, 1841. Their first child, Karen Bredesen born October 5, 1865 at Fægernes was my maternal grandmother. They moved to Aschim farm where Brede's brother Erik and his family were living. There, eight more children were born: Anders Bredesen b. May 3, 1868, to Des Moines, IA 1893; Ole William Bredesen b. January 29, 1871 to Stavanger; Edward Bredesen b. November 20, 1873; Anton Bredesen b. January 4, 1875; Anne Marie Bredesen b. April 15, 1878; Marta Bredesen b. October 6, 1880; Torstein Bredesen b. November 1, 1883, to Des Moines IA 1900; Gina Beate Bredesen b. July 4, 1887. In the 1900 census in Norway, Gudbjørg was living with Anton and Gina on the Aschim farm. Ole, Torstein and Gina worked for a time at the old Hadeland Hotel.

Karen Bredesen lived briefly in Des Moines, IA where an uncle, Anders Andersen (usually referred to as 'old man Andersen') was living. She later moved to Minneapolis where she married Adolf Olsen from Kopperud farm in Ullensaker, Akershus. There were four children born, Bert Olaf b. August 3, 1898, d. 1962. (He married Margaret Lutz, and had two children John Richard b. August 19, 1925 and Phillip Homer b. May 19, 1930.) Margaret and George, twins born and died in 1900. My mother, Gudrun Alida was born April 6, 1903, died July 4, 1988. Whereabouts of John, who was a lifer in the US Navy, and Phillip, who was a physician, is unknown.

Karen Bredesen c. 1901

On November 9, 1929, Gudrun married Anders Ludvig Schau b. January 21, 1899, d. April 16, 1978, Borgås farm, Rødenæs, Østfold, Norway. My mother spent her life as a homemaker taking care of her family with a combination of Norwegian tradition taught to her by her mother, and trying to involve

75

something of American life as well. My father was a painting contractor, which is the reason we moved from Minnesota to California in 1946. My brother Roald August was born September 9, 1932, is married with four children and lives in the high desert of Southern California. I was born September 6, 1939 and am a divorced single parent of one daughter, J'aime Brianna b. June 30, 1978, who is single and attends University of Oregon in Eugene. I am Credit Manager for a manufacturing firm and live in Long Beach, CA, but am seriously considering a move to Norway either to Hadeland or Tønsberg.

My great uncle, Anders Bredesen-Aschim followed his sister to America in 1893 and settled in Des Moines and pursued a career as a cabinetmaker. He outlived all three of his wives. First was Ida Melander with whom he had three children: Grace Evelyn b. December 6, 1905; Ruth Ione b. September 4, 1907; and Irving Martin b. January 11, 1912. Ida died February 5, 1912. In June of 1914 he married Klara Hillestad, born in 1886 and died in 1918, in Fjelberg outside Bergen. They had one child, Helen Elizabeth b. March 31, 1915. Helen (married name Niggemann) is the only surviving child and lives in Scottsdale, AZ where two of her daughters and their families live. Anders' third wife was Jenny Barber and there were no children of this marriage.

*A. B. Aschim
c. 1948*

My great uncle Torstein Bredesen-Aschim (we called him Uncle Stone) followed around 1907 to Des Moines where he married Selma Mickelsen in 1917. There were six children; Theodore Boyd b. May 7, 1918; Robert Leigh b. November 5, 1919; Donald Kermit b. October 11, 1923; Kenneth Richard b. August 3, 1925; and twins Dean Everett and DeLores Elaine b. March 27, 1928. Donald and DeLores are the only surviving children, and live in the Des Moines Area. An interesting point, in 1912

*Torstein & Selma Aschim
50th Anniversary, 1947*

Uncle Stone visited his mother in Norway and had a return ticket on the Titanic. Fortunately, he cancelled that passage because he wanted to return home earlier.

Relatives Anders and Mari Andersen came from Hadeland settled in Madison where their only child, Carl Thomas, was born 1865. Carl was the creator of the comic strip *HENRY* that first appeared in the Saturday Evening Post on March 31, 1932 and continued until his death in 1948. *HENRY* also appeared

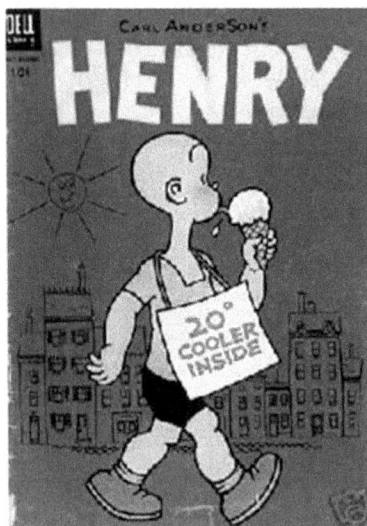

in 98 national and international Sunday newspapers. He worked with his father in his carpentry business for a time, and then studied to become an illustrator and teacher. HENRY was 'discovered' when Anderson was over 60 years old when he drew the first cartoon as an example to the class he was teaching in Madison. He is listed in the *Who's Who in American Art* and *World Encyclopedia of Comics.* Anderson never married.

In the cartoon below, the lady is said to be my grandmother.

Other family members known to immigrate, but with whom I have no contact and search for are:

Goro Andersdtr, Brandbu, Eidsand b. April 4, 1831, to America April 1852 (1)
Søren Torstensen, Tinglestad, Jønsrud, b. ??, to America April 1852
Anne Andersen, Brandbu,Eidsand, b. August 31, 1820, to America April 1852
Elling Andersen, Brandbu, Råssum, dates unknown.

(1)   I have a copy of a Hadeland newspaper article that says Goro lived in Minneapolis, married a ship builder named Prues (or Pruess) and moved to San Francisco.

Hadeland is my favorite place in Norway second only to Oslo. In Brandbu I stay with my cousin Annie Eid who has a Bed and Breakfast on the Eid farm overlooking the Randsfjorden. She appeared in the 1991 Hadeland calendar in a 1958 photograph as the first SAS hostess. She also is a regular volunteer at the Hadeland Folk Museum and teaches lefse and flatbrød making to young ladies in the Hadeland. Cousins Bjørn and Inger Eidsand, and their son Erling and his wife Brith and daughters Elin and Anne are other family members who I visit when in Brandbu. They live on the Eidsand farm and own the adjoining Eidsand Campground. The Eidsand family is very active in the community and cousin Brith makes her own version of Gjetøst, Anne is an accomplished hardanger fiddle player, Elin attends college in Hamar. I also have distant cousins living on the Jønsrud farm.

Anders Arnesen & Marthe Sørumseie

"Finding Their Roots" published November 2000   Form 492   Paul Anderson

Paul and Joan Anderson of LaCrosse, Wisconsin are photographed standing in front of the 200-year-old log house where Paul's paternal great-grandparents and children lived just prior to immigrating to Richland County, Wisconsin, in 1882. The log cabin on the tenant farm Avtjernlien is located in the northwest corner of Hadeland, just a few minutes drive west of Bjoneroa in Gran, Hadeland, Norway.

Paul's great-great-grandfather Arne Arnesen was born in Hedalen, Sør Aurdal, Valdres, in 1812 and he came to Hadeland and married Helvig Olsdtr. Askimeie, born 1813. They had 11 children all born at Fløybraten/Bjoneroa, Gran, Hadeland: Anders, Ole, Simen, Berthe, Siri, Mari, Inger, Simen, Anne, Andreas and Eleve.

Anders Arnesen, born 1833, was one of those 11 children and Paul's great-grandfather. He married Marthe Paulsdtr. Sørumseie, born in 1840 at Nesbakken, Gran, near Røykenvik, Hadeland. They had seven children born in Norway and one in the U.S.A.

Anders Arnesen changed his name to Andrew Anderson in the U.S.A. He and his wife Martha Paulson are buried in the Five Points Cemetery, Akan Township, Richland County, Wisconsin.

Anders and Martha's children Anne Andersdtr., Paul Anderson (*the author's grandfather*), and Marthe Andersdtr were born at the nearby tenant farm Fløybråten. Helene Andersdtr., Edward Anderson, Ole

Paul Anderson (1862-1936)

79

Anderson Log Cabin, Akan Township, Richland County, Wisconsin

Anderson, and Karen Andersdtr. were born at Avtjernlien. They all immigrated to Richland County, Wisconsin. Agnes Andersdtr was born in the U.S.A.

Paul and Joan met Kjell Henrik Myhre, a local genealogist in Brandbu, on their Norway 2000 Tour this summer. *Mange tusen takk* for the information that was provided by Kjell. Paul and Joan also wish to thank Paul's cousin Kari Odegaard, her husband Per Hoff and son Pål Audun for hosting them while in Brandbu, Hadeland. They had a marvelous time in Norway!

Tobias Gulbrandsen & Marte Christensdtr

published May 2001   *Form 461*

Excerpts from the book "Fjords and Fields" submitted by Jon Gilbertson

Brothers Anton Gilbertson, Halvor Bjertness, and Christen Tobiasen

Tobias Gulbrandsen was born June 5, 1820 at Greftegrev farm, Jevnaker, Norway, to parents Gulbrand Hansen and Magrete Halvorsdatter. He was baptized June 18, 1820, in Jevnaker Church. He died in February 1887, age 66, at Hatton, North Dakota.

Marte Christensdatter was born September 26, 1829, at Bjertness Farm, Jevnaker, Norway, to parents Christen Lagesen and Anne Pedersdatter. She was baptized October 11, 1829. She died November 20, 1908, at the Halvor Bjertness farm, Hatton, North Dakota.

Marte, age 24, and Tobias, age 35, from Sandvigen, announced their marriage in the Jevnaker Church on December 17, 26, and January 6. They were married in the Jevnaker Church January 12, 1856. After they were married they resided at Dalseje, sometimes spelled Dahlseje, most probably a part of the Bjertness farm in the Jevnaker parish. All their children were born and baptized while living at Dalseje except Torvald in 1873, but he died at Dalseje in 1874.

Their oldest son, Christen Tobiason, was born March 29, 1842, at Dalseje Farm in Jevnaker and was actually the son of Tobias and Marte Christensdatter's sister, Anne, who died when Christen was five years old. On October 25, 1866, he married Maren Andersdatter at Jevnaker Church. He was the first of Tobias' children to emigrate to America in 1868 and died May 13, 1906, age 64, at his farm home at Montevideo, Minnesota.

Tobias and Marte's first child was Anne Tobiasdatter Bjertness who was born on January 13, 1854. She was not married and came to America with her family in 1883 and made her home with her brother, Halvor Bjertness, north of Hatton, North Dakota. She died at the Deaconess Hospital in Grand Forks in 1906.

Their second child was Gustav Tobiason who was born February 22, 1856, at the Dalseje farm in Jevnaker. He died April 4, 1856, at the Dalseje farm.

The next son of Tobias and Marte was Gulbrand Velohagen, born March 2, 1857. He remained in Norway, married Kari Johannesdatter February 10, 1881, at Jevnaker, and died November 1923, age 66. He is buried in the Jevnaker Church cemetery.

The third son and the ancestor of Jon Gilbertson was **Anton Tobiason Gilbertson**, who was born May 25, 1859. He emigrated to the U.S. in the spring of 1882 to the Northwood, North Dakota, area and married Inger Mathea Hanson December 26, 1882, at her brother, Peter Hanson's, house near Northwood, North Dakota. She was born November 11 or 28, 1858 at Ringerike, Norway. Anton died November 4, 1939, age 80, at Grand Forks, North Dakota.

Halvor Bjertness was born to Tobias and Marte on February 3, 1861. He left Norway in March 1880, landing at the Port of Quebec, Canada in May 1880 at age 19. He settled first at Montevideo, Minnesota, where he was mailman for two years. He later moved to Dakota Territory and settled in Newburgh Township, Steele County, North Dakota. There he married Lottie Holter June 18, 1902, at his farm home in Washington Township north of Hatton, North Dakota. She was born December 28, 1870, at Northwood, Iowa, to Anton and Louise Holter. Halvor died May 17, 1925, at age 64 in Jamestown, North Dakota.

The next child of Tobias and Marte was a daughter, Margrethe Tobiasdatter, born August 3, 1863. No record has been found of her death but she apparently died between 1876 and 1883.

Lars Bjertness was born May 11, 1866. At age 17 Lars emigrated to America with his parents and worked on a farm near Hatton. He married Anna Syverson March 29, 1902, at the Halvor Bjertness farm near Hatton. Anna came to America from Norway in 1892 at age 29 and worked as a hired girl in Hatton. Lars died July 11, 1936 at age 70 at Hatton, North Dakota.

Inger Mathea Tobiasdatter Bjertness was born to Tobias and Marte on December 21, 1870, at the Dahlseje farm in Jevnaker. Inger also emigrated to the U.S. with her parents in 1883. She married Christian Fredrikson Fosse on October 2, 1889, at Hatton. She died February 23, 1943, at Williston, North Dakota, age 72.

The last child of Tobias and Marte was Thorvald Tobiasen, born October 11, 1873, on the Bjellumseje farm and died March 31, 1874, at the Dalseje farm.

Lars Bjertness with his violin

Tobias and Marte Gulbrandsen, with their children Anne, Lars and Inger, emigrated to the U.S. on the steamboat *Angela*, which left Oslo on June 8, 1883. Three of their children--Gustav, Margrethe and Thorvald--had died. Gulbrand, the oldest surviving son of their marriage, remained in Norway.

Jon Gilbertson's great-grandparents, **Anton and Mathea Gilbertson**, had nine children besides adopting and raising one boy. Their children were Hans, Anna, Marie, Thorval, **Gustav**, Albert, Inga, Dora, Helmer and Paul, their adopted son.

Gustav "Gust" was born August 2, 1890, near Northwood and married Johanna "Hannah" Andrina Dronen at Sharon, North Dakota. Gust's work experiences evolved from farming to the car and garage business at Sharon, North Dakota; Thief River Falls and Warren, Minnesota to a home bakery at Grand Forks, North Dakota, assisted by his family; and finally to the defense industry during W.W. II at Las Vegas, Nevada; and then to casino work until his death on December 22, 1953, at age 63. Gust and Hannah had four children: Gordon, Marcell, John and **Arthur**.

Arthur James Gilbertson was born April 25, 1927, at Thief River Falls, Minnesota. He married Lois Adele Otterson March 4, 1951, at Moorhead, Minnesota. He and Lois have four children: James, Jay, **Jonathan** and Jed.

Jonathan Lee Gilbertson, the author of this history, was born October 24, 1956, at Grafton, North Dakota. He graduated from Moorhead (MN) State University with a degree in mass communications in 1980. He spent several years in Salt Lake City, Utah, working in the printing industry before moving to Denver. Jon married Alice Marie Ringer on December 31, 1990. Jon has been employed at the Wells-Fargo Bank there as a graphic artist since 1985. He and Alice toured Norway and Sweden in 1995, including visiting relatives and seeing the Jevnaker Church.

*****

Brua Editor's note: Thanks to Jon Gilbertson for sending in his very complete family history. This was sent to Harald Hvattum to be added to the library in the *Hadeland Folkemuseum.*

Several items included in this history are excellent examples of genealogical situations which you find when you are researching your Norwegian ancestors. First is the announcement of the *banns* before a couple is married. Tobias and Marte's marriage banns were announced three times before they were married. This gave anyone who thought they had a "claim" on either of the partners a chance to protest or stop the marriage.

Secondly, Anton *changed his name* to Gilbertson, an Americanization of Gulbrandsen. That name is still used by the family.

Finally, the picture of the three brothers Anton Gilbertson, Halvor Bjertness and Christen Tobiason may be confusing because each brother used a *different surname*. Norwegians in the 19th century and earlier were given a first name at baptism. The surnames they used throughout their lives were patronimic--their father's name plus -sen (or -son) or -datter. They also had a farm name that in reality was a location or address for them because if they moved to another farm, that new farm name was attached to the patronym, replacing the previous farm name. When the emigrants came to America they had to choose a permanent surname. The oldest son, Christen Tobiason, apparently decided to use his patronimic name in America. Halvor Bjertness decided to use his mother's farm name. Anton used his father's patronimic, Gulbrandsen, but Americanized it to Gilbertson. Interesting!

Ole and Siri Rognstad
Eric and Thorine Thompson

published August 2001   *Forms 164, 430*   *Don Thompson*

Seven Hadeland Homesteaders c. 1882
Plano, Hanson, Fairview Townships, Hanson County SD
Front Row: Guttorm (George) Petersen, Iver Peterson, Brede (Willie) Rognstad
Standing: Jacob Lofsvold, Guttorm (George) Rognstad, Hans Lofsvold, Andrew Lofsvold
Iver is holding a wrench; Willie, an oil can. 4 are leaning on pitchforks. The field has been fenced.

Hans, Jacob and Andrew Lofsvold were three of the brothers of Thorine Lofsvold, the paternal grandmother of Donald Thompson. Thorine and her husband, Eric Thorstensen, also homesteaded in Plano Township, around 1880. Eric and Thorine took the surname Thompson when they reached America. Eric was born and raised in Hvendeneiet in Gran, Norway, which was close to Lofsvold where Thorine and her siblings were raised. Skirstad, which was nearby, was where the Lofsvolds attended school at the home of their paternal aunt Marthe Hansdatter Lofsvold, wife of Hans Amundsen Skirstad. Hans and Marthe are great-great-grandparents of Asmund Johnsrud, the current farmer of Skirstad. Two other Lofsvold siblings, Edmund and Ellen also immigrated to the U. S. They both settled across the Sioux River in Iowa, a few miles

85

east of Canton, South Dakota. The widowed mother of the Lofsvold siblings, Anne Sorine Jacobsdtr. Lofsvold, immigrated too. She lived with Thorine and Eric.

George Rognstad, the maternal grandfather of Donald Thompson, and Willie Rognstad were brothers, the sons of Ole and Siri Rognstad. George and Willie married cousins from Valdres, Norway. George and Iver Peterson were cousins of George and Willie Rognstad. The kinship line of this relationship isn't clear. Ivar's wife, Mary, was a sister of George Rognstad's wife, Gertrud Weflen.

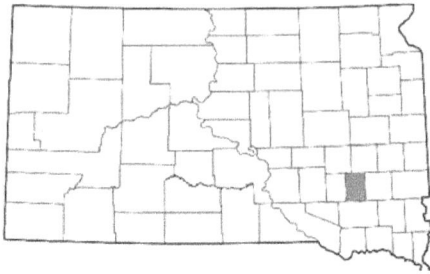

Hanson County, SD
Plano Township is in the upper left corner of the county; Hanson Twp is just below it.

The homestead claims of these seven Hadelanders plus Eric and Thorine were located within a six-mile radius in the Plano community. There were a number of Norwegian settlers in the community besides the Hadelanders, but the Norwegians were not a majority. The records show the Norwegians took an active role in the government of their community and in the building and maintaining of the schools and churches. They left substantial homesteads and farms, some of which had grown in size through the additional purchase of land. There were good crop years and bad years. The Norwegian Lutheran church was built three times, destroyed once by fire and once by a violent tornado. None of the schools or churches of the Plan community still stand on their original sites. The Methodist church has been moved to the grounds of the Middle Border Museum in Mitchell, South Dakota. Most schools and churches in this area are now centralized in the larger towns.

Almost all of the descendants of Eric and Thorine and the seven homesteaders in the photo have scattered across the United States. The last farmer among them, Raymond Thompson, will be retiring in Mitchell, South Dakota. The George Rognstad farm, which Raymond farmed, was recently sold to a nearby Hutterite settlement. The number of farmers in South Dakota grows smaller, a fact reflected in the census figures. Most of the farms are now much larger in acreage, and many are corporate holdings or other arrangements such as the communal ownership of the Hutterites.

OLE ROSSUM HOMESTEAD
Hudson, South Dakota
The Rossum homestead was located about 10 miles south of Canton, South Dakota. In 1866 Anna immigrated to America ahead of her parents, Ole and Siri Rognstad, and two younger brothers, Guttorm (George) and Brede (Willie), and was then lived for two years in Minnesota. They moved from Minnesota to the site of their homestead in Dakota Territory by wagon with

86

a team of oxen in 1871. Paul and Goro Schiager, the parents of their future son-in-law, Gunder Schiager, were very early settlers in the Canton area. Gunder was the second child born in the settlement.

Rossum Homestead c. 1896
Left to Right: Anna Olesdtr. Rognstad (Mrs. Ole Rossum); Anna's mother Siri Guttormsdtr. Klovstad (Mrs. Ole Rognstad); Ole Rossum; Ole and Anna's daughter Emma Rossum (Mrs. Ingebret Thormodsgard); Ole and Anna's daughter Mattie Rossum (Mrs. Gunder Schiager); Anna's niece Phoebe Petterson (Mrs. Olaf Lysnes); Ole and Anna's hired man Lauritz Hatlute.

After Ole Rognstad's death, Anna's mother, Siri Rognstad, spent her last years living in the homes of her daughters. Her second daughter, Margaret, was married to Edgar Petterson. The Petterson's homestead was next to Ole and Siri's, about six miles north of Canton, on the Sioux River.

Ole Rognstad and his siblings and other kin who came to America settled first in Wisconsin. Those who came early got land there. Those who came later stayed awhile in Wisconsin and then went westward as new land opened for settlement. By the time Ole's sons were ready to marry and establish themselves, they moved west 60 miles where new land was available for homesteading near Mitchell, Dakota Territory. Some of the following generation stayed on the family farms. Some found new ways of making their living through education and other training. Only two of Ole and Siri's great-grandchildren are known to be living on original homestead land. One of these farms recently sold out of the family. A great-granddaughter of Ole and Siri, Lois Schiager, is the wife of Sidney Rand, a former United States Ambassador to Norway.

Anna, Ole Rossum and their daughter, Emma, made a visit back to their families in Hadeland, circa early 1900's. Anna's Norwegian cousins, Kristine and Ingeborg Molstad, still remembered the family when Selma Sognstad Rilling and Donald Thompson visited Molstad farm in 1956.

Thron and Rønnou Håkenstad
Ole and Marie Håkenstad

published November 2001   Forms 85, 341   *Etta Hokenstad Berge*

Excerpts from a family history written in 1985 by Etta (Hokenstad) Berge, Hadeland Lag member who died in 1995. The history was submitted by Donald Thompson, Albuquerque, N.M., a distant relative of Etta's. Her story is a bit unusual because her parents were first cousins. However, it also means that all of Etta's ancestors are from Hadeland!

Brothers Ole and Thron Håkenstad

My Håkenstad Grandfathers

Thron was born 20 July 1842 and Ole, who was born 28 March 1846, as were numbers six and seven of the children born to Ole Hanson Haagenstad and Mari Tostensdotter Gagnum. As the parents had been, so were all the children both baptized and confirmed in the Jevnaker Church. This baptism font is still in use.

The early lives of Thron and Ole were similar and usual for that area: the common school education they received was equivalent to our sixth grade. As they reached the age of 15 he was apprenticed to become a cabinet maker. After about three years each became a skilled cabinet maker. In both this "trade school" and at home they gained business training and a lot of knowledge in mathematics partially because of the large farm their father managed. Both young men were avid readers and were very interested in politics.

Ole, on 17 May7 1866, was married to Marte Røisum, in the Gran parish by Rev. Soren Bugge. The young couple chose not to have a large wedding but instead used that money to come to the United States. Ole took with him his tool chest, tools, some clothes and a flute which he had played in an orchestra in Hadeland. This flute later became the possession of his son Winston.

After serving three years in the Calvary and being discharged, Thron also left for the U.S.A. On the day he left home a tree was planted outside the house; this stood until just a few years ago. Like his brother, Thron brought his tools with him; his brace and bit dated 1867 carved with his initials T.O.S.H. (Thron Ole's Son Haakenstad) which were carved from a tree root. He also brought his square and marker, and a number of planing tools which are in my (EHB) possession today.

Thron left Norway 24 April 1868 on one of the first steam boats. This was most likely a merchant ship which left when it was filled, as the cost of a regular ship ticket was an exorbitant $176.40. The landing was in Quebec 16 May 1868.

Marte Røssum

Marte was born 16 March 1850 as the fourth child of Gulbrand Gulbrandson Røssum and Margrete Torsdotter Lynn. She was born on Røssum; gaard 153, bruk 2, of the Brandbu parish. We know this is a very old farm because of the name ending in "um." Today the part with the buildings is used for their summer vacation time by a Røssum who lives in Oslo.

The Røssum farm was very large originally. We were told at least 16 farms originated from it. The school which was held in their home was also attended by their *husmenn*'s children. Thus Marte had more education than girls generally had at this time.

It is easy to picture this dark-haired, rather plump, short girl, a fairly quiet yet determined girl. She was just 16 at the time of leaving with her new husband for this unknown land, America. As it was Marte's choice to not have the large wedding she could have, as parents have always done – they packed a large trunk with a lot of clothes, including a hat so she would not look like a newcomer upon landing. She was also given some money. Ole and Marte also brought aboard the ship cheese, flatbread and a leg of mutton which was the envy of other passengers.

Rønnou Helmeid

Rønnou was the third child born to Borger Christenson Helmeid and Berte Johansdatter Almsengen on Helmeid 22 March 1843. She was baptized 15 April 1843 in the Sister Church in Gran by Rev. H. Heyerdahl. The baptism basin is still in use today.

Rønnou must have been taught to be independent and not be afraid of work. She was a slender woman of average height with red hair – which never did turn gray. As all children had to attend confirmation classes, Rønnou learned to read, but never to write except for a few words. She never learned to speak English.

In 1868 she came to America alone, by sailboat. Passengers in the sailboat had to bring their own bedding, clothes and food which, in her case, consisted mostly of flatbread. When in Norway, I was told by a guide at a museum that the sailboats of this time had three masts and two decks. The upper deck held two rows of double-decker bunks the length of the ship. The lower decks held barrels, trunks, etc. There were a couple of stoves and passengers stood in line to use them. The only light was through the portholes. The ticket cost between $50 and $90.

After 13 weeks she came to Quebec, Canada. Then it was by boat and wagon to Postville, Wisconsin. Her brother Ole had come to America the year before. He had gone to Minnesota, then on to Madison, South Dakota. Rønnou never saw him here. Their brother Brede came the year after, in 1869.

Here was this young woman who arrived alone and needing to find work to support herself in this strange land. Then Thron came! Whether she had known him before or not, it made no difference. He was from Hadeland!

Thron and Rønnou

Thron and Rønnou were married 5 July 1869 by Rev. K. Helland at the Free Lutheran parsonage at Wiota, LaFayette County, Wisconsin. They started their married life in Postville, Wisconsin. Postville appeared to have a good future. There was a general store, school and three churches (none Lutheran). Today there isn't much left. People still go to the old general store to vote and there are the remains of a blacksmith shop.

It was here the oldest three sons were born. On 8 May 1871, in Green County, Wisconsin. Thomas (Thron) Olson became a U. S. citizen. That same year they moved to Dakota Territory. "Thomas Olson" and his wife Rønnou built a sod house southwest of his younger brother, Ole and Marte. Here my father, Bello, was born on 2 March 1872.

Bello was the catcher on the Spring Creek Baseball Nine. He was of average height and liked to move fast, whether it be on foot or in horse-drawn carriages – then later automobiles.

Thomas gave up this claim and the family moved to township 102 in sections 1 and 2 where he took up homestead rights and secured his tree claim. Their first home was a combination dugout and sod house. As a carpenter theirs was one of the first frame houses in the area. In 1895 "Thomas Olson" changed his name legally from Olson back to Hokenstad.

Rønnou, while small in stature, was great in strength. Although babies came regularly she always had time to help a neighbor. Most of the time she walked, although at times she drove her faithful horse, Jack, on a single-seated buggy. Bello used to say that during emotional times and disasters, she was the calm one.

One day when she was driving back, the horse became frightened and shied, tipping over the buggy. Broken were Ronnou's left arm and leg and either the arm or leg on her right side. She never really recovered. In 1914 she was granted her wish to go to her Saviour and Friend on Easter morning.

The year after Rønnou died, Thomas went to live with a married son, Rudolph. I have fond memories of this bewhiskered grandfather. He taught love of family and country. He voted in the last election before he died in 1940.

Ole and Marte

The married life which began in Gran, Norway, continued to Monroe, Green County, Wisconsin. Ole worked here as a farmhand for about one year. Maria was born soon after they arrived. My heart goes out to this young mother, 16 years old with husband away working and cousin Margrete having to work out as a hired girl instead of helping Marte.

Then they moved to Janesville, Wisconsin. The next two daughters were born. Ole found work with a cabinetmaker so he thus continued in the trade he had learned in Norway. Even so, Ole must have become restless as he started out for Dakota Territory, leaving his wife and three children until he would send for them. Before leaving Janesville, he filed and was granted citizenship in the U.S. on 5 April 1870.

Ole arrived in Sioux Falls in April 1870, and staked a claim bounded by 12th Street on the north and on the west by (now) Minnesota Avenue. He figured this was poor farmland so he

91

relinquished it the same fall and moved near Canton where he filed a claim and built a sod house.

Marte left Janesville with girls aged four, two and six months and cousin Margrete Rognstad, taking the train to Sioux City, Iowa. Here a neighbor of Ole's met them with oxen and lumber wagon. Emma was born 15 November 1876, the sixth daughter of Ole and Marte, in a sod house on the family homestead. In 1878 they built what we would term a basement house. In 1885 a two-story house was built on top of the basement. Lumber was hauled from LeMars and Sibley, Iowa.

Emma spent practically all of her single life on this farm except for time spent working for others in their house, barn or field. She spent three months while in her teens in Canton, learning the dressmaking trade. She also wrote for a Canton newspaper, "The Sioux Valley News."

Ole was elected State Representative two terms during which the Republicans, who were mostly farmers, gained prominence. Ole was on the Public Health Commission for both his terms. He was Lincoln County Treasurer from 1904-1914, with his son George being his assistant the last years.

Because Ole was easy going and away from home a lot, Marte became stern and independent. She had the care of the house and farm the biggest share of the time. She found time to help their neighbors, especially by bringing food. She was president of the Ladies Aid of Canton Lutheran Church in 1888.

Ole and Marte celebrated their Golden Wedding on their homestead on 17 May 1916, with 13 of the living 14 children present. Ole had a stroke while uptown in Canton and died of this on 4 July 1916. Marte had jaundice and gall bladder problems and although she had surgery, she never recovered. She died on 23 June 1926 with her nine living children at her side.

Bello and Emma

Bello and Emma were married at the Lutheran Parsonage in Luverne, MN, on 1 June 1900. The witnesses were Bello's sister Bertha and his brother Conrad. The reason they were not married at home is that South Dakota had a new law against cousins marrying but Minnesota did not.

Their first home was on the 'Brewery Farm' northwest of Sioux Falls. In 1902 Dad, Mother, and daughter Blanch moved to what was known as the 'Carey Farm' near Booge, SD. Maurice was born in this farm home. In 1904 the family moved to the Thron Hokenstad homestead near Garretson, SD, and lived here for the next 11 years. In 1905 Telmar was born and in 1910 Etta was born to complete the family.

In 1915 Bello acquired 80 acres from Jens Hoff a half mile east of the homestead and the family lived there for the next four years. In 1918 Bello was offered the managership of the Co-op Lumberyard in Corson. They left the farm and rented it out, but sold it a year later. They moved into the 'Skalland' house, but soon built a new home.

Emma died of liver cancer in Sioux Falls 7 November 1945. Bello was never sick and peacefully slept to his death on 11 January 1962 at the home of Etta and Martin. Etta married Martin Berge 31 March 1933 in Brandon, SD. They had three children: Lyle, Lucille, and Linda.

(Brua Editor's note: Etta and Martin, who later lived in Marshall, MN, were active members of the Hadeland Lag for many years and their son Lyle and his wife, Billie, Colorado Springs, Colorado, are now members.)
'

Kristian Sorum
A Glimpse into Our Grand-Uncle's World

published February 2002   *Form 624*   *Terje Nilsen*

This article by Terje Nilsen was published in the "Oppland Arbeiderblad" on August 11, 2001, and is part of a series which he wrote about the trip to America taken by our friends from Hadeland. It has been translated by the Andersons.

"It is certainly strange to come here. I have never been here before." Solveig Sangnæs from Roykenvik looks at the old houses in an abandoned town on the Dakota prairie. For the first time she is in Sorum on Rabbit Creek, the place where her granduncle Kristian Sorum at one time worked and lived, than a small community of 30 souls.

A glimpse into the past: Solveig Sangnæs has traveled all the way from Roykenvik to the U.S.A. to see the place where her granduncle Kristian Sorum from Moen settled down and created a complete little town. But the store closed many years ago.

State Bank, Post Office, General Store + Wayside Inn.
Sorum, S. Dak.   Dec. 1910.

94

Now all is deserted. Progress came also to South Dakota in the end. People left the small close-knit community with a church, store and with its own high school. They would rather live in the nearby town with all of its attractions – in other words, like other Norwegians desired. This has happened with most of the small communities on the prairie.

While there can be individual deserted places in Norway, it is not so on the American prairie. Here one can drive mile after mile on a straight road without even meeting another vehicle. Only a herd of cattle now and then or a ranch on the horizon breaks the monotonous landscape. We met two cars in almost three hours of driving. It is a joke to refer to this as heavy traffic.

Solveig Sangnæs and her husband Johannes are on a trip around the Midwest together with other members of the historical societies of Hadeland. Now for the first time they see the place which Kristian Sorum changed into a small, but lively community early in the previous century. He settled down here in 1910 after emigrating from the Sørum farm in Moen Hadeland. Solveig remembers that Kristian, who was also her grandmother's brother, came to Norway to visit when he was a child and that he had light, fine clothes and a wide-brimmed hat. One of Kristian's sons, Dean Sorum, is on the trip and is able to tell how it looked when he was growing up. One of Solveig's cousins, historian and genealogist Hans M. Næss from Gran, added other information.

But there is actually not much to see. The pride of the area, the school and community hall, is used for storage by the only farmer who is at Sorum during the summer. The little church is` closed. The same is naturally true of the store and post office. The childhood home of Dean and his siblings is burned and the remnants have been buried. There is nothing left – only the flat, grass-covered landscape and the intense heat.

There was not much here either when Kristian Sorum got on the train and traveled west. When the train didn't go any further, he got a ride on a covered wagon and traveled even further. When he came to the Butte area in far western South Dakota he settled down and named the place after himself.

Kristian Sorum, or Chris Sorum as he is now known, was an enterprising man. He brought his saddle-making equipment with him from Moen, and these services were needed in the wild west. Therefore he built a workplace for this purpose. He also took the initiative to open a post office and had a postal route which was the longest in the U.S.A. He was the leader of a group which established a hotel, built a bank, general store, a church, school, and community hall.

Kristian also organized and built a telephone company which was started at the end of the 1920s. He also helped to bring electricity to the community. In other words, he was an important man, and had both servants and a large household.

In 1913 he married Ida Lowe, and the couple had three children – Christian Merle, who has now died; Pauline Stowman and also Dean. They survived the depression and poor times when enormous grasshoppers darkened the heavens and ate up everything that grew on the land. Both Kristian and Ida died in 1969.

Kristian emigrated from Moen in 1906, and worked the first years in the Minneapolis area. His brother Harald emigrated to America with Kristian, but Harald did not thrive well. In a letter which he wrote to his friend Oskar Jensrud, Harald recommended very strongly that Oskar should not emigrate and also that he wished he had never set foot in America. He also thought that "thousands would return to Norway again."

At that time Kristian probably did not thrive so well in the New Land either. In any case the two brothers agreed that they should meet at the train station in Minneapolis to begin the long voyage home to Hadeland. But Kristian arrived too late at the train station and therefore Harald returned alone. He later settled down in Røysumlinna at Jaren as a saddle maker, married and had four children.

Kristian remained in America and created a little, but bustling community in the middle of the desolate prairie. But as the years went on, the little community slowly grew smaller. That people would rather live in the nearby towns. Dean left Sorum in 1938, and early in the 1940s the school was closed for good. The store, which had been destroyed by fire many times, was relatively new when Dean left. In 1984 and 1985 both the store and post office were torn down. Such ends the lifework of Chris Sorum.

Kristian Sorum Revisited

published May 2002   *Pauline Stowman & Dean Sorum*
Children of Kristian Sorum

Chris Sorum was an adventurous fellow as we view his life from the comfort of the 21st century. But his life was not all about Sorum, South Dakota. In fact, he only spent about eight years in the town (1910-1918). Organizing the various community functions, starting the post office and mail route, and various businesses occupied those years.

He recognized the limits of the town as there was no railroad, major highway or county seat (government center) destined for Sorum. So they purchased a ranch and moved, including son, Merle, about two miles north of the town where they lived for 20 years. Through the good years of the 1920s and the brutal years of the 1930s their family increased, first Pauline, and then Dean was born when Chris was almost 50. They had busy lives with the church, school and social activities along with extremely hard work on the ranch. Their land consisted of one section (640 acres) which they owned and one school section (state owned) that they rented. Fortunately, a small creek wound its way through both sections so even during the dry years there was some hay for the cattle. The ranch house was not large by any standard and there were no "servants." However, there were "hired men" that helped with the outside work from time to time. The above terms may have been misused or misinterpreted in translation to Norwegian in the Old Country.

Charley Lafflin was a good friend and neighbor (25 miles away in South Dakota) and he had been a telephone foreman in Iowa. They decided to build a telephone line over 50 miles long from Bison through Sorum to Lafflin's ranch south of Slim Buttes with branch lines to several businesses and ranches along the way. After much fund-raising and hard work the line was built, but their connection to the outside world was threatened when the Bison telephone system was abandoned. So the ranchers took over the Bison system, hired a woman as the telephone operator and called it the Sorum Telephone Company. In the middle 1930s there was no money for repairs so Chris, Merle, and Charlie and his sons Fredrick and Charles (Chick) were doing the work as volunteers. In 1938 Chris borrowed money from a friend and bought the Abercrombie (North Dakota) Telephone Company and moved the family over 400 miles east and ran that company until 1954 when they sold it. After helping Merle with an automobile service station at Belle Fourche, South Dakota, for a couple of years Chris and his wife Ida retired to a small farm near Pelican Rapids, Minnesota. They had hundreds of laying hens for several years. They both died in 1969.

There are two versions of brother Harald returning to Norway. Harald lived in Benson, Minnesota, for about two years. The Norwegian version was in the February *Brua*. Chris' version is this: Christ first came to their uncle Lars Stensrud's farm *(History of Hadeland Lag in America, 1990, page 150)*. Next he worked for a Minneapolis contractor building sidewalks in nearby western Minnesota towns. He then worked in a hardware store in Marion, North Dakota (lots of Hadelanders, including "Per"). Chris and Harald decided to go to western South Dakota to homestead and they agreed to meet at Aberdeen, south Dakota, and take the train West. Chris went but could not find Harald in Aberdeen so he returned to Marion. Later he received a letter from Harald in Norway and then went to western South Dakota by himself. (He first visited Norway 40 years after leaving.)

97

Generations from Hadeland

Previously unpublished   *Dean Sorum*

Mikkel Sorum

Pauline Lunde Sorum

Christian Sorum and Ida B. Lowe Wedding Photo

Merle Sorum

Pauline Sorum Plowman

Harold Dean Sorum

Twenty year old Lars Stensrud stood at the top of the gang plank but before he walked down he picked up his former neighbor's four year old daughter. As he set her down in their new country he looked at her and said "I'm going to marry this little girl."

Mrs. Dorthea Hilden from Hadeland lost her husband when he was 54 years old. Four years later she and her three older sons and little daughter sailed to America bound for her brother's place in Fillmore County, MN. Their neighbor Lars Stensrud was on the same ship bound for a future in the new world. Dorthea's family worked hard for the next three years until they had acquired a team, farming equipment and knowledge sufficient to venture to western Minnesota. They immediately filed papers for homesteads. Lars Stensrud had also established roots in that area and as promised twelve years before, he married Ann Hilden in December, 1878. At the same time sister Kari Stensrud married brother Gilbert Hilden. Both families had many children (double cousins).

During 1905 Uncle Lars Stensrud provided a place for Christian M. Sorum to begin his new life in America. The Stensrud family had lived on the Dvergsten place for many years. But Lars' brother Mikkel somehow managed to buy the Sørum farm near the Moen Church in the Jaren, Hadeland area. Here Mikkel and his wife, Pauline Lunde raised their nine children and adopted the name of the farm, Sørum. Their children (including Christian) produced 61 grandchildren, three in America.

Christian Sorum worked on Lars' farm sacking oats out of the separator until it overflowed up to his waist. He later worked for a contractor building sidewalks in the towns nearby. Declining an offer to spend the winter in Minneapolis he took a job in a lumberyard/hardware store in Marion, ND. His brother, Harald, had been working in a shop in Benson, MN for a couple of years. Christian thought Harald would meet him in Aberdeen, SD and they would go to western SD and get homesteads. When he could not find Harald he went back to his job in Marion. Soon a letter came from Norway. His brother had returned to Norway.

In 1908 Christian went by train to Hettinger, ND. With another man they hired a man with a double team of horses and a wagon and loaded it with lumber. They threw their possession on top of the load and climbed on for the 50 mile trip south. Christian filed for a homestead and began the entrepreneur phase of his life.

Christian placed a mail box in his yard and periodically mail was placed in it by a carrier not only for him but for surrounding neighbors too. In 1909 Christian circulated a petition and in 1910 a post office was established in Sorum, SD with Christian Sorum as postmaster. Mail was delivered to the post office three times a week. A daily star mail route was eventually started between Newel and Lemmon with mail being exchanged at Sorum and the carriers returning to their bases every day. They even carried a few passengers and it was known as the stage.

The Sorum town-site on a railway survey route seemed to be very attractive. Several businesses were established besides Christian's post office-store. In 1910 a general store was built, The First State Bank of Sorum was started, a 16 by 24 blacksmith shop was built, then a pool hall-restaurant. In August a meat market and an ice house arose and a hardware store was moved in. In October a two story building was built for use as a hotel and much later as a high school then a church. A livery and feed barn did a thriving business with several saddle and driving horses. A newspaper, the Sorum Home Journal started publishing in January 1911. A young physician came to homestead with his mother and sister and provided health care in the area. A 24 by 40 auditorium was built and the first dance was held in November 1910 and a home talent play was presented the next February. Being that there were a large number of mostly young people nearby, the hall was busy not only for recreation but also for church, Sunday School and later for school. An accredited high school was started with four teachers, a matron, dean, and cook. In 1915 a milling company was incorporated and started operation the next year. They had a good business for several years. The farmers could bring their grain in and receive flour. This was appreciated, especially during the flour rationing days of WW1. In 1913 Christian and Ida B. Lowe were married. Ida, from North Dakota, had been homesteading about 10 miles north of Sorum near where her sister Mable homesteaded. Besides his store and post office, Christian Sorum drove Model T Fords from the factory in St. Paul, sold Delco light plants, and wired ranch houses in the area. However, with no railroad or decent highway they knew the limitations of the village and bought a ranch about two miles north of town in 1918.

There were three unequally spaced children in the Sorum family. For each child the year of birth, and the order of birth were equally important factors,. Christian Merle Lowe Sorum was the first, in 1915. This gave him at least 8 years to share hard labor with his parents on the ranch. He was also more inclined to operate machinery such as a tractor than his father. Thus the operation could be more productive. But his high school graduation was in the midst of the economic depression. Although he did well in mathematics and other subjects with his highly trained teachers there was no chance for higher education. He rode in boxcars to the west coast but came back with little money. In 1920 Mary Pauline Sorum was born. So she was available to help with the chores, garden, canning and babysitting Harold Dean Sorum, myself, born in 1931.

In October 1938 Chris and Ida sold the livestock and moved to Abercrombie, ND, about 400 miles away where they had purchased a small telephone company. The ranch was sold 20 years later. I, Dean, was in second grade and Pauline had started at Moorhead (MN) State College. There again, Merle was indispensable in the family enterprise until the 1950s. During the early 1940s Chris developed cancer and survived seven major operations. Since Merle was the only person to maintain the telephone plant he was exempted from military service during WW2.

During that time the economy improved while I progressed through the local school. I worked at the telephone company during high school, full time for one additional year and summers during college. I enrolled at the University of North Dakota graduating with a BS in Electrical Engineering in 1954. I was deferred from serving in the Korean War by being enrolled in the Air Force Reserve Officer Training Corps program at UND. Again, timing was fortunate as tuition and fees were only $48.75 per semester. I was the most fortunate of the three children, being especially indebted to my brother, Merle. The telephone Company was sold in 1954. Merle died of tobacco induced cancer in 1963 at age 47. Christian and Ida died in 1969. Pauline died at age 90 in 2011.

With some frugality and constant effort by parents and students, each able member of the next generation was able to receive one or more college degrees. With diligence but much less physical labor than their grandparents each has achieved considerable success. And the fourth generation is well on its way also.

*****

References:
- Stensrud Family History Including Sorum, Stokke, Hilden, Anderson, and Winger Families With Roots In Hadeland, Norway, 2008, Edited and self-published by Lorna Anderson, Perham, MN
- The Story of Sorum, SD and Vicinity (up to 1961) as printed in the Nations Center News, June 19, 1985 under Meet Your Neighbor Column by Linda Stephens, compiled by Mrs. Vivian Meyer and Mrs. Beatrice Jensen, The Bison Courier, May 29, 1985
- A Brief History of the Sorum Family and the Story of the Sod House by Paul Sorum

- A Taped Interview with Christian Sorum, 1968 , H. D. Sorum, Moorhead, MN

Other Sources of interest:

- Homestead Years, 1908-1968 by Mrs. L. I. Sudlow, The Bison Courier, 1968
- Dakota Panorama, Edited by J. Leonard Jennewein and Jane Boorman, Dakota Territory Centennial Commission, 1961, Brevet Press

Ole & Johanne (Hågenstad) Gulden

Published February 2002 Form 328 *Beverly Webster*

Beverly is the granddaughter of Marte Gulden and Peder Lanning.

Ole Olsen Tvet Gulden, baptized 2 Jun 1836 Tvet/Tvedt/Tveta, Jevnaker, Hadeland Norway; died 29 Nov. 1909, Montevideo, Chippewa County, Minn; buried Jevnaker Lutheran Church Cemetery, Mandt Township, Chippewa County, Minn., son of Ole Jørgensen Melaas and Marte Paalsdtr Oppen, who were married 29 Dec. 1860, Jevnaker Church.

Johanne Andersdtr Haagenstad, born 20 Sept. 1838, Haagenstad, Lunner/Jevnaker, Hadeland, Norway; died 3 July 1928, Mandt Township, Chippewa County, Minn., buried Jevnaker Lutheran Church Cemetery, daughter of Anders Johansen Haagenstad and Anne Jacobsdtr. Rud.

Ole's baptism witnesses: Halvor Tya, Gudrun Petersdtr. Tvet, Fredrick Raastad, Guri Haavland. At the time Anders was born, Ole and Johanne were living on the Kraggerud farm where Ole was a *husmann*, which means he did not own the place. A *husmann* was a person who contracted annually with a farm owner for work at that farm. In return, he received a place to live and in some cases a small plot of land to farm for his own use. For this he was obligated to work a certain amount of time for the farm owner. In addition he was obligated to be at the beck and call of the owner, so if there was a conflict about working his own plot or working for the owner, his first obligation was to the owner. These people are therefore often called "moonlight farmers."

In the 1865 census, their small plot of land and house was called Møllerstuen on Kragerud. Listed are:

Ole Olsen, 28, *husmand med jord* (farmer with land)
Johanne Andersdatter, 28, wife
Anders Olsen, 1
Marte Olsdatter, 6
Anne Olsdatter, 4 (all born Jevnaker, Lunner Parish)

Also living on Møllerstuen

Hans Andersen, *Logerende* (living with Ole and Johanne), cobbler, 21, born Jevnaker
Oline Andersdatter, his sister, 25, born Jevnaker
       The above two do not seem to be Joanne's siblings, perhaps they are cousins?

Also listed as a second household unit at Møllerstuen are:

Ingeborg Olsdatter (also living in the same house), 35, born Jevnaker (probably sister of Ole Olsen Tvet Gulden)
Karen Larsdatter (Ingeborg's daughter), 10 born Jevnaker

Kraggerud appears to be a complex of many farms, which include North and South Hytta/Hytten, Maakerud and Gronkjernt. Ole and Johanne were living on the Hytta farm in Jevnaker Parish where Olafus was born. Johan was born on the Gulden farm. His birth is supposed to be 8 Aug. 1869 according to the records in Chippewa County, Minn, U.S.A., but the emigration records of 11 April 1871 say he was half a year old. The emigration record was probably in error.

The passenger lists #18 show Johanne, 30 and their first five children Marte, 10; Anne, 98; Anders, 6; Claus, 3; Johan, 1/2; and leaving Oslo for Monroe (in Green County, Wisconsin, U.S.A.) on 15 April 1871 on the ship *Concordia*. The boat registrar was O.M. Sandberg. Their passage was paid for in America. They carried with them 41 SPD (specie dollars) and their destination was Monroe. We presume Ole immigrated in 1869 and Johanne in 1871. Ole was not in the 1870 census of Green County, Wisconsin.

The family stayed in Green County for a few years. Some of the Guldens say they spent time in Dane County, Wisconsin. Olava, Clara, Carl and Tillie were born in Wisconsin. About 1879 they moved to Erickson Township, Renville County, Minnesota, where they built a dugout near the old Krogfus Church and Cemetery. This was the church of Peder and Marte Lanning's family, who are buried in the Krogfus Cemetery. Ole and Johanne were "squatters." It was then that daughter Marte met Peder Lanning, who had homesteaded about 1 1/2 miles south of the old Krofgus Church. The 1880 census of Erickson Township, Renville County, Minnesota, lists Ole Gullen, Johanna Gullen and children: Marte, 19; Anna, 17; Andrew, 14; Olavi, 12; John, 10; Olava, 7; Chlora, 5; Karel, 3; and Tilda, 5 1/2. Herman was born there in 1882. Marte married Peder Lanning in 1881 and in 1883, the family moved to Mandt Township, Chippewa County, in the Montevideo area and lived there the rest of their lives. The last child, Jergen/George was born in Mandt Township, Chippewa County.

Taken from the "History of Milan Minn" by Marjery Burns: In Big Bend, Odd and Nils Halvorson owned a "Minnesota Chief" threshing rig. Their crew mas made up of Nils Hagen and son Knut, Ole Gulden and son Olous, E. P. Alstad, Gabriel Gabrielson, Mikkel Mikkelson, Knute Johnson, and sons James and John, Halvor Knutson, Joe Oddan, Mr. Oddan and his father, Ole Oddan. This is how the machine worked: "Odd Halvorson, after the machine was pulled between stacks, leveled and blocked, checked off the tumbling rods laid out straight. The horse power was pulled into position, staked and chained and five 'sweeps' put in place to which five teams were hitched up around the power. Gabriel Gabrielson, tallyman, screwed the tallybox on a hind wheel of the separator. The straw carrier was about 10 feet long. Ole Gulden held up the sacks for the measurer. Then Odd stepped onto the feeders stand and grabbed two cylinder teeth to help start the works. The driver, Olous Gulden, was on the power, swinging his large whip and 'get-upping' and soon the Old Chief was humming like a mocking bird. Mr. Odden and E. P. Alstad hauled the grain in bags from the machine, and by night they were very tired."

The question arises concerning the Gulden name. The last farm in Norway that this farm lived on was the Gulden/Gullen farm, Gran, Hadeland, where son Johan was born. John was baptized in one of the Sister Churches, Gran, Hadeland. Naming patterns in Norway were that the first son and daughter were named for the paternal parents. This holds true in this family. The patronymic names were used until about 1900, which for this family was Ole Olsen, Johanne Andersdatter, Marte Olsen, Annie Olsen, Andrew Olsen, etc., and the third name used was the farm that they were on at that time. Their third name changed often as Ole was born on Tvet and then we find him on various farms when the children were born: Larshus, Gullen, Kraggerud, Hutta, and Gulden/Gullen. Soon after they arrived in the U.S.A. they chose for their family name the last farm that they were on, which was Gulden. They were becoming Americanized.

In the 1910 census in Mandt Township are listed: Johanna, 71, with sons Carl, 30, and Herman, 28, and grandsons Hjelmar 10, and Lloyd, 6. In the 1920 census, Johana "Guden?" 80, widow, was living with her sons, John O., Carl and Herman in Mandt Township, Chippewa County, Minnesota. Also listed was Tillie's son that Johanna raised: _____ (probably Lloyd) Gulden, 17. They were all farming and Johanna was probably the woman of the house.

From the Decorah Posten, 20 July 1928:

>Our beloved mother and grandmother, Mrs. Johanne Gulden, born 20 Sept. 1838 in Norway, died 3 July at the age of 89 years, 9 months, and 13 days. Her husband, Ole Gulden, passed away 19 Nov. 1909. They were blessed with 12 children of whom five survive her, namely Anders, Johan, Carl, Herman and Jørgen, all of whom were at the funeral.

>She came to America in 1871 with her husband (Ole probably came in 1869) and their children who were born in Norway. Since the death of her husband, she has lived with her sons Carol and Johan. Since neither of them were married and since she needed more care, she lived during the summer of 1927 and from the spring of 1928 until her death with Anders and his family. Besides her own children, she has also raised two sons of her youngest daughter from the time they were infants until they were grown.

>The funeral was conducted 6 July from the funeral home and she was laid to rest at the Jevnaker Church Cemetery beside her husband. Funeral services were conducted by Pastor Strom, whom we dearly thank for his comforting words. He spoke both at the funeral home, in church, and at the graveside.

>Peace be with her remains, blessed be her memory!

>*Her two sorrowing grandsons (children of the youngest daughter)*
>*Hjalmer O. Gulden and Lloyd O. Gulden*

The inscription on Johanne's gravestone says: *"Gjemt Ikke Glemt"* which means "Gone but not forgotten."

The Guldens from Norway to U.S.A. can be traced by baptism and census records:

- 1860 Marte, born on Larshus farm, Lunner, Hadeland, Norway
- 1862 Anne, born on Gullen/Gulden farm, Gran, Hadeland
- 1865 Andrew, born on Kraagerud farm, Lunner, Hadeland
- 1867 Olaf, born on Hytta farm, Lunner Hadeland
- 1869 Ole came to the U.S.A. alone to Green County, Wisconsin (not found on 1870 census)
- 1871 Johanna and the first 5 children came (per immigration record)
- 1879 Family moved from Green County to Erickson Township, Renville County, Minnesota
- 1881 Marte Gulden marries Peter Lanning in Erickson Township, Renville County, Minnesota
- 1883 Family moved from Renville County to Mandt Township, Chippewa County, Minnesota

Note from the author:
I found the clipping from the Decorah Posten in the files at St. Olaf College, Northfield, Minnesota (translation by Priscilla Sorknes, genealogist for Romerike Lag). The obituary states that Ole and Johanna had 12 children. Only 11 children were accounted for. I suspect another child with the same name (Ole/Olaus) was born and died before Olaus was baptized on 18 Aug. 1867. Under their customs of naming their children, the first son and daughter were named for the paternal grandparents (Ole/Olaus and Marte) and the second son and daughter were named for the maternal grandparents (Anders and Anne).

Marte Olsdatter Larshus Gulden
How My Hadeland Grandma Got Her Man

Published May 2011   *Beverly Webster*

My grandmother, Marte Olsdatter Larshus Gulden (born 1859) came to America with her parents Ole Olsen Tvet Gulden and Johanne Andersdatter Haagenstad in 1871 on the ship *Concordia.* The family was in Green County, Wisconsin, for a few years before going to Erickson Township, Renville County, Minnesota. This family were squatters about a mile north of where my grandfather Peder Lanning homesteaded in 1873. He was born in Wisconsin. His father was born in Valdres, Norway, and his mother was from Land.

In 1880 Grandpa heard that there was a pretty young gal about a mile north of his farm. Grandpa wanted to see "this pretty girl." He went up to this farm and found they were living in a dugout. In order to take a look at this gal he decided to climb onto the roof of the dugout and take a peek. He was too shy to knock on the door. Peder made a grand entrance into their dugout. He climbed up and promptly fell through the roof! Apparently Marte's parents were impressed, as she and Peder were married soon after in 1881.

Peter Rosendahl

Published May 2002   *Form 475*   *Dean Johnson and Georgia Rosendahl*

Robert Rosendahl, Decorah, Iowa, sent us articles written about Peter Rosendahl, creator of the comic strip, Han Ola og Han Per. Peter's parents were immigrants from Hadeland. Below are printed excerpts from the articles.

Who is this Guy? *By Dean Johnson*

Peter Julius Rosendahl was truly a remarkable man. He was a good farmer, a fine humorist, a talented cartoon artist and poet. He held convictions that enabled him to overcome his innate reticence, and make his mark on the literary and artistic world through his cartoon strip *Han Ola og Han Per* (He's Ole and He's Per) that was published in the Norwegian language newspaper "The Decorah Posten."

Born in 1878 in Houston County, Minnesota, he lost his father at the tender age of two. Fortunately he inherited his father Paul's intelligence. Unfortunately he did not inherit his outgoing personality. Paul had been a state legislator, but his youngest son Peter was content to be a tiller of the earth.

The event that triggered his cartoon was brought about by the carnage and anti-foreign hysteria of the First World War. The comfortable era of Spring Grove's "Golden Age of Norwegian Culture" was challenged by America's involvement in its first truly global conflict. "Ola and Per" was this thoughtful man's response to that. Humor has always been a way of dealing with difficult times and the war followed by the Spanish influenza was terrible in the extreme. Peter had a fine sense of humor and loved a good joke. He epitomized through his cartoon strip the self-deprecating humor that is a hallmark of Norwegian culture.

But the slapstick antics of "Ola and Per" do not capture the entire persona of the man. His sensitive poetry gives us an insight to a person that spent a great deal of time studying the technical changing of the world around him, its unavoidable impact on people and the deeply felt quest for peace that was at the heart of Peter's soul.

Ola and Per gave humor and solace to our ancestors. It is a humble, yet magnificent contribution. We are allowed a rare glimpse to a little known genius that gave comfort and laughter to the *Decorah Posten's* 45,000 weekly Norwegian readers. But nothing that is precious lasts forever. After a slight rebuff over one of the cartoons submitted to the *Decorah Posten*, Peter Rosendahl quit writing his strip. The familiar characters of Ola, Per, Polla, Dada,

Lars and Væmor flew back to Norway.

In the year 1942 Norway, our beloved homeland, lay occupied by the Nazi invader. France had fallen and Britain had stood alone for over a year. Russia was in flames from Leningrad to Stalingrad. The Japanese stood triumphant in the Pacific although they had received a check in the decisive Naval Battle of Midway.

Against this background, beset by health problems, his sons facing the draft, and America being different to Peter in his old age than it must have been to the first immigrants, he took his own life for reasons that only he knew.

Life in our comfortable community fits most of us like a glove. Peter Julius Rosendahl gives us an insight into how this came to be. His life had many facets. He was our Henry David Thoreau, our Al Capp, our Benjamin Franklin, and at the end, our Ernest Hemmingway. He was Spring Grove's first truly remarkable man.

Peter Rosendahl *By his daughter-in-law Georgia Rosendahl*

The author, Peter J. Rosendahl, of the Norwegian-American comic strip, *Han Ola og Han Per,* was born on April 14, 1878. The farm on which he grew up on was off the main road in a beautiful valley running north to south, about one mile southwest of Spring Grove, Houston County, Minnesota. The driveway to get to this homestead was by several private lanes. The Rosendahl farm consisted of around 240 acres.

Peter's parents were immigrants from Norway. His father, Paul Hanson Rosendahl, who was born on October 18, 1839, came to America with his parents in 1851. They first settled at Jefferson Prairie, Wisconsin. Then in 1854 they continued on to Spring Grove where they stayed with their relative, Anders Kroshus.

Peter lost his father when he was a little over two and a half years old. Peter being the youngest in the family had to depend on his older siblings and mother for his nurturing when growing up. His mother Gunhild, with the help of hired men, was able to manage their large farm. One has to believe that most of the work fell onto the shoulders of her sons, namely Oliver, born in 1871, Otto, born in 1875, and Peter, when they became older.

Peter also had two sisters, Julia born in 1866 who was married to Edward Pedersen in 1886, a pastor of the Norwegian Evangelical Lutheran Church, and Hannah who was born 1869, married Narve Narveson in 1898. Gunhild died in 1933 at the age of 95 years.

Peter never went beyond grade school. Just how many months this involved, one has to speculate. Usually school was held during the winter months when there was no fieldwork – just the everyday chores. But Peter must have had a thirst for knowledge as we find that he not only purchased many, many books during his lifetime, he also subscribed to many magazines, some of which were *The Youth's Companion* and *Scientific American.* Above all, he liked to draw. Neighbors would tell how he would draw pictures in the dust on the threshing machines in the fall. Many of those pictures would resemble the men who were working with the threshing.

It was believed for many years that Peter never traveled much outside his home in spring Grove. But we have found that in 1904, Peter and his brother-in-law Narve Narveson took a train trip to the West Coast. Peter and Othelia Melbraaten were married December 20, 1905. After they married, they took a trip to North Dakota to visit the Stoas. Mrs. Stoa was Gunhild's sister. He also went to the Cities to paint his brother's house and while there wrote a poem about life in the city. He would go to Bemidji to visit his brother Otto who did summer work in connection with his job at the University. He would also send his children to visit at the lake and there were many happy memories connected with these events. In turn Otto's sons would visit the farm in the summer and get to know first-hand what all was entailed in producing milk and butter, plus pork chops and eggs.

4. "Are you soon through, Polla?" "My goodness! I haven't even got her started up yet."

Peder Gulleneie and Ingeborg Wahl

Published May 2002　　　　　　　*Form 940*　　　　　　　*Diane Resvick*

Ingeborg and Peder Wahl
c. 1913 in Canada

How deep are the roots of your Hadeland tree? How wide do your branches extend? Have you ever wondered if you still have "family" in Norway? Hopefully, this article will inspire at least one person to begin or continue his/her own search for the answers to these questions.

There may be many obstacles to overcome in searching for information about your family history. For me, it began with having little information to start with about my great-grandparents. I had a half-sheet of paper with a few dates and places mentioned on it about my great-grandfather, Peder Johnson. The only information about my great-grandmother was from family stories. We weren't even sure about her actual surname. Many family members believed that it was Dahl. However, one family member had a rubber stamp and believed that it once belonged to my great-grandmother. Once the "old Gothic" typeset was deciphered, the name attached to my great-grandmother then became Ingeborg A. Wahl.

Another obstacle that was encountered was my lack of proper research techniques. The development of effective research techniques was very frustrating, a little disheartening and very time consuming. Many in my family felt that there was no hope of finding out more about your relatives.

I quickly learned, however, that in doing family history research 'perseverance' has to become your middle name. You need to look at the search as a 5,000-piece jigsaw puzzle that you want to assemble. You may have only a few pieces of the border or you may have small-connected pieces from the middle. Don't let this discourage you. Even with a half-sheet of paper or a rubber stamp, you must believe you can find more information!

Start with reading, reading, reading all you can about Norway. If you are looking for good sources of information regarding genealogy searches and Norway there are several available on the Internet. My e-mail address is located at the end of this article. I would be happy to send you the URL addresses for those sites I found the most useful.

My family searched all we could here in the United States with the information we had. No new information was located and the search seemed hopeless and discouraging. But, I quickly learned that you don't give up. Did no new information in the United States mean no new information in Norway for us?

111

To answer this question, it seemed that the next likely place for us to look for information was in Norway. I wrote the Norwegian Emigration Center in Stavanger, Norway, with the limited information I had about great-grandfather Peder. Six months later I received a letter from the Center with the names of my great-grandfather's parents, his birthday and birthplace, his confirmation date and place, his date and port of emigration. It also included the names, ages, and birthplaces of his siblings.

There is a charge for this information but personally I feel it was worth every dollar. The staff and volunteers at the Norwegian Emigration Center continue to do their research work by hand. Check out the following website for more information: http://www.emigrationcenter.com.

One of the responses I received sent me on an adventure into my family's past that I would have never imagined could happen. It was the beginning of a journey that would end with a trip to Norway to meet my Norwegian family! Here's what happened.

That one special message was from Gunnar Thon, who lives in Oslo, but was raised in Hadeland. He was conducting research about the same Aaslund farm in Lunner that I had requested information about. We exchanged several e-mail messages regarding the farm, but quickly decided there was no connection between our two families.

One would think that would have been the end of the communication between us. However, with what we now know, the communication was probably meant to be. There's more about our connection to each other later.

Gunnar continued to assist my family in locating information about my great-grandparents. Thanks to his expertise guidance and patience, I learned more than I ever could from my book, video, website or class.

We quickly discovered that there was a possibility I still had family in Norway. That's when the first "miracle" happened. Gunnar visited a local genealogist in Jevnaker. Gunhild Myhrstuen, a new Lag member, helped him to discover that descendants on my great-grandfather's side still lived in Norway. In fact, my third cousin was a neighbor to Gunnar's late mother!

The impossible dream had come true. To find my third cousin and her family was more than my family had ever imagined would happen. Contact was quickly established with letters traveling back and forth on a regular basis between Norway and the United States. Once translation difficulties were resolved, we quickly learned more about each other.

The desire to meet our family in Norway blossomed into a trip to Norway in July 2001. I still find it difficult to express the feelings I felt as the day of the trip arrived. I was nervous, scared, excited and so overly happy that I couldn't sleep on the 14-hour trip to Oslo. A second "miracle" was indeed happening,

Three cousins who met in Norway were (left to right)
Ethel Resvick, Gina Gullheim, and Mary Bergestuen.

The family I so longed to meet met my mother and me at the Gardermoen Airport. As we left the arrival gate Mary Bergestuen and her son, Ulf, greeted us with a sign welcoming us to Norway. It was so heart-warming and will always remain one of my many special memories.

I made many observations about Norway, its people, its culture, and the land while I was there. The one that remains the most predominant in my mind is the kindness and cordial manner in which we were treated no matter where we traveled. From my family to the strangers we met along our travels, there wasn't a single person who was impolite, rude or unwilling to assist us when help was needed.

My family took time from their own busy lives and summer holiday schedules to take us on many trips around the Jevnaker area. We met many other relatives and got to know each other quite quickly. There are many similarities and differences between our families.

Gunnar Thon visited us many times during our time in Norway. We traveled with him on several occasions visiting various communities and areas of Hadeland. We attended a festival celebration at the *Hadeland Folkemuseum.* In my opinion, this is a must place to visit for anyone with ties to Hadeland!

The archives at the *Folkemuseum* house a wealth of information and has a very knowledgeable staff. It's through the information we found at the archives that the third "miracle" happened. Gunnar and I found out there was indeed a reason for our friendship to continue. His great-great-great-grandparents were baptismal sponsors for my great-great-grandfather! My family worked for his family on the Aaslund farm in the 1880s.

To think that our ancestors knew each other and now the paths of our two families had crossed again! Miracles are not impossible! You may remember that I mentioned the Aaslund farm earlier. Yes, the archive information took us back to the Aaslund farm where my contact with Gunnar first began. This, in turn, leads me to another point. Never give up on those puzzle pieces. You might have to turn them around or look at them from a different angle, but the pieces will eventually fit together.

Gunnar and I continued to discover new information about our families and surprisingly, we usually discovered new information about the other person's family, too. We continued to work as a genealogy team long after I let Norway. Each of us relied on the strengths and resources of the other. In that way, our family trees continued to grow and our friendship prospered until his death in 2004.

In closing, I hope that Lag members will pursue their interest in locating their Hadeland roots. Who knows what you may find along the way? Remember to read and learn all you can about genealogy resources, believe in miracles and, within time, that 5,000 piece puzzle will be closer to completion. Your branches will extend into a beautiful tree and those roots will take you back into the past and an adventure of a lifetime. Cherish your Norwegian heritage!

I publicly wish to thank Hadeland Lag members, Gunnar Thon and Gunhild Myhrstuen, for their assistance in making my family's dreams come true.

The Hval (Wahl) Family Journey to America

Previously unpublished   *Diane Resvick*
With thanks to family members for many of the photos in this article

By 1884, every member of the Anders and Berthe (Syversdatter) Wahl family journeyed to North America from Hadeland, Norway. However, for this family, the process did not happen all at once. Actually, it took over 15 years for the entire family to set foot in the New World. This is their story.

The Wahl family was a typical tenant family. Anders and some of the family are living at Ulverud, in Gran, on the 1865 Norwegian Census. Anders is identified as a *husmann med jord*, meaning that he leased a small piece of farmland for a limited time, and either leased or owned the home on the property for the family to live in. (One might assume that they leased the home because most of their 11 children were born at different locations.)

Providing for a large family was difficult at this time in Norway. This is evident on the 1865 census. The older children are not listed with the rest of the family as they were working "out of the home" to provide for their own survival. The census also describes the size of the farm where the Wahl family lived. Anders had 2 large cattle (probably cows) and 6 sheep. As for what he grew on the land...he had 4 bushels barley, 1 bushel mixed grain (usually barley/oats), 4½ bushels oats, ½ bushel peas, and 8 bushels potatoes. By today's standards this would be a very small farm. Not hard to understand why it would be difficult to feed a family of 13 with these provisions and that these circumstances may have triggered their emigration to America.

What follows tells of each family member's journey to the New World. None of the histories are complete. However, every attempt has been made to locate and confirm as much information as possible about each family member. Information about living descendants and their spouses has only been included with permission.

If any information differs from what descendants today know about their ancestors, the difference is not meant to offend anyone. Accuracy is of the upmost importance. But it is only as good as information that others are willing to share.

The individual histories of the Wahl family are in order of emigration. First, Elise; then Ingeborg; Martha; Edward and Anne Maria (together); Andrew; Syver; Berthe, Karen, and the parents (Anders and Berthe); and lastly Lars.

Elise Wahl Risem

The first member, in this Wahl family, to emigrate was Else/Elise. She was Anders Larsen and Berthe Syversdatter Wahl's fourth child. Else was born 27 October 1850, at Hvaleie in Gran. Elise had already left her family's home to work at the young age of 15 in 1865. She had gone to work at the Dœhlen farm (under Lysengen) in Gran.

On 21 February 1873 Elise signed out of the church. She indicated that she was going to Oslo. She may have moved there to work. There's also the possibility that she went there to help her oldest brother Lars and his wife, with their first child who was born in September of that same year.

Eventually, Elise boarded the *S/S Angelo* headed for America. The ship set sail from Oslo on 30 October 1874. Elise indicated that she was headed to Boston, Massachusetts.

Elise may not have had any choice as to where she was going in America. She had an agreement with the shipping agent to pay off her fare when she arrived at her final destination. The contract may have specified the location of her final residency.

What Elise did for work during those first years is unknown. She must have been a strong-willed young woman setting off by herself for America, by taking on debt to pay once she got there.

In Norway, Elise had worked as a domestic. Like other Norwegian females, she more than likely knew how to sew, too. This might have been the way in which she met her future husband who was a tailor.

Elise and Erland Rasmussen (R.) Risem married, 27 July 1879, in Boston. Erland was the son of Rasmus Olsen and Ronnaug Erlandsdatter Risem. He was born 4 September 1846 in Lom, Oppland, Norway. It's not known when Erland immigrated to America.

Following their marriage Elise worked at keeping house and Erland continued his work as a tailor. They were blessed with three sons. Within months of the birth of their youngest son, Erland and Elise became naturalized American citizens on 25 October 1887. The naturalization laws at the time permitted immigrant women to be naturalized with their husbands.

Their oldest son Edward/Erland/Eddie Sidney was born 24 April 1883. He only lived 2 ½ years. He passed away 18 January 1886 of diphtheria. He was laid to rest at the Forest Hills Cemetery in Boston in plot 369, Heth Field, Section 30.

Elise's strength was tested once again when Erland died suddenly, 18 January 1890, of pneumonia. He was buried at the Forest Hills Cemetery in Boston, Massachusetts. He was laid to rest in Plot 367, next to his beloved son, Eddie Sidney, who preceded him in death.

Erland's death left Elise with two young children to raise on her own. What she did to provide for the family remains unknown. She never remarried. The oldest son, Andrew Rasmus (sometimes Andrew Rufus) was providing for the family at the young age of 20. He was born 30 April 1880 in Boston. In 1900 he was working as a shipper for a photography lab and was listed on the census as the head of the house with his mother and younger brother living with him.

Later in life Andrew was a letter carrier for the US Post Office. He married his first wife Ellen Gould (Nellie G.), 26 September 1910. She was the daughter of Irish immigrants Mark Gould and Mary McHugh. Ellen was born in Boston 3 November 1883. Unfortunately, tuberculosis took her within three year's time. Ellen died 26 November 1913. She was laid to rest in the Forest Hills Cemetery, Field of Manoah section, grave 1872.

Andrew then married Catherine E. Skinner on 6 December 1916. She was the daughter of Donald Skinner and Susan Parker. Catherine was born 11 March 1877 in Nova Scotia, Canada. She emigrated in 1901 and worked as a domestic before marrying Andrew. Catherine died 16 November 1929. She was buried next to Ellen in grave 1873.

Andrew followed Catherine in death shortly after. He passed away 26 March 1930. He was buried with Catherine and Ellen at Forest Hills Cemetery.

Erland and Elise's third son, Bernard Edward Oscar Risem (Edward Oscar and sometimes Oscar E.) was born 4 March 1887, in Boston. Edward O. worked as a clerk/auditor in Boston's City Hall. He also served 9 years as of 1917, in the U.S. Army Coast Artillery. Edward passed away 18 October 1946. He was laid to rest in Field of Heth, Section 30, Plot 369, in Forest Hills Cemetery.

Elise's sons must have felt a strong commitment to their mother. She lived with both of them at some point throughout her life. Elise died, 29 May 1929. She was buried in Forest Hills Cemetery, in plot 368, next to her husband. Catherine and Elise died within 6 months of each other. There are no known grandchildren for Erland and Elise. This was probably yet another tribulation for this strong Norwegian immigrant.

Ingeborg Wahl Johnson

Taken about 1900 in Moorhead, Minnesota
Seated: Ingeborg (Andersdatter Wahl) Johnson, Peder Johnson, and Anna Matilda
Standing: Josephine Emelia, John Bernhard, Oscar Tederman and Bernard Anton
Missing from photo is oldest daughter, Anna. Ingeborg and Peder are the author's great-grandparents.
Oscar T. is her grandfather.

Ingeborg was the second member of this Wahl family to immigrate to America. She was the sixth child of Anders Larsen and Berthe Syversdatter Wahl. She was born 23 September 1855 at Hvaleie in Gran. In 1865, Ingeborg was residing with her parents and younger siblings, at Ulverud (under Hval).

Just like her older siblings had done, Ingeborg probably worked outside of the home once she was old enough. In 1875, she was employed at the north Bratvold farm in Jevnaker. There she worked as a servant. The north Bratvold farm was located just west of the Braaten farm where Ingeborg's older sister Anne Maria worked.

However, Ingeborg decided to follow yet another older sister to America the following year. She left Oslo aboard the *S/S Angelo* 13 October 1876. Her fare was paid in full and she indicated that she was headed for Boston. This was a logical location for her to go as Elise had settled in Boston the year before.

Once in Liverpool, England, Ingeborg transferred to the *S/S Marathon*. It arrived in the port of Boston 29 October 1876. Ingeborg indicated that she was a servant. She also indicated that she was 20 years old, when in actuality she was 21. This is of significance when researching Ingeborg as she seldom told her correct age!

117

In 1880 it is known that Ingeborg worked for the Heinrich and Inger Lootz family as a servant. They too were Norwegian immigrants. Due to their involvement with the merchant and petroleum oil business, they became fairly prominent in Boston after the Civil War.

Mrs. Lootz wrote a letter of reference for Ingeborg that same year. In the letter, Mrs. Lootz says that "Ingeborg Wahl has lived with me two years, and I can cordially recommend her, as a good cook, good laundress, strictly honest, always pleasant, and willing to do what is required of her."

Sometime after, 2 June 1880, Ingeborg moved to either Lafayette or Iowa County, Wisconsin. There she would marry her husband, Peder Johansen Gulleneie.

The Bratvold farm mentioned earlier was also near the Gullen farm in Jevnaker. Several researchers believe that the Wahl and Johansen families may have known each other quite well. Recently, it was discovered that there is a Peder J. Gulleneie listed as a baptismal sponsor for Anne Maria's first child, born in 1875.

This raises several questions though. If they knew each other prior to coming to America, why didn't they travel together? How did they manage to maintain contact with each other, being they settled in different locations upon coming to America? Were they 'in love' or was this an arranged marriage?

Despite these questions, it's known that Ingeborg Andersdatter Wahl and Peder Johansen Gulleneie married, 4 June 1881, with the Reverend C. C. Aas officiating. There is reason to believe that the ceremony took place at the East Wiota Lutheran Church, in South Wayne, Lafayette County, Wisconsin.

Their marriage record does not appear in the church records. This apparently was not unusual. Many ministers entered only the names of those who financially supported the church.

Peder Johansen Gulleneie was born to Johan Andersen Aaslandeie and Berthe Toresdatter Guldeneie 4 March 1858 at Jevnaker. They resided on the Masserud farm (under Gullen) in 1865.

Peder left Norway from Oslo 31 August 1877 also aboard the *S/S Angelo*. In Liverpool, England, he transferred to the *S/S City of Chester*. The *City of Chester* arrived in the port of New York (Castle Garden) 15 September 1877. He indicated that he was headed for Monroe, Green County, Wisconsin.

Even though Peder indicated Monroe as his final destination, he was probably traveling to the neighboring Lafayette County. Peder's brother Anders and several other relatives had settled there years earlier. Lafayette County was also an area highly populated by immigrants from Hadeland. By 1880 Peder had acquired employment as a tinsmith. He was more than likely working as an apprentice with Herman and Hermana Lund, in Blachardville, Lafayette County. They were also Norwegian immigrants.

However within the next year Peder and Ingeborg moved once again. This time it was because the family was growing in number and Peder's oldest sister Tolline lived in Goodhue County, Minnesota and she could help the young couple.

That's because Tolline was well known as a midwife. Ingeborg and Peder's first child was a daughter. Anna Matilda, was born, 6 June 1882. A son followed the next year. John Bernhard was born 23 December 1883. Both were born near Prairie Island or Welch Township in Goodhue County.

Ingeborg's siblings weren't the only ones to stay together once arriving in America. Peder's siblings somehow stayed connected, too. In 1884 Ingeborg and Peder moved to Kilkenny, Le Sueur County, Minnesota. Peder's older brother Anders was living there with his family. They are recorded next to each other on the 1885 MN Census. Peder worked as a farm laborer while in that area.

In 1886 the family moved yet again. Ingeborg and Peder settled their family in Erhards Grove Township, Otter Tail County, Minnesota. Several of Ingeborg's siblings and Peder's brother Anders had already established themselves there.

Peder indicated on his 1941 autobiography that he "bought a piece of land" while in Erhards Grove. It's possible Peder bought his piece of land from a family member and they never registered the transaction.

A second son, Bernard Anton, was born in Erhards Grove, 15 September 1887. Their second daughter Josephine Amelia was born in Fergus Falls, also in Otter Tail County, 2 January 1889. Around 1892, according to the 1895 MN Census, the family moved to Moorhead, Clay County, Minnesota. They lived there for over a decade, while Peder worked as a janitor at several schools in the area. His longest position was at the State Normal School. Today, the State Normal School and the house in which the Johnson family lived are part of the Minnesota State University-Moorhead.

During their tenure in Moorhead, Peder became a naturalized citizen of the United States. His first papers had been filed in Lafayette County, Wisconsin some 13 years earlier. Another significant event during that time was the birth of their third son, Oscar Tederman. Oscar was born 15 October 1896.

Sometime after 1900, the family moved across the river to Fargo, North Dakota. Little is known about their lives there. It's possible that North Dakota may have provided them with more opportunities being it was a fairly new state.

In 1905 once again, Ingeborg and Peder moved the family further west. This time, however, it was only Peder, Ingeborg, and Oscar. Anna, John B., Ben, and Josephine had now started their own lives.

Ingeborg, Peder, and Oscar settled near Ruso, McLean County, North Dakota. They were actually some of the first residents in that community. Ruso, founded in 1906, grew rapidly for several years. The Johnson family was part of that growth. They even purchased several lots in town where they built their home. Peder was a laborer of odd jobs while in Ruso. At some point Anna Matilda and her husband as well as Josephine and her husband lived there, too.

Flyers for "free" land in Canada were circulating throughout the United States. Peder more than likely saw these flyers. So early in September 1910, Peder was on his way to Canada. Ingeborg and Oscar joined him sometime in 1911.

The family settled in the Melfort, Saskatchewan area. Ingeborg and Peder became citizens of Canada and received a homestead patent in 1913. The homestead was located along the Carrot River.

Despite the growth going on in Saskatchewan at that time, Ingeborg and Peder returned to the United States in June 1914. They lived in Ruso for a couple of years and then moved to Minot, Ward County, North Dakota in 1917. Peder worked for the Great Northern Railroad as a cook and a bridge carpenter.

In August 1918 the District Court Judge of Clay County, Moorhead, Minnesota informed Peder that his U.S. citizenship was cancelled and that it was null and void. This was due to them taking citizenship in Canada. So within two weeks Peder filed yet another Declaration of Intention to become an American citizen in Minot, Ward County, North Dakota.

Unfortunately Ingeborg would never again be an American citizen. Sometime in 1920 she became seriously ill. She eventually went to Weldon, Saskatchewan, to live with her daughter Anna Matilda.

Ingeborg died there, 10 June 1922. She was laid to rest at the Kinistino Cemetery, Saskatchewan, Canada. Authorities in Kinistino feel that she may rest with or between two of Anna's children who were also buried there.

Peder received his American citizenship again in May 1922. He worked at the Sather Restaurant as a cook until his death. Peder passed away 28 May 1942. He is buried in the Granville Cemetery, McHenry County, North Dakota, near their youngest son Oscar.

Oldest daughter Anna Matilda married Hiram Butler Munger around 1904, in either North Dakota or Minnesota. Hiram was born in 1879 in Iowa, to Warren J. and Alice E Munger. Hiram died 24 January 1927 in Chilliwack, British Columbia, Canada. Anna Matilda later married Alex Broten. Anna Matilda died 21 May 1969 in North Saanich, British Columbia. She was laid to rest in the Royal Oak Burial Park, Victoria, British Columbia. Hiram and Anna's children were Violet Lucille (1905-1906), Warren Benjamin (1907-1910), Howard Orville (1909-1992), Pearl (b. 1912), Orval (d. 1916), Roland James (1920-1956), and Gordon Hiram (1926-1997, married Doris).

John Bernhard married Hilda A. Pederson, 1 February 1904. Hilda was born 13 April 1882 in Rothsay, Minnesota, to Christian and Dordi Pederson. John died 25 April 1950 in Hubbard County, Minnesota. Hilda died 2 October 1970 in Fargo, Cass County, North Dakota. They were buried in Greenwood Cemetery in Park Rapids, Minnesota. Their children were Chester William (1904-1977, married Sarah E. Wallschlager), Eleanor Charlotte (1906-1995, married Martin J. Bearson), and Kermit W. (1912-1961).

Bernard (Ben) Anton married Vera D. Shurtliff 3 October 1910, in Dickinson, Stark County, North Dakota. Vera was born 27 March 1892 in Big Flats, Adams County, Wisconsin. She was the daughter of Henry Shurtliff and Susan Pells. Bernard died 21 March 1955 in Auburn, King County, Washington. Vera died 9 June 1958 in Pacific City, King County, Washington. They are buried at the Mountain View Cemetery, Auburn, King County, Washington. Their children were Vera Nevada (1911-2002, married Harold Reddy), Naomi Ione (1915-1992, married Paul Pohlman), Juanita Anita (1917-1987, married James Ingram), Marvel Belle (1919-1988), Wayne Bernard (1921-1995), and Alma Lorraine (1924-1956). Their youngest daughter is still alive.

Josephine Emelia married Russell Holmes Simmons on 5 November 1906. Russell was born 21 November 1886 in Mercyville, Missouri. Russell died 14 November 1982 in Abbotsford, British Columbia. Josephine died 21 May 1984 in Clearbrook, British Columbia. Their children were Donald Robert (1907-1934), Harold Leo (1908-1985), Mildred (1910-1999, married Ted Hermanson), Nina (1913-2004, married Herman Hermanson), and Russell Dean (1915-1999, married Emily Friesen). Josephine and Russell's two youngest daughters are still alive. ,

Oscar Tederman married Bessie Addie Geddes 22 December 1920, in Minot, Ward County, North Dakota. Bessie was the daughter of Jason Geddes and Maria Jane Boutilier. Oscar passed away 10 October 1941 in Oregon City, Clackamas County, Oregon. Bessie passed away 1 May 1990 in Minot. Their children were Ethel Mae (1926-2008, married Jean Francis Resvick), and JoAnn (b. 1941, married Paul L. Buriak).

Martha Wahl Johnson

The third member of the Anders Larsen and Berthe (Syversdatter) Wahl family to immigrate was their seventh child, Martha. Martha/Martha A. was born 28 May 1858 at Hvalseie in Gran.

There's little information about her early life in Norway. More than likely Martha worked out of her family home at an early age, as did many husmann's children in Norway.

On, 26 April 1878, Martha left Oslo on the *S/S Hero*, headed for Boston, Massachusetts. She probably went to join her older sisters, Elise and Ingeborg. Her fare was paid in full and might have been paid by her siblings being they were already established in America. This was a common practice among the immigrants.

Martha found employment with a Dr. Horatio G. Morse. Several sources say that Dr. Morse was a general practitioner in the Roxbury (Boston, Massachusetts) area. Martha was working as a servant for him at his place of residence.

On, 3 June 1882 in Boston, Martha married Axel Johan/Axel J. Johnson. He was the son of Johan Lorentz and Charlotte Amelia Aas. Axel was born 21 July 1858 in Trondheim, Sør-Trondelag, Norway. Records vary as to what year Axel came to America but it seems to be between 1878 and 1880. Axel was employed as a cornice maker and a sheet metal worker throughout his life.

Martha and Axel were blessed with one child. John Axel was born 20 March 1883 in Boston. He went on to graduate from Boston University with a degree in law. John practiced general law in the Roxbury area.

It seems to have taken an extended period of time for Axel and Martha to naturalize. However, they completed that process 20 October 1892.

Axel died 17 October 1928. He was laid to rest at Forest Hills Cemetery, Boston, Massachusetts.

Following Axel's death, Martha went to live with her son John and his wife. She remained in their care until she passed away 13 August 1937. She was laid to rest next to her husband at Forest Hills Cemetery.

John married Marguerite E. Cleveland about 1918 in Boston. She was the daughter of Earl and Mary J. (Simpson) Cleveland. Marguerite was born in Boston 20 February 1883. John was 30 days younger than his wife (except in a leap-year)! John and Martha had no children.

Marguerite passed away 18 March 1959. She was laid to rest in Forest Hills Cemetery. John A. passed away 26 November 1964. He was laid to rest in Grave 7214 at Forest Hills Cemetery, next to his wife.

Edward Wahl

* Every attempt has been made to locate a primary source which confirms that the individual described in this history, is the son of Anders Larsen and Berthe Syversdatter Wahl. However, none of the documents found thus far in the United States give his full birth date or the name of his parents. The writer of this history felt that a disclaimer needed to be made for this reason.

The first male, in this Wahl family, to immigrate was Edvard/Edward. He was Anders Larsen and Berthe Syversdatter Wahl's ninth child. Edvard Anderssen Wahl was born, 27 August 1861 at Hvalseie in Gran. This happy event followed the death of his infant sister, Elina, 3 ½ months earlier.

In 1875, Edward along with his younger brother, Anders, was with their older sister Anne Maria at the Braaten farm under Gullen in Jevnaker. Anne Maria worked for the owner of the farm. She had just had her first child, a daughter. So the brothers may have been there to visit their sister or to help her with her responsibilities on the farm.

Edward signed out of the church, 16 April 1880. Four days later he was aboard the S/S Baldur in Oslo headed for America with the name of Edward A. Wahl. He traveled with his older sister, Anne Maria, her husband Hans Larsen, and their children.

From passenger records, it is known that they transferred to a transatlantic ship somewhere along the way. The *S/S Weser* arrived in New York harbor (Castle Garden), 10 May 1880. It had sailed from Bergen, Germany. How they traveled from there to Minnesota is unknown.

Edward indicated that he was a shoemaker. It is not known whether, Edward went to Fergus Falls, Minnesota, with Anne Maria. He may have ventured to the Duluth area of Minnesota instead.

Edward married Olivia/Olava J. Melby, 8 January 1891, in St. Louis County, Minnesota. She was born 14 August 1850, in Norway, and immigrated to America in 1881. She is known to have been a dressmaker. Edward was a laborer of some type, such as a painter, during those early years of marriage.

Edward and Olivia moved to Otter Tail County around 1893. There may have been a two-fold reason for this move. Fergus Falls was where several of Edward's siblings has settled and established themselves. It was also the closest state-ran hospital to Saint Louis County.

Edward was a patient at the Fergus Falls State Hospital (now known as the Regional Treatment Center) in Fergus Falls, Minnesota. "The hospital accepted patients that were mentally ill, developmentally disabled, or had a chemical dependency." [*"The History of the Fergus Falls Regional Treatment Center: 1890-2004,"* provided by the Minnesota Department of Human Services, Fergus Falls, MN, Print.]

His first admission was 20 October 1892. According to hospital records, he was admitted at least two more times throughout his lifetime. He was in the hospital during the time of both the 1900 and 1910 US Censuses.

` "Most patients in 1894 had some type of mental illness and were committed by legal actions.

photo from Sandra Frojen, Minneapolis, MN

However, the Superintendent at that time, worked diligently to change the laws governing the establishment. He felt that allowing individuals to be admitted on a voluntary basis would change the attitude of the public toward such hospitals. This law went into effect in 1910. This is also the same time a contagious hospital was opened on the grounds of the center." [*"The History of the Fergus Falls Regional Treatment Center: 1890-2004,"* provided by the Minnesota Department of Human Services, Fergus Falls, MN, Print.]

Edward died at the hospital, 4 April 1913, of phthisis pulmonalis or tuberculosis. He was laid to rest in the Fergus Falls State Hospital Cemetery in Cemetery 2, Section 12, Grave 26. A headstone was placed on Edward's grave in 2014 using monies from private donations and a grant from the State of Minnesota. ["*Fergus Falls State Hospital Cemetery Burials,*" Friends of the Fergus Falls State Hospital Cemetery. Web. http://www.tc.umn.edu/~vanes002/FFSHBurialsRWD.html]

Olivia had died the year before on, 10 March 1912. She is buried at Bethlehem Cemetery, Fergus Falls, Minnesota. Edward and Olivia had no children.

Anne Marie Wahl Larson

Anne Maria was the first member of this Wahl family to emigrate with a husband and children. Anne Maria, the third child of Anders Larsen and Berthe Syversdatter Wahl, entered the world 22 December 1848 at Bjørgeeie in Gran.

By the age of 17 Anne Maria resided and worked outside of her parent's home. She more than likely served as a domestic at a neighboring farm in Gran. There's no indication that she left Hadeland and migrated elsewhere.

Between 1865 and 1875 Anne Maria moved to the Rønnerudeie farm in Jevnaker. She worked at the Braaten under Gullen farm, also in Jevnaker, as a domestic. Her responsibilities included sewing, knitting, weaving, and probably other household chores.

Her two younger brothers, Edward and Anders, visited her at the time of the 1875 Norwegian census. They may have also been there to help her with her responsibilities around the farm. Anne Maria had just had a child prior to the census.

A daughter, Anne Lovise Hansdatter, arrived 7 October 1875 at Rønnerudeie in Jevnaker. Hans Larssen Gulleneie, the son of Lars Hansen and Anne Engebretsdatter, was her father. He was born 7 November 1849 at Gulleneie in Jevnaker.

Anne Maria and Hans married 3 April 1877 in Jevnaker. They continued to live at the Ronnerudeie farm for several years after their marriage. On 21 August 1877 Anders, their second child arrived. Their third child, Lars, came on 25 January 1880.

However, Lars did not live in Norway for long. Within four months of his birth, his family was leaving for North America. The Hans Larson family signed out of the church 19 April 1880. On the 22nd, they boarded the *S/S Baldur* in Oslo bound for America. They indicated that they were heading for Fergus Falls, Otter Tail County, Minnesota. O. Svenson served as their agent. Hans and Anne Maria would have debt upon arriving in their new country due to their passenger fare being only partially paid. Edward Wahl, Anne Maria's brother, traveled with them.

The travel route that they took is uncertain. From passenger records it is known that they transferred to a transatlantic ship somewhere along the way. The *S/S Weser* arrived in New York harbor (Castle Garden) 10 May 1880. It had sailed from Bergen, Germany. How they traveled from there to Minnesota is unknown.

Upon arriving at their final destination Hans immediately went to work to provide for his family and settle their debt. He rented and worked as a farmhand at the Toso farm in Trondhjem Township.

The farm owners, Hans Andersen Toso and his wife Gjerturd, were probably not strangers to Hans and Anne Maria. They too had come from Hadeland years before. Hans, born 1846 at Gulleneie in Jevnaker, and his wife, Gjertrud, born 1841 at Vaterud, immigrated to the United States in 1868. They were well established in Trondhjem Township when Hans and Anne Maria arrived there. This was probably a great comfort to the newly arrived immigrants.

The Larson family continued to grow. Berthe, the first one born in the United States, arrived in February 1882. Jennie Mathilda followed on 13 February 1884. Another son, Albert, came four years later, in May 1886. Then three more girls joined the family. They were Hilda, born December 1888, Ottilda born December 1891, and Seigfreda, born 22 November 1894.[2]

In order to make his entire family American citizens, Hans began the naturalization process sometime between 1881 and 1886. He received his final papers and citizenship in 1897. From there on out, Anne Maria, Anne Lovise, Anders, and Lars, were also American citizens.

Eventually Hans and Anne Maria moved their large family to their own home. In 1900 they were living in Erhards Grove Township, Otter Tail County. The land must have provided nicely for the large family, as they were able to buy the farm and own it mortgage free.

Years went by. The children stated to marry and grandchildren started the next generation. Then in 1910 tragedy struck the Larson family. The story, as told to me by a descendant, is that it was a hot summer day. Unfortunately in an attempt to comfort her children and herself, Anne Lovise took water from a 'bad' well and they all drank it. Within two weeks, two family members, including Anne Lovise, were dead from typhoid fever. Another child died later of pneumonia. Remarkably, two children lived through the ordeal to adulthood.

Anne Lovise married Olaf Hans Orstad, in 1901. Olaf, born July 1872 in Norway, immigrated to America, in 1893. Anne Lovise died 13 September 1910 in Erhard, as a result of the typhoid tragedy. Olaf died 1 February 1951. They are both buried at Maplewood Lutheran Church

Cemetery, Otter Tail County, Minnesota. Their children were Henry Leander (1903-1991, married Bernice Raboin), Orvill Melvin (1905-1910), Edna Louella (1907-1910), and Selma Mattilda (1909-1988, married James Hauge).

Anders (Andrew H.) married Emma Pederson around 1905. Her birth occurred about 1882 in Wisconsin. Anders died 27 May 1951. Emma died 10 March 1960. Anders and Emma are also buried at Maplewood Lutheran Church Cemetery. Their children were May O. (1906-1906), Baby boy (1907-1907), and Alma Sylvia (1909-1995, married Arthur Anderson).

There is little confirmable information about Lars. One source says that he married and moved to North Dakota.

Berthe (Borgine) married Adolph B. Nelson (born 1882) on 6 December 1908 in Hillsboro, North Dakota. Adolph died 29 June 1950. Berthe died 2 April 1971. They are both buried at Conrad Memorial Cemetery, Kalispell, Flathead County, Montana. Their children were Evelyn T. (1909-2006), Altona L. (1912-1993, married Dale Gorton), Arlind A. (1914-1967, married Grace Lenon), Janet M. (1916-2013, married Clayton Donovan), Anna P. (1918-1999, married Melvin Wik), and Beatrice M. (1922-2008, married Eugene Havens). Their youngest daughter is still alive. There was possibly another brother, Adolph L., who died the day of his birth, in 1925.

Jennie Mathilda married Lars/Lewis Swenson (born 1884) in about 1908. Lewis died 17 February 1964. Jennie died 13 August 1972. Jennie and Lewis are buried at Bagstevold Cemetery, Otter Tail County, Minnesota. Their children were Myrtle A. (1909-1988, married Leonard Island), Lloyd I. (1911-2001), and Clifford O. (1914-1989). Their two youngest daughters are still alive.

Albert married Alice Elmina Carlson (1889) about 1912. Albert died 19 August 1958. Alice died 23 October 1957. They are buried at West Hills Memorial Park, Yakima, Yakima County, Washington. Their children Vernon L (1916-1992)and Grace (1925-2006) have a sister who is still alive.

Hilda Johanna married Ingval Gustave Anderson (1886) in March 1910 in Barron County, Wisconsin. Hilda died 21 November 1955. Ingval died 25 November 1966. They raised a girl from Wisconsin, Helen I. (c. 1913-1992). Hilda and Ingval are buried at Bagstevold Cemetery.

Ottilda married Holley Leonard Allerson (born 1893) in Sibley County, Minnesota around 1925. Ottilda died 5 July 1945. Holley died 5 January 1967. Ottilda and Holley are buried at the Clear Lake Swedish Lutheran Cemetery, in Sibley County, Minnesota. They had four sons, Arlin William (1926-2000), Warren Merlan (1927-2005), Robert Donald (1928-1993), and Roger Edward (1932-2000). Ottilda also raised another son of Holley, Virgil.

Seigfreda married Alfred Wilhelm Anderson (1888) about 1917. Alfred died in 1965. Seigfreda died in 1979. They are buried at New Scandinavia Lutheran Cemetery in Dallas Township, Barron County, Wisconsin. Their children were Verna L. (1920-2006), Warren W.

Anderson (1921-1991), and Evelyn Bernice (1923-2010). Olaf and Anne's oldests daughter may still be living.

The original roots of this Larson family, Anne Maria and Hans, are buried at the Central Swede Grove Lutheran Church Cemetery, Otter Tail County, Minnesota. Anne Maria passed away 30 October 1917, following a stroke 17 years earlier that left her paralyzed. Hans passed away 11 years later 19 November 1928.

Andrew Wahl

Next to leave Hadeland for America was the tenth child of Anders Larsen and Berthe (Syversdatter) Wahl. Anders A. Wahl, was born 17 October 1863 at Ulverud, in Gran. He more than likely followed the footsteps of his older siblings, attending school when he could, and working out of the home at an early age.

Anders/Andrew A. immigrated to America 13 May 1881. He indicated that he was headed for Boston, Massachusetts. He left aboard the *S/S Rollo* and his fare was paid in full. Two of his sisters had immigrated there years earlier. As was common among immigrants, they may have helped with payment of Andrew's fare.

As early as 1889 Andrew worked as a cornice maker. Cornice was popular in houses in that period of time. Therefore, it more than likely was a profitable form of employment. Andrew did this type of work the rest of his life.

Andrew married Caroline J. Brauner on 8 June 1889 in Boston. She was born in August 1865 in Vestre Aker, Norway. Her parents were Julius and Andrea Brauner. Caroline immigrated either in 1882 or 1883 to America.

An interesting note to Caroline's history is that she attended four years of high school according to the 1940 US census (ancestry.com). One might consider this a significant clue about her family's status in Norway. It was highly unusual for immigrants to have attended higher education.

The young couple settled in the Roslindale area of Boston. Andrew's older brother, Lars, and his sisters Elise and Marthe, also lived there. Actually, Andrew's family lived next to Marthe's family, for over 20 years! The two homes still exist today.

Andrew and Caroline were blessed with two children. Their daughter Martha Josephine Bergine was born 13 January 1891 in Boston. Their second child was a son. Carl Arthur was born 8 October 1893.

Andrew and Caroline naturalized on 1 October 1892. It's fortunate that this process was completed when it was. Andrew died of consumption 9 March 1895. He had suffered for two years. Andrew was laid to rest in the Pine Grove section, Grave 568, Mt. Hope Cemetery, Boston, Massachusetts.

This left Caroline to raise two small children on her own. She never remarried. Caroline worked as a dressmaker according to the US census.

Then Carl passed away 1 March 1908, at the age of 14. His life was shortened by heart disease. He was buried at Mt. Hope Cemetery near his father, in Grave 570.

Josephine never married. She worked in the business sector as a stenographer, typist, and bookkeeper. At one point her employer was the City of Boston. She also cared for Caroline until her death.

Caroline died 13 October 1948. She was laid to rest next to her husband at Mt. Hope Cemetery in Grave 569.

Josephine died 25 February 1980. She was also laid to rest at Mt. Hope Cemetery. She was buried with her brother in Grave 570.

With the death of Martha in 1980, this branch of the Wahl family came to an end but hopefully their lives will not be forgotten with the writing of this history.

Syver Wahl

Syver A., even though a Hadeland native, immigrated to America from another region of Norway. Syver was the second child of Anders Larsen and Berthe Syversdatter Wahl. He was born 26 August 1846, at Lundereie within Lunner Parish in Jevnaker.

At the age of 19, Syver was living and working at the Løkken farm in Gran as a farmhand. But within a couple of years, Syver left Gran. However, his migration was not recorded in the church book until, 22 March 1869. The reason for the delay is uncertain. A notation does indicate that he left for Røken, which is in Buskerud.

Syver married Anne Marie/Marie S. Svendsdatter, 1 October 1871, in Røken Parish, Buskerud. Anne Marie was born about, April 1846, in Fogelvik, Varmland, Sweden. Syver and Anne Marie's marriage record indicates that her father was Svend Erlandsson. No name is given for her mother.

Anne Marie Svendsdtr Wahl

Their first child, a son named Anton S. was born 19 June 1871 at Huseby in Røken Parish, Buskerud. Didrik/Dedrick S. arrived 1 January 1874, also born at Huseby. Otto Bernard came along 8 July 1875, born at Bjørnestad in Røken Parish (birth record indicates 9 July). Their last son, Siem/Sam S. was born 20 September 1879 according to his obituary.

Syver, Anne Marie, Didrik, Otto, and Siem left Norway from Oslo, 14 May 1881, aboard the *S/S Kong Bjørn*. They indicated that their destination was New York. They are listed under the surname of Anderson Huseby. Huseby is one of the farms on which they lived in Røken Parish in Buskerud.

The *S/S Kong Bjørn* sailed from Oslo to Hamburg, Germany. The means of travel from there to Bremen, Germany is unknown. However, Syver and his family successfully made that journey. In Bremen they boarded the *S/S Salier* on 25 May and arrived in New York harbor (Castle Garden) 6 June 1881.

It is important to note that the oldest child, Anton, is not listed with the parents and siblings on either of the passenger lists (Norway or New York.) Anton remained in Norway for some reason with his grandparents, Anders Larsen and Berthe Syversdatter Wahl. It would be a year before Anton would rejoin his family. Anton is listed as Anton Larsen on the Police Protocol when he left Oslo.

The family made their way to Minnesota. The "History of Erhards Grove, Otter Tail County, Minnesota and it's Earliest Settlers" (Pearson and Thompson), says that the Syver Wahl family first lived with a man named Axel Knutson and then later Nels Lanskov in Trondhjem Township. According to the 1905 Minnesota Census, they did this for about one to two years.

Eventually, Syver and Anne Marie settled on a piece of their own land in Erhards Grove Township. Anne Marie through hard work and determination was able to receive the homestead patent for that land on, 21 July 1900.

Two more children were born to the family in the United States. Inga Marie arrived 24 August 1883, and Emma Caroline came 31 December 1886.

In order to make his entire family, American citizens, Syver began the naturalization process in June 1884. He filed his Declaration of Intention in Otter Tail County. Unfortunately, Syver passed away before becoming an American Citizen.

Anne Marie completed the naturalization process by filing her final papers on, 26 May 1899. Anton was able to sign as a witness for his mother as he had received his citizenship 3 April 1899. Didrik received his citizenship 30 October 1896, in Barnes County, North Dakota. Otto's citizenship occurred sometime in 1898. Siem followed suit 14 June 1905.

Syver died 20 June 1894 following being sick for only three days with lung fever. It is believed that he was laid to rest in the Bagstevold Lutheran Cemetery, Erhards Grove Township, Otter Tail County. Anne Marie/Marie S. died about 25 August 1919. She was laid to rest in the Bagstevold Lutheran Cemetery.

Anton married Helena Gilbertson Wick (born 1877) 7 December 1895. Anton passed away 24 March 1927. He was laid to rest in the Bagstevold Lutheran Cemetery, Erhard Township, Otter Tail County, Minnesota. Helena died 18 February 1965. She was laid to rest next to her husband. Their children were Sophie Christine (1897-1987, married Olaf Gilbertson), Melvin Bernhard (1899-1986, married Esther Odland), Betsy Amelia (1901-1984, married Edwin Knobel),

Anton & Helene Wahl

129

Oscar Norman (1902-1987, married Lillian Nelson), Alma/Alina Katherine (104-1984, married Ernest Rasmussen), Carl Edward (1906-2001, married Lillian Rippie), Hilda Andrine (1908-1985, married Helmer Sundblad), Arthur Henry (1911-2003, married Ruth Putnam), Olga Mathilda (1913-1987, married Alfred Klovstad), Alice Emelia (1914-2005, married Wilbur Klovstad), Ella Josephine (1916-1998, married Palmer Nelson), Ethel Florence (1918-1994, married Fred Hughes), Harvey Arnold (1920-2007), and Kenneth Marvin (1923-1995, married Ruby Strandlien).

Didrik married Mathilda Nelson (born 1878) in 1898. Didrik died 23 August 1937. Mathilda died 2 April 1975. They are more than likely buried in Bowman County, North Dakota. Their children were Simon Henry (1899-1973; wife, Vera), Melvin (1900-1938, married Alvine Rivinius), Dina Marie (born 1901), Carl Siem (1903-1988; wife, Hilda), Emma K. (born 1904, married Solomon Wahl), Helen Marie (1906-1998), Nora Amelia (born 1909), Norris Oliver (1910-2003), William Dedrick (1913-1988, married Ruby

About 1910 in North Dakota: Didrik and children: Karl, Melvin, Simon, Dina, Emma, Helen, and Nora

Schradleck), Henry Melvin (1914-1998, married Lily Svendsgaard), Myrtle Mathilda (1915-1998), Clarence Irvin (1917-1977), Geneva Lillian (1919-2014), Walter Eddie Norman (1921-2006; wife, Blanche), and Roy Alvin (1923-2008, married Bonnie Alexander).

Otto married Sigrid Mathilda Peterson (born 1881) 22 August 1897. Otto died 28 December 1955. Sigrid died 25 June 1977. They were laid to rest in the Bagstevold Lutheran Cemetery, Otter Tail County. They had one daughter who died as an infant.

Siem/Sam married Anne Marie Anderson (born 1885) 18 November 1905. Siem died 2 April 1958. Anne Marie died 4 October 1965. Both were laid to rest in the Bagstevold Lutheran Cemetery.

Otto Wahl

Their children were Donald Vernon (1909-1974, married Lillian Skalstad), Lila Irene (1914-1914), Eunice Olga (1915-1923), Marlo Kenneth (1918-1999, married Helen Wentzel), and Doris Ruby (1926-2010, married Robert Shol).

Inga Marie married Gilbert O. Gilbertson (born 1883) 22 December 1905. Inga died 28

October 1951. Gilbert died 3 May 1955. They were buried in the Bagstevold Lutheran Cemetery. Their children were Olof Sigurd (1906-1978, married Kathleen Sha), Joseph Magnus (1907-1953, married Nora Soldner), and Christian Theodore (1910-1979, married Selma Gilbertson), Ida Galene (1912-1963, married Loren Gilbertson), Helen Caroline (1915-1982, married Iver Fossen), Hilda Marie (1915-1968, married Clifford Oak), Clara Josephine (1917-1975, married Orris Christianson), and Gladys Irene (1919-1988, married Obert Wold).

Emma Caroline married Ole Stephenson (born 1885) between 1910 and 1920. Emma died 18 September 1945. Ole died 12 April 1965. They were laid to rest in the Bagstevold Lutheran Cemetery. It appears that Emma and Ole may not have had any children.

Berthe Wahl Molden

Dedicated to Ole Gamme, Iver Molden, and Kjell H. Myhre. Their assistance made this history possible. Iver gave his permission to include living family members.

With life being so difficult in Norway during the 1800's, why would someone emigrate and then return to Norway? Immigrants probably had many reasons for returning to their Homeland. This story tells of one such immigrant. It might just be a 'true love' saga as well.

Berthe Wahl and Hans Molden
Photo from Iver Molden

Berthe Andersdatter Hval/Wahl was born 1 Oct 1852, at Hvalseie in Gran. She was the fifth child of Anders Larssen and Berthe Syversdatter. It's almost impossible to know the exact tenant farm where Berthe was born. However her parents Anders Larssen and Berthe Syversdatter who residing at Ulverud (which belonged to Hval) in 1865.

Like other Norwegians, Berthe probably thought about going to America. She signed out from the church on 15 April 1880. Within the next week, her younger brother Edward and her older sister Anne Marie along with her family, did the same thing. Possibly they planned on travelling together. But, Berthe's plans changed.

It was two more years on 21 April 1882, when Berthe finally emigrated with her parents and her youngest sister Karen. They indicated that they headed to Rothsay, Minnesota. The Rothsay/Fergus Falls area of Minnesota had a high concentration of Norwegians. It's also where Berthe's siblings Edward and Anne Marie had immigrated a few years earlier.

Her time in America was apparently short. Hans Paulsen Molden traveled to Rothsay to get Berthe on 1 June 1882. One might wonder if true love drove Hans to America to get Berthe.

They married 26 June 1882 in Fergus Falls, Minnesota with the Rev. O. N. Fosmark officiating. Sometime after that they returned to Norway to begin their life together.

Hans Paulsen Molden was born 19 April 1838 at Gjerdingen (another tenant farm of Hval). He was the son of Paul Halvorsen and Eli Hansdatter. His parents married 23 March 1822 at Lunner in Hadeland. Somehow Hans managed to save enough money to buy one of the six Molden farms in about 1860 [later known as farm nr. 252/3 in Gran]. Indications exist that Hans, or rather his parents, soon forgot their former life as tenant farmers. Sources in Hadeland say that Han's parents didn't feel that Berthe was a worthy wife for Hans, being she was a 'humble tenant farmer's daughter'!

Berthe and Hans had two daughters. Elise was born 1 April 1883 and died 7 June 1883 at Molden. Their second daughter, also named Elise, was born 21 December 1887 at Molden.

Berthe passed away at the age of 73 on 16 August 1925, as the result of a stroke. Hans died 27 February 1929. They are buried at the Sister Churches in Gran.

Berthe and Hans' daughter Elise married Iver Hansen Molden on 19 April 1910 in Gran. Iver was born at a neighboring Molden farm on 31 July 1877. He was the oldest son of Hans Iversen Molden and Kirsti Bredesdatter. The couple lived at the Molden farm where Iver was born. This is farm number 253/1 in Gran today. The land formerly belonging to Elise's family was added to this farm in 1915.

Berthe and Hans lived in their farm home the rest of their lives. Following their deaths, other families inhabited the home. The building was eventually destroyed in the late 1970s.

Elise and Iver had no children of their own. They did, however, adopt a neighboring three year-old boy in 1923. Peder Bredgaten was born 17 February 1920. He was the son of Elise Pedersdatter Bredgaten and Peder Johannsen Lynnebakken. After the adoption Peder was given Molden as his new surname. Elise Molden passed away 16 May 1940. Iver passed away 26 July 1969. They're buried at the Aal Cemetery in Gran.

Peder Molden married Helga Hvattum of Gran in 1942. Helga was born 17 May 1919. She was the daughter of Gudbrand Paulsen Hvattum and Randi Iversdatter. Peder inherited the Molden farm from his stepfather in 1947. Peder and Helga had three children: Iver born in 1942, Gudbrand born in 1945 and Erik born in 1948. Peder Molden passed away on 22 December 1996. He was laid to rest in the same grave as his parents. Helga passed away 9 March 2014.

Iver married Kari Helene Gagnum, of Gran in 1969. She's the daughter of Thorstein Gagnum and Magnhild Bråstad of Lunner. Iver and Kari Helene's also had three children: Hans Peder born in 1970, Else Marie born in 1972 and Thorstein born in 1984. Iver has run the Molden farm 253/1 since 1974.

Karen Wahl Bakken

Karen was the youngest member of this Wahl family to emigrate. However, she Karen was the youngest member of this Wahl family to emigrate. However, she wasn't the last. Karen, the eleventh child of Anders Larsen and Berthe Syversdatter Wahl, joined an already large family on 5 February 1867, at Hvaleie in Gran. It's unknown, though, whether Karen got to see her older siblings often. By the time she was 10, many of them had moved to other places in Norway or emigrated to America.

This may have triggered a desire in her to immigrate, too. Somehow, Karen (considered a minor in Norway) purchased a passenger ticket. She registered with the Norwegian police indicating that she was going to travel with her older brother Anders. They were to leave on the *S/S Rollo* 13 May 1881, from Oslo. For some reason, Karen did not leave with him.

It's known that Karen immediately returned to Gran. She was confirmed 9 days later (22 May 1881), at the Sister Church there.

It would be another year before Karen actually immigrated. This time she signed out of the church with her parents on 14 April 1882. Within a week, Karen, her parents, and older sister, Birthe, were aboard the *S/S Rollo*. They indicated that they were headed for Rothsay, Minnesota. The *S/S Rollo* set sail 22 April headed for Hull, England. Records of her transatlantic trip have not been located at this time.

In April 1887 Karen married Simon E. Bakken. Simon was born in Ringebu, Oppland, Norway on 6 November 1850. It is believed that he emigrated to America, 3 October 1879, aboard the *S/S Hero* from Oslo, Norway. His parents were Engebret Hansen and Sophie Syversdatter. It's possible that Simon used the name of Engebretsen until he naturalized sometime around 1890. The couple eventually settled in Maplewood Township, Otter Tail County, Minnesota. The farm they established there supported the family for at least 50 years.

Karen and Simon had nine children, according to both of their obituaries. Their first child, Sina B. was born January 1888. Their first son, Anton Edwin, was born 21 October 1889. Louis S. followed 28 December 1891, and John E., 30 March 1894. Anna B. then joined the family 23 October 1896, followed by Henry Samuel 31 January 1901, Ida Matilda 19 July 1903, and Ruth Josephine 26 November 1905. There may have been a newborn death, a stillborn birth, or a miscarriage at some point in time. The 1900 Census indicates the child died prior to the census.

Sina B. appears on the 1895 and 1905 Minnesota Censuses with her parents. She also appears on the 1900 US Census with them. From that point on, there is no confirmable information about Sina. However in her brother Henry's obituary there is mention of a Sina Wangen, who preceded him in death. From this, one can assume that she did marry. One can also assume from Simon's obituary that she died before 1923.

Anton Edwin married Katie Pfaff in October 1923. Anton passed away 27 October 1929, following complications from appendix surgery. Anton was buried at the Evanston City

Cemetery, Evanston, Uinta County, Wyoming. Anton and Katie had no children.

Louis S. married Charlotte Cornelia Anderson (born 1898) in 1927. Louis passed away 30 November 1961. Charlotte passed away 10 November 1988. They were buried in Maplewood Cemetery, Otter Tail County. They had one son Loren Ladean (1933-2010) and one daughter, Charlotte LouAnn (1939-1939).

John E. married Ella A. Bollingmo (born 1905) in November 1933. John passed away 1 March 1956. Ella died 5 August 2004. They were buried at Bethlehem Lutheran Cemetery in Fergus Falls, Otter Tail County. Their children were Duane Edward (1936-2007) and two sons and a daughter who are still alive.

Anna B. married Archie B. Cole (born about 1896) sometime between 1910 and 1919. Archie passed away 31 March 1925. They children were Margaret Louise (1919-1983) and Melvin Leonard (1921-1936). It is unclear when Anna married Joseph Melvin Klovstad. Their child was Eugene Edward (1936-1993). Joseph died 5 March 1954. He was buried at West North Immanuel Church Cemetery, Otter Tail County. Anna died 31 July 1984. Anna was buried at Mound Union Cemetery, Hennepin County, Minnesota.

Henry Samuel married Alice E. Springer (born 1920) in October 1941. Henry passed away 3 February 1983. Alice died 21 December 2005. They were laid to rest in the Saint Leonard's Catholic Cemetery, Pelican Rapids, Otter Tail County. They had one daughter Patricia Ann (1942-2004) and one son, Charles Francis (1944-2012). Both children died as a result of injuries sustained in vehicular accidents.

Ida Mathilda married Elmer Henry Klovstad (born 1900) in April 1935. Elmer died 24 October 1977. Ida passed away 17 October 1986. Elmer and Ida were buried at the West North Immanuel Church Cemetery, Norwegian Grove Township, Otter Tail County. They had one daughter, Helen Ione (1939-2008) who married Clifford Dow.

Ruth Josephine married Carroll Lewis Klovstad (born 1903) in November 1928. Ruth Josephine died 4 April 1977. Carroll died 21 December 1990. They are buried at Maplewood Lutheran Cemetery, Otter Tail County. Their children were Kenneth Norman (1929-2012), and four sons who are still alive.

Simon passed away 21 February 1923. From then on, their son Henry, who remained single until 1941, operated the family farm. Karen lived with him until her death 2 July 1940. Simon and Karen were laid to rest in the Old South Lida Cemetery (Scandinavian Christian/Free Mission) Cemetery, Otter Tail County.

An added footnote: The two Klovstad men documented in the Syver Andersen Wahl history and the three Klovstad men written about in this history are all brothers! They are the children of Peder Pedersen Klovstad and Nellie Jensdatter Haugstvedt. Peder Pedersen Klovstad was also born in Hadeland. Obviously, the families enjoyed each other's company!

Anders Larsen and Berthe Syversdatter Wahl

Anders Larsen Wahl, the patriarch of this Wahl family, was born 20 March 1821 at Lundereiee in Lunner. His parents were Lars Anderssen and Else Syversdatter. At some point Anders left Lunner/Jevnaker and moved to Gran. There he married Berthe Syversdatter on 2 January 1845. Berthe was born 15 April 1824, at Hval in the Gran. She was the daughter of Syver Christenssen and Anne Marie Eriksdatter.

Anders and Berthe had eleven children. All but one of those children are told about in their own histories. One of their middle children, Elina, died as an infant. She was born 14 May 1860, at Braaten under Østre Alemnningen, and died 6 May 1861 at Ulverud.

By 1882 all but three of their children had immigrated to America. Their oldest, Lars, was established and with family, living in Oslo. Berthe and Karen were still near them in the Gran area. They also had their grandson, Anton Syverssen Wahl/Anton S., living with them following his parents emigrating a year earlier.

So, the time came for Anders and Berthe to make the journey. They signed out of the church on 14 April 1882. Anton is not listed with them in the church records for some unknown reason.

Anders and Berthe Wahl

By 21 April, Anders, Berthe, Berthe (their daughter), Karen, and Anton were aboard the *S/S Rollo*. From NorwayHeritage.com, we learn that the ship left Oslo headed for Hull, England. They indicated that they were headed to Rothsay, Otter Tail County, Minnesota. First order of business once in the New World, would be to reunite Anton with his parents and siblings in Otter Tail County. Information on their journey from Hull to the United States has not been located at this time.

Anders and Berthe settled in Erhards Grove Township according to the 1885 Minnesota Census. This put them in close proximity to several of their children or their *w*descendants. Syver, Anne Maria, and Karen already lived in Otter Tail

County. Ingeborg and Edward would be in the area within the next five years. The means of support for Anders and Berthe is unknown. But one might think that the children were instrumental in making sure they were taken care of.

At some point after 1885, Anders Larsen and Berthe Syversdatter Wahl moved from Erhard to Boston, Massachusetts. This would again put them close to their rest of their children or grandchildren. Elise, Martha, Andrew and eventually Lars all lived in the Boston area.

It seems amazing that this large family was able to "stay together" with it taking over 15 years for them to all emigrate. The 1,200 miles between Minnesota and Massachusetts didn't seem to stop these parents from seeing their children again.

It is believed that Anders and Berthe lived with their daughter Martha and her family the rest of their lives. Anders died 10 April 1897, after being struck by a train while attempting to cross the railroad tracks near Clarendon Hills station. Berthe passed away 18 August 1908 following a stroke three days before. Anders and Berthe were laid to rest in the Forest Hills Cemetery in Boston, Massachusetts.

Lars Wahl

For this Wahl family, emigration from Hadeland ended with Anders and Berthe's oldest child, Lars Anderssen Ulverud Hval/Wahl. He was born 29 Oct 1844 at Hvaleie in Gran.

As a young adult (1865) he lived and worked at the Hvattumshagen farm in Gran to support himself. But within a year he signed out of the church and indicated that he was moving to Oslo. There is little other confirmable information about his younger years.

Lars married Charlotte Olivia Nielsdatter. She was born 16 Sep 1848 in Oslo. Charlotte was a foster/adopted daughter of Lars Nielssen Hogstad and Maren Karine Sundby from Løhreneie in Østre Aker. Her biological parents were Carl Oscar Bredberg (Swedish) and Anne Severine Nordstrøm. It's unknown as to why the Nielssens raised Charlotte.

Descendants say that Maren either worked as a "lady-in-waiting" or as a maid in the Royal Palace. It is known that Lars served as a Sergeant in the King's Guard, so this is probably how Lars and Charlotte met. They were married 6 Apr 1873 at Grønland Parish, Akershus.

Lars and Charlotte had three daughters. Maren Bertha Lovise was born 2 Sep 1873. Anna Borghild Karine was born 9 Jun 1875. Sigrid Charlotte Lagerta was born 25 Mar 1877.

Charlotte and the girls arrived in the port of New York 30 Nov 1885, aboard the *S/S Geiser*. It is unknown the exact year that Lars came to America. However, since their fare was paid in full, one might assume that Lars had already arrived and sent money for them to join him. (The 1910 US Census indicates he came in 1884.)

The family settled in the Roslindale (Boston, Massachusetts) area. Lars worked as a painter during his first years in America. Later in life, he worked as a watchman at a factory. Descendants tell that young family members loved pulling Lars' red-haired beard like 'milking a cow'!

Charlotte died 14 Aug 1892 of tuberculosis. She is buried at Mount Hope Cemetery, Maple Grove section, plot 3610, in Boston, MA. There is no known headstone.

In little over a year Lars married Christina Enarson. They were united 28 Oct 1893 in Boston. Christina was born 1 Aug 1846 in Älvsborg, Sweden. Her parents were Johannes Enarsson and Cajsa Jonsdotter. Christina immigrated to the United States in 1882.

On 17 Oct 1894 Lars became an American citizen by naturalization. In 1898 Gustav Newberg, Christina's son, joined Lars and her in Boston. He was born March 1872 in Sweden. He worked as a cornice maker while living with Lars and Christina. Little more is known about Gustav.

Lars died of nephritis 26 Apr 1916 at the age of 71. He is buried in the same plot as Charlotte at Mount Hope Cemetery. Christina died 31 Aug 1920. She is buried in Forest Hills Cemetery, Field of Heth section, Plot 1652, Boston, MA.

Maren Berthe Lovise married Sydney Herbert Parsons 24 Mar 1905 in El Paso, Texas. Sydney was born 1 January 1873 in London, England, to Albert Edward and Margaret Jane (Cowan) Parsons. He immigrated in 1874. Maren and Sydney had one child: Sydney Herbert Parsons, Jr. (1906-1985). He married Zena "Marie" Rinaldi. Sydney, Sr. died, 20 Mar 1949 in San Diego, and was laid to rest in the Valley Center Cemetery, Valley Center, California. Maren died 15 Feb 1960 in San Diego, and was laid to rest next to her husband. Sydney, Jr. and his wife are buried next to Sydney and Maren.

Anna Borghild Karine married Arne (Arnold) Martinussen Kenseth 24 June 1894 in Boston, Massachusetts. Arnold was born 21 Apr 1866, in Ringsaker, Norway, to Martinus Haavelssen Kjendset and Eline Arnesdatter Mœhlum. He immigrated 1884. They had eight children: Erling Leif (1895-1961, married Eleanore L.); Sigrid Charlotte (1897-1975, married Christopher Shaw); Mildred E. (1899-1997, married Theodore Collins); Dagmar Ingrid (1901-1999, married Irving Hendry); Anna Magda (1904-1978, married Philip Gahm); Arne Wahl (1905-1910); Harold Edward (1910-1973, married Ruth P. Beers); and Arnold Martinus (1915-2003, married Betty J. Amey). Arnold died 20 November 1923 and was laid to rest in the Milton Cemetery, Milton, Massachusetts. Anna died 19 May 1965 and was laid next to her husband.

Sigrid Charlotte Lagerta married Hans Petter Kristian Hansen (known as Peter) 11 Aug 1900, in Boston Hans was born 5 Aug 1871 in Eidsvoll, Norway, to Petter Eugenius Hansen and Oline Mathea Olsdatter. He immigrated in 1888. They had two children: Trygve Sverre (1901-1959) and Astrid Ingeborg (1902-1996, married Herman Heinz). Sigrid died 23 September 1965. Hans is believed to have died, 6 February 1950 (not confirmed).

Descendants of Lars and Charlotte Wahl still live in the Boston area and throughout the United States. An interesting footnote to this Wahl history is that even though Lars was the first to leave Hadeland, he may have been the last to immigrate to America from Norway.

Gulbrand Andersen Köln

Published August 2002   *Form 435*   *Alton Quanbeck*

Family of Gulbrand's grandson Andrew Ostlie taken about 1938.
Seated: Adolph, Andrew P. Ostlie, Dorothea Halvorson, Wendell
Standing: Emma, Olga, Hilda (mother of the author), Anna, Stella, Evelyn, Doris and Esther

Gulbrand Anderson Köln, my great-great-grandfather, was born in Gran, Hadeland, 17 March 1796. At age 64 he emigrated with his family to America where he lived until 1901, being just seven days short of 105 years old when he died on 10 March 1901. His longevity was remarkable since the life expectancy of a male during his time was about one-half of the age that he attained.

The parish record of Gran, Oppland, shows the marriage of Anders Ingebrethson Horgen to Berthe Olsdatter Helgager on 11 December 1788. Their third son, Gulbrand, was christened on Palm Sunday, 1796, in Gran. Three generations of the family are shown in the 1801 Norway census living on the farm Kolden, Brandbu subparish, Gran parish. That record identifies Gulbrand Anderson living with his parents, twin brothers Ingebret and Peder (age 10) and sister Marthe (age 3). That census also shows Gulbrand's grandfather, Ingebret Jenson (age 80) and grandmother, Pernille Erichsdatter (age 60). To find three generations of one's ancestors in one record was a windfall.

In his twenties, Gulbrand Anderson moved eastward from Gran to the farm Rundhagen in Hurdal, Akershus, where he was a *sagmester* and *husmann*. The *Hurdal Bygdebok* indicates that he was from the farm Kollen in Gran. In Hurdal he met Marthe Pedersdatter from the farm

Gjodingsetra. She gave birth on 12 January 1826 to a son Anders where Gulbrand Anderson is listed as the father even though they were not married. Two years later they did get married three weeks before the birth of my great-grandfather, Peder Gulbrandson, on 10 December 1828. Other children followed: Marie, Katrine who died in infancy, Martin and Karine.

The parish record for Nannestad in Akershus shows the family of Gulbrand Anderson and Marthe Pedersdatter moving into the parish on 7 December 1854. Their departure for America in 1860 is then recorded for Gulbrand (age 64), Marthe (age 47), their daughter Karine (age 21), her husband Lars Hanson (age 23) and child Gulbrand Larson (age 1). During some period of their six-year stay in Nannestad, Gulbrand lived on the farm Østli, a name which most of his descendants chose as their surname in America.

I have not been able to find the migration route for the family from Norway to America since passenger records for that time are incomplete. In any event, the 1870 United States census records Gilbert Anderson (age 75, retired farmer), Marthia Anderson (age 70, keeping house) and son Andrew Gilbertson (age 44) in Grand Meadow township, Clayton County, Iowa. The census enumerator took the liberty of anglicizing their names. After the 1870 census, Marthe Petersdatter disappears from the records and it is likely she died in Iowa sometime between 1870 and 1878. Unfortunately the death records for that locality in Iowa in that time period do not exist.

The Northwood, N.D., *Diamond Jubilee, 1884-1959*, tells that Gulbrand Anderson, a native of Hadeland, settled in Section 28 of Northwood Township at the age of 82 years. Together with his son Peder, they had with them a herd of Norman horses. The same publication provides more detail about his life and family:

Gamle Gulbrand, A man who lived in three centuries

Gulbrand Gulbrandson was the oldest pioneer to homestead in Northwood Township. He left Hadeland, Norway, with his family in 1857 and came to Dakota Territory and filed on land in 1878. Having been born in 1796, he was 82 years when he homesteaded. When he was 100 years old, he pumped water for 35 head of cattle and remained in fairly good health until he died in 1901. He is the only pioneer whose life spanned three centuries.

Gamle Gulbrand's son, Peder G. Ostlie, purchased the first Woods Binder in the township in 1884. His grandson, Lauritz Ostlie, bought one of the first steam threshing outfits in the township. This granddaughter, Mrs. Hans Buraass, lived in the first frame house built on the prairie east of the Goose River, and great-great-grandson, Vincent Buraas, purchased the first airplane in the township in 1944. Vincent also started the first airport and flying school here, and is the first to operate an airplane spraying service.

After the death of his son Peder on 15 January 1889, Gulbrand returned to Iowa to live with his eldest son Anders, his daughter Karine and her husband Lars Hanson. The 1900 U.S. census finds the family together in Grand Meadow Township, Clayton County, Iowa, where the occupations of Lars Hanson and Andrew Gilbertson are shown as 'capitalist' and 'landlord,' respectively. Less than a year after the 1900 census was enumerated, Gulbrand Anderson died near Clermont, Iowa, on 10 March 1901."

E.M. Lundt, Elgin, Iowa, wrote an obituary in April 1901 which follows in its entirety, including misspellings and inaccuracies:

105 Years Old Gudbrand Anderson Kolan
Fulfills His Long Life at Clermont Iowa

Gudbrand Anderson Kolan is dead in Clermont, Iowa. He was born in Grans Prastegjeld Hadeland Norway March 17 1796. He was confirmed in Akers Church by Pastor Heierdal in October of 1812 and served after his confirmation in Maridalen for a salary of 6 to 10 dollars per year. When he was 30 years old he was married and moved to Hurdalen, where he was caretaker of a house and acreage until 1860. While there he saved himself enough money so he bought himself an acreage in Nannestad. With this marriage he had 5 children who came to America with him in 1875. They settled near Clermont, Clayton County, Iowa. The land here was already taken up and high priced. He then moved to the Red River Valley, Minn with his oldest son and took up free land there. His son died after a few years there and the old man was now 95 years old. He then moved back to the Clermont settlement with his daughter Karen where he lived until he died on March 10, 1901. He was lacking 7 days of being 105 years old.

The underwriter visited him last fall. He told me many things about old times. He told me that at one time back in Norway he was assigned a Swedish Officer who had been taken prisoner by the Norwegians and to take him to a place in Hadeland. When they reached their destination the officer sat dead in the saddle.

In the morning he sang hymns with a strong voice. Hymns from both Guldberg and Kingo's Hymnals. He had an exceptional good voice and had always been close to God and had always lived a quiet, busy and moral life.

His aged daughter and son-in-law, Lars Hanson, did everything possible to make his last days happy and pleasant. Yes, Gudbrand waited for the Lord and now sleeps in the East Clermont cemetery until the morning of his resurrection. Peace be with his remains and pleasant be his memory.

The reader will note that the farm name in Gran that Gulbrand Anderson chose to use appears as Killen, Kolden, Kolan and Köln. The inscription on his tombstone is Köln. It is also noteworthy that some of the information presented in the local history and his obituary is inconsistent with the historical church and census records.

During the summer of 2001, my wife Susan and I found his gravesite in the front row of the cemetery of the classic East Clermont Lutheran Church. In addition to the birth and death dates, there is the following inscription on his tombstone:

Fred med hans støv,
(Peace be with his dust)
Nu har jeg seier fan-get,
(Now I have captured victory
Lov
(Praise)
Ske den gode Gud's Son,
(to the good God's son)
Som høver en Synder saa bange.
(who hears a Sinner so frightened.)
Gud giv os den evige Løn.
(God give us the eternal reward.)

It is likely that Gulbrand Anderson Köln has several thousand descendants living in the United States today. My great-grandfather, Peder Gulbrandson, adopted the surname Ostlie after the farm Østli in Nannestad. He had 10 children who were in turn very prolific. A check on the Internet shows more than 3,000 hits for the name Ostlie.

My cousin, Cindy Ostlie, who lives in Columbia, Missouri, and I have shared the results of our research into our family history. She had uncovered some matters that were a deep mystery to me and I am indebted to her for much of what appears in this article.

Andrew P. Ostlie (grandson of Gulbrand Koln) and wife Dorothea Halvorsen in 1938 at their farm in Newburgh Township, Hatton ND. He was a farmer, director of the bank and owner of the Chevrolet dealership in Hatton.

Gulbrand and Marthia Anderson Family

previously unpublished   Form 435   *Cindy Ostlie*

Gulbrand Anderson, his wife Marthia, and all four of his living children (Anders, Peder, Maria, Martin, and Karine) emigrated to America, although not at the same time. There was another daughter Karine who was born December 26, 1835 and died on January 26, 1836 in Hurdal. Gulbrand, Peder, Martin, and Karine's husband Lars Hanson eventually took the last name Ostlie. Anders kept the last name Gulbrandson until his death; and Maria married Ulrick Hanson, who eventually took the last name Buraas. Peder's daughter Mathia married Hans Christianson who also took the last name Buraas.

Gulbrand Anderson was born 17 Mar 1796 in Gran and his wife Marthia Pedersdatter was born 4 Jul 1802 in Hurdal. They were married 22 Nov 1828 in Hurdal.

The first to arrive was Peder Gulbrandson, born 10 Dec 1828 in Nannestad, his wife Maria Olsdatter, born 2 Mar 1830, in Grasmo, Nannestad, and their eldest child Mathia who was born 20 Mar 1856. Oral family history says that the second daughter Gustava was born on the ship; however, her death certificate says that she was born in Iowa on 19 Apr 1857. The remaining eight children (Gulbrand, Lauritz, Olaf, Emma, Andrew, Caroline, Syver, and Jacob) were born in Iowa from 1858 through 1876. Naturalization records for Gulbrand Anderson and Peder Gulbrandson show that both came through the port of Detroit but the dates of entry are reversed for them. (Gulbrand's has a date of June 1857 and Peder's has a date of June 1860.) Both Gulbrand and Peder signed with their marks and the person filling out the forms recorded them incorrectly. The Nannestad bygdebok shows Gulbrand Anderson, age 64, fra Østli , his wife Marte Pedersdatter, age 57, Lars Hansen, age 23, fra Østli, his wife Karine Gulbrandsdatter, age 21, and their child Gulbrand, age 1, leaving Norway to go to Amerika in 1860, which agrees with an entry through the port of Detroit in June 1860. Based on the years of birth of Peder's children, he was present in Iowa in 1857. Peder, his wife Marie, their 10 children, a son-in-law and two grandchildren moved from Iowa to Northwood Township, Dakota Territory in the late 1870's and homesteaded there. Gulbrand Anderson went with him. When he signed some of the homestead papers in 1879, he stated he was single. When and where his wife died is unknown; she is not listed on the 1880 census for Dakota Territory.

The oldest child of Gulbrand Anderson was named Andres Gulbrandson and he was born 12 Jan 1826 and died 22 Nov 1913 in Grand Meadow Township, Clayton County, Iowa. He never married. On the 1860 Iowa census he is 34 years of age and living in Marion Township, Clayton County with a farmer, his wife, and their two children. In the 1900 Iowa census, his name is given as Andrew Gilbertson and he is living with Lars and Carrie Hanson and Gilbert Anderson, age 104. The 1900 census says that he came to the United States in 1859. His occupation in 1900 is listed as "landlord" and Lars' occupation is listed as "capitalist." Lars, Carrie, and

Gilbert Anderson list their year of arrival in the United States as 1860. After his death in 1913, his estate was probated and the probate records were very useful in determining who the descendants of his brothers and sister were.

It is likely that Marie Gulbrandsdatter, her husband and two children traveled with Andres Gulbrandson to America. The Hurdal bygdebok shows Ulrik Hansen Burås, age 47, his wife Marie Gulbrandsdatter age 27, and children Inge Gustava, age 3, and Hanna Birgitte, age 6 months leaving in 1859. Marie was born in September 1832 and Ulrik was born 19 Sept 1812. Marie and Ulrik were residing in Hurdal when they married on 05 May 1856. Their first child born in America was Herman who was born 27 Oct 1860. Gilbert, born 1864, Mathilda, born 1866, Ole, born 1868, and Mina, born 1871, followed. Ulrik died in 1876 and Marie died in 1885. Their daughters Inger Marie and Mathilda and husbands moved to Northwood Township, Dakota Territory. Their son Gilbert was living in Northwood Township in 1880 when he was 16, but his whereabouts after that are unknown. In 1880, Inger and her husband Peter were using the last name Erikson and Gilbert was living with them under the name Gulbran Ulrikson. Another son Herman and his wife tried Northwood Township but moved back to Iowa. Eventually Inger Marie, her husband and children moved to Polk County, Minnesota, where they used the last name Bjerke.

In 1860, Karine, her husband Lars, and child Gulbrand arrived in Clayton County, Iowa. Daughters Hilda, Kristine, Mina, Inger, and Josephine were born from 1861 through 1878. All of Karine's children except for Josephine remained in the Clermont, Iowa area. Josephine settled in Fillmore County, Minnesota with her husband.

Martin Gulbrandson was the last of Gulbrand Anderson's children to leave Norway. His naturalization papers show he came through the port of Boston in June of 1883. His wife Ellen Marie Halvorson was born in Nannestad 24 Jan 1834 and their children Herman and Johanne Marie, born 24 May 1869 and 16 Mar 1871, respectively, came with him. Herman was a carpenter and built houses in Northwood and also built the Spring Valley Lutheran Church in Plaza, ND when he lived in that area. Johanne died eight days after the birth of her son.

Homestead papers for Peder Gulbrandson and his father Gulbrand Anderson show that they were in Dakota Territory in 1879. At that time, Gulbrand Anderson was 83 years old and he was single. Where and when his wife Marthia died is unknown. She appears with him on the 1870 Iowa census for Grand Meadow Township, Clayton County. At that time they were living with Andres Gulbrandson (note that the census taker Anglicized the names Gulbrand and Gulbrandson to be Gilbert and Gilbertson.) Also living in the household was Marthia Peterson (Anglicized from Pedersdatter), age 40 who is listed as a house helper. This is actually the 14 year-old daughter of Peder Gulbrandson.

Gulbrand Anderson died 10 March 1901 at the home of his daughter Karine in Grand Meadow Township, Clayton County, Iowa. He was 7 days short of his 105th birthday. He was buried under the name Gulbrand Anderson Køln in the East Clermont Church cemetery. His original tombstone was replaced by the church as they were proud to have someone who lived in three centuries buried in their cemetery. His son Peder died 15 Jan 1889 and oral family history says that Martin's wife Marie took Gulbrand back to Iowa. The 1895 Iowa census shows him living with Karine. The following obituary for him was published in Skandinaven on 10 April 1901 and was written by E. M. Lund. (Translated by Marion Lind, son-in-law of Clara Aanes who was a granddaughter of Karine.

"Gudbrand Anderson Køln is dead in Clermont, Iowa. He was born in Grans, Hadeland 17 Mar 1796. He was confirmed in Akers Church by Pastor Heurdal in October 1812 and worked after confirmation in Maredalen for a salary of 6-10 dollars per year. When he was 30 years old, he was married and moved to Hurdalen where he was a custodian until 1860. As custodian, he had saved enough money to buy a small acreage in Nannestad. To this marriage 5 children were born who immigrated to America in 1857. They came to Clermont, Iowa, and found most of the land was already taken and was high priced so they moved to the Red River Valley, Minn., with his oldest son and took up free land. The son died a few years after this move so now the old man was nearly 95 years of age and moved back to Clermont settlement and lived with his daughter Karen where he lived to his death on March 10, 1901, lacking 7 days of being 105 years old.

The undersigned visited him last fall. He told me much about the old days. Once he was to escort a Swedish officer, who was taken prisoner by the Norwegians during the war to a camp near Hadeland. Upon arrival there, the officer sat dead in the saddle.

In the morning he sang with a strong voice several hymns for me of both Guldbergs and Kingos hymnals. He had an unusually beautiful voice. He had always kept close to God and his whole life was of a quiet nature, a busy and moral life. His grey haired daughter and his son-in-law Lars Hansen did everything humanly possible to make the old man's last days comfortable and happy.

Yes, Gudbrand waited for the Lord and now sleeps in the Clermont Church cemetery until the morning of his resurrection. Peace be with his remains. Blessed be his memory.

Elgin, Iowa, April 1901

E. M. Lund"

The East Clermont Lutheran Church in Iowa was organized in 1851 as the Norwegian Evangelical Lutheran Church of Clermont and was composed of 40-50 families. It extended from Gunder on the east, Clermont valley on the west and south to the Turkey River. The first called pastor was U.V. Koren, 1853-1862, who visited the Clermont congregation once a month.

In preparation for the church's 100th anniversary, Mrs. Hilda Aanes (daughter of Lars Hanson Ostlie and Karine Gulbrandsdatter Ostlie) was interviewed in 1949 when she was 88 years old. The following is what she related:

"Lars Hanson (Ostlie) came from Norway in the fall of 1860, with his wife, Karine, and one son Gudbrand (Gilbert) and .50 cents in his pocket, when he landed in McGregor.

That first winter they stayed with kind neighbors, Arnulf Knudson (Aanor) and here their second child Hilda was born on Sept. 20, 1861.

This kindness was not forgotten. Every Christmas as long as the Knudsons lived, they received a gift of $1.00 from Lars.

Woodcutting was the main source of work to be had and 35 cents a day was the usual pay. Lars traded his overcoat for his first cow. He paid $1.00 an acre for his home farm and while most of the houses at that time were of logs, he obtained lumber and built a two room house with upstairs.

The first twelve years or so oxen were used for all work and transportation, but Lars as most all pioneers of the time, often walked to town with his eggs in a sack, to exchange for the few groceries needed.

Mrs. Aanes recalled that once when her parents were away, some Indians came. While the younger children were frightened and hid, she gave the Indians some freshly baked "donuts," which her mother had prepared. This pleased the Indians and they soon departed peacefully, but they took with them what donuts they had not eaten.

About 1875, Lars moved his house further south to the location of the home place of Selmer Erickson. A new house was now built, the old house serving as a summer kitchen and as the entrance to a storm or sub-cellar, which is still in use. This was their refrigerator as it was an ideal place for the storage of meat and vegetables. It had a constant cool temperature around the year. It was also a place to run to if a bad storm was approaching.

Lars had been able to get a cook stove for their first house, but many of the pioneers of that time were living in "dugouts" and log houses with the open fireplace (peis) where all their cooking was done.

Like many others, Lars sent money to Norway, to help his father and brother come to America. His father had his home with them as long as he lived. Later, Mrs. Ostlie's father, Gudbrand and brother Anders, lived with them. The father, Gudbrand Anderson, was born in 1796, lived through the 1800's and into 1901 and became 105 years old. On his 100th birthday he sang many songs from memory for the assembled guests. Lars was an experienced tailor in Norway and supervised the making of many of the family's clothes. He used to tease his wife by telling that he made her wedding dress (it was true) but she countered by saying she wove the material of pure wool.

When death had entered the home of his friends and taken one of their loved ones, Lars often helped prepare them for burial."

The following is a listing of the descendants of Gulbrand Anderson:

I. Andres GULBRANDSON, born on 12 Jan 1826 in Norway; died 22 Nov 1913, Grand Meadow Township, Clayton County, Iowa.

II. Peder G. OSTLIE, born 10 Dec 1828, Nannestad, Akershus, Norway; married Maria OLSDATTER, 27 Dec 1855, Nannestad, Akershus, Norway; died 15 Jan 1889, Grand Forks County, Dakota Territory; buried in the South Cemetery, Northwood Township. Maria OLSDATTER, daughter of Ole HANSEN and Berthe LARSDATTER, born 2 Mar 1830, Grasmo, Nannestad, Akershus, Norway; died 19 Mar 1911, Grand Forks County, North Dakota. They had the following children:

    1.   Mathia OSTLIE, born 20 Mar 1856, Norway; married Hans Christianson BURAAS, 1873, Iowa; died 1 Dec 1932, Northwood, Grand Forks County, North Dakota.

    2. Gustava OSTLIE, born 19 Apr 1857; married Engebret O. BERG, 16 Feb 1879; married Phillip BARLOW, 25 Sep 1920, died 28 Aug 1934, Grand Forks, Grand Forks County, North Dakota. .

    3, Gulbrand OSTLIE, born 13 Dec 1858 in Iowa; died 14 Jan 1879 in Fargo, Cass County, Dakota Territory; buried in the South Cemetery, Northwood Township, Grand Forks County, North Dakota.

    4.   Lauritz P. OSTLIE, born 5 Mar 1859, Iowa; married Amanda Wilhelmine LINDSTROM, 14 Apr 1881; married Mathilda LINDSTROM, 22 Jan 1882; married Bergit OLSON, 21 Dec 1904; died 19 Jun 1914.

    5. Olaf P. OSTLIE, born 7 Nov 1863, Iowa; married Johanna KRILING, 20 Jul 1884; died 25 Feb 1933, Northwood, Grand Forks County, North Dakota.

    6. Emma OSTLIE, born 28 Jul 1866, Iowa; married Gilbert NELSON before 1886; died 30 Oct 1887, Grand Forks County, Dakota Territory.

    7. Andrew P. OSTLIE, born 23 Feb 1868, Iowa; married Dorothea HALVORSEN, 29 Jun 1889; died 1 Mar 1951, Grand Forks County, North Dakota.

    8. Caroline OSTLIE, born 23 Oct 1871, Iowa; married Martin HAAKENSON, 23 Mar 1891, died 28 Nov 1940, Warren, Marshall County, Minnesota.

9. Jacob Hans OSTLIE, born 20 Nov 1873, Iowa; married Caroline KNUTSON, 6 Feb 1894; died 29 Oct 1954, King County, Washington.

10. Syver OSTLIE, born 22 Jul 1876, Iowa; married Josephine Marie KNUTSON, 8 Jun 1897; died 11 Jan 1964, Grand Forks County, North Dakota.

III. Marie H. GULBRANDSDATTER, born Sep 1832, Norway; married Ulrik Hansen BURAAS, 5 May 1856, Hurdal, Akershus, Norway; died 28 May 1885. Ulrik, son of Hans ULRICKSON and Berte Marie NILSDATTER, born 19 Sep 1812; died 22 Nov 1876. They had the following children:

1. Inger Gustava BURAAS, born 3 Feb 1856, Gulbrandsdalen, Norway; married Peter Edward BJERKE, 8 May 1878, Iowa; died 8 Dec 1941, Hill River Township, Polk County, Minnesota.

2. Hannah BURAAS, born 12 Mar 1859, Norway; married Lauritz JOHNSON about 1888; died 14 May 1932, Geddes, South Dakota.

3. Herman H. BURAAS, born 27 Oct 1860, Clayton County, Iowa; married Rachel OLESON, 17 Nov 1883; died 7 Jan 1943, Clermont, Iowa.

4. Gilbert BURAAS, born in 1864.

5. Mathilda BURAAS, born 15 Feb 1866, Marion Township, Clayton County, Iowa; married Iver Martinus THINGELSTAD, 16 Mar 1883; married Joseph P. THINGELSTAD, 1897; died 5 May 1949, Northwood, Grand Forks County, North Dakota.

6. Ole BURAAS, born in 1868.

7. Mina BURAAS, born 15 Dec 1871, Clayton County, Iowa; married Martin ANDERSON, 6 Nov 1895; died 1 Jun 1953, Albert Lea, Freeborn County, Minnesota.

IV. Karine GULBRANDSDATTER, born 26 Dec 1835 in Hurdal, Akershus, Norway; died 26 Jan 1836, Hurdal, Akershus, Norway.

V. Martin G. OSTLIE, born 12 Dec 1837, Norway; married Ellen Marie HALVORSON, 7 Dec 1871; died 4 Feb 1909, Northwood, Grand Forks County, North Dakota. They had the following children:

1. Herman M. OSTLIE, born 24 May 1869, Norway; married Martha GRINA, 29 Dec 1895; died 10 Sep 1936.

2. Johanne Marie OSTLIE; born 16 Mar 1871; married Lars THOMPSON 6 Oct 1887; died 20 Dec 1887.

VI. Karine GULBRANDSDATTER, born 14 Feb 1839, Norway; married Lars Hanson OSTLIE, 18 May 1859, Nannestad, Akershus, Norway; died 17 Feb 1907, Grand Meadow Township, Clayton County, Iowa. They had the following children:

1. Gilbert L. OSTLIE, born 4 Jun 1859 in Nannestad, Norway; married Anna NELSON 1 Dec 1881; married Anna JACOBSON 7 Sep 1886; died 20 May 1945.

2. Hilda OSTLIE, born 20 Sep 1861, Grand Meadow Township, Clayton County, Iowa; married Ole AANES 17 Nov 1881; died 28 Jun 1950, Clermont, Fayette County, Iowa.

3. Kristine OSTLIE, born 3 Apr 1864, Clayton County, Iowa; married Knudt KITTLESON 23 Nov 1882; died 20 Dec 1948.

4. Mina OSTLIE, born 23 Jan 1867, Grand Meadow Township, Clayton County, Iowa; married Gustav OLSON Jan 1888; died 11 Jul 1950, Postville, Allamakee County, Iowa.

5. Inger Marie OSTLIE, born 23 Jun 1869, Clayton County, Iowa; married Even Olson LIEN 7 Oct 1893; died 14 Feb 1949.

6. Josephine Louise OSTLIE, born 4 Aug 1878, Clayton County, Iowa; married Thomas O. LIEN 28 Oct 1899; died 30 Sep 1963, Spring Valley, Fillmore County, Minnesota

Iver and Anne Kanten

published November 2002   *Form 274*   *Shirley Kanten and Anne Sladky*

This brief biography was written in 1981 by Shirley Kanten (1914-2001). Shirley was a granddaughter of Iver and Anne Kanten. She was the acknowledged authority on Kanten family history and an esteemed member of the Chippewa County Historical Society. This story was submitted by Anne Sladky, a great-granddaughter of Iver and Anne.

Iver and Anne Kanten about 1900

Iver Halvorsen Kanten was born in Gran, Hadeland, Norway on 15 February 1825. He was educated (learned the tailor's trade), grew to adulthood and married in Norway. He married Anne Gulbrandsdatter Hilden. She was born 18 December 1826 in the same area. They came to the United States in June 1864 and made their home with Anne's brother John Thinglestad, in Winona County, Minnesota, for two years and then moved to Fillmore County, Minnesota where they lived until 1869 when they moved to Tunsberg Township, Chippewa County, Minnesota.

The first settlement in Chippewa County was in 1865. The Kantens homesteaded 80 acres of land in Tunsberg Township, section 20, one mile west of Watson, Minnesota. It was on this land that they constructed a dugout in which the family lived for some time before a substantial farm home was built. These dugouts were mainly dirt cellars with a pole, brush, hay or sod roof, a small window or two and a door fashioned of split logs. The dugout was followed by a log house built in about 1870. This log cabin, with additions and improvements, was used by various owners until 1964 when a new house was built by the present owners, the Earl Ostlies. The Yellow Medicine County Historical Society acquired the log cabin, which was made of heavy oak logs. The log cabin is now furnished as a pioneer church and is on the historical society's exhibit area near Granite Falls, Minnesota.

Iver and Anne worked hard and in time had a good farm developed from the wild prairie sod. They prospered and became the owners of 352 acres and here they spent the rest of their lives. They assisted in the founding of Zion Church northwest of Watson. Iver H. and his oldest son Hans were on the building committee in 1875-1876 when the congregation was being organized and the church built. Iver H. was one of the early treasurers of the new congregation. He also was in charge of the loading of the lumber that was hauled from Benson. The Zion Ladies Society constitution was adopted at a meeting at their home in 1885.

Iver's first vote was cast for General U. S. Grant for President. The Kantens were active in all local, social, and religious activities of the community.

Iver took interest in all civic matters and did much in the way of development and growth of the township and county in which they lived. School District #14, Watson and the surrounding countryside was organized in January 1871. Before any schoolhouse was built, school was held in various places including the log cabin owned by Iver.

Iver Kanten died in 1910 at the age of 85. Anne Hilden Kanten died in 1908 at the age of 82. Kanten was the gårdnaven (farm name) in Norway. All the sons of the Iver H. Kanten family used the surname Iverson except Christian who lived in Big Bend Township, Milan, Minnesota (although he also used Iverson for several years as some of his children's birth records are recorded Iverson) and Andrew who moved to Canada.

Additional Information *from Anne Sladky*

Iver and Anne and their six sons boarded the ship *Norden* in Drammen. A report about the accident the killed their infant son Iver appeared in the *Ringeriges Ugebled"* on July 8, 1864. It reads:

"The emigrant ship "Norden" which in a few days will leave for America reported on June 30 a terrible accident involving a little child who fell through an open hatch (trapdoor) to the room (deck) below and injured himself so severely that, according to the medical officer's report, the child died a few hours after the accident."

Iver and Anne are buried in Zion Lutheran Church Cemetery, rural Watson. Their children were:

- Hans Iverson (1845-1927)
- Gulbrand Iverson (1850-1927)
- Kristian Kanten (1853-1932)
- Helger Iverson (1855-1928)
- Mikkel Iverson (1858-1932)
- Anders Kanten (1860-1944)
- Iver Iversen (1863-1864)
- Karen Martia/Mrs. Peter J. Canton (1865-1958)
- Ingeborg/Mrs. Bernt Borgerson (1867-1893)
- Peder Iverson (1870-1945)
- Anne/Mrs. Hans Alm (1872-1957)

Iver and Anne's youngest daughter Anne is Anne Sladky's grandmother.

Ole Ericksen Alm and Johanne Hansdtr

published November 2002   Form 8   *Anne Sladky and Mary Margaret Gibson*

Ole Ericksen, son of Erich Eriksen Blekan, was born August 10, 1829 on Solbjøreie in Hadeland. When his confirmation was recorded on September 29, 1845, it shows he was *lagd på Østen* (cared for at Østen). His mother Ragnhild Augedahl had died in 1832 and it would seem that his father was unable to take care of him. Children raised outside their family faced prejudice and many obstacles in the culture of the times. We can assume Ole had a very difficult childhood.

Ole married Johanne Hansdtr Dvergsten on December 4, 1853, at Grinaker Church in Tingelstad. A daughter of Hans Pederson and Marthe Johansdatter, she was born June 20, 1832 on the Brenna *husmannplass* on Dvergsten.

Perhaps owing to the difficulties of his childhood, Ole grew to be an embittered man without much ambition. He worked as a laborer (tree cutter and lumberjack) on a series of farms and his family received poor relief at various times. According to his son Hans, Ole had a drinking and gambling problem.

Hans paid for his parents and sister's immigration in 1888. He often said he would not have done this for this father, but he held his mother and sisters in high esteem and wanted them to find what ease and opportunity they could in the New Land. According to Hans his mother was a hard-working, gentle and generous woman who was supportive of her children and held the family together throughout their tumultuous childhoods. When she died in 1896, he felt her loss deeply.

Ole lived with Hans and Anne for a time after his wife's death. He had so alienated his children that no other sibling was willing to take him in and, although they tried, Hans and Anne quickly tired of his self-centered, unhappy ways. Ole was living on the poor farm in Tunsberg Township by 1900. He died of a stroke there on May 4, 1915. Ole and Johanne were buried at Sunset Memorial Cemetery in Montevideo, Minnesota. The exact locations of their graves is no longer known.

Excerpt from "From the Old Country to the Prairie" published in February 2007
Written in 1981 by Mary Margaret Rekstad Gibson, granddaughter of Erick Rekstad and Martia Alm.

In the Tingelstad congregation, a part of the then Brandbu parish, in the district of Hadeland

152

there lived a *husmann* named Ole Ericksen. During his lifetime in Norway he lived on various farms – Solbjørgeie, Dvergsteneie and Almseie. He also lived in the *husmann's* cottage Badstua. He was born on Solberg (Solbjørgeie) on August 10, 1829. His father was Erick Eriksen. On December 4, 1853, while living on the Dvergsten farm, he married Johanne Hansdatter in the Grinaker Stave Church in Tingelstad. Johanne was born on June 20, 1832 on Dvergstenshagen. Her father's name was Hans Pedersen Dvergsteneie who, as the name indicates, was a *husmann* on the Dvergsten farm. (*Brua Editor's Note:* A *husmann* worked as a laborer on the main farm but was not a member of the family that owned the farm. In exchange for his day labor, a *husmann* was allowed to live in a small cottge which was owned by the farm. This cottage usually had a small amount of land, a couple of acres, on which the *husmann* could grow a garden and could probably raise a cow, some sheep and a few chickens.)

Ole Ericksen was a small man, but he had a tough reputation. His parents both died when he was very young (*other records indicate he was abandoned by his still-living father)* so he was only acquainted with one of his siblings, a sister. She later emigrated to America and became the mother of Lars Stensrud and Mrs. Gilbert Hilden of Watson, Minnesota. Later Ole found one of his brothers. It is told in the family that Ole introduced himself by yanking his brother out of his girlfriend's bed and throwing him out of the house! They became acquainted when they tried to beat each other up! The brother later emigrated to Wisconsin.

Ole earned a living by felling trees and serving as a guide in the woods. He also snared live birds which he sold to Germany. These birds were native to Norway and German officials were trying to establish them in the forests of their country. It is thought that the birds were large game birds, probably similar to the American wild turkey. During the winter, Ole wove baskets which he sold. His greatest love and also possibly his greatest vice was gambling at cards. His daughter Martia remembered her father coming home late one night with a gambling buddy and at the door handing over his overcoat – he had lost it in a card game.

Ten children were born to Ole and Johanne. They were:

- Randi, born November 1, 1853; married Even Andreassen Svenrud on December 27, 1872, emigrated on August 30, 1901; died November 4, 1945 in Morrison County, Minnesota.
- Marthe, born March 7, 1856; died January 12, 1863 on Dvergstenseiet, Hadeland.
- Erik, born April 3, 1859; married Lisa Mathea Martinsdtr on June 8, 1883; emigrated in 1893; died July 3 1927 in Clough Township, Randall, Minnesota.
- Anne Marie (Mary), born April 21, 1862; married Nils Kristoffersen on May 30, 1886, Gustave Johansen in 1889. Emigrated as a single woman with son Nils on March 20, 1889, and married Johan William Johanesen Moe; died on March 3, 1924 in Chippewa County, Minnesota.

- Hans, born September 9, 1864; emigrated in 1885; married Anne Iversdatter Kanten on May 31, 1890; died September 2, 1931 in Binford, North Dakota.
- Marthea (Martia), born February 13, 1868; emigrated with her parents in 1888; married Erick Anderson Rekstad on July 5, 1890; died on January 17, 1940 in Chippewa County; buried in Jevnaker Lutheran Church cemetery, Montevideo, Minnesota.
- Oline, born June 24, 1870; emigrated with her parents in 1888; married John Olson; died on November 24, 1942 in Randall, Minnesota.
- Johan, born March 13, 1873; died September 8, 1876 at Badstua, Tingelstad, Hadeland
- Ole, born February 25, 1875; died on September 5, 1876 at Badstua, Tingelstad, Hadeland
- Johanne, born May 11, 1879; emigrated with her parents in 1888; married Henry Paulsrud on May 9, 1906; died on April 24, 1939 in Bismarck, Burleigh County, North Dakota.

Three of these children died in Norway before the family emigrated. Marthe died in 1863 at the age of six and a half. Johan was three and a half and Ole was only a year and a half when they died of scarlet fever in September, 1876.

Randi Alm Svenrud Family

Mary Alm Moe Family

Hans Alm Family

Martia Alm Rekstad Family

Oline Alm Olson Family

Johanne Alm Paulsrud Family

Hans Oleson Alm and Anne Iversdtr Kanten

published November 2002   *Form 7*   *Anne Sladky*

Anne and Hans in 1929

Hans O. Alm was born to Ole Erickson and his wife Johanne Hansdatter in the parish of Tingelstad in Hadeland, Norway on September 9, 1864. Hans' youth was one of grinding poverty as he followed his parents from farm to farm. As a boy he herded cattle and as he grew older did the full range of farm work He recalled living in a bunk house with other farm workers at a very young age. Each man (and boy) had a spoon hung by the door. Meals were eaten from a large common bowl in the center of the table. All too often it was nothing more than old bread and a bowl full of souring cream. The famous "Cream and Berad" that gave rise to a series of humorous books was not remembered fondly by Hans! On his own initiative, he became an apprentice to a house painter and learned the trade he practiced for the rest of his life.

Hans migrated to the United States in 1885 at the age of 21. His maternal uncle John Dvergsten of Watson, Minnesota, paid his passage and provided a home for him. After repaying his uncle, Hans underwrote the cost of his parents' immigration with two of his sisters and helped them establish themselves. His father did not repay him.

It was in Watson that Hans met Anne Kanten, the youngest child of Iver Halvorsen and Anne Gulbrandsdtr Kanten. She was born on May 23, 1872 in Watson. They were married in May of 1890. It was Anne who taught Hans how to read and write English. He became a naturalized citizen in Chippewa County in 1898. Unlike so many immigrants drawn to America by the availability of good farm land, Hans vowed that once he left Norway he would never have anything to do with farming again. Although it was a decision his father-in-law would often argue against and never understood or approved, Hans never did!

In the mid-1890s Hans and Anne joined his sister Oline and her husband John Olson in Ashland, Wisconsin. This seems to be where their father Ole's brother was living, and may be why they made the move. It is likely that two of Hans and Anne's young children died while they were living there, and that may be one of the reasons they returned to Watson. A true daughter of the prairie, Anne would shake her head when recalling their time in Wisconsin – "It's an awful place with too many trees. The only way to see the sky is looking straight up!"

Anne's brother Andrew Kanten married Hans' first cousin Anne. They homesteaded in Foster County, North Dakota and Hans and Anne soon followed, making their home in McHenry, North Dakota. By 1904 drought sent Andrew and his family across the border into Saskatchewan. Hans and Anne moved a few miles down the road to the new town of Binford, North Dakota. As the town was being built, Hans was able to secure regular work as a painter and wallpaper hanger (working with Hadeland Lag genealogist Leslie Rogne's father). Before their McHenry house was moved to Binford, the family lived in the West Hotel where Hans held the position of manager. Hans was busy on the new construction in town, so along with caring for her 5 young children, Anne managed the books and handled all the cooking and cleaning in the hotel. A tragic store fire took the life of 7-year-old Alvin Gerhardt just before Christmas 1905.

Hans purchased a spacious lot at the north end of town and added a second floor to the McHenry house when it arrived in Binford in the spring of 1905. Anne tended a garden and canned most of the produce to feed the family in winter. She was an expert seamstress and made and kept in repair almost all of her family's clothes. She and Hans rose early, talking quietly in Norwegian as Anne prepared breakfast. Hans enjoyed playing the violin and sang with a men's quartet for many years. He would sit each night and read the Norwegian and English newspapers to which he subscribed before retiring about 9 p.m. Anne could usually be found alone, quietly mending and sewing – with bread rising in the kitchen – at midnight.

After the initial 'building boom' in Binford, Hans found little work in his chosen profession. He spent a summer in Fargo, North Dakota, and did quite well, but resisted moving the family to what was to him a 'big city.' Although he didn't like farming Hans was an ardent Norwegian Lutheran who felt at home in the quiet of the prairie and saw nothing good in the noisy bustling and 'loose ways" of a large town. Anne agreed with him completely. Hans acquired a small but steady income as the janitor at the local school. He held the position until a year before his death, when his worsening heart condition left him an invalid.

Hans did not permit liquor in his house (no doubt as a result of his father's drinking problems) and was an active member of the Sons of Norway. Hadeland Lag *stevner* were a time for a reunion with his siblings and their families and, although there was little money for extras, there was always enough to cover the trip.

His daughters reported that Hans was in demeanor distant and strict, as was typical of many Norwegian fathers. When they wanted something they approached their mother, not their dad. His outward sternness was only superficial – he took great interest, was supportive and held a deep affection for each of his children. Hans finally succumbed to his heart condition in 1931.

Her children never recall Anne raising her voice in anger. She lost three children as infants. She gently cared for Alvin's burns for the last painful hours of his life and comforted her husband and children in the difficult days thereafter. Without hesitation Anne left her own young family in 1910 to care for her father back in Chippewa County during the last few months of his life. She outlived her husband by more than 25 years. Two of her adult sons preceded her in death. Through it all she was the emotional anchor for her family and all those around her. She was a strong, stoic Norwegian woman who trusted God and, when hardships arose, patiently faced them with dignity and grace.

After breaking her hip, Anne was confined to a wheelchair for most of the last five years of her life. She suffered a stroke and passed away just after her 85th birthday on May 28, 1957.

Hans and Anne are buried in the Binford Cemetery in Binford, North Dakota.

Family photo taken in 1915
Back row: Julia, Iver, Oscar, and Alice
Front Row: Arthur, Hans, Ruby, Anne and Helen

The children of Hans and Anne Alm:

- Iver Herman, born October 18, 1890, in Watson MN married Clara Hanson in Moorhead MN on Valentine's Day 1915. Iver died in Jamestown ND on May 11, 1939. Their children were Helen (Schmit), Wallace, and Jeanne (Jensen).

157

- Oscar Alfred Alm, born January 12, 1893, in Watson married Hazel Jean Maurer in Binford on June 24, 1920. Oscar died December 8, 1951, in Binford. Their children were Ross and Kent.
- Alvin was born in 1894 and died in 1895 in Ashland, Wisconsin.
- Julia was born and died in 1895 in Ashland, Wisconsin.
- Alvin Gerhardt was born December 26, 1898, in Watson MN. He died on December 20, 1905 in Binford ND.
- Julia Emile born January 29, 1901, in Watson MN married Harold Skrove in Binford on November 10, 1925. Julia died April 24, 1980, in Fort Collins, Colorado. Their children were James, Patricia (Walberg/Jacob), and Saundra.
- Alice Elnora born March 3, 1903 in Watson MN married Charles Keeney. Alice died November 12, 1979 in Grangeville ID. Their children were Connie (Tryon/Akers), Pat and Dennis.
- Helen Margaret born December 8, 1905, in Binford married Manfred Knapp in 1931 in Poulson, Montana. Helen was 100 years old when she died on September 16, 2006 in Jamestown ND. Their son was Richard.
- Arthur Gilman born in Binford on January 28, 1908, married Margaret Mary "Maye" Curran on June 12, 1938. He died in Asheville, North Carolina, on January 23, 1998. Their children were Michael, Thomas, and Mary.
- Rudolph Melvin was born in Binford on August 16, 1911. He died April 23, 1912.
- Ruby Mildred born March 5, 1913, married Gerald Grover in Moorhead MN on May 27, 1950. Ruby died in Fargo ND March 3, 2002. Their children were A Anne and Ralph. Ruby is the author's mother.

Julia, Ruby, Arthur, Alice, and Helen with their mother Anne, c. 1955

Martia Alm and Erick Anderson Rekstad

Published February/May 2007 *Form 8* *Mary Margaret Rekstad Gibson*

Mary Margaret is the daughter of Rudolph and Eleanor Rekstad, and the granddaughter of Erick Anderson Rekstad and Martia Alm. The life stories of these ancestors were included in a paper entitled "From the Old Country to the Prairie" written for a college course at Southwest State University, Marshall MN in 1981. She spent her teaching career in the Montevideo MN High School and Alternative Learning Center. She and her husband Dennis live in rural Montevideo. Their son, lag member Shaun Gibson, submitted his mother's article for publication.

Erick and Martia (Alm) Rekstad Family
Seated: Jennie, Martia, Erick, Helga
Standing: Anna, Edwin, Ole, Andrew, Rudolph

Martia's memories of her childhood in Hadeland

Children attended school to learn reading and writing; however, the girls were not taught arithmetic because it was considered unnecessary. All the teachers were men. The pastors taught the confirmation lessons in church. Martia was confirmed on October 1, 1882 in a large class of about 40 boys and girls. At the time of catechization when the confirmands were asked questions about Bible history and Luther's Catechism, they stood along the outside walls of the church and in the center aisle. The pastor walked around and asked them questions. One of Martia's fellow confirmands was Erick Anderson. Martia and Erick would some years later, after they emigrated, be married on July 15, 1890.

159

These are some of the memories that my grandmother Martia told my father about her childhood. Martia remembered that in the summer she and her sisters and brothers picked large yellow berries called *molte* (cloudberries) which were about the size of large raspberries. They sold some of them to get extra money for the growing family.

When she was fifteen years old, Martia was sent out to work on the large Tingelstad farm where she had the sole care of the cattle. She milked the cows, fed them, cleaned their stalls, and in the summer went with them up to the *seter* (summer dairy, usually near the top of the hills or mountains). There she stayed all summer, herding and milking the cows and helping to make butter and cheese for the coming winter. One summer she did not go up to the *seter*, but stayed on the farm to help cut grain with a sharp scythe with a curved-hooked blade. She said that she cut twice as much as the other workers did. Martia was satisfied working at Tingelstad. She liked her duties. She had a room of her own and especially remembered looking forward to a week full of festivities at Christmas. During that time, she and the other hired help could go *julebokking* to neighboring farms – a different farm each night – and dancing until morning! The night's festivities ended by returning to the farm in time to do the morning milking!

Shoes were made by itinerant shoemakers. They would come to the farm and work for two or three weeks at a time. The softer leather was usually used for shoes for the farmer's daughters and the cheaper leather for the hired girls. The sympathetic shoemakers would often spend extra time softening the leather for the working girls so that their shoes fit more comfortably and wore better than those of the daughters' shoes!

Martia always sang at her work. Many times, an old man in the farm would ask her to sing *The Husmann's Vise*, a ballad about the difficult lot of the *husmenn*. After hearing the song, he would say "Every word of that song is true!" and would shed a few tears.

Emigration to America

On May 5, 1888 on the steamship *Rollo*, Ole Ericksen and his wife Johanne Hansdatter emigrated to America, together with three of their daughters: Martia, age 22, Oline, age 18, and Johanne, age 9. Their son Hans had emigrated three years earlier. There he worked on the Dvergsten farm in Watson, Minnesota, and had by that time earned enough money to send passage money to his parents and his two younger sisters. Mr. Dvergsten was Johanne's brother. Martia's $40 passage was paid by Gulbrand (Gilbert) Hilden of Watson. She was obligated to work for him to repay her passage – at the rate of one dollar per week. The passage from Christiania to New York City took only about three weeks. They traveled on a steamship in which the cattle had been hauled the previous year. Although the cost of their passage included food, they brought their own dried meat, sausage, cheese and flatbread. They only food she remembered eating from the ship's fare was the potatoes. Nearly everyone in the family was seasick most of the journey. Only her father Ole did not get sick. Erick Anderson, Martia's future husband, was also a passenger on the same emigrant ship and heading to Watson MN, too. He was traveling alone and like her father Ole, Erick did not get seasick. Both of them liked to play cards so that was their pastime on the trip.

Erick Anderson, his life and recollections of Hadeland

Erick Anderson was born on January 17, 1868, the son of Anders Amundsen and his wife Siri Eriksdatter. She had inherited the small *husmann's* farm Rækstadbraaten in Tingelstad. It was only a few acres, but large enough to raise a few sheep and chickens and a couple of cows. Anders made his living as a carpenter. Erick had a younger brother, Anton, born in 1870 and a sister, Bertha, born in 1877.

Erick went to school and learned to read well and to write a little, although he did not enjoy it. His father was fairly successful in those early years so Erick did not have to work very hard. When he was 18 years old, his mother died. Two years later he got a chance to emigrate to America. A neighbor, Peter Canton, who had emigrated to America a few years before, sent a ticket to his brother to come to America. At the last minute the brother decided that he didn't want to go. "I'll take that ticket," said Erick. His father encouraged him by telling him that going to America was just like taking a trip to Christiania and saying, "If you don't like it, you can come home again." They certainly knew very little about the immensisty of this decision! Since there were no real opportunities for Erick in Norway and because he was only 20 years old with no responsibilities, the trip seemed like a big adventure to him!

When the time for Erick's departure came, the father walked with him all the way to Christiania – more than 40 miles – so that he could see his eldest son off to America. That was the only time that Martia saw her future father-in-law. She described him to her children as big and husky with dark curly hair.

The train trip from New York to Watson, Minnesota, went without incident. Ole and Johanne's son Hans was there to meet them. Erick arrived in America with exactly fifty cents in his pocket and promptly began working for his friend Pete Canton to pay off the cost of his ticket to America.

After Erick Anderson Rekstad had worked for Peter Canton long enough to pay for the cost of his ticket from Hadeland to America, he went to work for Gilbert Hilden. On this same farm, Martia Ericksen Alm was working as the "hired girl." They had met on the steamship *Rollo* that had taken them to America the year before. While working on the Hilden farm, their courtship developed. On July 5, 1890, Mrtia and Erick hired a team of horses and a buggy from Hilden for one dollar, drove into Montevideo, and got married. Martia's brother Hans and his wife were attendants at their marriage. One of their most appreciated wedding presents was a hen from Oste Peterson. They soon moved into Watson where Erick built what has later been known as the "Gary house." While they lived in Watson, their four oldest children were born:

1) Andrew, born 24 December 1890
2) Ole, born 14 January 1893
3) Jennie (Johanna) born 12 December 1894
4) Helga, born 19 October 1896

Notice that Martia and Erik continued the Norwegian tradition of naming their first-born son for his paternal grandfather and the second-born for his maternal grandfather. Erick worked on the railroad until 1897 when they sold their home and moved to a farm owned by Hans Kanten which was located about a mile and a half west of Watson, Minnesota.

In 1901 the Rekstad family moved. They moved to the Peterson farm, five miles north of Watson. There their last three children were born:

5) Anna, born 4 January 1901
6) Edwin, born 29 December 1901
7) Rudolph, born 26 June 1905 (*Rudolph was the father of the author*)

In retrospect, Erick could have rented that farm for the rest of his life since it was always owned by non-farmers. He was very successful when they lived there. He owned some of the best horses in the area; his children had the advantage of being near school, church, and town. However, Erick's brother Anton, who had immigrated to America in 1904, had settled in Grace Township, nearly 20 miles from the nearest town. In 1905 Erick chose to buy a 160-acre farm near his brother for 25 dollars an acre, or $4,000. There was a small 3-room house with a loft, a new granary and a stable on the farm. The soil was heavy black gumbo and on this acreage there were many sloughs or "pot-holes" as they are often called. Because of heavy annual rains, no crops were harvested during the first four years! With no crops, a mortgage that had to be paid and a large family to feed, Erick was forced to sell his fine horses. In 1920 the county started building a drainage ditch through the area which was finished in 1923. This helped lessen the risk of crop loss because of flooding, but just a few years later, the dry 1930s arrived!

By 1914, when a new house was built, the three oldest children were no longer living at home. Andrew had been working outside the home for seven years. Later he married Hilma Haug, the daughter of the people he worked for in South Dakota. Andrew and Hilma settled in the Willow Lakes, South Dakota, area. They had one daughter, Arlene. Andrew lived in South Dakota the rest of his life and died there on January 26, 1949. Ole worked for neighboring farmers during the summer and was home in the winter. Jenny married James Jones, an Irishman, in 1918. The had three children: Charlotte, Elwood and Arlene. Helga still lived at home in 1914. On March 14, 1937 she married a fellow Norwegian-American, Jens Jolstad. Martia approved of him. Erick really liked him, too; he was another farmer from Norway! After living on a farm near Kerkoven, Minnesota for a short time, Jenny and Jens later moved to a farm only a mile from Erick and Martia's farm.

Erick and Martia in front of their year-old house in 1915

Erick Rekstad was a handsome man, quite small in build with a big mustache and large, powerful hands. He was a gentle, quiet man who while resting was happy just smoking his pipe. He never said much around the house, never disciplined his children except with a hard look and then only if Martia demanded it. His only failing was that he didn't like to work; however, he did like to visit often with his friends and neighbors. When he took a load of grain to town to sell, he would usually not get home until after midnight because he loved to visit with all his neighbors, coming and going!

Martia was an untiring worker, an organizer and a leader. She had natural musical abilities and a love of writing. Her greatest joy in spare moments was to write letters to her schoolmates and to Erick's stepmother in Norway. Though she was sharp and sometimes stubborn, she was loving but tough. She, too, loved to visit but she preferred not to learn to speak English although she must have understood it. There were Irish, Germans, and Norwegians living in Grace Township. Somehow, she communicated with the women in the neighborhood and the peddlers who came to her door. She did not like it when her children spoke English in her presence. She never encouraged her children to marry. In 1937, Edwin, at the age of 34, married Angeline Bjorgan. They bought the Hendrickson place that the whole family had lived on in 1913 so they also lived near her parents. Ole and Rudolph married after their mother died. Anna never married.

On January 17, 1940, Erick celebrated his seventy-second birthday with a house full of sons, daughters, in-laws and grandchildren. Rudolph remembered noticing how strange his mother's eyes looked as they were sitting visiting. After all the visitors had left and before the family had settled down for the night, Martia suffered a heart attack. She died instantly. After picking up Ole (who was living with Helga and Jens), Rudolph then picked up Edwin and the three of them drove to the Burgess store on the 17-mile corner in order to telephone Dr. Bergh. The doctor arrived shortly in his new Cadillac. It was so cold that he wore two overcoats! The next day, Anderson Mortuary came to get Martia's body.

In 1934, Rudolph met the new country school teacher. He had seen her before when he was shopping at the Montgomery Ward store where her brother worked. The teacher's name was Mildred Moen. Herman Bang introduced them in the A & P Store in Montevideo. She taught in the local school until the spring of 1938. For years, Rudolph did not ask her for a date, although tthey were often at the same social gatherings. Two years later, in the fall of 1940, Rudolph finally asked Mildred on a date to the local movie theatre. They were married February 8, 1941. Rudolph bought the home farm from his dad for $50 per acre.

In August 1941, Erick and Anna moved to Montevideo. Ole stayed on Helga and Jens' place until he married Mabel Iverson, a widow with two children, in 1943. Later they moved to Montevideo and bought the house next door to Erick. Erick died on March 4, 1951, and his daughter Anna died on February 22, 1959. Jennie also moved to Montevideo after her husband's death in 1942. Edwin died on July 9, 1969. Jenny died on September 9, 1969. Ole died on February 24, 1970. Rudolph died June 6, 1985 and Jennie (Johanna) died on January 25, 1986. Now they are all gone.

My brother John Rekstad has a son. He lives on the East Coast and works for the U.S. Patent Office as a video patent analyst. He is a great-grandson of Erick and Martia. His name is Erick Rekstad. Erick's name lives on!

Recollections of Pioneer Times

published May 2007 – written by Mary Margaret Rekstad Gibson

Sunday was a day of rest at the Rekstad home, but it was uncommon for the whole family to go to church. They belonged to the Jevnaker Norwegian Lutheran congregation located in rural Montevideo, Minnesota, and named in honor of the church in Hadeland where many of the local immigrants had lived in their youth. Erick would drive the buggy to church and take with him the children who were "reading for the minister"* at the time. However, everyone went to the congregation's Christmas Tree (program) which eventually evolved into the annual children's Christmas program. Rudolph, the youngest Rekstad son, remembered being in his first program when he was five years old. Prior to the program, money was collected annually from among the church members. With this money they bought apples, oranges, and Christmas

candy. Each child reeived a small paper bag of these goodies together with a present after the program. Rudolph say that each of the other children received a present, but he did not get one. All the presents were distributed and there was none for him. He remembered crying all that day and the next! The following day his father Erick hitched up the horses and drove

> * reading for the minister is a literal translation of the Norwegian phrase *lese for presten*, an idiom which means being enrolled in a confirmation instruction class in the local Lutheran church.

twenty miles to town to get a present for Rudolph. He never forgot that present – a toy with a bell on it awith a hammer to make it ring.

Baseball was Rudolph's first love. He began playing with a rag ball and a homemade bat and ended by being one of the most sought-after players among the local teams. Nearly every township and small town had a baseball team. Each team had official uniforms and every Sunday afternoon there were games, played according to a pre-arranged schedule. The teams were allowed to "import" players to ensure future victories. There was even a black pitcher from Minneapolis on the Milan (MN) team. Rudolph paid for his baseball uniforms, balls and gloves with money he earned trapping muskrats (32 cents a pelt), mink ($10 a pelt), and skunks ($5 a pelt).

Rudolph remembered the wild strawberries that grew in the Randall (MN) area in those days. There had been a forest fire one summer and the next year the strawberries were so numerous that they picked milk pails full of them.

In 1915 the whole family went to a Hadeland Lag meeting in Montevideo. Ole, Edwin and Rudolph went in a buggy. The rest of the family rode with Lars Olson, the man who built their new house on the farm and who owned a Model T Ford. Ole and Andrew bought a new Model T Ford in 1917 for $360, but shortly afterwards they were both drafted into the army to serve in the First World War. While they were in the army, Erick learned to drive and used their car. Later, in 1919, when Ole and Andrew returned, Erick bought himself a car, but the price of cars had gone up during those past two years. His car cost nearly $700!

Both Andrew and Ole saw military action at the front lines in Argonne, France. Ole was under fire for six weeks and narrowly missed being injured when his pant legs and backpack were peppered with bullets. Andrew was in the front lines for two

Ole and Andrew Rekstad in their WWI uniforms

weeks before the cease fire came on November 11, 1918. The brothers had trained in Fort Lewis, Washington, but they were split up when they got to France. When they came home, Andrew took off his uniform and never put it on again, but Ole wore his around the neighborhood on special occasions for some time.

Every spring the Rekstads would butcher both a steer and a pig. The pork was put into crocks and covered with salt brine. Later it would be fried in preparation for the table. The beef was dried or made into sausage. In later years, much of it was canned. During the canning process the meet was first browned and then packed into glass jars and placed in a hot water bath for several hours which then hermetically sealed the food for future use. This meat was later served with a cream gravy that was "Oh, so good!" Chicken was also boiled, but never fried. Martia's garden provided almost everything else they needed for the daily table – tomatoes, beets, cabbages, onions, radishes, carrots and cucumbers. Potatoes and corn were grown out in the farm fields. Gooseberries, cranberries, apples and ground cherries were made into sauce. The first peaches were bought in 1913. They were processed into sauce, but Rudolph remembered that he stole one and rearranged the peaches so that no one ever found out about it! Whenever the family entertained company for dinner, fruit sauce was the dessert. Pie was served only to the threshers. Martia baked bread every day for her large family and for the relatives who often would come to stay, sometimes for months at a time.

From the time that Rudolph was old enough to work, Erick let him make the farm decisions – what and when to plant, what machinery to buy, when to harrow, cultivate, harvest, plow, etc. Ole, Edwin and Rudolph had a bank account together and farmed all the land as one unit. They got along very well, letting the youngest be the 'boss.' They farmed with a Farmall F-20 tractor and an F-23 for planting corn, oats, wheat and occasionally flax. The corn was harvested by hand. The family owned a threshing machine, a corn sheller and a truck. These were also used when they threshed and shelled corn for their neighbors. At one time the three brothers farmed 680 acres. Erick got all the crop from his 160 acres. Edwin got the crop from his 120 acres. Helga, whose husband Jens was accidentally killed while hunting in 1905, got the crop from her 160 acres and Rudolph and Ole split the renter's share of the remaining 240 acres.

The family was able to avoid financial tragedy during the Great Depression of the 1930s, although Erick lost $1,000 when the bank in Watson closed. The DeGraff Bank also closed, but he was able to get his money out of his account in the Benson bank. The farm was paid for, but the family took out loans to build a new barn in 1920. In 1924, a new chicken coop was built. Martia was very excited about her new chicken coop and wanted everything in that new building to be made of new lumber. Rudolph liked to tease his mother about this. One day Martia asked, "What's dad doing?" "Oh, he's in the chicken coop putting up the old nests," said Rudolph. Martia grabbed her shawl, threw it across her shoulders and ran to the newly built chicken coop, only to find that Erick was not even working there!

These recollections are mainly those that my father Rudolph told me. He had an accurate memory for details and the stories his parents told him. My parents respected and revered their parents and provided for their personal needs and listened to their stories. These are some of their recollections and stories they passed on to me.

Nils and Lottie Tovson

"Recollections of Pioneer Times" published November 2002   Form 500   Marie Gleason

Nils and Lottie

My sister Lorraine and I learned to know our grandmother Lottie through our family research.

Lottie died in 1908 when her own children were small. Of course, as adults we knew her name, Aletta Karolina Peterson, knew that she was one of Annie and Andrew Peterson's 13 children, and knew that in 1899 she married handsome Nils Tovson, left the white frame house her now-prosperous parents had built on their homestead just outside of Mayville, N.D.

Born in Gran, Hadeland in 1849, Lottie's mother Annie was baptized in one of the *Søsterkirker*, and brought shortly after to Wisconsin by her Hadeland parents, Christiania Ingebretsdotter and Halvor Larsen. In the early 1870s Annie, with husband Andrew and two infant sons, was in one of the first wagon trains that settled Dacotah Territory. Together with their numerous kin, the Petersons had their choice of the rich and fertile land along the Goose River.

Many Mayville-area settlers looked to their Hadeland home and to the *Søsterkirker*; the small white church they erected near the Goose was called "The Gran." Before many of their homes were built, the settlers' energies went into providing a pastor and building the church in which they could worship.

It was in the Mayville Gran Church that Lottie was baptized and confirmed in Norwegian. As a young woman she worked for the Norwegian-language school on the premises. And it was in Gran that in 1899, Lottie was married. The Skrivseth Studio's wedding photo shows a tiny, sweet-faced woman standing by her groom. He is seated in an ornate Victorian chair, one arm resting on a Victorian table. Wide-eyed, focused, Lottie stares into the camera. A gifted seamstress whose specialty was elaborate dresses for women and children, Lottie designed and sewed her wasp-waisted gown with its beribboned kick-pleats. Lottie's face is framed in a halo of flowers.

Really, there was very little chance that Lottie and Nils would live happily ever after. The newlyweds pioneered on a remote tree claim and lived on a sandy soil Minnesota homestead, little like the rich land the Petersons had homesteaded in the Red River Valley. There were several miscarriages and five living children born in less than 10 years. For most of her laying-ins, Lottie returned to her parents in Mayville. Both Annie and Lottie's grandmother Christiania were well-regarded midwives, but the fifth birth did not go well. From this distance, we can only conjecture what happened. Lottie did not die immediately; she lingered in a slow and painful month-long decline that exhausted and tore family members in ways we can only guess.

Left to Right: Arthur, Nils, Oliver, Olga, Alice and Olive Tovson

We sisters have a black-and-white family photo taken perhaps two or three years after Lottie's death in 1908. Nils and Lottie's five children are grouped around her tombstone in the Gran churchyard. But it is Nils, her bereaved husband, still a young man, who draws the eye. In his black suitcoat he stands, shoulders bowed like those of an old man. He looks down at the gravestone, not even at his children; only Alice, the eldest, appears aware of why they are there. The other children are too young, uncomprehending. "Aletta Karoline, *døde* Feb. 1908," reads the tombstone's lettering. Some of the text is legible with a magnifying glass.

Fast-forward to the 1980s: My sister Lorraine and her husband have moved to Mayville, where they have a business on the town's main street (which appears little changed from the last turn-of-the-century). As a resident Lorraine discovers numerous second cousins and "The Gran," still painted a pristine white among Dakota fields of grain and sunflowers. On one of my visits from Newfoundland, Lorraine and I conclude we may have seen this little white church as visiting children, but we're not certain.

We wander the well-tended cemetery lots and afterwards lie in the stubbly grass and speculate about these long-dead ancestors of ours, none of whom we've ever met. There's the grave of our Hadeland-born great-great-grandmother Christiania Ingebretsdottir Larsen Erickson; we had no idea she had such a parade of names. (Most were misspelled in the family album.) She died within a year of Lottie, we learn, but Christiania had lived an eventful 90 years and was buried separately from the rest, with an imposing tombstone. In death as in life, "Momma," with her exalted pioneer status, was accorded special treatment.

Lottie, our own grandmother, auburn-haired Lottie, who bore five children and died before her 30th birthday, Lottie, we discover, was buried in the midst of the Petersons. Buried witih her parents Annie and Andrew, are her sisters Sarah (who died as a child) and the young adult Emma. A long, low monument houses all the Peterson graves; each Peterson has a simple name and date identification. "Why," Lorraine and I ask each other, "was Lottie buried with her original family and not with her husband?" "And what happened to Lottie's four-foot grave monument? The one we saw in the black-and-white print with Nils and his children?"

Lorraine and her sons, as well as another family of Nils-Lottie's descendants, searched the old cemetery. No one found a trace of Lottie's tombstone; its whereabouts remained a mystery.

In May 2002, Lorraine sent me an e-mail: "Marie, better write all this out for you while it's fresh in my mind. It really was very strange. The dream: Ross (her son) and I were walking the river bank south of the Gran Church looking for pieces of Lottie's tombstone. I don't recall there was any conversation but we found two pieces of the stone. One piece had the letters TOV, the second LETT or LETTA. Don't remember which, but it was definite proof to us we had found two pieces of what we were looking for. The dream ended right there, with feelings of elation.

"Then to have Ross show up at 9:00 the next morning! No warning; it was a Monday and he never comes on a weekday, but he just had a feeling that he should take a day off and come for a visit. So I told him the dream right away and that we should go looking.

"Well, we walked the river bank but found nothing at all. Then Ross spotted this man mowing the lawn at the old Peterson place and said, 'Let's go talk to him.' The man introduced himself and said he was the nephew of a pioneer friend of ours. After we talked a bit, we showed him the photo of Lottie's tombstone with Nils and the children gathered round. He said he remembered the stone, remembered it well. As a boy of 9 or 10 it was his job and that of his cousin to mow the grass in the cemetery. Said they always wondered who Tovson was – not a name familiar to them and why was it on the Peterson lot?

"Then he remembered there had been a big electrical storm, thunder and lightning, in the 1960s. A herd of cattle, terrified, had broken through the Gran fence, trampling and breaking down maybe a half-dozen stones. The families whose names they knew were told of the stampede and given the broken pieces of their family tombstones, but no one knew anything about the name 'Tovson.' By now the two cousins were young men and they were asked to dispose of the broken pieces that were not claimed. They felt bad about just doing away with someone's stone, but they didn't have a choice. So they loaded the pieces and then left them in the woods near the river, but not down the bank."

Lorraine interjects: "Ross and I walked the woods for an hour, but found nothing."

The man who had been mowing told us later that several years ago his cousin built a dike on his land along the Goose and may have used these broken pieces along with boulders. He said he'd ask his cousin and if they found anything of Lottie's stone they'd try to retrieve it for us.

"Then the man added: 'It was odd that you'd find me mowing the grass at the old Peterson place. I did it as a favor for the person who normally does it. I'm an insurance salesman and I travel a lot; I'm not easy to find!'"

We have never heard anything further, but Lorraine and I believe we now know where Lottie's broken tombstone lies. Just like Lottie's bones, her stone never travelled far from "The Gran."

Anders Larsen Røykeneie and Ole Larson

published February 2003   *Form 518*   *Diane Teigen*

Anders Larson with his two oldest grandsons, Peter and Arthur

My great-grandfather Anders Larsen Røykeneie was born 31 May 1826 in Gran, Hadeland, Norway. He was the youngest of three sons born to Lars Jensen Nes and Gudbjørg Jacobsdatter Røykeneie (married 1817). Their sons were Jacob, born 1818; Jens, born 1821; and Anders, born 1826.

Anders emigrated as a single man in the spring of 1851 with his brother Jens and wife Anne Iversdatter, their son Lars Jensen, and some partners. Their sailboat landed in Quebec. Anders and his traveling companions spent three years in Quebec, probably working to earn travel money.

Next they journeyed to Chicago. They worked on the railroad. Chicago at the time was a small town built in a low swamp (Anders' words). The cholera epidemic came and hundreds died, including his brother, some relatives and his partners from Norway. The immigrants moved north and then westward in Wisconsin. In 1855 they were at Lake Koshkonong (between Milwaukee and Madison) where Anders married Maria Iversdatter Amundrud (sister of his brother Jens' wife, Anne).

I believe Maria and several of her brothers were traveling with Anders. (This would explain how some Iversons are known to be our second cousins.) Iver Jacobsen-Røykeneie in 1817 married Gjertrud Julsdatter Heggen. Their children were Jacob, 1818; Marte, 1821; Kjersti, 1823; Kjersti, 1825; Anne, 1827; Maria, 1830; Jul, 1834; Ole, 1837; and Iver, 1840.

The good land in Wisconsin was taken or too expensive, so the group moved on. Areas of public land were opened up in Minnesota. It was 245 miles from Lake Koshkonong, Wisconsin, to Scott County, Minnesota. Traveling was hard and babies, small children and others died along the way. (Were they traveling in winter to cross the Mississippi River on ice?) Anders and his family reached Scott County, Minnesota (just south of Minneapolis) in 1863, a year after the Indian outbreak and in the middle of the Civil War.

We can assume that they were small farmers, raising most of their food and some wheat to sell. Maria died in 1875. Anders commented many times that after she died everything went wrong (grasshopper plagues 1873-1877). Anders chose to go north and homestead property on the fringe of the Red River Valley. The land looked more like his home in Norway: rolling hills, trees, lakes and swamps. Anders came to Humboldt Township, Clay County, with three children in 1879. Lars, born 1858 in Wisconsin, died in 1879; Ole, born April 16, 1867 in Scott

171

County; Josephine, born November 24, 1870 in Scott County. Six children had died previously on the trail or in Scott County (two Oles, two Annes, two unnamed). The official homestead deed was signed in 1891 by Benjamin Harrison after 10 years and buildings were built. The certificate is in possession of the owner of the Larson land, my brother Greg Larson.

My grandmother Karoline Pedersdatter was born December 26, 1880, in Brandbu, Hadeland, Norway. Her father was Peder Gudbrandsen Bleikeneie (Saddler), born September 9, 1851. In 1880 he married Berte Johansdatter Nessie, born Nesteggeeie, June 7, 1850.

Peder's parents were Gudbrand Hansen and Kjersti Gudbrandsdatter, married in 1843. Berte's parents were Johan Peter Hansen and Berte Amundsdatter, married in 1840.

Karoline emigrated at three and one-half months of age with her parents Peder and Berte and Berte's father, Julian Hansen. The Parish Register (*Kirkebok*) states that they traveled on the ship *Rolla* and their final destination was Barnesville, Minnesota. Peder, Berte and Caroline changed their last name to Blegen. I believe the Blegens lived one to two miles north of the Larson homeplace. Caroline was confirmed at Gran Lutheran Church November 10, 1895 (about three miles north of the Larson place). Caroline Blegen married Ole Larson in 1899 or 1900. They had 10 children, seven survived to adulthood.

Syver, their seventh child, farmed the original Larson land. My brother, Greg Larson, who now owns and farms the land, lives in Barnesville.

Sources for this history are oral histories, information from Delores Larson, research in Norway by Gunnar Lee (a second cousin once removed on my mother's side), Minnesota and Wisconsin highway maps, Karoline's papers from the Parish Register (permission to leave Norway), and Minnesota: A History of the State by Theodore C. Blegen.

Obituary of Andrew Larson
Received from Delores Larson

Andrew Larson died at his son's home June 25, 1921 (the family farm) in Humboldt Township, Barnesville, Minnesota, one of the county's oldest men. He lived in this settlement since 1879.

He was born in Gran Prestegjeld, Hadeland, Norway, May 2, 1826. He went to America in the spring of 1851 and was one of the first emigrants from that place. He often talked about the trip on the old sailboat to America. They stopped at Quebec, Canada, for three years, then worked on the railroad. Chicago at that time was a small town built sort of in a low swamp. The cholera epidemic came and hundreds died – among them his brother, some relatives and his partners from Norway.

In 1855 he moved to Koshkonong and the same year was married by Pastor Muus. They also lived in Muskego where they were members of the well-known Muskego Church, the first

Norwegian Lutheran Church in America, which is now restored and stands on the grounds of Luther Seminary, St. Paul.

In 1865 Larson, with his family, moved to Scott County, Minnesota. In 1879 he came to Clay County where he lived on his farm until he died. Larson was a typical pioneer. Time and again he was always along to help with new ideas, willing to do his share in a lot of the heavy work that was needed to break new ground.

Ole Larson was one of the country's strongest men and healthiest. He had never been to a doctor until the last years when his son called the doctor for his blindness, so it was hard for him to help himself.

He was a member of Gran Congregation and took an active part to the last. The funeral was on Monday, June 27. He was laid to rest in Gran Cemetery. There was a nice sermon by Pastor S.G. Hauge, minister of Gran Congregation. There were services at the house and at the church. He is survived by two children, Ole and Josie Larson, and several grandchildren. His wife died in Scott County in 1875.

Peace with him. Blessed is his memory.

Biography of Ole Larson *Diane's grandfather*
Text from "A History of Clay and Norman Counties," volume 2, published 1918 by B. F. Bowen & Company of Indianapolis; pages 445-447; photos courtesy Delores Larson

Ole Larson

Ole Larson, farmer in Humboldt Township, Clay County, was born in Scott County, Minnesota, April 16, 1867, a son of Andrew and Mary (Engen) Larson, both natives of Norway, from which country they immigrated to America, single, in 1851, making the voyage on the same boat, landing at Quebec, Canada. Their family consisted of nine children, six of whom died in Scott County. Lars died in Clay County. Ole, the subject of this sketch, and Josie are the only ones who survived to adulthood.

Ole Larson attended the early district schools of Clay County. He has worked hard all his life, assisting his father, who was a typical pioneer, with the general work of developing farms in a new country. He was one of the organizers of the Farmers Elevator Company in Barnesville and a heavy stockholder in the same. He was its first president.

Caroline Blegen Larson

Mr. Larson was married in 1897 to Caroline Blegen, a native of Norway and a daughter of Peter and Bertha (Tingelstad) Blegen*, both natives of Norway, where they grew up, married and established their home; but later brought their family to America, locating among the early pioneers of Humboldt Township, Clay County, Minnesota, where they became very comfortably established through their industry, buying railroad land in section 13. After living there a number of years they moved to Beltrami County, Minnesota. Six children were born to Mr. and Mrs. Blegen, namely: Caroline, Nettie, Gilbert, Vent, Peter and Henry.

The following children were born to Ole Larson and his wife: Arthur, Peter, Ida Louise, Lars, Clara, Anna and Sever. Mr. Larson was an active member of Grong Lutheran Church of which he was a trustee for many years.

> *Brua Editor's Note: According to an Ancestor Chart received from Delores Larson, Peder's birth name was Peder Gudbrandsen Bleikeneie, born at Eggeeie, Norway. His wife was Berte Johansdtr. Neseie, born at Nesteggeeie, Brandbu, Norway. The Ancestor Chart does not give Tingelstad as her name.*

Obituary of Syver Larson, *Diane's father*
from the Fargo (ND) Forum

Syver Norman Larson, 87, Barnesville, died Wednesday, Sept. 4, 2002, in his home. Mr. Larson was born Nov. 7, 1914, near Barnesville, where he grew up and attended school. He farmed with his family. On June 14, 1942, he married Mildred Thompson in Moorhead. They lived and farmed near Barnesville. In 1977, his son took over the farming operation, but he continued to help and live on the farm.

He is survived by two sons, two daughters, a brother, a sister, seven grandchildren and three great-grandchildren.

Visitation was held at Dobmeier Funeral Home, Barnesville with the funeral in Gran Lutheran Church, Barnesville and burial in the church cemetery.

Ole Gulbrandsen & Berthe Borgersdtr

published August 2003   Form 487   *Bruce Plomasen*

When the emigrant ship *Argo* sailed from Oslo, outbound from Norway to the New World on April 23, 1869, it numbered among its passengers peering over the bow down Oslofjord my great-grandparents, Ole Gulbrandsen, age 64, his wife Berthe Borgersdatter, age 63, their unmarried daughter Mari (or Maria), age 24, and possibly also their unmarried son, my grandfather, Anders Olsen, age 22. They had each paid 123 *sp.daler* for their passage. Their destination was Chicago.

Ole Gulbrandsen had been born in 1806 at the Sogn farm in Jevnaker and in 1832 had married Berthe Borgersdatter (born in 1807 on the Plomasen farm at Jorstadeiet located several kilometers west of the Sister Churches at Granvollen). They had six children: Gulbrand, Borger, Jens (who emigrated to America, but apparently not with his parents), a first son named Anders who died in infancy, a daughter Mari (or Maria) and a second Anders, my grandfather (born in 1848 and baptized in the Saint Nikolai Church at Granvollen), who either emigrated with his parents on the ship *Argo* in 1869 or emigrated separately, perhaps with his brother Jens maybe a year or two earlier or later.

I remember my father saying that his father, Anders, had landed at Milwaukee, Wisconsin. They made their way to an area near Clermont in northeastern Iowa settled by emigrants from Norway. There my grandfather Anders met a young lady, Gro Thorson, who had been born there in 1851 of parents who had emigrated from Hallingdal, Norway in 1850. They were married in 1872. Realizing that the last name "Olsen" was very common among immigrants from Scandinavia, they changed the family name to "Plomasen" after the name of the farm near Gran where Berthe and several of the children had been born.

In 1873 the family traveled 300 miles to Rock County, Minn., in covered wagons. The trip took three weeks. There were no roads as such, only faint trails. They had to ford streams as there were no bridges. What later became the county seat of Rock County, Laverne, consisted of only one single-story multi-purpose log building. It was a lodging place, store and post office all in one. They homesteaded near Hardwick where their first houses were built of sod, with dirt floors and few windows. They later built log houses, but as this was prairie country, they had to travel a day's journey to timberland where they cut down trees, hewed logs and hauled them home. The winters were severe, with temperatures dropping sometimes to 40 below zero. Under blizzard conditions, cabins could be nearly buried under drifting snow. In winter men went to town on skis only when necessary to buy items that they could not raise or grow, such as coffee or sugar.

175

Anders Plomasen and Gro Thorson

Anders and Gro Plomasen had five children: Lise Giorne (born 1875, died 1906), Ole Theodore (born 1878, died 1945), Bertil Adolph (born 1881, died 1891), my father, Thor Garfield (born 1883, died 1978), and Amelia Georgine (born 1886, died 1970s).

The family photograph was made in Laverne, Minn, in 1888. My father is the little five-year-old boy in the middle foreground with his right arm on his father's chair. His father Anders died the next year in 1889. His mother Gro remarried and the siblings had a half-sister Bertina. After Anders died, the family had a difficult time making ends meet. They later moved to Laverne. They were so poor that they would gather straw from the fields after harvest and twist the straw into bundles to burn in the stove. Another source of heat was obtained when the children would go down to the railroad tracks and throw stones at the hoboes, who might throw pieces of coal back at them. They would pick up the coal to use in the cast-iron stove at home. My father Thor Garfield had only four years of schooling. When his mother Gro died in 1899 the surviving children were sent to live with relatives until they were considered old enough to look out for themselves (14 or 15 years old).

Of the five children, only three lived long enough to have their own children. These were Ole Theodore, Amelia Georgine and my father Thor Garfield. All three of them went west into South Dakota. Ole Theodore met and married a young lady named Grace. They later moved to Montana and on to Kelso, Washington where Ole operated a sheet metal shop. They had two boys and two girls. Most of their descendants currently live in Washington and California. Their story will be told at another time. Ole died in 1945 and Grace lived many years after her husband's death.

Amelia Georgine met and married in South Dakota a young railroad telegraph operator named Ira Seeger. They moved successively to North Dakota and Minnesota before settling in Sabula, Iowa where Ira operated the swing railroad bridge across the Mississippi River. They had five children. One particularly attractive daughter was chosen as "Corn Queen of Iowa" in the 1930s.

Thor Plomasen and Ragna Anetta Lund

My father, Thor Garfield, was born on the last day of 1883. His father carried him six miles on skis across meter-deep snowdrifts to be baptized in the little country Lutheran church. As a young teenager he followed the then popular admonition, "Go west, young man, go west" and traveled to South Dakota where he drove the chuck wagon for a cowboy outfit. The boss cowman, upon seeing a rattlesnake, used to pride himself on his ability to leap in the air and come down with his boot heel on the snake's head, killing it before it could bite him.

One of my father's favorite early recollections was of crossing the Missouri River at Pierre, S.D. in a primitive ferryboat and noticing a particularly dirty, unkempt and despicable-looking old woman among the passengers. A fellow passenger nudged him and said, "That old woman is the famous Calamity Jane."

Thor Garfield settled in Golden Valley County in western North Dakota where he worked in a barbershop, became Justice of the Peace, and bought a 640-acre farm a few miles from the Montana border. There he met and counted as his friends a number of men who had known Theodore Roosevelt and the Marquis DeMores, both of whom had come to live in and love the North Dakota Badlands some years earlier. He worked as an apprentice for the county engineer and studied highway engineering through correspondence courses. He helped survey the first real road through the Badlands from Dickinson, through Medora to Beach and the Montana line. Since road work could not be done effectively during the cold North Dakota winters, he and a friend spent several winters in Cuba where, for a time, they purchased and operated a sugar cane plantation.

I remember as a young boy an occasion in the early 1930s shortly after the lifting of the prohibition against consumption of alcoholic beverages, my father took me into the bar at the famous old two-story "Rough Riders Hotel" at Medora in the heart of the Badlands. After he had ordered a beer for himself and a Coca Cola for me, he introduced me to an old friend of his named "Six-Shooter Slim" who thrilled me with stories of the old time cowboys. He pointed out a number of holes in the ceiling of the bar that he claimed had been made by some drunk cowboys who had ridden their horses into the bar and discharged their revolvers vertically, causing some distress among the sleeping occupants in the hotel rooms on the second floor.

My father met my mother, Ragna Annetta Lund (whose father had emigrated from the Gudbrandsdal Valley and whose mother's family came from a small farm in Tingvoll on the

Thor and Ragna's wedding portraits

northwest coast of Norway) who had graduated from Valley City State Teachers College and was teaching school in Beach. They were married in 1918. They had two children: Bruce William (the author) born in 1922 and Jeanne Thora born in 1926. When the North Dakota State Highway Department was formed, Thor was appointed District Engineer. Then moving to the capital city, Bismarck, he became State Highway Maintenance Engineer and rose to become Highway Commissioner. He later became Chief Engineer for the WPA in North Dakota. He and my mother moved to Long Beach, California where he died in 1978 and she died in 1971.

I, Bruce William Plomasen, was born in Bismarck in 1922. I joined the Navy at age 19 and went on to graduate from the U.S. Naval Academy at Annapolis. My sister Jeanne Thora attended St. Olaf College and graduated from the University of California at Long Beach where she received her teaching degree. She taught school in California and Nevada for many years. She married Melvin Keith, a men's clothing store manager, in 1953. They had two children: David born in 1958 and Tamara who was born in 1961 and died in 1995. Melvin Keith died in 2001. My sister currently lives in Las Vegas, Nevada.

During my career as a naval officer I served in cruisers, destroyers, minesweepers and gunboats in World War II, and the Korean and Vietnam conflicts. While serving as commanding officer of a U.S. Navy ship, my ship was transferred to the Royal Hellenic (Greek) Navy. I met my future wife through the Greek Navy Commander who had replaced me as captain of my ship. She is Julia Anna Calpaca who was born and raised in Athens. Her father was a retired officer of the Greek Army Corps of Engineers. Her primary and secondary school education was at the Ecole Saint Joseph, a convent school operated by French Roman Catholic nuns of the Order of Saint Joseph where the language of instruction was entirely French. She graduated with the Deuxieme Baccalaureate degree in Philosophy awarded the by French government. She also had attended the University of Athens majoring in chemistry. We were married in Athens in 1950. We have three daughters, Marcia Anne born in 1954, Diana Marie born in 1955 in Athens while I was serving with the Joint U.S. Military Assistance Group to Greece, and Sylvia Ruth born in 1958.

I was at sea when two of our daughters were born, proving the old adage that "You have to be there for the laying of the keel, but you don't have to be there for the launching of the ship." All three daughters graduated from Salisbury University in Maryland. Marcia was married to Felix Irwin, a lawyer in 1989 and they have a daughter Julienne born in 1993. Sylvia married Scott DeLong, a mortgage banker, in 1988 and they have a daughter Madeleine born in 1994. Both Marcia and Sylvia with their husbands and children live in Bel Air, Maryland. Diana was married to Thomas Kollecas, a builder and development executive, in 1982 and they have a son Christopher who was born in 1984 and a daughter Lauren born in 1987. They live in Darnestown, Maryland, a suburb of Washington, D.C.

My wife and I moved from the Washington, D.C. suburbs to Ocean View, Delaware in the late 1990s and we hope to spend the rest of our lives here near one of the most pristine beaches on the Atlantic Coast.

Anders Plomasen

published February 2006   Form 487   *Jane Brosius*

My Hadeland ancestry is rooted in Gran where my great-grandfather, Anders Plomasen, was born June 10, 1848. His parents were Ole Gulbrandsen and Berthe Borgersdatter. Berthe had been born on the Plomasen farm near Granvollen. Anders was baptized in the Nikolai church in Gran. He came to the United States in 1868. His family settled in homestead country in Minnesota. There were three sons and two daughters from his first marriage to Gro Thorson whom he married in 1872. One son, Bertil, died at age 10. My grandfather, Ole Theodore Plomasen, was born in Luverne, the county seat of Rock County, March 31, 1879. His brother was Garfield; the daughters were Amelia, born 1886 and died in the 1970s; and Lise, born 1875, who died in 1906. There was a half-sister of Amelia, Bertina, when her mother remarried after Anders' death. The Plomasen name had been adopted at the time Anders married Gro Thorson and was taken from the farm the family had come from.

Since grandfather Ole died when I was only five I never got a chance to hear firsthand from him about his travels and their family voyage from Minnesota to eventually Kelso, Washington. I owe a debt to his sister Amelia (married name Seeger) for the booklet she put together in 1965. I also owe much to my father, Ted Plomasen, for his frequent telling of stories from North and South Dakota, Montana, and the eastern side of Washington state in Davenport, Washington. My father's cousin is Bruce Plomasen whose father was Garfield, the younger of the two remaining sons. Family resemblance in pictures is remarkable. This past summer of 2005 Bruce, his sister Jeanne and I, with other family members, went to Gran, Hadeland, for a visit and a tour of Norway. I pay tribute to the pioneers who left that lovely valley and came to the U.S. I know why Norwegians like Minnesota and Washington state -- they are very similar to Norway in many ways.

My grandfather (his name is variously spelled Plomasen and Plomason) was married to Sara Grace Richardson in Luverne in 1903. They may have met at a Grange meeting along that Minnesota-South Dakota border. Grace (as she was always called) was from Mitchell, South Dakota, and the Corn Palace was an important landmark in her life stories. I found some ruby glass goblets from Miller, S.D., among her belongings that

Ole T. Plomasen & Sara Grace Richardson
1903

were honeymoon souvenirs. The young folks joined other family members in the Parkston, S.D. area to homestead. The first child was Charles Garfield, born Oct. 7, 1904. My father, Theodore Anthony, was born June 12, 1906. Neoma Alice was born July 27, 1908 and Vivian Florence was born July 7, 1910.

Vivian was only a few months old when the family, along with Garfield and Ole Plomasen's sister Amelia (now Seeger) and her husband Ira and three small children migrated to North Dakota. My father, known forever as Ted, could recall the slow journey north in a covered wagon across the plains to North Dakota. The 11 members of two families, all seven children under 7 years of age, spent a winter in a sod house waiting for spring and crop time.

Ole Plomasen was a man of many skills and he ran restaurants and dairy farms and managed other farms. He ran restaurants in Minnesota and South Dakota; Miller, S.D. documents him as running the Owl

Vivian, Neoma, Ted and Charles in 1914

restaurant in 1901. His horse skills included making shoes and he worked many kinds of metals; his last business in Kelso, Wash. was making sheetmetal ducting and manufacturing metal things that householders needed. I know there were turkey skewers and cookie cutters in family kitchens that he had made. The family moved slowly westward. There was time spent in North Dakota in the Beach and Sentinel Butte area while Ole managed the Roosevelt ranch. My father recalled one-room schools and a dairy route that the horse wouldn't deviate from even on the way to church.

Ted Plomasen

My grandfather was a man who liked being part of organizations. He and his brother played baseball. In spite of meager education Ole and Garfield were talented builders; there's a picture of them both assisting with the construction of the St. Peter and Paul Church in Star, S.D. in 1908. He was very involved in the Eagles fraternity and also in farmers' groups. He could mend anything. One vivid recollection of my father's was having Ole tape his (Ted's) ear back on after it was clipped by a horse. The scar was visible until his death, but he had his whole ear. Ole could sew and cook as well. There were always huge vegetable gardens and fruit trees. He made wine and raised rabbits and chickens. Grace canned everything that would fit in a jar. She also crocheted, and made tablecloths, decorative pillow covers and many doiles for all occasions. I have a tablecloth which Amelia finished for me in 1961 after Grace died. There were no idle hands among that group.

There were many changes in the country and culture while the family moved West. Ted Plomasen recalled seeing automobiles for the first time and the barnstorming pilots after World War I came through Montana and left legends behind. The family traveled by "emigrant car" on the railroad to move from place to place. Ole and the boys rode with the cattle and goods, the girls and Grace in the passenger car.

The moves were necessitated by weather-caused crop failures. In 1917 the whole wheat crop was pouned into the ground in a horrible hair and thunder storm. Christmas goodies had already been ordered from the Sears-Roebuck catalog and were delivered, but paying for them was very difficult.

In the early 1920s the family found themselves in Davenport, Wash., the self-advertised "Wheat Capital of the World." There were jobs, high school friends and Ole managed the country poor farm. The red barn still stood in 1994 when my son (also a Ted) and I visited that spot. Charles graduated from Davenport High and went off to what was then The State College of Washington; today it is Washington State University and world-famous for scientific work in wheat. Charles graduated in engineering in 1930; his career would lead him to Rochester, N.Y. and Eastman Kodak. He also was part of the super secret work in Oak Ridge, Tenn. and Los Alamos, N.M. that created the atomic age. He and his wife, Helen May of Sequim, Wash., never had any children, but royally spoiled their nieces and nephews. Ted and his wife, Ethel, and children Jane and Jim visited Charles and Helen in Rochester in 1957, part of a six-week trek around the United States that touched in many places where cousins lived, from North Dakota to Pennsylvania.

My father Ted graduated from Kelso High School in 1927. He told me of construction work, driving Model T Fords across the state, looking for work which was very scarce as the farm economy crumbled. He began to attend Pacific University in Forest Grove, Ore. in the late 1920s. He lettered in several sports and believed he would go into teaching and coaching. Ted graduated from Pacific in 1933. It was there he met my mother, Ethel Bradford, whose family ancestry included some famous founding fathers of the United States. Her immediate background was in the logging camps of Oregon and California; her father was descended from Mayflower arrivals in Massachusetts. They were married in Portland in 1933 and settled in Longview, Wash. Ted worked for the Long Bell lumber company until 1945. Ethel was employed as a secretary, having taught school in Oregon in the early 1930s. The wartime industry drew him to Tacoma, Wash.; very abruptly the war ended and so did the lumber boom. He found a new job at Brown and Haley Candy Company where he would supervise the plant operations for the next 27 years. He also served on several community boards, most especially the YMCA where he was their top fundraiser for about 20 years.

Two children were born to Ted and Ethel: Jane Ellen, June 17, 1940, and James Theodore, November 10, 1943. Ethel returned to school teaching in 1956 while Ted continued at the candy factory. Jane graduated from Stadium High in 1958 and went to the other corner of the state to attend Washington State College, which became WSU in 1959. Her graduation in 1962 in political science led to a job in Washington DC at the Central Intelligence Agency. Her early months in DC were spent in the home of Bruce Plomasen (her dad's cousin) and his family.

Jim Plomasen graduated from Wilson High in Tacoma and attended various colleges and universities but never got a full degree. He has spent many years in both clothing retail and as a sales rep for ski companies and ski clothing manufacturers, and presently lives in Sun Valley, Idaho, where he can be guaranteed snow in winter. He has no children.

Jane married William Brosius in Washington DC in 1965. Their children are Caroline Cecelia, born Setp. 13, 1967 and Theodore Bradford, born Setp. 13, 1973. Caroline lives in Washington DC where she works for an engineering firm and on the side does adventure races and paddles different racing water craft from dragon boats to canoes and outriggers and kayaks. She attended Mills College in California and also Trinity College in Dublin, Ireland. Ted (at 6 feet tall he doesn't like Teddy) is a church youth director for a United Methodist Church in the Bremerton area in Washington State. He also graduated from Pacific University in 2000. Since a divorce in 1992, Jane has lived in Tacoma, Wash. Currently she is employed with the Social Security Administration as a telephone service representative. Jane (the author) has served her United Methodist Church in many capacities and sings in the choir.

Ole and Grace had two daughters. Neoma married Ruel Anderson in 1927 and moved to California. Their son is Conrad Ruel Anderson, born Dec. 4, 1928. He grew up in Santa Monica, joined the army when young and was mustered out early because of illness. Neoma worked many years for McDonald-Douglas aircraft, particularly in the interior decorating line of the plant. Conrad marriage Angela Bianco in 1950; they had three children: Connie Rae, born August 1952; Glen Ruel, born August 27, 1955; and Kenneth James, born May 26, 1962. Conrad and Angela were divorced. Today he lives in San Diego with his wife Beverly, Connie Rae married Dave Ballard in August 1972; they have four children: Aubrey, Josh, Daniel and Bethany. Presently they live in Scottsdale, Ariz. area. Glenn lives in Las Vegas and has a daughter. Ken, who has two children, Chad and Alexis, also lives in Las Vegas. We were able to be together for Conrad's marriage to Beverly in September 2002.

Vivian Plomasen married Helge Johnson Aug. 31, 1935. They adopted a daughter, Linda, in the 1950s, having no children of their own. At this writing I have no idea what has happened to her, as she separated herself from family many years ago. Vivian and Helge skied, he played bass fiddle in a dance band and also played violin and piano. They spent their adult lives in Kelso, Washington.

Ole Plomasen died on Thanksgiving Day, Nov. 22, 1945 after having prepared the turkey for dinner. My father, Ted, always created the turkey dressing/stuffing and passed along the recipe and mixing techniques to my son, Teddy. Grace died in March 1961 in Kelso. Ted Plomasen, my father, died Nov. 24, 1998 after a stroke and a struggle with Parkinson's disease. Charles Plomasen died in July 1986 from Parkinson's complications. He and Helen had retired to Sequim, Wash. Vivian died in February 1988 in Kelso, and Neoma in September 1982 at Santa Monica, California. I regret none of them ever got to Hadeland to see the wonderful valley that was their ancestral home.

I felt very much at home among the Norwegian hosts and hostesses and the landscape. The faces of those in Gran had a resemblance to my grandfather, my great-uncle Garfield, my father and his brother Charles. Many thanks to the Hadelanders for their gracious hospitality. Now they need to come visit this farthest corner of the continental U.S. to see its wonders and visit their Norwegian cousins.

Martin G. Peterson

Recollections of Pioneer Times, August 2003   *Form 160*   *Verlyn Anderson*

In the November, 2002, issue of the *Brua*, "Emigrant Searching" Family 9 inquired about Gudbrand Peterson Brynsaas. It stated that one of his sons, Martin, had settled in Fertile, Minn. I asked my good friend Robert Heckman, who lives in Fertile, Minn., if he could find out anything about him.

Indeed he did! Martin Peterson is buried in the cemetery of the Little Norway Lutheran Church, where Bob is a member. Inside the church is a beautiful miniature stave church which was built and donated by Martin G. Peterson.

We visited the church in rural Fertile in May, 2003, and took the following pictures. On the left is Peterson's cemetery stone, and on the right is the church in its attractive rural setting.

185

Bob Heckman also visited the archives of the *Fertile Journal* and found Martin's obituary in the December 18, 1924, issue of the newspaper:

Martin G. Peterson
Another Pioneer Laid to Rest

One by one the sturdy old pioneers who came into Minnesota's northern wilds to seek homes and transform the prairie sod and dense woodlands into productive fields are passing away. Monday, Martin G. Peterson, who died Dec. 9, 1924, as announced in last week's issue, was laid to rest.

Funeral services were held in Little Norway Church of which he had been one of the most active members; interment took place in the picturesque cemetery by that church. Business places closed their doors during the afternoon in honor of the departed and many from distant points were in attendance out of respect for one whose personal influence in life had extended beyond his immediate neighborhood.

Since his arrival here in 1882 when he settled on a homestead in Garden Township, the departed has been closely connected with the activities and development of this community; for he was an active and earnest worker in public affairs, held numerous offices, served on important committees, was a valuable asset in organizing and pushing to successful completion, various enterprises of civil and church matters.

The following is from *A History and Biography of Polk County* published in 1916:

Martin G. Peterson of Fertile, an eminent citizen and leading businessman of Polk County, has been widely identified with the history of northern Minnesota and is a member of a well-known pioneer family of Nicollet County. His parents were natives of Norway and crossed the ocean on the *Christina*, a sailing vessel, that was 13 weeks in making its destination and it was during this voyage on May 17, 1854, that Martin Peterson was born. A brother of his father was then living in Dane County, Wisconsin, and Gilbert Peterson set out with his family for that place. At Whitewater they reached the end of the railroad and the father continued his journey on foot and on arriving in Dane County, dispatched Knute Nelson, now U.S. Senator, with a wagon to convey his wife and four children. This wagon was of home manufacture, the wheels constructed from sections of logs and was drawn by an ox team. A most interesting account of the trip has recently been recorded by Peter Peterson, the eldest son, in his recollections of the early days. Peter Peterson and Knute Nelson became close companions and schoolmates in Wisconsin, a comradeship which was further strengthened during the troublesome times of the Civil War, and was continued throughout the various experiences of their busy careers. Peter G. Peterson was a member of Company H of the Fourth Minnesota Regiment and active service in important campaigns under Grant and Sherman. In 1856 the Peterson family moved from Wisconsin to Minnesota, making the trip in a lumber wagon with oxen, there being but one span of horses in the party which included seven families. They located in Nicollet County, where Gilbert Peterson took a preemption claim, four miles north of the village of Nicollet and here experienced the hardships and triumphs of pioneer life. Gilbert Peterson took an active part in public affairs and served in various offices. His death occurred on his 85th birthday, on the old homestead which has since been operated by Peter G. Peterson who, like his father, is widely known in the public activities of the county and served as township clerk for many years. Martin G. Peterson grew to manhood on the farm and received his early education in the country schools and later spent two years studying in a school in Illinois and in Luther College in Decorah, Iowa. His marriage to Ingeborg Brekkethus, who was born in Norway, occurred in his 25th year and for three years they made their home on the Peterson farm. In 1882 he came to Polk County and took land in the northeast quarter of section 17 of Garden Township, eight miles east of the present site of Fertile, being one of the early homesteaders to settle in that township. In 1892, failing health demanded the cessation of such arduous labor and he sought recuperation during the winter months in Norway, enjoying the mild climate of the west coast. He returned to his farm the following summer and again resumed his agreicultural pursuits until 1898 when he was summoned to public service by an appointment from the county commissioners to the office of county treasurer. Mr. Peterson had previously served as township clerk and chairman of the township board and his appointment received the hearty approval of his fellow citizens as was evidenced in the next two elections when he was returned to the office, serving for five years as county treasurer, and discharging the duties of the office in the notably capable and conscientious manner which has characterized the many services in public interest of his busy career. At the close of his second term, in January, 1903, he located in Fertile and entered the commercial circles as a member of the firm of Nesseth & Peterson, dealers in flour and feed and agricultural implements and engaged in that business for three years when he returned to his farm. In 1905 he again took up his residence in Fertile soon after which he became the secretary of the Farmers Mutual Insurance Company. Mr. Peterson retains his farm interests and has added 40 acres to his original quarter section in Garden Township and is further associated with the business activities of the community as a director in the Farmers State Bank of Fertile. He has ever been a leader in the political arena and has given particularly forceful support to the temperance cause. Mr. Peterson is a member of the United Lutheran Synod.

Brua Editor's Note: The United Lutheran Synod joined two other Norwegian-American Lutheran Synods to form the Norwegian Lutheran Church in America in 1917.

Johanne Olsen Husby

published November 2003 *Form 594* *submitted by Delores Cleveland*
Printed by the "Sioux Valley News," Canton SD in June 1951

Diamond Club Member
Started Life in "Fashionable" Prairie Home

Johanne Husby in 1881

Mrs. Johanne Olson Husby, a pioneer woman who observed her 88th birthday last Sunday, has recently completed writing a series of incidents that are a part of her life. She has been a resident of this community since 1888. For 10 years she lived in Canton and recently she located at the Bethesda Home near Beresford.

Here she is remembered as the wife of the late Even Husby and the sister of the late Rev. I.S. Olson. Most of the years she has lived in Lincoln County her home has been on a farm. In 1920 Mrs. Husby and her husband moved to Canton. Later Even suffered a stroke and died January 21, 1931. After his death Mrs. Husby moved back on the farm. Last March her daughter Emma and family moved to the home place which they purchased.

Although certain infirmities have beset her body, illness long ago deafened her ears and shut out much of the world about her. Mrs. Husby is still blessed with clear vision and therefore can enjoy books and magazines and Scripture. With her ready pen she quickly jots down thoughts that arise, at times in prose but more often in verse. She has written a number of editorials to Scandinavian papers. Her interests are wide – wide as the world about her – and to anyone who will sit down with her she will speak thoughts that have accumulated during long silences.

Johanne in 1951

Mrs. Husby is a maker of collars, laces, rugs and throws, with which she is busy a good portion of the time. From her own autobiography came much of the following information about her life which was compiled and submitted by Sidsel Thormodsgaard.

188

In Hadeland, Norway, June 1, 1863, Steffen and Anna Olson became the parents of a daughter, their 3rd child, christened Johanna.

When spring returned to the mountains and valleys the Olsons made their departure from the homeland and sailed to America. On the boat a brother was born and named Olaf, the name of the boat. No parson was on board the ship, so the captain baptized the baby.

The family traveled from the Atlantic to McGregor, Iowa, and only strange scenery and untried experiences passed in review until they reached the depot where an uncle met them to bring them to his home. On the way to his home the oxen became frightened, overturned the load, and mother and tiny brother were thrown far down beside the creek. The mother regained consciousness, but the baby died on August 23.

The Civil War was over and so on Independence Day celebration was to be held with great fervor. Not that this newly arrived family had opportunity to attend the festivities, but Johanne and her sister each received a dress that had belonged to two small girls, who had met with violent death upon the explosion of a cannon. They were daughters of Ole Grina.

The father sought work in the community and was kept quite busy. In the spring of 1869 the family departed for Dakota Territory via covered wagon and two yoke of oxen. On one wagon was nailed a box containing a few cackling hens. In the procession were also a few cows. For three weeks the wagon moved on from Clearmont to Gayville. Very often great streams had to be forded and the wagons almost floated on the waters. On the way they met other immigrants – once there were 14 wagons in the company.

Arriving at Gayville they were received into the A. Solem home where they all dwelt together in a little shanty. The preparation of meals was done out under the blue heavens where in rain or shine the old stove stood ready for service. Once a fearfully long serpent crept across their table, but the mother quickly seized a board and disposed of the reptile. Johanne was then only six years old but she was fearful at mealtime for a long time after this experience.

Their first home was a little sod house built by the father. He dug down a couple of feet and built up the walls with sod. It was a thrill then to have a place to call one's own. The winter was very severe with a snow storm raging for three full days. An opening had to be made from whence the family made their exit. When the snow began to melt the earthen floor was flooded and so the mother dug a trench just before the door. When the trench was filled, the water had to be carried out.

Prairie fires raged in dry seasons and grasshoppers were a burden, but valiantly they harvested a small supply of corn and by hand ground meal for making the bread and mush. There was plenty of butter because little of this could be sold as markets were too distant. Never did the family go to bed in hunger.

And the joys of Christmas! Then the mother would prepare a small dough of white meal, add raisins and from this make very small loaves about the size of two biscuits, and each child was given one of these. This *Jule Brod* was too precious to eat and often the children saved them until they were stale and hard.

Indians often prowled about the hut, but did no harm. They were satisfied to receive handouts of food.

Mrs. Husby tells of how these pioneers made their way to religious services. The wagon box was filled with hay and boards were laid across the box whereon sat the riders. Johanne had neither overshoes nor coat – only a shawl over her shoulders and cloths of wool to spread over their knees. The place of meeting was filled to capacity. Once there was such a throng that the stove pipes leading from the chimney were pushed down and soot went flying in all directions.

In 1881 winter raged long and desperately. West of their simple hut lay such piles of snow that it was impossible to see the sun for some time. Great tunnels had to be dug so that a passage to the stable could be made. This was followed by a flood. The water reached nearly to the hay loft, where all living things on the homestead found refuge. For two full weeks 12 humans, 2 calves, a sheep and 2 lambs were sheltered in the loft which was 16'x16'x3'. All other livestock perished.

Boats were used that spring to bring the families to safety. The boats were of such a size that six men were necessary at the oars. After some days when the water subsided the heads of the households rowed back to determine what could be done.

Disease and contagion stalked the countryside after this flood. The mother was constantly making her way from place to place seeking to alleviate pain and suffering.

Johanne grew to young womanhood and finery was then a dream. She made a grand purchase of a hat for 35 cents which served her well for many a season. A calico dress at 8 cents a yard was the pride of all her gowns. Once at Christmas time she indulged in a piece of silk ribbon at 10 cents.

December 10, 1885, Even Husby and Johanne Olson were married by the Rev. H. Carlson. After spending some time in her parental home, Even purchased a small horse and was then able to do more carpentry inasmuch as distance was not then such an item.

In 1888 they moved to their very own home and soon a structure 16'x16'x8' became their "home sweet home." The bride was proud to purchase a "stove with 4 covers." One evening after work was done, Even made a little table

Wedding Photo of Even and Johanne Husby

whereon their meals might be served. It was midnight before he finished the task. Then he woke his wife and invited her to arise and drink coffee with him by the table. But her eyes were too heavy and they closed again in sleep. But when morning came, breakfast was served thereon. That day Johanne was busy making a cloth for her new table.

She was also the proud possessor of an old lace curtain given her by a lady for whom she had worked. This curtain she cut into two pieces and hung one before each of her two windows. They brought a great wooden box with them and Even fitted this with shelves. This became their cupboard. One day a trim little mother of the prairie came to the door of the new home. It was Mrs. August Asper. When she beheld the glory within: the cupboard, the curtains, the table with the white cloth, she exclaimed, "Well, it's not so hard to be a pioneer when you can begin in such a fashion."

The Husby home has been visited with both light and shadows. Those who know them best praise them for their fine neighborliness and their cheerfulness which was contagious. Their daughter Anna left them in her prime and this was to them a grief. Long illness did not keep her from serving her fellow men. She sent good literature to camps and persons serving overseas in the first World War. Mrs. Husby still has with her Ida (Mrs. Alfred Wevik) of Alcester; Johnny, ex-soldier, of Beresford; Simon of Canton; Emma (Mrs. Andrew Ekanger) of Alcester; and William.

The Even and Johanne Husby Family c. 1914
Seated: Even and Johanne
Standing: William Ida (mother of Delores), Johan, Anna, Simon and Emma

Additional notes from Delores: Johanne died Oct. 17, 1952. Even and Johanne and her brother Peter are buried at Romsdal Cemetery in rural Hudson SD. Their daughter Anna and sons John and William are also buried in the family plot there.

Johanne's father Steffen died in January, 1909, and her mother Anne in September 1919. Steffen and Anne Olson and their son Rev. Ingebrigt Olson and his wife Anna are buried at Trondheim Lutheran Church Cemetery in rural Irene, SD. Johanne and Even Husby had six children: Ida (Mrs. Alfred Wevik), Anna, Johan, Simon, Emma (Mrs. Andrew Ekanger) and William. They had 12 grandchildren: Judith, Olive, Irving, Ernest, Delores and Delmar Wevik; Esther, Charles, Ernest and Bertha Ekanger; Clarion Dahl and Lois Husby. There are now 21 great-grandchildren, 25 great-great-grandchildren and four great-great-great-grandchildren.

191

RECOLLECTIONS OF PIONEER TIMES

More excerpts from memories written by Johanne Olson Husby. These were written in Norwegian and later translated into English. – *sent in by her granddaughter, Delores Cleveland*

Psalm 77:1 I cry aloud to God, aloud to God that He may hear me.

Even and Johanne Husby farm. Date unknown, but a Model T is parked near the house

I was born June 1, 1863 on Engereiet in Jevnaker, Hadeland. My father was Steffen Olson (Olsen in Norway), who was born on Toso in Jevnaker, Oct. 21, 1829. My mother was Anne Jonasdatter who was born July 15, 1830, on Breieneiet in the Norderhov parish in Buskerud County. The name of their *husmann's* place was Rådårud. My parents were married on April 6, 1857. My sister Dorothy (Dorothe in Norway) was born August 8, 1857, while our parents were still living on the Breieneiet farm. My brother Peter was born January 14, 1860. He died before I was born.

In the spring of 1866 we left for America – father, mother and we two little girls. (Editor's note: the records in Hadeland indicate that they got their Emigration Certificate from the Jevnaker parish pastor on April 14, 1866. Their sailboat, *Olaf*, left Oslo on April 22, 1866). My brother Olaf was born during the time we were crossing the Atlantic. He died just a few months later.

We arrived just after the Civil War. Two years later Peter was born on April 7, 1870. We lived in a sod house on Jacob Brorby's farm. Father worked wherever he could find work.

During the winter of 1871-1872 we had terrible snow storms. Both people and cattle froze to death. On April 9, 1874, my youngest brother Ingebrigt was born. He was a mission pastor

192

in the Hauge Synod and was known as Rev. I. S. Olson.

1875 was a bad year with Scarlet Fever and Diphtheria. My youngest sister, two brothers and I were all sick at the same time. I lost almost all of my hearing and oldest brother was sick the rest of his life. I didn't get much schooling because of my hearing.

In the late winter of 1881 we had an awful flood. Beyond the grove we saw large houses go by. One morning Mother saw a big structure floating, it was either a church or an elevator. My parents lost almost all their cattle. My father sat on the roof and saw his horses struggling for their lives, jumping as high as they could and when they couldn't jump any more, they sank and drowned. I remember father came in through the upstairs window and cried sorely. Then Mother said, "Do not cry for we are all here. Let us pray to God that He will hold his hand over us and ours." He then fell on his knees and the rest of us did too. Many prayers were prayed to God those days. At the end of two weeks so much of the water was gone that they came with large boats to take us out.

My brother Peter and I accompanied J. Andriasen's son; we took Peter out of bed, the rest of the family followed. When Pastor Andriasen came home we were already there, and stayed over night. The next day John Johnson came for us and we were there several days. Then my father and I left for home to see what we could do. Part of the way we went by boat and then we waded through the water. Oh, what a sight we saw when we got home – dead horses, cattle and pigs. The hens, sheep and calves that were upstairs were so weak they had to be carried out. The house, what a sight! We had taken in some sows with baby pigs and thought we could save them, but they were all dead. There was 5 to 8 inches of sand and mud on the floor. Father used a shovel to clean the floor and I threw water on the floor and swept it out. When we finally could see the floor, it looked like a plowed field. The walls were black as coal and we scraped and swept when the water receded. Father began to bury the dead animals.

I was 18 years old and had to go out and work to earn some money so I could help to buy horses and other things so we could get along. I wasn't so well after I had the scarlet fever, but had to get out to earn a living. Wages were poor and sometimes nothing. The first summer I worked in Canton. Sometimes I got a dollar and a half per week and sometimes nothing. Whatever I earned I sent home to my folks. I came home and stayed home all winter. It was almost impossible to find work during the winter. When spring came I went to Sioux City, Iowa with Rønnaug Ringstra. Later I went to Sergeant Bluff, Iowa and worked with Anton Bruvik. There I got $2.00 a week. Their son Ole was born while I was there. We were 12 people and I washed clothes and cooked meals for all of them. I often worked into the night. At harvest time I went home and helped harvest the grain and shocked the bundles. Then I went back to Sergeant Bluff. This time I took what work I could find. I washed and ironed, scrubbed floors, and cared for sick people. When spring came I found work at a hotel. That was a lot of hard work. The "Mrs." was a practical (mid-wife) nurse who took care of mothers and their babies. Often I was left alone to wash clothes on a scrub board and tub for 5 to 19 people.

That fall I worked for Ingebret Husby. Their son, Ingvold, was born September 10, 1883. They were good to me, as one of the family. I didn't spare myself, but struggled all I could. I went barefoot to spare on shoes and stockings.

On December 10, 1885 I was married to Even Husby in my parents' home by Rev. F. H. Carlson. For our wedding text he took Psalm 128. You can believe it has helped me greatly many times. He declared what is most important in this life and it has been like a secure symbol to me. In 1886 we lived in Sergeant Bluff, Iowa. In 1887 we lived with my folks. Even built a barn for my father. I helped in the home and did some sewing. We were given a small horse for carpentry work. In 1888 we moved to our farm, Norway Township, rural Hudson, S.D., Lincoln County.

The fall of 1891 Even became sick and was ill all winter. He lost a finger when he worked in the brick-yard in Sergeant Bluff. He became depressed and lost his beard – it came out from the roots. I was afraid I'd be left alone. Feb. 28, 1892 our daughter Anna was born. She was so weak, being born two months too soon, but gained strength and grew to be an adult.

We built a small shanty for cooking. In the spring of May 21, 1894 our son Johan (John) was born. He was a big healthy boy. In 1895 we bought out Erland Jacobson, NE 1/4 - 96-49. The next year we moved our house next to the Jacobson house. We plastered the whole house, upstairs and cellar. We had bought 1,000 bushels of corn for our hogs. We had over 100 head. When they had consumed most of the corn the hogs began dying – every single one from hog cholera. That was a terrible blow, we owed for the corn and fixing on the house and nothing to sell. Corn was 9 cents a bushel, if we could have had good luck with the hogs things would have gone well. We were young and healthy and began over again, but to no avail – for three years we lost our hogs.

June 12, 1897 our son Simon was born. In 1899 our daughter Emma was born on October 9. In 1900 we built a large barn, 40' x 56' x 16' high. Anders Hangeraas and Nils Erickson were the carpenters. John Melan was our hired man. Ida and Anna were going to Elmwood Country School and Emma was one year old.

My father Stephen Olson, passed away January, 1901. I received $200.00 from his estate. I purchased a sewing machine, a hat and a side board cupboard with my money. This antique piece of furniture was passed to Ida (Husby) Wevik and then to granddaughter Delores (Wevik) Cleveland. It has three large drawers on the bottom, a writing desk in the center section and the top has glass doors with four shelves. December 12, 1901 our son William was born. Johnny and Anna were sick with scarlet fever. Johnny was very sick for six weeks, we had the doctor many times for them.

The 23rd of June 1902 we had a terrible storm. A tornado wrecked everything in its path. Our new barn was thrown all over, pieces were found in our neighbors' fields. Horses and swine lay everywhere, some injured, others died. We had to kill the injured animals. Our living house was saved except most all the shingles were gone. We and our children were alright. "Praise be to the Lord," I said to Even. "I shouldn't have spent that $200.00 I got last year." He replied, "Those were items you needed, we'll get the barn and house fixed up again."

In the fall we built a small barn from pieces of salvaged lumber. We put a straw roof on it. The 8th of January, 1903 another wind storm came and the straw roof blew off. It surely was a tough time. We lost 10 head of horses and cattle, besides what we lost in the tornado a few months earlier.

Anders Ellingson Halbakken

published February 2004   *Form 590*   *submitted by David Halbakken*

Originally published in the Fergus Falls (MN) Daily Journal, March 10, 1934

Mari and Anders Halbakken family about 1892

Back, left to right: Syver, Anne (Ronningen), Fritjof "Fred," Emil "Martin," Maria (Christianson); Second Row: Edwin Adolph, Anders, Nils Theodore, Mari, Ottilde (Hovland), Johanne (Rude); Front Row: Anton "Melvin" on Anders' lap, Thea Nekoline, David Julius on Mari's lap; Sitting in front: Nora (Helsvig)   Not pictured: Iver and Nikolai

Andrew Halbakken Came Across in "Sailor's Coffin"
Trondhjem Pioneer Tells of Early Experiences and Privations

One of the few surviving pioneers of Trondhjem Township, Otter Tail County, Minn., is Andrew Halbakken, now residing in Pelican Rapids. His life in this part of Minnesota is another of those gripping tales of courageous pioneers who began with nothing and through privation and undaunted effort wrested from the wilds comfortable homes and valuable farms.

Mrs. Halbakken's (Mari Johansdatter Heier) death, May 19, 1930, recalled to Mr. Halbakken many memories of mingled joy and sorrow; hardships and suspenses which they had shared together during the nearly 63 years of married life. Some of them are recounted here.

196

Nine Weeks Crossing Ocean

Mr. and Mrs. Halbakken were married in Jevnaker, Norway, June 2, 1867. The following year they decided together with a group of townspeople to go to America. At this time they had one infant child but very few belongings.

Two sailing vessels lay at anchor in the harbor of Christiania (Oslo) ready to undertake the long and hazardous trip to America. The ship which the Halbakkens boarded was both old and unseaworthy and was known to sailors as a coffin.

The trip over the North Sea was perilous; one storm cracked the mast but on they went in spite of winds and weather; the captain was a determined man and an able seaman.

Halfway across they sighted the other ship which had left the Oslo docks some time after them. It soon overtgook and passed them amid the hurrahs and cheers of its passengers. The captain of the slower vessel asked his people to kep quiet, which they did.

Thus they kept on as best they could until they reached Newfoundland, where they went into dock for repairs. When they finally arrived in Quebec, nine weeks and four days after leaving Oslo, on the Fourth of July, 1868, water and food were at a low ebb. From here they proceeded in fright cars to Clermont, Iowa.

Worked for 50 Cents Per Day

The Iowa harvest was just beginning and both men and women found work in harvest fields, binding grain. Wages were 50 cents a day. Persistent rumors reached them about the wonderful Red River Valley in Minnesota. Mr. Halbakken became filled with a consuming ambition to secure free land and a home of his own in this favorably reported valley.

This ambition wa realized after two years in iowa. The man who had advanced the money for their passage agreed to wait with the remaining $150 if Halbakken wished to go on to Minnesota.

There were now two children in the family but they still had no wagon or oxen. However, he secured conveyance for his wife and children with a man by the name of Hans Molden whose party consisted of only three adults.

In the covered wagons were placed the early possessions of these two families except that there was not room for a keg of salt pork which the Halbakkens had to send by rail to St. Cloud. This key wa slater sent with Ole Tollerud, who together with a number of Otter Tail County newcomers was in St. Cloud buying supplies. The precious keg of salt pork was in dur time delivered to an acquaintance of Halbakken's living 3 miles from Mr. Tollerud's home in Norwegian Grove Township, where the Halbakkens were headed.

When Mr. Halbakken and the company arrived in Elizabeth they followed the trail up along the Pelican River cutting across to the northwest to the home of an acquaintance who had the keg of pork in his care.

Walked to Alexandria from Rothsay

All homestead land was taken. However, Mr. Molden was bound for the neighborhood of the present village of Rothsay, where his brother had settled the previous year and the Halbakkens decided to accompany them there. There vacant claims were still to be had and they were soon busy hunting section and quarter stakes in the tall, waving prairie grass.

Mr. Halbakken filed his claim on a quarter section (160 acres) which he had selected but at the land office he noticed another more desirable quarter which seemed, contrary to expectation, to be vacant. Upon his return he found to his surprise that this quarter was still unclaimed. He immediately trudged back to Alexandria afoot and changed his filings. On this trip he set out with only a few slices of bread and no money. He slept where night overtook him, spending one night in the open and another on some shavings where a building was being erected. But he got his choice quarter.

With the enthusiasm of youth he and his wife tackled the mighty job of transforming the wilderness into a pleasant home and a splendid farm. They had little or no equipment. Practically all their earthly goods except the clothes they wore and the keg of pork were contained in their one Norwegian chest. They could not live in the chest, so a sod cellar had to be dug. With a borrowed spade the work began. Meanwhile, shelter was found for Mrs. Halbakken and the children with a neighbor who had homesteaded the previous year. When this sod cellar was completed and a little of the prairie land had been put under the plow by their considerable exchange work, they felt at last this was their home sweet home.

Some sorely needed funds were eked out by cutting wheat with a cradle for neighbors, and working on railroad construction hear Dayton, a neighboring community.

Recalls Prairie Fire

The first fall a terrible prairie fire driven by a violent west wind bore down upon the settlement. The settlers fought desperately to save their belongings and homes and many a one lost eyebrows and whiskers in the close battle. Many hay stacks were burned. Mr. Halbakken was able to save his, but some timber intended for their home was destroyed. This had been hauled from the woods near the river and had cost hard exchange work. There was nothing to do but continue to live in the sod cellar. After three years, however, a small log house was erected. This was later succeedd by a larger structure of the same material. In due time that again gave way to a modern frame building.

During the first year in the sod cellar Mrs. Halbakken baked her bread in an iron kettle, as they did not have an oven. Then they had an opportunity to buy a secondhand stove on credit. When the time came for payment there was no money, and the seller insisted on his pay. Under the circumstances there was nothing to do but offer their pig, although it was intended for butchering. However, the pig solved the problem by successfully hiding. Later the man received his full pay.

Raised Large Wheat Crops

One of Mr. Halbakken's serious handicaps during the early years of his homesteading was the fact that he didn't have a team of horses and a wagon. His plowing and hauling had to be paid for by doing exchange work. Not for three years was his credit substantial enough for the purchase of a yoke of oxen and a wagon. From that time on his progress was rapid. As a wheat farmer he was very successful and remembers that one fall he shipped three carloads of wheat to Duluth. At that time he was farming a section of land.

The privations, perseverance, and achievements of Mr. Halbakken and his faithful wife are typical of the sturdy manhood and womanhood which paved the way for succeeding generations throughout this part of the northwest. However, it can surely be said of Mr. and Mrs. Halbakken that they began with as little as any, much less than many, and succeeded.

Mr. and Mrs. Halbakken were the parents of 15 children. As stated, Mrs. Halbakken passed away May 19, 1930, and of the large family only five children survive. They are David and Iver of Fergus Falls, Syver and Martin of Rothsay and Fred of Rhame ND.

Mr. Halbakken is in his 87th year and is still quite active. In spite of a strenuous life of many hardships and sorrows his disposition is still sunny and cheerful. He is patiently awaiting the call to move on to the Father's House Where There Are Many Mansions.

The Halbakkens in later life Photo may have been taken for their 50th Anniversary

Brua Editor's Note:

With the assistance of our Lag's genealogists in Hadeland, Ole Gamme and Gunnar Thon, I was able to determine from primary sources and our on-line Emigrant Database the following information: "Anders Ellingsen Halbakken was born December 6, 1846, the son of Elling Lagesen Svendsbraaten and Mari Larsdatter Ruud. On June 6, 1868, he married Mari Johansdatter Heier, born January 31, 1847, daughter of Johan Hansen Heier and Marte Olsdatter. On August 20, 1868 their daughter Johanne Mathia was born on the Skaarrud farm. On April 20, 1869, Anders, Mari and Johanne Mathia emigrated from Christiania (Oslo) on the sailboat *Johan*; they arrived in Quebec, Canada, on June 20, 1969." Then, as Andrew states in the interview, they traveled on to Clermont, Iowa, arriving there several weeks later, in time to find work in the harvest fields.

The Brothers Western of Lunner

published May 2004   *Forms 438,690*   *Laurel and Barry Peterson*

The John Peder Western Family about 1912 in the yard of their Clarksfield MN farm
Left to Right: Johnny, Julia, Melvin, Ingeborg Bergen Anderson Western, Alma, and Jon Peder Western.

The family that became known as Western goes back a long way in the Lunner, Hadeland area and some still live today on the Western farm between Lunner church and Grindvoll. It is just north of Grindvoll.

The family of Jon Pedersen and Anna Ericksdatter lived on the Western farm. Let's begin with Anna because she is the first Western of this pair. Anna was born 28 July 1793 to Erich Hansen Western and Anne Steffensdatter. She was the youngest of four boys and three girls in the family according to the 1801 census. That census shows Marthe, Hans, Stephen, Jacob, Lage and Rangdi in addition to Anna. Erich was an owner of the farm where two families lived. The other family was that of Thore Andersen and Anne Gulbrandsdatter.

Anna grew into adulthood at Western, or as it was called in the 1801 census, Weesteren. When she was 28, she married Jon Pederson Høyby (or Høiby). Jon was born nearby at Høyby 13 July 1794 to Peder Olsen and his second wife, Giertrud Jonsdatter (Svendsbratten). Jon

200

moved to Western after the marriage and he evidently farmed there until he retired.

It is here, at the Western farm in Hadeland, where their 8 sons were born:

- Peder Jonsen, 28 June 1821 - 15 July 1821
- Erick, 28 Aug. 1822 – 2 April 1890
- Peder, 29 Oct. 1824 – 20 Sept. 1904
- Lage, 16 Jan. 1827 – 3 June 1829
- Anders, 11 Jan. 1829 – 24 Oct. 1905
- Lage, 1 Jan. 1831 – 14 June 1918
- Johannes, 22 Dec. 1833 – 10 Dec. 1921, and
- Ole, 25 Aug. 1836 – 5 May 1914

One can see here that two sons, the first Peder and the first Lage, died as infants and we shall see that all the surviving sons except Johannes emigrated to America.

We shall examine the lives of the sons based upon when they emigrated from Norway to America and discuss the life of Johannes and his descendants. The first to emigrate were Anders and Lage in 1852. It appears that both eventually arrived in Moscow, Iowa County, WI and that Anders remained a resident of Wisconsin until he died. Anders served in the Civil War from 1864-65. He farmed in Dodge County and later lived in Stevens Point, WI 24 Oct. 1905. He married Anne Salvesdatter in Wisconsin 18 Nov. 1855. Anders was also known by the names Andrew Johnson, Anders Johnson, Andres Johnson and Anders J. Western in the USA.

Anders' brother Lage immigrated with him in 1852 to Moscow, WI. He evidently lived in the Moscow area for several years as he married Petronelle Estensdatter Aasen in nearby Franklin (now Highland), Iowa County 16 Aug. 1854 before moving to Fillmore County, MN not far from the town of Lanesboro in Amherst Township about 1855.

Sometime after immigrating, Lage dropped the farm name, Western, and was known as Lage Johnson (except on the 1870 census where he is called Lagger Johnson). Lage and Petronelle had 11 children: Gea, Amelia, Henry Oscar, Anna Maria, Josephine, Oline, Peter Louis, Tilda, Wilhelm Nicholai, Julia and Sophie Evaline. All of them used the last name of Johnson. We think the youngest child was Sophie who was born 11 March 1877. We don't know when the first four listed above were born. The 1870 census showed Lage owned 160 acres in Amherst Township that he probably homesteaded. Ninety acres were broken farmland, 55 were unimproved and 15 were wooded. The farm value was listed as $250, with machinery at $175 and livestock values at $700. Wages paid were $300. The census lists 4 horses, 4 milk cows, 4 other cattle, 3 sheep, 9 swine and he produced 1,159 bushels (bu.) of wheat, 300 bu. corn and 450 bu. oats.

The Elstad Lutheran Church records show Lage was one of the early pioneers and that he took a lead in setting the location of and constructing the present church.

201

That was the same year Peder Jonsen Western, wife Kari Hansdatter and their four children left her parents on the Askelsrud farm in Jevnaker parish for America. Their four children are John Pedersen Western (2 Feb. 1851 – 3 April 1920); Hans (15 Feb. 1854 -); Gubjør (7 Jan. 1857 -) and Anne (26 Aug. 1861 – 29 July 1947). John is Laurel Western's paternal great-grandfather (*farfars far*). Kari was born at the Kalasjø farm and her parents are Hans Jensen and Gubjør Pettersdatter, both born about 1803. We think Peder farmed for a short time in the Moscow, WI area before moving to Fillmore County, MN to continue farming.

Kari died sometime between 1866 and 1873. We are still searching for this information in Wisconsin and Minnesota, but there seems to be a lack of any records about her life or death in the USA. Peder married Ingeborg Andersdatter Berven, the widow of Anders Hansen Baalerud (Bollerud) 10 Feb. 1873 at the Elstad Lutheran Church and they had one child, Julia Allene (12 May 1875 – 19 Feb. 1942). She and her youngest brother Mons Anderson emigrated from the Berven farm in Gran parish on the west side of the Randsfjørd in 1861.

The youngest son of Jon Pedersen and Anna Eriksdatter, Ole Jonsen Western, emigrated in 1867. He had married Karin Cristoffersdatter in 1860 and they had four children in Norway. The first died early. The others were Anne Bolette, Ida and Caroline born in Norway and Henry Oschar, Anton and Johan, born in the USA. All of the children used the name Johnson. Ole used both Johnson and Western during his life in the USA. When the family arrived, it moved first to Lage and Petronelle's home and then to another farm in Fillmore County.

The last brother to arrive in America was Erick Johnsen Western, his wife, Berthe Christiansdatter Kinge (22 Sept. 1830 – 1900) and five daughters, Anne Maria, Karin, Johanne, Helene and Emma. Two sons and a daughter had died as children in Norway. Augusta Bolette was born in Fillmore County the year after they immigrated. They first settled in Fillmore County and were the last to move on, except for Peder who remained in Fillmore County until his death.

When Erick left Norway, that meant that the only brother remaining was Johannes. Because of the system providing for the eldest son to inherit the farm, Johannes then became eligible for the farm. But Johannes had married a girl from the Løken farm named Marthe Gulbrandsdatter and was operating that farm and teaching school. Erick's parents lived on the Western farm in 1865 according to the census and they died prior to the 1875 census, so we don't know where they lived in the interim. It appears that Erick sold Vestern (*gaard*) to operators of another Western farm, Johan Olsen and his wife Mari Hansdatter.

We think the original Western farm has gone down through that family (currently Halvor Western) and has now been reunited with the line of Jon Pedersen Western in that Halvor married Karin Løken, a great granddaughter of Johannes. Halvor and Karin were married in 1965.

Most of the Western (or Johnson) boys farmed in southeastern Minnesota. Only Anders stayed behind in Wisconsin and fought in the Civil War. The other brothers farmed in Fillmore Co. from 7 to 19 years before deciding to move west again. First Lage and Ole decided on places in the Starbuck, Pomme de Terre, and Ashby area of west central Minnesota.

Ole's new wife, Marthia Hofstad, along with his five surviving children, accompanied him in a covered wagon arriving in Pope County in October 1874. He was accompanied by Lage and his family and (because Lage was considered well off) two covered wagons. They settled here for only a short while. Ole and Lage explored Norwegian Grove in Otter Tail County and finally settled on places in Grant County. Ole obtained a 200-acre farm just north of the Pembina Trail in Pelican Lake Township probably in 1878. He lived in a home near a pond and just over a half mile west of Pelican Lake. Marthia died about 1879 and Ole moved into the home of first one daughter Mrs. Carl Ellingson and later with Mrs. Christ Peterson and worked as a carpenter. Ole is buried in the Ashby Cemetery. We understand he used the name Johnson until he moved to Pelican Lake Township and then changed his name to Western.

Lage, a very pregnant Petronelle, and the family moved with Ole's family, first going to Starbuck and a year later moving on to Pomme de Terre between Elbow Lake and Ashby. Lage, by this time 43 years old, may have given up farming and decided to try business. He built and operated a general store in Pomme de Terre and became its first postmaster in 1882. Soon afterward, there was a hotel, saloon and other small businesses. A gristmill predated Lage's store. Lage and Petronelle bought three lots in Portland, Traill County, ND and lived there for a while but moved back in 1885 where he remained in business until 1893. He again lived on a farm nearby and in 1896 he moved with Petronelle to their daughter's home. After Petronelle died in 1897, Lage remained in Aastad Township in nearby Otter Tail County, MN with his daughter, Mrs. Amund (Oleana) Johnson. The family typically used the Johnson name in the USA.

The next to move was the son of Peder Jonsen Western, John Pedersen Western. He left Fillmore County to homestead in Yellow Medicine County, MN in 1875 with his bride Ingeborg Berven Anderson (25 June 1856 – 9 March 1947). Ingeborg was the daughter of Peder Western's second wife and Anders Hansen Bollerud. We are not sure when they married, but they took their oldest two children, Charoline (Lena) and Alfred, with them on the covered wagon ride to the Clarkfield area where they homesteaded on 160 acres in Lisbon Township. John was granted a patent on the farm 10 June 1882 as John Pedersen. They had a total of 11 more children: Ida, Henry Gilbert (Laurel's grandfather), Albert, Hana, Olaf, Peter, Johnny, Johnny E., Melvin, Julia and Alma.

When looking through the old family Bible of Ingeborg's at the kitchen table at the farm home one day with Ingeborg's grandson Alton Isaacs, we found the notation *"Jane er født deb 4 Juni og døde den 19 de Juli 1889."* This really puzzled us for awhile as we knew of no Jane in the family. Finally, several cups of coffee later, we realized that Ingeborg was spelling one of her sons John as Jane (or Johnny / Yanny). This corresponds with the dates for the first Johnny Western in their family. There was a good laugh over our inability to recognize the name as it would sound when spoken by great-grandma Western.

Alton was born on the farm and lives there to this day. He tells the story of when his grandfather was out in the fields spreading manure one winter day and it got so windy and snowy that he couldn't see his way back to the farmyard. He then left finding home to the senses of the horses, dropped the reins until they stopped walking and he could tell they were behind the barn. Alton also tells of a time long ago when Mr. and Mrs. Western had gone to visit the Westerns up near Ashby. It must have been in 1910, as they all saw a bright light in the sky and thought the world might be coming to an end. They considered opening the pasture and farmyard gates to release the livestock. But, the incident was the passing of Halley's Comet and all was well.

Ingeborg Western at the spinning wheel with her grandson Lawrence Western and his oldest child, Ingeborg's great-granddaughter Laurel

Erick Western's son-in-law, John Haakensen (Hogenson) decided to explore eastern Dakota Territory and went to the area north of Valley City in the spring of 1880. It was a difficult trip but he found a spot slightly northeast of Mt. Franklin. He and a friend, Peter Mathison, built a log house in Section 16 of Romness Township, broke five acres and put up some hay before returning to Fillmore County for their families.

On 1 Sep 1880, John started back overland to Romness with a yoke of oxen hitched to a prairie schooner with his wife, Karin, daughter Hellene and son Edward. They traveled with the Peter Mathison family. The Sheyenne History indicates they drove 26 head of sheep and 16 head of cattle covering a distance of about 20 miles per day. While passing through St. Paul, the sheep crowded onto a streetcar track so that the horse-drawn streetcar stopped to allow them to pass. John took an active role on the frontier. He was Romness' first postmaster, the town clerk and one of the organizers of the Romness Methodist Church among other things.

Karin's father, Erick, decided to make the move to Romness in 1883. We are unsure if the remainder of the family moved to Romness that year or in 1884. Emma Ellingson (a granddaughter of Ole Western) in her book "The Life of Caroline Western Ellingson" tells a fascinating story of the trek west. Remember that Ole lived within a half mile of the old

Pembina Trail. Emma says, "On the hill to the south they could see the stage road. Here they saw covered wagons moving westward into Dakota or the Red River Valley. They would see large droves of cattle that settlers in these regions were driving eastward to market. Sometimes cattle grazing on the prairie ran to join the herds and it was sometimes difficult to get them home again. Frequently people passing on the road at dusk would come for water or maybe to buy food. One evening, a man knocked on the door (of Ole Western – Caroline's father) and asked to buy bread. When he came into the kitchen, he turned out to be Ole Johnson's brother Eric, who was moving to Dakota. They were camping for the night not half a mile away so there was much visiting back and forth as the families had not seen each other for several years. Eric had expected to look up his brothers in Pomme de Terre."

Once Erick, Berthe and their family made it to Romness, they found land about 1 mile north of Mt. Franklin. Three other daughters and husbands built near each other and the Sheyenne River. The *Griggs County History* details many firsts by this extended family. The *History* shows that they joined the Romness Lutheran Church in March 1883.

The Brothers Western lived full lives in their native Norway, on the high seas coming to the promised abundance of 'Amerika' and in the communities in which they lived. They have provided an important legacy for us.

John Pedersen Dybdahl

published August/November 2004   Form 407   Ann Urness Gesme

This is a story from "Look to the Rock ..... The Dybdahl/Anderson Episode," by Ann Urness Gesme, copyright 1991. John Pedersen Dybdahl is Ann's great-grandfather.

The surname Dybdahl (Dybdal, Djupedal) means deep valley and comes from the name of a *husmannsplass* on the Smedshammer farm in Brandbu, Hadeland, Norway. This is where John Pedersen lived immediately before emigrating from Norway. The farm is located in the northern part of Brandbu, and is situated on the east side of Lake Randsfjorden, a short distance southeast of the Eidsand farm, where John P. Dybdahl's first wife was born. Dybdal was abandoned many years ago, and does not exist as a farm in Norway today.

John Petersen Dybdahl emigrated from Norway with his first wife, Anne Andersdatter Eidsand, and two little boys, Peter and Andrew, in 1852. He was the first of my Norwegian great-grandparents to emigrate, and the only one who came from Hadeland. He came to the Koshkonong Settlement in the southeastern corner of Dane County, Wisconsin where he lived a short time. By the end of 1854 he had moved to Vermont Township in the same county, and there he purchased a farm a mile south of the village of Black Earth. Anna died 21 October 1861, and seven months later John married Thora Eriksdatter Eid. John and Thora Dybdahl are my great grandparents.

John and his second wife Thora Eriksdtr Eid with Albert, Caroline, and Edward (1873)

John became a leader in church and township affairs in Vermont Township, becoming Americanized as quickly as possible. Perhaps this explains why little or nothing of his experience as a youth in Hadeland was handed down orally in the family, and nothing was known about any family members remaining in Norway. However, I was fortunate to make contact with Hans Næs, genealogical authority from Gran in Hadeland, who provided me with valuable genealogical information. In addition to Hans Næs' information I used church and census records, as well as *Hadeland Bygdenes Historie, Volume IV, Oslo, 1953*, and other printed sources with information about this place and time in Norway. Mr. Næs explained that the family moved often, probably because they were looking for a better cotter's place to live, or had been evicted from the hut where they were living by the owner of the farm.

John Dybdahl's children
Back: Caroline, Christopher and Albert (the author's grandfather), all born in the US
Front: Andrew and Peter, born in Hadeland, and Edward, born in the US

John Peterson Dybdahl's Father

John Peterson Dybdahl's father was Peder Jørgensen, son of Jørgen Torsteinsen and Brithe Pedersdatter. His mother was Kari Olsdatter, daughter of Ole Larsen and Rangdi Olsdatter. All were from Hadeland in Oppland. Jørgen Torsteinsen, John P. Dybdahl's paternal grandfather, was born about 1750 in Hadeland. He was first married July 17, 1777 to Anne Olsdatter Lyseneie, with whom he had several children including: 1. Child (name omitted in record) born at Lyseneie and baptized April 4, 1779. 2. Ole, born at Lyseneie and baptized in February, 1781. 3. Tosten, born at Blekeneie and baptized June 6, 1784. 4. Marthe, born at Blekeneie, baptized in January, 1788; died at Egge age 6 months old, buried May 2, 1788. 5. Hans, baptized July 18, 1790. The family was living at Raasumeie when the mother, Anne, died. A burial service was held April 4, 1792.

Seven months after his first wife died Jørgen married a second time. He was 42 years old when he was married November 15, 1792, to Berte Pedersdatter Røiken (John Pedersen Dybdahl's paternal grandmother). Tosten Alm and Mons Svinning were witnesses to the marriage. Jørgen's children with his second wife were: 6. Peder, baptized June 30, 1793 from Raasumeie; died and was buried July 29, 1793. 7. Marthe, baptized October 12, 1794. 8. Peter, baptized December 26, 1797. His sponsors were Joen Pedersen Egge, Peder Olsen Alm, Lars Hansen Naes, Anne Nilsdatter Egge, and Kiersti Stephansdatter Alm. Peter was the father of

John Peterson Dybdahl.

At the time of the 1801 census, the family lived near the Brandbu church, at Øvre Nes. Nes was a relatively large place. There were 17 households with a total of 75 people living there at that time. In the main household lived the proprietor, in four households were the families of farmers, and the remaining 12 places were those of the *husmannsfolk* (cotters), one of which was occupied by Jørgen Torstensen, his wife, and 3 children. He was then 51 years old, his wife, Brithe, was 43 years old, and their children were Hans 11 (from his first marriage), Marthe 7, and Peder 4.

John Peterson Dybdahl's Mother

John Peterson Dybdahl's mother was Kari Olsdatter Alm, whose baptism is recorded December 8, 1793, in the records of the Gran parish. She was the youngest daughter of Ole Larsen and Rangdi Olsdatter Almseiet. Witnesses at her baptism were Torsten Olsen Hilden, Sven Eriksen Helmey, Niels Larsen Grynmyr, Johanne Hansdatter Alm, and Mallene Olsdatter Helmey. She was one of seven known children born to Ole Larsen and Rangdi Olsdatter, each born at a different farm in Hadeland. The children were: 1. Lars, born 1777 at Drøvdalseie, 2. Anne, born 1780 at Helgakerseie, 3. Ingeborg, born 1783 at Rekkeneie, 4. Kari, born 1787 at Hildeneie, 5. Ole, born 1791 at Helmeeie, 6. Lars, baptism not found, but said to be 7 years old in 1801, and 7. Kari, born 1793 at Almseie.

Kari's parents and her two youngest brothers were living at Hilden at the time of the 1801 census. The two oldest children were probably servants on farms in the area, and Kari had probably been placed in a home by the local poor relief organization, as it appears her parents were destitute. The census indicates that her father was 58 years old, blind, and a pauper; her mother was 50 years old and also a pauper. The poor relief system of the district provided a living for them at Hilden, and probably paid for Kari's care at another farm in the community.

While researching my ancestors in Sogn and other parts of Norway, I learned that many of my forefathers in Norway were *husmenn*, but none seemed to be quite as destitute as Kari's family. It seems as though impoverished families in eastern Norway had a more difficult time of it than those in western Norway and the inner valleys. The following quotation from an article by Arvid Sandaker, in *Norwegian-American Studies*, Volume 26, page 51, tells what Ivar Aasen, a poet from west Norway, said about this very situation in 1845: *"There are two agrarian classes, and these differ greatly. One class is the farm owners with their families, even though they may not possess much else. The farmer here is a real squire; he is no mere petty farmer, like those in Hallingdal, Telemark, or the Bergen area. He is a little lord or baron. His family resembles those of the rich merchants in the trading centers, his house is elegantly furnished, and the family's life style seems to be the same as that of the affluent burghers . . . The conditions of the cotters, to the contrary, is not very enviable. They are the ones who are to till the farmer's fields and be his servants. Consequently, they have to toil so much on the main farm that they can do little on their own plots. The cotter class is said to be very numerous in this area. We may probably assume that the landowners have established as many cotters as possible in order to have a permanent staff of laborers on their farms."*

Aasen did not explain why cotters were treated with so little consideration in the eastern part of Norway. Perhaps it had something to do with the more cosmopolitan influence from Sweden, for in some instances it seemed that the Swedes were not shy about showing their authority and superiority over the Norwegians. Might some of the land-owning upper-class farmers apply the same attitude in dealing with their cotters and the servants? Another influence in the attitude of class distinction in this part of Norway might have been their close proximity to Kristiania (Oslo). Perhaps city folks tended to be more aware of status than was common in the rural areas.

At the time John Dybdahl's parents, Peder and Kari, were born, Norwegians were not yet subjects of the king in Sweden, but were still subjects of the Danish king. Kari was 16 years old in 1810 when she was confirmed in the Lutheran church, and Peder was probably confirmed about 1813 at a similar age. Denmark and Norway were at war with Great Britain at that time (1807-1814). Peder was too young to be a soldier, so after his confirmation in the state church he probably went to work as a farm hand, and Kari most likely became a servant girl on one of the farms in the community.

Confirmation in the state church of Norway was required by law, and failure to comply was punished. In addition to the religious significance and the legal ramifications of confirmation, it was a sort of "coming of age ritual," placing high honor on the one confirmed. Following this milestone in their young lives, Peder and Kari became adult citizens, entirely responsible for their own welfare.

It was not a kind world that poor cotters' children faced when they went out to make their own way in Norway, and it was especially grim during the war years. In addition to problems directly related to the war, several years of crop failure created a shortage of food, which brought about famine and poverty. The war ended January 14, 1814, with the signing of the Treaty of Kiel. By the conditions of this treaty, the Danish king signed Norway over to Sweden. Needless to say, this idea did not meet with agreement in Norway, so some of the country's leaders gathered at Eidsvoll, a little place about 30 miles from Brandbu. Here Norway's Constitution was adopted on May 17, 1814. A Danish crown prince, Christen Frederik, was elected to be Norway's king, but the Swedes, under Karl Johan's leadership, objected. After a few skirmishes, the Norwegians decided it was best to negotiate with the Swedes, and on Friday, November 4, 1814, Norway became a constitutional monarchy under the rule of Sweden's king.

Although the war was over and the issue of political leadership resolved, our ancestors in Hadeland, as well as the rest of Norway, continued to experience great hardship. When Karl

209

XIV Johan became king of Sweden and Norway in 1818, conditions in Norway remained much as before. Under the new king, Norway experienced severe economic depression and bankruptcies were numerous, particularly in the eastern and southern part of the country where our Dybdahl ancestors were living. Bitter resentment toward the new government prevailed, and hard times continued. During these difficult years, while working as farm servants in Hadeland, Peder and Kari decided to get married.

It was customary to wait until a cotter's place became available before a couple married, but Peder and Kari did not wait, and were married before they had a place of their own. According to the church records of Gran in Hadeland, Peder Jørgensen Eggeeiet and Kari Olsdatter *nedre* Alm, were married in Brandbu, on Saturday, January 2, 1819. Witness to the marriage were Peder Halvorsen and Hans Olsen Gullerud. At least five children were born to them: 1. John Pedersen, born January 8, 1821 at Svinning, 2. Kari, born October 9, 1823 at Svinning, 3. Brithe, born September 24, 1826 at Svinning, 4. Martha, born July 12, 1829 at Raasum, and 5. Oline, born November 10, 1831 at Alm.

John Dybdahl's parents remained *husmenn* their entire lives. According to Volume IV, *Hadeland Bygdebok, husmenn* in Brandbu increased from 198 in 1825, to 260 in 1855; while the number of farmers decreased to 130. The last years they lived, John's parents were residents at the Raaum farm, which is located a short distance from the cotter's place where John was living when he emigrated. John's parents died four days apart. The church records show: Peder Jørgensen Braaumseiet, 66 years old, died on Monday, July 17, 1865. Four days later, on Thursday, July 21, 1865, his wife, Kari Olsdatter Braaumseiet, age 76, also died. They were buried at the cemetery by the Nes church in Brandbu, where the pastor conducted a *jordfesting* (interment) service for both of them on Sunday, August 6, 1865.

John Peterson Dybdahl

John Pedersen was born Jan. 8, 1821, at the Svinning farm in Brandbu, Hadeland, Norway, to Peder Jørgensen and Kari Olsdatter Svinningseiet. The ending *eiet* tells us that John's parents were not farm owners, but lived on a *husmandsplass* (cotter's place) at the Svinning farm. It is not known how many people were living at Svinning in 1821, but when the census was taken twenty years earlier, there were 45 people living there. In addition to the farmer and his family, there were 5 cotters' places in 1801. It is likely that there were even more cotters' places at Svinning by 1821.

John was only 6 days old when he was taken to the Nes church at Brandbu on Sunday, Jan. 14, 1821, to be baptized. It is interesting to note how soon after birth the child was taken to the church for baptism, considering it was winter and everyone had to walk to the unheated church with the newborn baby. In early times, it was the rule that a baby must be baptized by the time it was eight days old, but when the minister served several churches located several miles apart, he did not get to each church every Sunday, so the rule was modified. In spite of the modification, most Norwegians felt it was critical to have a baby baptized as soon after birth as was possible. Sometimes, when a baby died very young, it is noted in the church records that the baby died from "being brought too early to the church for baptism."

John spent his early years on farms along the east side of Randsfjord. His vaccination record was not located, but we know this had taken place, for without it he could not have been confirmed. Confirmation records of Oct. 15, 1837 show that 7 boys and 35 girls were confirmed in the Gran parish in Hadeland. At that time John was a resident at the Kjos farm, about 1 ½ miles north of the place where he was born. He was most likely a farmhand there.

One of the girls in the 1837 confirmation class was Anne Andersdatter, who became John Peterson Dybdahl's first wife. She was born Friday, Dec. 6, 1822, to Anders Isaksen and Anne Torstensdatter at the Eidsand farm. The following Sunday, when she was only 2 days old, Anne was taken to the Nes church in Brandbu for baptism. Eidsand is about 4 or 5 miles north of the church and about 3 miles north of the farm where John was born. Nov. 22, 1824, when Anne was almost 2 years old, she was vaccinated for small pox. She grew up in the same neighborhood as John Pedersen, and was confirmed with him on Oct. 15, 1837.

The archives in Hamar, Norway contain the marriage record of John Pedersen and Anne Andersdatter Eidsand. There it is stated: *"The bachelor John Pedersen, born at Svinningseiet, now at Nes, aged 25, son of Peder Jørgensen; and the girl Anne Andersdatter Eidsand, age 23, the daughter of Anders Isaksen; were married in the Gran Parish, January 2, 1848."* The baptism of their first child is recorded 2 ½ months after they were married. Their first child was a son, named Peder after his paternal grandfather. He was born March 14, 1848, and was baptized March 26 when he was 12 days old. He was the son of farm laborer, John Pedersen Eidsand, and his wife Anne Andersdatter.

It was not unusual for our ancestors in Norway to have babies within the first few months or weeks of marriage, and sometimes even before a marriage had taken place. In the early 19th century, engagements were often long, and having a child during this period was usually overlooked, as the engagement was nearly as binding as the marriage itself. Engagements were seldom broken, but when one was, it was considered almost as culpable as desertion by one of a married couple. It is said that some authorities believe that it was no accident that the bride was pregnant at her wedding, or had already had a baby. Inheritance laws made it desirable to have a child to inherit property, so if a man intended to marry, it was prudent of him to assure his intended wife's fertility, and first make certain she was capable of producing an heir.

For property owners it was of great importance to have an heir to inherit the farm and keep it in the family, as well as to provide security for the farmer and his wife when they got old. The oldest son usually took over the farm, but if there were no sons, a daughter and her husband could fill this role. The heir to the farm provided a home and pension for the parents.

The older couple did not retire but continued to contribute many valuable services to the farm work and household activity as long as they were able. Even landless cotters, as well as cotters with a little land, had some rights of inheritance as set down by the landowners.

John and Anne's status as *inderst* at Eidsand, indicates that they were probably living with Anne's parents until after their first child, Peter, was born. By the time their second child was born they were cotters or *husmansfolk* at the Smedshammer farm. Anders (Andrew) Johnsen was born August 1 and baptized August 17, 1851. He was named for his mother's father. At this time the family was living at the *husmansplass*, Dybdal, on the Smedshammer farm.

Smedshammer was not a large farm. In 1801, the census of Norway recorded 11 people living in two households at the Smedshammer farm. In one residence was the farm owner, his wife and five children; also a 73-year-old widow who was a pauper, supported by the community. In the other household was a *husmann* with land, his wife and one child. From these bits of information we can assume that it was still not a big farm 50 years later when John and Anne Dybdahl lived there. As *husmansfolk* (cotters) at Smedshammer, John Dybdahl and his family were provided with a little house, and maybe a small plot of ground where they might grow potatoes and/or other crops.

Such were conditions in the household of my great-grandfather, John Pedersen and his wife, when they began making preparations for emigrating. There is no record of the exact reason why they chose to leave their homeland, but contributing factors most certainly included the lack of economic opportunity in Norway. It was virtually impossible for a landless laborer or cotter to rise above his existing status in Hadeland in 1852. Once a cotter always a cotter. In the middle of the 1800s the population of Norway had increased greatly without significant industrial development taking place to employ the surplus labor supply. It became necessary for people to look outside the community to make a living. It was at this time that "America Fever" reached even the most isolated communities, providing an alternative for the struggling peasants.

The Norwegian church records contain a section headed *Utflyttning*, which means moving out. It was not until 1848 that people living in the Gran parish first went to America. The following year a few more people left the district, including several people from the Svinningseiet and Kjos farms in Brandbu. Emigration quickly caught on, and by 1852, when John and Anne emigrated, many of their acquaintances and/or relatives had gone to America and were already settled in the Norwegian immigrant communities of Wisconsin.

As was true of all emigrants, the John Dybdahl family began making preparations for emigration well in advance of their departure. Emigrant ship captains required each family to supply food and provisions, as well as bedding, for a 2- to 3-month journey. Prospective emigrants butchered sheep or hogs and salted or dried the meat. They made cheese, baked flatbrød and other relatively non-perishable food, which was packed in wooden containers to take with them on the ship. Trunks and chests were made in which to transport clothes, tools, and whatever equipment they thought would be needed in their new home. Before leaving their home district, they sold what could not be taken along, and with the money they got from the sale of these items, paid for their passage to America. Considering their economic status, John and Anne probably had few possessions that accompanied them to America.

In March and April of 1852, 112 people signed out of the Gran parish, 102 of whom showed America as their destination. On Wednesday, 14 April 1852, John Pedersen Dybdahl, his wife, Anne, and their two little boys, Peter 4 years and Andrew 8 months old, signed out. Also signing out the same day were Anne's two brothers and their wives. They were Anders Andersen Eidsand 26 years old and his wife Mari, 22; and Torsten Andersen Eidsand 30 years old with his wife Goro 20 years old. Although our Dybdahl ancestors left no record telling exactly how they traveled from Brandbu to Koshkonong, it is possible to describe the trip with a reasonable degree of accuracy, based on other emigrants' accounts.

After many months of preparation, the emigrants' food, bedding, and other possessions, including the baby's cradle, were packed in boxes, trunks, chests, barrels, and other sturdy containers. These were transported on the backs of packhorses and/or in two-wheeled carts, to a waiting boat on the shore of Randsfjord, probably not far from the Smedshammer and Eidsand farms. They traveled by boat to Jevnaker at the southern end of Randsfjord, where they loaded their possessions in a cart to carry them to Tyrifjorden, where they boarded another boat, traveling as far as possible in that manner. They probably walked the final distance to the harbor at Kristiania (Oslo), pulling carts heavily loaded with their belongings. Exactly how many days it took them to reach Kristiania is not known, but it most certainly took several days to travel the 50-plus miles. There were places along the way where travelers could spend the night, but one wonders if they had the funds to waste on such a luxury. In one way or another they found shelter and were able to rest along the way to the harbor in Kristiania.

The cost of the trip from Norway to New York was about $20 to $30 for adults, half that for children, and babies traveled free. They were required to report to the police department in Kristiania to secure their passports. It is assumed that they had arranged for their ocean passage in advance, and an emigrant ship was waiting for them when they arrived at the harbor. The sights and sounds of the busy port city presented a new experience for the emigrants, although a few of the men in the group might have visited the city when hauling lumber from Hadeland, or when attending the semi-annual market held there.

John, Anne, the little boys, Anne's brothers and their wives, as well as others from Brandbu, were to sail for America on the emigrant ship *Cobden*, which was probably waiting in the harbor. After their possessions were loaded in the hold of the ship, the passengers took with them their food and bedding to the area between decks. This was to be their home for more than two months.

In her book, *Norway To America*, Ingrid Semmingsen describes accommodations between decks on a typical sailing vessel. There were two rows of bunks on each side of the ship from front to back, each bunk accommodating up to five people. After filling the bunk with straw, they covered it with sheepskins and coverlets for sleeping. Their baggage and some food items hung from nails and pegs in the bunk. Food chests were used as tables at meal time, and for chairs at other times. Water was provided for the emigrants, most of it used for cooking.

Since the members of the Dybdahl emigrant group were all young, they were probably in good spirits and enthusiastic about what lay ahead. It would be interesting to know if this spirit was still intact on Wednesday, June 30, 1852, when they arrived in New York – or several weeks later when they reached the Koshkonong settlement in Dane County, Wisconsin.

Peder H. Nelson

"Peder H. Nelson" published November 2004/February 2011   *Harald Hvattum*
Originally published in the "Oppland Arbeiderblad" in 2004   *Form 691*

Peder H. Nelson, in a photo originally published in "The History of the Hadeland Lag 1921-1990." He is wearing the St. Olav Medal.

In 1914 a 14-year-old boy and his mother emigrated from Jaren. 72 years later he died as an old man in Northwood, North Dakota. The obituaries written about him referred to the great contribution he made for Hadeland by writing articles about Hadelanders in America. 2014 was the centennial anniversary of his immigration to America.

Peder H. Nelson was a Hadelander born on the Løvset farm in Jaren on May 21, 1900. Like many other emigrants, Peder H. Nelson had not planned to stay long in America. But the years passed and there was no return move to Norway. He had nevertheless strong roots in both countries and compensated his longing to go back to the old country by writing about *Hadelendinger* in America.

Nelson published Norwegian-American material in Norwegian-American publications in America. This started in 1926 with *Vikingbygden Hadeland* (The Viking Community Hadeland) in *Normanden* (The Norseman) which was published in Grand Forks and Fargo ND. He wrote for them until 1937. From 1929 he also produced articles for *Norden Literært Tidskrift* (The North Literary Magazine) and *Skandinaven* (Scandinavian) in Chicago.

The articles for Norwegian publication began in the spring of 1930 in the *Hadeland* newspaper with the article "A Hadeland Community in America," about Northwood, North Dakota. This continued by him sending articles to this newspaper until he was an old man. A bibliography in *Årbok for Hadeland* (Yearbook for Hadeland) 1975 shows a total of 55 articles.

In the beginning of the 1930s Nelson was asked to write an article about *Hadelendinger* in America for *Hadeland Bygdebok.*

At about the same time the Hadeland Lag of America became aware of this man who sat with "writer's itch" up in North Dakota. The Lag had, in 1921, begun publishing its own newsletter which they entitled the *Brua* (The Bridge). But there were other publications that wished to use Nelson's excellent knowledge of Hadeland emigrant history. In 1942 Jacob Moldstadkvern

215

began a publication he called *Gammalt frå Hadeland* (Old from Hadeland). This publication was randomly published until 1964. Nelson was represented in the first issue with the article *Nybeggerliv i det ville Vesten* (Pioneer Life in the Wild West), an article about Peter Gjerde from Lunner, and wrote for *Gammalt frå Hadeland* until its last issue. That was a special edition about Hadeland in America and in that edition there were many nice remarks about Nelson.

In 1968 the *Årbok for Hadeland* was started. Again, Nelson was a good person to turn to. A total of 30 articles written by Nelson were published in these yearbooks. His last article was published several years after Nelson's death. For the Norwegian-American self-taught writer, there were also publications outside Hadeland. In the 1930s Nelson wrote a little for the *Buskerud Blad* (newspaper) in Drammen; from the 1950s for a couple of decades he wrote articles for *Nordmanns Forbundets Tidsskrift* (The Norseman) in Oslo. His wife Clara was of Halling ancestry. This put Peter Nelson in contact with that part of Norway. He was editor of the Hallinglag membership publication *Hallingen* for 30 years. His only book, *Vien og Vidden (The Way and Open Country)* published at Geilo in 1976 is a more general emigrant history than Hadeland or Halling history. According to the *Foreword* in the same book, Nelson had many different occupations in America. The later years he worked for the town of Northwood, but it was not specified what he did.

Was he honored in his life? Yes he was. In 1957 he was presented the Norseman Federation's *Medal of Merit*. Later he was honored by the country of Norway with the King's St. Olav Medal of Honor. In 1980 he received an honor from his home community when the *Hadeland* paper presented him with the *Hadeland Prize*.

Peder H. Nelson returned to Hadeland twice. The first time was in 1974, the second time in 1976. The last time was scheduled so he was here when Gran Historical Society was organized. Nelson naturally was at the organizational meeting and thus was one of the founding members of the Gran Historical Society.

In the fall of 1986, the calendar was September 29 when Peder H. Nelson died. He is buried at the Northwood (ND) Cemetery.

Nelson was a great collector of Norwegian-American literature. This he willed to Harriet Foss, who like Nelson was enthusiastic member of the Hadeland Lag of America. She was uncertain what she should do with this large collection of books, but decided to send about 3,500 volumes to the Gran Historical Society. With good professional help from the Gran Library the collection was catalogued at the branch library in Vassenden where it was housed until it was moved to the Hadeland Folkemuseum.

The Peder H. Nelson Collection was opened to the public in March 1999. Harriet Foss was on a tour of Norway at that time and could personally present the collection to the Gran Historical Society. Erik Bye was also present at that time. Peder H. Nelson had especially been a good supporter of Mr. Bye when he, a few decades earlier, had made a series of television programs from Norwegian-America for the Norwegian National Television.

Peder H. Nelson: Northwood's Norwegian

The following article was written by Kathy Freise and published in the 'Fargo Forum' on Sunday, June 8, 1986:

One day after his 86th birthday, Peder H. Nelson has little to say. Words come less easily these days, and he no longer writes. "That's all in the past," Peder says, as though he left little behind — as though a lifetime of work could be shrugged away. But a brightness appears from within his eyes, and they shine.

In Norway, Nelson is one of the country's most honored authors on American-Norwegian immigration and culture. He received several national awards – including the St. Olav medal from H.M. King Olav V – for his work to promote and preserve the Norwegian cultural experience. The cabin where he was born in Norway has been converted into a museum in his honor.

In Northwood, N.D., Nelson spends quiet days at the city's nursing home. His tidy room gives clues to the heritage he's spent much of his life preserving. A calendar with a Norwegian verse hangs on the wall. Norway's flag, in postcard form, hangs upon a bulletin board. A book of Norse stories in their original language lies upon the bedside table.

Nelson's work has attracted acclaim from his home country but has gone largely unnoticed here in America. He only smiles at that, enjoying a personal secret. During the day, he worked as a laborer. Nights, he sat at a sturdy wooden desk with a typewriter, writings and words — which a friend calls " his love and his life."

Nelson sits in a wheelchair, two medals pinned to his suit. One is the St. Olav Medal, awarded in 1970 by the King of Norway and the Norwegian government. This medal is awarded to outstanding contributors of cultural exchange between Norway and other countries.

The other is a Medal of Merit from *Nordmanns Forbundet*, an international Norwegian cultural association.

On this bright, warm day, all Nelson says about the medals given for his style of heroism, is "Yah, I did some writing once in awhile."

The quiet, slight man came to Kloten, N.D., from Hadeland, Norway, with his family when he was 14. At family and neighborhood gatherings stories of pioneer immigrant life inspired Peter H. Already a poet, Nelson interviewed settlers and their descendants to set their memories into print.

In 1918, his first published story appeared in a Fargo-based Norwegian-language newspaper, *Normanden* (*The Norwegian*).

During the next 60 years, he wrote hundreds more for other Norwegian-American newspapers. Norwegian newspapers, yearbooks, and other publications linked to Norwegian

217

ancestry.

Much of Nelson's literary career appeared in *bygdelag* publications, for people who have roots in the same Norwegian districts. He edited two *bygdelag* magazines, the Hadeland *Brua* and the Hallingdal *Hallingen*.

Though he's never visited Hallingdal, Norway, Nelson assumed leadership of the *Hallingen* as a favor. He edited the magazine for three decades, from 1947 to 1977.

Starting in the 1930s and continuing through World War II, Nelson was a correspondent about emigrant farm history for a newspaper in Drammen, Norway.

His book, *Veien og Vidden* (*The Road and the Wide Open Country*) was published in Norway in 1970. It is sold out and has been translated into English.

He's made little money from his writing. Nelson says his profit was delight in helping preserve a culture "for the fun of it."

Along with his research, Nelson built a library which has been reported to be one of the largest private collections of Norwegian culture in this country.

Nelson says he has collected nearly 4,000 volumes. The library easily fills four walls floor to ceiling. Rows of hard-cover volumes encompass much of Norwegian history, including complete sets of Norwegian-American magazines.

Harriet Foss of Northwood keeps Nelson's library and has worked as his assistant. "His collections aren't worth as much without him," she says. "He knows the authors, if not personally, then through their writings."

Likewise, people have sought out Nelson through his writings. They have visited him in Northwood, this modest man who keeps a can of Copenhagen chewing tobacco ever close.

Nelson married Clara Johnson in 1929. Drought forced them to move from Wild Rose, N.D., to Northwood in the late 1930s. He farmed and worked 15 years as street commissioner for the village of Northwood. Clara died in 1973.

The following year – 60 years after he'd left – Nelson returned to Norway. During that visit, wearing a borrowed Norwegian costume, Nelson had a 30-minute audience with H.M. King Olav V.

He made a second, final trip to Norway in 1976. He revisited his birthplace and its surrounding   *bygd*. (A *bygd* is a community or small rural district.) His written goodbye is a testament to the country that his soul never left.

"The sun sinks now in the west, but lights up the forest high up on Raanaasen in the east. It was as if the sunbeams embraced me in the fall evening's splendor, and gentle rays greeted me from the windows up on the hillsides . . . If only I in the last evening of my life could lie here and look out on the beautiful *bygd* where I was born. . . . I know that I begin to become old now, and that this is the last time I should see my dear old Hadeland with its old memories. Farewell, you dear old *bygd*."

Brua Editor's Note: Less than four months later, Peder H. Nelson died on September 29, 1986.

In 2001, the Hadeland Lag arranged a tour for a large group from Hadeland. One of the important stops they made was in Northwood, North Dakota. This photo shows them gathered in Northwood Cemetery.

The visitors placed a wreath on Peder Nelson's grave.

Photos provided by Harald Hvattum

Lars Halvorson Grinaker

published February/May 2005   *Forms 54, 704*   *Larry Grinaker*

   The death of my father, Floyd Grinaker, prompted me to compile a history of the Grinaker family. While much of the information about our early descendants is sketchy, I am able to provide a significant amount of first-hand information about my father, and to a lesser degree my grandfather, Albert Grinaker. Leslie Rogne of rural Kindred, N.D., provided most of the history of my great-grandfather, Lars Grinaker, and my great-great-grandfather, Halvor Lageson. He worked countless hours in providing extensive genealogical information of his family and ours and I am grateful for his contribution.

   It is important for my children and their descendants to know the history of their ancestors. These memories fade all too easily, and by recording them they will be preserved for generations to come. It is my sincere desire that my descendants continue this task.   *Larry Grinaker*

History written in 1989, revised in 2004

Lars and Martha Grinaker and their children, circa 1900
Lars and Martha are seated in front with their two youngest daughters, Lillian (Severson) and Ann (Johnsen) Standing are Sophus, Albert (the author's grandfather), Hilda and Henry.

Early Ancestors

The earliest records of our ancestors, which Mr. Rogne was able to obtain, date back to the 1700s in Norway. In those days people were named from their parents' names and also from the area in which they lived. This added some confusion since a brother and sister could have different names if one moved to a different area. The name "Grinaker" was derived from a farm to which Lars Halvorson moved at an early age. He took the name Lars "Grinaker" since he lived and worked on a farm by that name. Lars' father's name was Halvor Lageson. His parents were Lage Halvorson Lovlien and Valborg Jensdatter. The records indicate that Lage Halvorson was born in 1777 to Halvor Lageson Olim (born in 1745) and Else Ingebretsdatter Biertnas (born in 1750). Records also indicate that they were married July 15, 1772.

In describing the area of Norway from which our descendants came, I will quote a section of Mr. Rogne's account: "Hadeland, Norway, is a part of the county of Oppland, about 30 miles northwest of Oslo. In the county of Oppland are North Gudbrandsdal, South Gudbrandsdal, Valdres, Land, Toten and Hadeland. The southernmost part of Oppland, Hadeland, contains the municipalities of Gran, Jevnaker and Lunner. Early records from the 1700s and the census of 1801 indicate that Jevnaker was the name of an area now divided into Jevnaker and Lunner. The Ericksons (Grandma Mollie's family) came from the area now called Lunner. The Grinakers came from farms in Gran."

The name "Lovlien" may be an early spelling for the *gaard* (farm) "Lauvlia" which appears on modern maps northeast of the town of Brandbu. Gran, Hadeland, was the area where the church records of the first ancestors were found – those of Lage Halvorson and Valborg Jensdatter Lovlien. Lage Halvorson (Lovlien) died in 1851 at the age of 74 and Halvor Lageson Lovlien was born in 1810. Our family history continues with him.

Halvor Lageson

Halvor Lageson was born in the area called Lovlien of Gran, Hadeland, Norway, in 1810 to Lage Halvorson Lovlien and Valborg Jensdatter Biertness. There were six sons and at least one daughter in this family. In 1847 he married Siri Stephansdatter Haug. She was the daughter of Stephan Larsen Aschiem. Three children were born to Halvor and Siri. Since they moved to the *gaard* (farm) Olerud, all their children were baptized with that name. Stephan Halvorson was born in 1849, Valborg Halvorsdatter in 1851 and Lars Halvorson in 1853. In 1856 Halvor Lageson died at the age of 46. Siri, with her three small children, then moved to a farm called Grinagereiet. The letters "eiet" mean they rented a *husmannsplass* (a little house with a small acreage) on Grinager. In 1866 Siri died so the children were orphaned. Stephan was 17, Valborg 16, and Lars 13. Stephan was old enough to find work and since he took the name Vamstad when he moved to America, he had probably worked on a farm by that name. In the 1865 census of Hadeland, Valborg was listed as a servant on Grinager. Stephan immigrated to

America in 1885 with a son, Julius, and a daughter. Lars immigrated to America in 1879 going directly to Fargo in Dakota Territory. (North Dakota achieved statehood in 1889). We continue our history with Lars.

Lars Halvorson Grinaker

Lars Halvorson Grinaker was born in 1853 to Halvor Lageson and Siri Stephansdatter Haug on the *gaard* (farm) Olerud. He had a brother, Stephan, and a sister, Valborg. Church records in Norway indicate the children were baptized under the last name of "Olerud" since they were living on that farm as small children. However, when their father died they moved to the *gaard* (farm) Grinager with their mother, Siri. Apparently Lars and his siblings took the name Grinager at that time. Emigration records from Gran, Hadeland in Norway, indicate that when Lars immigrated to America in 1879, he spelled his name "Grinaker" as it is to this day. (It is not known why the spelling of his last name was changed. It simply could have been a spelling error on the emigration record that Lars decided to accept upon departing for America.) Records also indicate that he had $20 in his pocket and his destination was listed as "Fargo, Dakota Territory."

By 1882 a new life lay ahead for Lars since two important events took place that year. He married Martha Eriksdatter Wien at Sheyenne Lutheran Church (currently named Norman Lutheran church) located a few miles northeast of Kindred, N.D. She was 17 years old and Lars was 28. Also, in 1886 he filed for a tract of land noted as NW 6-136-49 which is the northwest quarter of Section 6, range 49 of Walcott Township in what would eventually be located in Richland County of North Dakota. This quarter section remains today in the ownership of Larry Grinaker and the Elaine Elker Trust.

According to a mortgage deed dated June 10, 1890, Lars and Martha also purchased a quarter section of land for $1,360 from a Mrs. Chambers of West Oakland, Calif. The location of this land is described as "the northeast quarter of section number one in township number one hundred and thirty-six (136) north of range number fifty (50) west of the fifth principle meridian containing one-hundred and sixty acres more or less according to the U.S. Government Survey." Carroll Johnson, a grandson of Lars Grinaker, currently owns this land.

Lars Grinaker became a citizen of the United States on Jan. 22, 1885, more than four years before North Dakota achieved statehood. The original certificate of citizenship is still in my possession as well as the envelope in which it was mailed which, incidentally, cost two cents to mail!

It appears that Lars farmed two quarters of land (320 acres) after 1890 which probably was a fairly large farm (not to be compared to the bonanza farms in the Casselton and Amenia areas of North Dakota) for one person. The major crops were small grains such as wheat, barley and

222

oats. Wheat was a profitable cash crop and yields of 40-50 bushels per acre were not uncommon. Teams of horses provided much of the farm labor during this time.

Lars and Martha had six children; Hilda (she eventually married Pete Erickson, Molly Erickson's brother), Albert, Henry, Sophus, Anna (Johnson) and Lillian (Severson). We continue the family history with Albert Grinaker, my grandfather.

Albert Lars Grinaker

Albert Grinaker was born on April 12, 1884 to Lars and Martha Grinaker. He had two brothers, Henry and Sophus, and three sisters, Hilda, Lillian and Anna. Albert worked on the farm with his father during his childhood and when he was 19, Lars rented "his whole farm" to Albert. An agreement written up by Albert dated April 14, 1903 explains that Albert would rent the land for a term of five years. The profits would be divided equally. The contract continued on: "A.L. Grinaker is to have all the hay and millet except what L.H. Grinaker needs for his use. That L.H. Grinaker is to have free use of team (of horses) to haul his grain to town or to the elevator. That L.H. Grinaker is only to pay for his own thresher bill and that A.L. Grinaker is to pay all other expenses. That A.L. Grinaker is to have free use of all the household goods."

It is interesting to note that Lars rented the farm to Albert and not to any of the other sons. It is also interesting that Lars rented out the farm at a relatively young age of 50 years. In past conversations with my father it seems that Albert was a rather industrious person and "tended to business." He apparently knew the value of a dollar and applied this to his farm operation. Thus Lars may have favored Albert and decided to rent the farm to him. (This is all speculation, of course!)

On April 25, 1905, Albert married Molly Erickson. They had three children: Floyd, Delia and Lois. Floyd was my father, Delia married Selmer Jordheim in 1940 and Lois never married. Lois moved to Minneapolis in the 1930s and worked for the Boos Dental Lab until her retirement in 1974. In 1975 she moved to Moorhead, MN and resided there until her death in April of 1988.

Albert and Molly Grinaker - wedding photo

Early recollections of my grandparents, Albert and Molly, begin with their moving to Kindred from Walcott around 1952. When my parents were

223

married in 1940, they lived with Albert and Molly on the farm. Since those were not the best living arrangements, my grandparents moved to Walcott perhaps in 1942 and then to Kindred about 10 years later. They moved their house to a lot on Main Street in Kindred which was later purchased by Tollef Lee, after Albert's death in 1961.

Delia, Floyd and Lois Grinaker

One of the most vivid memories of Albert and Molly was Christmas Eve at their home in Kindred during the 1950s. Our family, along with the Jordheims (Selmer, Delia, Sharon, Gary and Neil) and Auntie Lois, would gather for our traditional Christmas meal: lutefisk (boiled cod fish cured in lye), lefse, oyster stew, meatballs and mashed potatoes. Molly was an excellent cook and it was one meal which we all awaited with limited patience. Afterwards we would open presents as any other American family.

Albert worked with Dad on the farm and helped out quite a lot during the 1950s. As I remember, his specialty was cultivating soybeans. He would spend hours on our 1939 Moline tractor with its two-row cultivator. Years later when he was unable to work on the farm, the job of cultivating was passed on to me. I must say my heart was simply not in it as it was such mundane work.

Grandpa loved to tease. During the summer of 1954 when I was six years old, Dad and Grandpa built a grainery. While I was "helping" them one day, Grandpa took the end of my belt strap and nailed it to one of the studs. I remember becoming quite anxious since I didn't know how to get myself free. To this day, I could walk into that grainery and locate that very nail hole made by Grandpa's hammer.

I always looked forward to Grandpa Albert driving out to the farm from his home in Kindred because without fail, he had a candy bar in the glove compartment of his 1951 Ford Coupe. Another memory was his incessant teasing about "Miranda," a fictional girlfriend he conjured up in his mind. "So how's Miranda?" he would say, much to my dislike. During his last months he would repeat the same phrase several times an hour since he was suffering from Alzheimer's disease, an illness that eventually claimed his life in January 1961.

Grandma Molly was everything one would visualize in a grandmother. She was very loving and caring and also very sociable. She took her own life after suffering for several months from a mental condition over which she had no control. I will always remember her big smile and hearty laugh.

Albert and Molly were very religious and attended church regularly at Norman Parish northeast of Kindred. Albert, in fact, had seriously considered becoming a pastor. He was well respected in his church and community and much loved by his family. In addition to becoming a good farmer and prudent in his financial affairs, he was also an excellent carpenter – a skill perhaps possessed by many in those days. He was a heavy smoker, consuming two or more packs of "Old Gold" cigarettes daily. My most vivid memory of him is sitting in his rocking chair, smoking an Old Gold cigarette and asking me, "So how's Miranda" which was followed by his hoarse laugh. I will never forget him.

FLOYD GRINAKER

Floyd Grinaker, my father, was born on March 18, 1906 to Albert and Molly Grinaker and was the oldest of three children. His sisters were Delia (Jordheim) and Lois, who never married. His childhood was perhaps typical for young boys growing up in a rural environment. Farm work would become a familiar activity, even at an early age since he was the only male in the family. As he grew into his teen years, farm work would become a top priority as far as his dad was concerned and he missed a great deal of school. Since farm work began early in the spring and extended late into the fall, school attendance for Dad was limited to only the winter months. During these months, he lived in Kindred with his grandparents, Lars and Martha, and attended school there. Previously he had attended school at the "consolidated" which was located a few miles southeast of the farmstead. By the time he started his ninth year of school (high school), he realized he was so far behind his peers in schooling that he knew he would not be able to catch up. He became frustrated and one day, upon returning home from school,

he told his dad he was not going back. He held true to his word and never set foot inside a school again. Despite his realization that working long hours on the farm for most of the year was a matter of survival, he became bitter about having to make this sacrifice while his sisters completed high school and went on to college. This scenario was no doubt played out in many rural families during this period, particularly when there was only one male child in the family.

Floyd and Anne Grinaker (c. 1985)

Dad remained and worked on the farm and met Anne Ehlers, a schoolteacher in Viking Township of Richland County. His sister Delia was also a schoolteacher, who taught in another school in the same township. During the Christmas season the two schools performed their Christmas program together and Delia was instrumental in introducing Anne to her brother, Floyd. Apparently the magic worked and the two eventually became engaged and were married on Oct. 4, 1940. During the first years of their marriage, they lived with Dad's parents on the farm. Eventually Albert and Molly moved to a house in Walcott and Mom and Dad remained on the farm. Elaine was born on August 19, 1945, and I was born July 21, 1948. In 1949 they built a new house which remains today on the farmstead.

225

My memories of Dad are fond ones. He worked hard and was a good father and husband. We never had a lot of money but our basic needs were always met. He was very prudent in his business affairs. In fact, all his farm machinery was usually old and worn out but the farm work always got done.

Dad farmed until 1973 and then cash-rented the land to Martell Erickson of Kindred. Mom had taught school in Center and Viking Townships during the 1930s before she married Dad. She resumed her teaching career at Hickson from 1958-1960 where she taught junior high, and then taught in the Kindred Public School at the second grade and junior high levels from 1960 until her retirement in 1972. She was an excellent teacher admired by both her peers and students.

Mom and Dad enjoyed many years of retirement together. In April of 1987 Mom and Dad sold the farmstead to Greg and Bonnie Plath of Kindred, and they moved to a new home at 2602 Southgate Drive in Fargo. Since they were advancing in age they felt it was time to move off the farm and move into Fargo. Surprisingly, the transition from the farm to the city was an easy one and they enjoyed city life immensely. Dad was suffering from chronic chest pain and as the years passed his pains became increasingly more intense. In spite of his discomfort, he remained quite mobile and clear-minded up to his final day. The day before he died he and Mom made lefse! Then during the early morning hours of Nov. 19, 1988, he suffered a heart attack and passed away. He was 82 years old. Mom passed away in 2007 at the age of 95.

Dad was a kind and gentle man who deeply loved and cared for his family and friends. He was honest, sincere, warm-hearted and always friendly to everyone he met. He especially liked children and they had an affinity for him as well. He never had an enemy. As a child and on into my early adulthood, we worked many hours side-by-side on the farm and, in spite of all the hard work, we enjoyed working together. At times, I didn't demonstrate the kind of enthusiasm for farm work that he expected and he would show his displeasure with me; but for the most part, we had a great relationship.

The Larry Grinaker family, 2013
Front: grandchildren Sarah & Christopher Nichols
Left to right: Kathy & Larry Grinaker, daughter Peggy and husband Justin Kitsch, daughter Jackie and husband Josh Nichols, and son Ryan Grinaker

226

Hans Andreas Hansen Blegen

published August 2005   *Form 777*   *Lynne Hogan*

Hans and Anna Marie Blegen Family -1908
Back Row: John, Ellen, Peter and Olaf
Front row: Hans, Hannah, Nora, Joseph and Anna Marie

Hans Andreas Hansen Blegen

Born: Dec 2, 1859, Nes, Hadeland, Norway
Married: Anna Marie Nesset, May 29, 1891, Decorah, Iowa
Died: March 14, 1941, Leeds, North Dakota
Buried: Leeds Lutheran Church Cemetery, Leeds, N.D.

Hans Andreas Hansen Blegen was born on Dec. 2, 1859 at Nes, Hadeland, Norway to Hans Pedersen Blegeneiet and his wife Anne Oldsdatter Grinna. After attending the district school and being confirmed by Provost S. B. Bugge, he attended the Gran secondary school during the years 1875 and 1876.

Hans and his older brother Peder took passage on the Anchor Line at Oslo via Hull and Glasgow. At Glasgow they boarded the steamer *Bolivia* and arrived in New York in July of 1876. From New York they traveled by train to Lansing, Iowa; and then traveled by foot to an uncle's farm at Washington Prairie, Iowa.

Hans then attended Professor Breckenridge's Decorah Institute, where he received the necessary education for teaching school, which he followed for several years. From 1882 to 1886, he attended Luther College at Decorah, Iowa, where he received the Bachelor of Arts degree. In 1886, he came to Wahpeton, Dakota Territory, where he was engaged in teaching school. Later he attended the Luther Theological Seminary, which at that time was on the move, one year at Madison, Wis.; one year at Minneapolis, Minn.; and one year at Robbinsdale, Minn. He graduated at Robbinsdale, Minn., in June 1890 receiving a Candidate of Theology degree.

In the summer of 1890, Hans came to Mayville, North Dakota, and on September 1890 he was ordained a minister. He received a call as a pastor for the Lake Ibsen congregation and for five other congregations: Viking, North Viking, St. Olaf (these three in Benson County) Big Coulee, and Norway congregations (these two in Ramsey County). Besides being a pastor for the six congregations, he had the missionary work of organizing the scattered settlers and helping them in getting churches and schools established. He traveled over the counties of Nelson, Ramsey, Benson, Towner, Rolette, Wells, Pierce, McHenry, Ward and Bottineau.

Hans and Anna Marie - wedding photo

Rev. Hans Blegen was married on May 29, 1891 to Anna Marie Nesset at Glenwood near Decorah, Iowa. Anna Marie Nesset Blegen was born Sept. 11, 1869 to Ole Einarson Nesset and Johanna Hakonsdotter Nesset at Decorah, Iowa. After their marriage, Rev. and Mrs. Blegen returned to Leeds the latter part of June 1891, and resided in rooms above the O. P. Larson store. Later, on advice of the president of the church district, Rev. B. Harstad, Rev. Blegen filed on a homestead and borrowed money to build a house on the claim. From 1890 to 1899, Rev. Hans Blegen was pastor for the Lake Ibsen Lutheran congregation and various other congregations, and continued his missionary work in the surrounding counties.

Rev. Hans A. Blegen was appointed manager of the Wild Rice Lutheran Orphans' Home at Fossum, near Twin Valley, Minnesota, in the spring of 1899. He continued there for several years, until Mrs. Blegen found that the work of caring for the children was impairing her health. After the Orphans' Home was firmly established, he resigned as manager primarily on account

228

of his wife's health. In the work at the Orphans' Home, he became a pioneer also in caring for the unfortunate in the church. He advocated the idea of placing orphaned children in private homes rather than in institutions.

In 1903, the family moved to Decorah, Iowa, where Mr. Blegen was a member of the staff of the Lutheran Publishing House for a period of about 10 years until it closed because of church mergers.

Hans and Anna Marie returned to Leeds, North Dakota in 1915 to make their home on the old homestead where the family continued farming. Hans also continued his interest in education by teaching school at various times. During these years, Rev. and Mrs. Blegen spent their time actively involved in the Leeds Lutheran church and the Leeds community. In the fall of 1937, Rev. and Mrs. Blegen moved from the homestead into the city of Leeds. Hans Blegen often wrote articles for *The Leeds News*. In 1935 he began to write articles about his memories of his life as a prairie minister in the Leeds, North Dakota area. These articles were called "Ten Years in a Buggy."

On March 14, 1941, Rev. Blegen at the age of 81 passed away after a brief illness. He always took an active part in school and civic affairs. He carried the gospel to hundreds of prairie homes bringing words of condolence and comfort.

Rev. and Mrs. Blegen were blessed with eight children. One child died as an infant, and two died as teenagers, and the five who lived beyond their 70s were Olaf, Peter, Nora, Hannah and Joseph.

Excerpts from "Recollections of Pioneer Times," published August/November 2005
"Ten Years in a Buggy"
By Rev. H. A. Blegen, published in "The Leeds (ND) News"

Hans Andreas Hansen Blegen is my maternal grandfather. My mother Nora had a scrapbook in which she placed many items about the family. The collection included newspaper clippings, obituaries, and several clippings from "The Leeds News" entitled "Ten Years in a Buggy" ...My cousin in Bismarck ND and I went to the North Dakota Archives and searched the microfilm of "The Leeds News." We reached the year 1934 and started to find the articles. We also found many other articles written by him on other subjects...These are his reflections of the time period from 1890 to 1899. Hans Blegen was a Lutheran prairie minister in the Leeds, North Dakota, area.
Lynne Hogan

April 9, 1934
I have been asked by some friends, including the editor of *The Leeds News,* to tell about pioneer days but have hitherto been reluctant to comply because I have no right to the title of pioneer. Neither can I point with pride to any great achievement that would entitle me to be their spokesman or historian. I cannot even boast of any noteworthy suffering and hardship endured.

It is only 44 years since I started traveling trails already blazed by other pastors and missionaries and tried to follow them for ten years or so. But since the ranks of the pioneers are growing smaller and smaller and there soon will be none of them left to tell their own story, I thought that perhaps it would be possible, by brushing up the memory, to retrace some of the trails traveled. If you care to go with me on this tour, perhaps we will see how others lived. We start from a farm a few miles southest of Mayville, Trail County. We will stop here to visit for awhile.

The farm itself does not look much different from other farmsteads in the neighborhood, if anything it is plainer and simpler. But I am more anxious to have you meet the owner, Rev. B. Harstad, than to show you the farm. He is at the time of our visit "President of the Minnesota District of the Synod for the Evangelical Lutheran Church of America," generally known as the "Norwegian Synod" or simply, 'The Synod." The territory over which he has supervision includes, besides Minnesota, all the territory to the west clear to the Pacific...

Through Rev. Harstad I received a call as pastor from the Lake Ibsen congregation in Benson County, North Dakota. After stating what they demanded of the pastor, they stated the inducement they had to offer. "We are unable to offer any definite salary but promise to do what we can to assist in the support of the minister." Accompanying the letter to Lake Ibsen congregation from three other congregations, St. Olaf, Antelope Valley (the present Maddock), and Viking. This letter gave no promise of any kind, only asking to be served by the pastor coming to Lake Ibsen...the committee in charge would endeavor to assist to the extent that the total income would amount to $500 per year including whatever the congregations could donate either in salaries, offerings or gifts of any kind.

Well, the call was accepted and I was told to come back to Trail County. After being ordained in the Mayville church, I started out to procure an outfit for my future work. I bought a pair of small buckskin ponies, Tom and Jerry, with harness for $100 and ordered a buggy but it failed to arrive in time for me to meet the appointments already made. I was told to go to Devils Lake and call on Rev. O. H. Aaberg for further instruction about my field and future work. Harstad let me have his buggy and he was going to travel on horseback until the newly ordered buggy arrived. So I started out in grand style while President Harstad plodded along on horseback or foot.

(date unknown)

When speaking of the hardships of the Pioneer, it does not mean only the hard work that Mr. has to do. Mrs. certainly has her share in the work and hardships as well as the success of the pioneer. She is a pioneer as well as he is. Her work may be different but it is not of less importance nor easier than the man's. They both have their hands full. Take one concrete example of many that was told to me. One summer all the men in the settlement of Willow

Creek, 50 or 60 miles northwest of Leeds, went to the Red River Valley for harvest and threshing, leaving only women and children to care for the homestead, or I should have said, leaving only the women folks to care for the homestead and the children.

Of course it was hard for the men – hard to leave their families, hard work tramping almost 200 miles before they found work, hard work in the fields, and it was hard work going back to Willow Creek carrying the flour and groceries on their backs from Larimore, the nearest railroad station. But wasn't it also hard for these women to see their husbands leaving? Did it take less of courage? Did thye have less anxiety, less loneliness, less responsibility? The pleasure of meeting their only possible visitors, the red men, was as may easily be imagined, of a rather doubtful character.

And when it comes to church work and the building of churches, it is a recognized fact that you find the women in the front rank of workers. By their vision, industry, and sacrifice, they not only gather the first pennies, but also inspire the men with hope and courage to take up the same work....

May 24, 1934

....After getting somewhat acquainted with the field of work, I was to lay out a route and work out some kind of timetable. To being with it looked something like this: Every third Sunday at Leeds, the two Sundays in between and one whole week at other points, with school and sometimes services on weekdays. To be sure it wasn't much of a school, only little more than hearing lessons, but the mothers assured me that it was a great help to them.

President Harstad advised me to get hold of a piece of land. Accordingly I bought the improvements on a quarter section and filed on it, using my preemption right. When the two years were up, and there was no $200 on hand with which to prove up, I had it changed to a homestead entry and continued living there for five years more when I got a document called "Patent" signed by President McKinley. The Registrar at the Land Office pronounced it the best proof he had taken.

The house we built on this farm served as a church, schoolhouse, and boarding house for children from outlying districts and their teachers – sometimes too crowded, at other times with a depressing lonesomeness, but always work, work for the housewife. But with brave courage, sustained by faith and hope, she bore it all without complaint. We sometimes hear the words "Good Old Times." Although often spoken with a sneer and a trace of irony, the wordsa re far from being all bosh. There were many things good and nice about the early days. It was not by any means, all drudgery and hopelessness. The blessings were too many to count. The outstanding ones to my notion were: The absence of class distinction, the priceless treasure of good neighbors, and everybody doing what he could to help the other fellow.

Ole Olson Tingelstad

published November 2005   *Form 837*   *Lawrence Onsager*

Ole Olson Tingelstad was the brother of the author's great-great-grandmother, Siri Olsdatter, who married Lawrence's great-great-grandfather, John Andersen Onsager.

Ole Olson Tingelstad
as a young man in 1859

Ole T. Olson, the son of Ole Borgerson Helmeid Tingelstadeiet and Anne Nielsdatter Nedre Alm, was born on November 27, 1824 on Tingelstadeiet in Gran Parish, the district of Hadeland, Oppland County, Norway.

His father, Ole Borgerson, the son of Borger Christenson Helmey and Malene Olsdatter Nedre Hilden, was born in 1783 on the Helmey farm in Gran Parish. Ole, 18 years old and unmarried, is listed in the 1801 census on the Helmey farm with his mother and stepfather. He was married on April 17, 1815 in Gran Parish to Anne Nielsdatter Nedre Alm. Anne was born about 1790. Ole and Anne had 8 children born on the Nedre Alm and Tingelstad farms. Ole was a cotter (renter) on the Tingelstad farm when he died on October 13, 1834. Anne appears in the 1865 census as a 75-year old widow living on poor relief with her daughter, Siri, and son-in-law, John Anderson, on the subfarm Braaten under the Onsager farm in Gran Parish. She probably died before her daughter, Siri, emigrated in 1881.

Today, the Tingelstad farm is part of the *Hadeland Folkemuseum*, the regional museum for the Gran, Jevnaker and Lunner municipalities. The *Hadeland Folkemuseum* is an open-air museum located a short distance from Gran at Tingelstad *hogda*. It is built around a Viking era burial mound which tradition says holds the torso of King Halvdan the Black. Twenty-five historic buildings, many dating from the 1700s, have been moved to the site. Its greatest treasures are Old Tingelstad church and Tingelstad farm.

The museum's collections of over 10,000 artifacts trace the cultural history of Hadeland and it serves as the repository for an extensive historical archive. The Old Tingelstad (St Peter's) Church was built in the first half of the 12th century and was used for worship until 1866. The stone walls are 2 meters thick. Its small narrow windows resemble archery slits. The stone altar dates to the Middle Ages.

According to his obituary, Ole was a shoemaker from the time he was 11 years old. On March 5, 1847, Ole Olsen Tingelstadeiet left Gran to join the *Norske Jægercorp 1. compagnie*. That is the only reference that he might have been a soldier (*Migrants from Gran, 1825-1900, and Jevnaker, 1837-1901, Digitalarkivet.no*).

 Ole was married in Norway on Feb. 14, 1850, to widow Siri Peterson. Siri Ingebretsdatter Allergot, the daughter of tenant Ingebret Jacobsen Framstadeiet and Christine Olsdatter, was born in Gran, Hadeland, Norway, on July 15, 1821. She was baptized on July 22, 1821. Her baptism sponsors were Hans Egge, Peder Egge, Iver Egge, Malene Jacobsdatter Egge, and Mari Jacobsdatter Egge (*Digitalarkivet.no*). Siri was first married on November 26, 1845 to Iver (Ever) Pederson Lysenseiet. Ever was 26 and Siri was 23. Iver, the son of Peder Iversen Lyseneiet and Christiane Nielsdatter, was born on November 20, 1818 in Gran. He was baptized on November 22, 1818 in the Gran Parish. His baptism sponsors were Ole Dæhleneiet, Ingbor Dæhleneiet, Lars Lysen, Iver Lyseneiet, and Marthe Lyseneiet. Siri and Iver had one son: Peter A. Everson.

Ole was a farmer and a shoemaker. On April 2 1853, Ole and his family left Gran for America. The party consisted of Siri's parents, Ingebret Jacobs. Allergodt, born in 1789, a *selveier* (owner or freeholder); Christine Ols. Allergodt, born in 1796, his wife; Ole Ols. Allergodt, born on 11/27/1824, *inderst* (renter or tenant), born *Nedre* Tystad; Siri Ingebretsd. Allergodt, born on 7/15/1821; Peder Ivers. Allergodt, born on 9/17/1845 (Ole's stepson), born Brandshagen; Iver Ols. Allergodt, born on 10/10/1850, born on Juliødegaard; and Christine Olsd. Allergodt, born on 1/14/1852 (*Migrants from Gran, 1825-1900, and Jevnaker, 1837-1901, records 799-805, Digitalarkivet.no*).

There were many preparations that had to be made before an emigrant left Norway. The emigrants had to have provisions for up to a twelve-week voyage, particularly foods that would not spoil. Usually an auction was held and nearly all of their household goods were sold because freight rates were high. At this early time many of their neighbors would come to say goodbye and pity them because they were going to that "heathen" land, America.

The Olsons landed in Quebec, Canada and came into the United States at the port of Buffalo, N.Y. in May 1853. The Olsons located in the Muskego Norwegian settlement in Racine County, Wisconsin where they lived for two years. The Muskego settlement was founded in 1839 near Lake Muskego in Waukesha County. The low marshy area was unhealthy and the settlers suffered from malaria. In 1840 many settlers moved south into Racine County. A thriving settlement soon grew up in Norway, Yorkville, Raymond, and Waterford townships. The name "Muskego" was retained for both settlements.

The land in the Koshkonong Norwegian settlement in Dane County, Wisconsin was more attractive than in Racine County and many Norwegians had settled there beginning in 1840. The settlement of Norwegians in Juneau County began in 1850. At that time Juneau was part of Adams County. In 1857, Juneau County was created. The Juneau settlement was a northward extension of the Koshkonong settlement. Probably hearing of available land as Adams (Juneau) County was opened up, the Olsons moved in June 1856, settling on a farm west of Mauston in Lisbon Township. B. C. Dockstader hired Ole to run a shoemaking shop, which he established in Mauston. In the autumn of that same year Ole took charge of the store. Ole's obituary gives 1858 as the date the family left the farm and moved to Mauston. However in the 1860 census, they were residing on a farm in Lindina Township. Eventually they moved permanently to Mauston where they resided except for two years in La Crosse, Wisconsin from 1867 to 1868. Ole operated a shoemaking or repair shop the remainder of his working life.

Mauston was named for Milton M. Maughs who came into possession of the lumber mill there in 1849. Maughs platted Mauston in 1854. Mauston was incorporated as a village in 1860. Ole T. Olson saw much of the early history of Mauston.

Ole Tingelstad

Ole and Siri joined the East Lemonweir Church located in Fountain Township, Juneau County, Wisconsin on August 24, 1857. They received communion from Pastor Herman A. Preus that same day. Since Siri's parents did not join the church, they had probably died prior to August 1857.

Ole T. Oleson, 36, male, shoemaker, real property, $150, personal property, $90, born in Norway, is listed in the 1860 census

Siri Tingelstad

for Lindina Township, Juneau County, Wisconsin with Sarah Oleson, age 38, female, born in Norway; Peter Oleson, age 14, male, born in Norway; Ever Oleson, age 10, male, born in Norway; Christina Oleson, age 8, female, born in Norway; Edward Oleson, age 4, male, born in Wisconsin; Anton Oleson, age 2, male, born in Wisconsin; and Ann Maria Oleson, age 2 months, female, born in Wisconsin. *(1860 U.S. Census)*

On February 25, 1863, Ole's stepson, Peter A. Everson, enlisted in Company K, 6th Wisconsin Volunteers. At Gettysburg, PA on July 1, 1863, Peter received gunshot wounds to both legs during the charge of the railroad cut. He was discharged because of this disability on May 11, 1864.

According to his obituary, Ole moved his family to LaCrosse, Wisconsin in 1867 and returned to Mauston in 1868.

Ole and his family appear in the 1870 census in Mauston. He had $800 in real property and $300 in personal property. His occupation was given as a boot and shoe manufacturer. The business had $200 in capital. Ole had one hand powered sewing machine. He was the sole employee and worked twelve months a year. His materials on hand included: sole leather, 25 sides, $200. Kip boots, 24 pairs, $168. Kep shoes, 25 lbs, $50. Calf boots, 25 pairs, $225. Calf shoes, 100 lbs, $150. Shoes, 75, $225. Sheep shoes, 3 doz., $30. Repairing, $125. Pegs, wax, & thread, $12. The household included Ole, age 45; his wife Sarah, age 47; Ever, 19; Christina, 17; Edward O., 12; Anton, 11; and Ole Johnson, 23, a laborer. Ole was his nephew, Ole Johnson Onsager, who emigrated in 1868.

Ole and his son, Ever, appeared on the rolls of Captain John Turner's Mauston Light Guards, Wisconsin State Militia on September 30, 1874. The guards were organized in 1870.

Siri died on August 1, 1895 in Mauston, Wisconsin and was buried in the Mauston Cemetery. Her obituary states that she had been a member of the Methodist Episcopal Church for many years. She was also a member of the Rebekah Lodge. In 1905, Ole was living with his daughter, Christine Campbell and her husband, James, on a farm in Lindina Township.

Ione Nelson Duranceau, the daughter of Mabel (Campbell) Nelson, wrote:

> Ole Olson (my great-grandfather) was a shoemaker by trade. He made the shoes. My mother said he used to make theirs when they were children. He lived with my grandparents. He died when he was almost 97 yrs. I can remember him sitting in his rocker, reading his Bible (the size of a big dictionary). We were afraid of him as he would thump his cane at us if we got noisy! I never knew my great-grandmother (*Duranceau Correspondence, LW Onsager files*).

Ole died on January 21, 1921 in Mauston, Wisconsin and was buried in the Mauston Cemetery. Gilbert Siebecker purchased the O. T. Olson farm in Lindina Township. (Juneau County Genealogy Society, *Cemetery Book 5*, p. 544).

Ole and Siri's Children:

- Ever (Iver) O., b. Oct 10, 1850, on Juliødegaard; bp. Oct 27, 1850, Gran (sponsors: Kari Pedersdtr. Gubberud, Malene Olsdtr. Granvolden, Torger Mikkelsen Gubberud, Borger Olsen Helmeneiet, Peder Larsen Bildeneiet); m. Helen E. Valleau February 28, 1875, Mauston, WI; he was a physician in Osseo, WI; one child.
- Christine, b. Jan 14, 1852, on Juli in Brandbu; bp. Feb 8, 1852 (sponsors: Ingeborg Pedersdtr. Gudmundshagen, Kari Olsdtr. Midtegge, Gudbrand Pedersen Gudmundshagen, Jacob Ingebretsen Allergodt, Iver Olsen Drøvdalseiet); m. James H. Campbell; 4 children.
- Andrew, b. Sep 3, 1853, WI; not listed in 1860 census.
- Annie, b. October 18, 1854, WI; not listed in 1860 census.

- Edward Olaus, b. Nov 27, 1856, WI; bp. Aug 24, 1857, East Lemonweir Church (sponsors: Niels Bjornsen, Niels Nielsen, Gabriel Olsen, Karen Hansdtr., and Martha Asmundsdtr.); d. Aug 17, 1895.
- Anton Julius, b. May 15, 1858; bp. Aug 20, 1858, East Lemonweir Church (sponsors: Gunder Johannesen, Lars Olsen, Johannes Gundersen, Endre Narvestad, and Karen Hansdtr.); m. (1) May 11, 1879, New Lisbon, WI, Carrie Bell Southworth; m. (2) June 1919, Mrs. Harriet Smith; operated hardware store in Tomahawk, WI; 2 children.
- Anne Maria, b. May 11, 1860; bp. Jul 24, 1860, East Lemonweir Church (sponsors: Lars Olsen, Christen Christensen, Augund Lawrencesen, Marie Ormsdtr., and Torbjor Nielsdtr.); d. 1865.
- Sem (Samuel) Marcus, b. Sep 29, 1861; bp. Nov 20, 1861, East Lemonweir Church (sponsors: Gabriel Oddsen, Torstein Thorbjornsen, Maria Hansdtr., and Kristine Hansdtr.).
- Marcus Samuel, b. Jul 14, 1864; bp. Aug 30, 1864, East Lemonweir Church (sponsors: Ole Hansen, Karl Pettersen, Karen Hansdtr., Aguet ?)

Olaf A. Lee

"Hadeland Folkemuseum" published May 2006   *Kari-Mette Stavhaug*

Emigrants from Norway at the end of the 19th Century were often families, both young and old. From 1900 younger and unmarried men and women dominated among the emigrants. They were adventurous and they wanted to earn money for a few years and return to Norway. About one-fourth of the emigrants after 1880 returned to Norway.

One emigrant who returned to Hadeland was Olaf A. Lee. While staying in the U.S. from 1907 to about 1915, he bought himself a camera. Olaf A. Lee was a good amateur photographer and kept several photos from the U.S. After his death they were donated to the Hadeland *Folkemuseum.*

We choose to show you some of the pictures to give you insight in this valuable documentation of the emigrants' daily lives.

Olaf A. Lee

Olaf Anderson Lee was born out of wedlock in Brandbu in January 1887. His parents were farmers Anders Olsen Dælen and Anne Andersdatter (born 1861). In 1907 he emigrated to stay with one of his mother's brothers. The pictures show he lived in North Dakota and lived on farms. He returned to Norway after 7 or 8 years and married Marie Andersdatter in Tinglestad Church in 1915. He worked as a postman in Moen and Brandbu. Olaf A. Lee and his wife had no children. Lee died in 1969 at Jaren in Gran.

Brua Editor's Note: The little town of Westby still exists. The town received its name because it was the farthest west town in North Dakota. When the train arrived, the station was built on the westside, and is actually in Montana. Only a small part of the community is now in ND.

Six Morstad Siblings from Gran

published May 2006   *Form 825*   *J. H. Fonkert*

Author's note: Information sources are only mentioned in passing in this account. Some information has been contributed by Denise Wallack and Richard Rowe, both Morstad descendants.

Six children of Johannes Nilssen and Kirsti Christensdatter emigrated to America between 1886 and 1905. Although their families were centered in Minnesota and Wisconsin, before their deaths they scattered as far as California and Alberta. All six were born in Gran Parish in Hadeland County, Norway. Nils and Anna Marie married in Norway and brought young children to America. Mathea, Johan, Karen and Kirsti married and had families after coming to the U.S.

Sometime in his 20s, their father, Johannes Nilssen, wandered some 70 miles over the hills from Vårmland region of Sweden to Gran parish in Hadeland, Norway. No one knows why he left Sweden, but he became committed to Gran when, while not yet married, he fathered a child with Kiersti Christensdatter in January, 1857.

Johannes, born in June 1833, was about a year and a half older than Kiersti, born December 1834. Johannes was 23 and Kiersti 22 when their first child, Iver, was born in January 1857. Johannes was a smith at Vøyen farm, Kiersti a maid at Skiakereiet farm. They were married later that year in November. Over the next 21 years, they had 8 more children, as recorded in the Gran parish register.

Iver, born 1857, Skiakereiet farm
Niels, born 1858, Skiakereiet farm
Mathea, born 1860, Skiakereiet farm
Christiane, born 1863, Morstadeiet farm
Anne Maria, born 1866, Morstadhagen farm
John, born 1869, Vestre Morstad farm
Karen, born, 1872 Morstad farm
Margrete, born 1875, Morstadhagen farm
Kristi, born 1878, Morstadhagen farm

Iver, Christiane and Margrete remained in Norway. Most of the children at some point used the Morstad farm name as a surname. For convenience, the family here is referred to as the Morstads, although Karen went by various names and Johan chose to call himself John Welhaven.

Mathea

Mathea left Gran for Rothsay, Minnesota, in March 1886. Her obituary says that she went to

Above are the Morstad sisters, left to right: Mathea, Karen (Clara) and Kiersti (Kate)

Oscar Township (Otter Tail Township) and lived with relatives. Rothsay is just into Wilkin County from Oscar Township. The identity of these relatives is not known, but the township was heavily Norwegian. Several Gran-Jevnaker emigrants gave Rothsay as their destination when they left Norway, including two young men that departed on the same ship Mathea.

Mathea was also known as Martha or Mattie. She married Norwegian-born Andrew Christofferson in Fergus Falls, Otter Tail County, Minnesota, in 1886. The family lived near Barnesville in Wilkin County in 1895, but by 1900 were back in Fergus Falls. "Martha" and Andrew had six children: Betsy Karine, b. 1888, Carl Johan (Oscar), b. 1889, Gustav, b. 1891, Clara, b. 1893, Olaf, b. 1896, and Maud Genette, b. 1902.

The family was again in Wilkin County in 1905. Andrew died in Akron Township in 1908. Mathea remarried in 1912 to another Norwegian, Andreas P. Overland, a tailor in Fergus Falls (not to be confused with Anton P. Overland of Fergus Falls, a photographer, and also Norwegian-born and of virtually the same age). Mathea's youngest daughter, Maud, died in 1918 from pneumonia contracted while attending a Lutheran Bible school in Grand Forks, N.D.

Andreas Overland died in 1923. Mathea lived for a time with her daughter Betsy (Mrs. Paul C. Weinrich), and in her later years lived in Fergus Falls with her daughter Clara (Mrs. Einar Blikstad). Mathea died in Fergus Falls in 1951.

Karen

Karen was probably the next to leave Norway. She was in Superior, Wisconsin, by the summer of 1892, when she married a Norwegian saloon-keeper, Ole Petersen. She used the name "Carrie Nelson." Her emigration date is not certain and it is not clear what attracted a single woman, not much past 20 years old to Superior. There is no evidence she had relatives in the area.

239

By 1901, she was divorced from Ole, who died drunk in jail in 1907. The Superior newspaper made some note of Ole's death, calling him a "pioneer saloonkeeper of the city," who had made a "small fortune," but died virtually without funds.

Ole and Karen had two children: Sigrid Caroline, born 1893, and Hjalmar Peder Oldin, born in 1894. Sigrid was later knows as Vivian. Hjalmar was known as Earl as a young man. In 1910, Karen was using the name "Clara" and was living in Minneapolis. Her trail becomes faint for the next 20 years. Hjalmar/Earl was living in Spokane, Washington in 1917 and later married Camille Purdy. They had a daughter in Victoria, British Columbia. Vivian married Arthur Stratton, and lived in the Los Angeles area. Descendents of Hjalmar are still living up the coast from Los Angeles.

Karen, now probably known as Clara, married a Mr. Franklin sometime between 1910 and 1917. It is known the marriage occurred by this time, because her son was using the name Earl Franklin when he registered for the military draft in 1917 in Spokane.

An unsubstantiated family story tells that Clara was engaged to marry a doctor in Cloquet, Minnesota – probably sometime between 1910 and 1920 – but her fiancé died in an automobile accident a week before the wedding. She supposedly inherited a large amount of money, moved to California and became a close friend of the famous childhood actress, Shirley Temple. While no evidence has been found to support most of the story, there may be some truth to the part about Shirley Temple. Clara's great-granddaughter in California remembers her mother saying that Clara lived in the same triplex in Los Angeles as Ms. Temple's manager. Clara was in Los Angeles by at least 1931, when she ordered a delayed Wisconsin certificate for her daughter, but her death certificate says she had lived there since about 1923. Clara died in Los Angeles County, California, in 1948.

Johan

Uttflytta records from Gran indicate that Johan left for Kristiania (Oslo) in 1884, and that he went to the United States in 1893. He used the name "John W. Welhaven" when he filed his declaration of intent for citizenship in September 1893 in Chicago. His obituary says he served in the Spanish-America War (1898-99) but this has not been substantiated.

By 1899, John was a tailor in Minneapolis and in 1900 he was working as a men's clothing salesman in Minneapolis, where he lodged in the home of an Englishman. In the same home was Swedish-born Mary Ahlm, whom John Welhaven married soon after (based on a marriage age given in 1930 census).

In 1905 the Minnesota census indicated that John's family had been living in Scanlon, Carlton County, MN, since about September

1901. The Welhavens, as well as John's sister Kirsti (Mrs. Kate Jackson), were living in a hotel operated by another sister, Anne Marie, who had arrived in Scanlon in late 1902 (see below).

In January 1908, John Welhaven filed a homestead application for 160 acres of land near Scanlon. He had settled on the claim in August 1905, and built a small house and very small barn, but apparently never cleared more than a few acres. His attempt to prove-up claim in 1908 was at first rejected because he had been absent from the ensuing winters because of ill health, but he received a patent for the land in 1909.

In 1901, John had his own tailor shop in Cloquet, Carlton County. John's obituary says he made uniforms in Chicago during World War I. The 1920 and 1930 censuses placed the Welhaven family in Duluth. Both his sisters Kate and Anna Marie lived in Duluth in 1920. John died in 1940 in Duluth.

Kirsti (Kate)

Kirsti, later known as Kate, traveled from Oslo to New York when she was only 17 years old in 1896. Since she was young and single, she likely went to relatives, possibly her sister Mathea or brother John. The better likelihood may be John, since Kate lived near him in later years.

Kate has not been found in the 1900 census, but soon she married Burt Shepard. The 1905 Minnesota census locates them in a boarding house run by Kate's sister Anna Marie (see below) in Scanlon and indicates both Kate and the Welhavens had been living in the district since about spring of 1901. The census gave the same timing for Kate's residence in Minnesota, raising the possibility that she lived outside Minnesota for some period after her arrival in the U.S.

Kate and Burt had two children while at Scanlon: Burt Jr., born 1903, and Dorothy (Mrs. George Simmons), born 1905. The marriage ended sometime after 1905, but it is not known whether due to death, separation or divorce. Kate and her two children were living in Superior, Wisconsin in 1910. She was listed as widowed, but her husband Burt may have still been living in Duluth.

Kate remarried to Samuel Jackson in 1917 in Minneapolis. In 1920, they and Kate's son Burt were living in Duluth, where Sam was a riveter in the shipyards. Although ages given in the census are not a perfect match, Sam and Kate were probably living in Gnesen Township of St. Louis County in 1930.

The 1951 obituary for Kate's sister, Mathea, says the Jacksons were living north of Seattle in Snohomish County, Wash., where it is believed they had a farm. Mathea's sons Oscar and Olaf were living in Seattle at the time. Sam Jackson died in Snohomish County in 1952 and is buried in the G.A.R. Cemetery. Kate died in 1969, more than 90 years old.

Anna Marie

Anna Marie married a military officer, Marthin Kolberg, and moved to Drøbrek, not far from her husband's home in Onsøy, Ostfold, south of Oslo. The couple had five children before

Marthin died in 1900. Anna Marie sailed with her five children to America in 1902. The children were: Kirsten (Katherine), born 1888, Peder (Peter), born 1890, Barbra (Barbara) born 1891, Johannes (John), born 1893, and Anders (Andrew, born 1895.

Her obituary says Anna Marie came to Superior,

Marthin and Anne Marie (Morstad) Kolberg Family
Left to right: Anne Marie, Peder, Johannes,Kirsten, Anders, Barbra, Marthin

Wisconsin 1902. When Marie and her children arrived in New York in July 1902, the passenger manifest said they were going to meet Anna Marie's brother, John Welhaven, in West Superior, Wisconsin. The 1905 Minnesota census found the family in Scanlon, Carlton County, Minnesota, where she was a hotel keeper. The census indicated she had been in Scanlon since 1902. According to the census, her sister Kate and brother John were already in Scanlon before her. Kate and John were living in Anna Marie's boarding house in 1905.

Anna Marie soon moved to Superior where she and her children are listed in city directories from 1906 to 1912. Her sister, Karen/Clara, had lived in Superior for many years but by this time was divorced and was in Minneapolis by 1907. For at least part of her time in Superior, Anna Marie operated a small hotel or boarding house. The 1913 directory reports she had moved to the small town of Gordon, about 40 miles southeast of Superior. Anna Marie moved to Two Harbors, Minnesota, where she operated a millinery store with her daughter, Katherine and Barbara (Mrs. Charles Falk). Her daughter Katherine and son Andrew were still living with her in 1920. John was still living in Gordon and Peter was living in Minneapolis. Anna Marie died in 1927 in Two Harbors. Peter moved frequently, living in Minneapolis, Moose Jaw (Saskatchewan) and other places in Minnesota, North Dakota and Montana. At the time of Anna Marie's death, John and Andrew had moved to Ashland, Wisconsin. Barbara (Mrs. Charles Falk) lived most of her life in Two Harbors.

Nils

Like his younger sister, Anna Marie, Nils had a family in Norway before he came to the U.S. He left Jevnaker in 1889, and by 1900 was married and living in Oslo with his wife and first two children: Ruth and John. Another daughter, Mary, was born in 1902. Nils left Oslo bound for New York in January, 1905, but there is no obvious record of his arrival in America. Nils' wife Marie and three children passed through Ellis Island in October, 1905, giving their destination as Nils' residence in Hoboken, New Jersey.

It is not clear where the family first settled, but Nils filed his first naturalization papers in Burleigh County (Bismarck), North Dakota in August 1906. In 1910, the family was living on the other side of the Missouri River near Altmont in Morton County, N.D. Nils Morstad received a government patent for 160 acres of land (NW 1/4, Sec.12, T137N, R86W) in Morton County in 1911.

Nils did not stay long around Altmont. The April 22, 1911 edition of the Altmont *Arena* newspaper reported: "Mrs. Nels Morstad and children left for Castor, Alberta, Canada to join husband and father who had preceded them to that place, where he has a homestead." He received a land grant near Castor, about 50 miles east of Red Deer and the 1911 census recorded the family at Bawlf, about 50 miles northwest of

Rev. Nils and Maria (Ahlm) Morstad with daughter Ruth. Photo taken in Norway.

Castor and closer to Edmonton. Nils was a Lutheran preacher.

The children and probably their mother returned to the U. S. in 1914, as indicated on both John's and Ruth's declaration for intent of U.S. citizenship, which were filed in Minneapolis in 1914 and 1922 respectively. Ruth gave her last residence as Castor, Alberta.

Alien registration records (January 1918) for Marie Morstad indicated that her husband was a Canadian citizen and living in Fort George, British Columbia. The whole family was back living together on 15th Ave. S. in Minneapolis at the time of the 1920 census. They were still living in Minneapolis in 1930, but the parents used the name "Hagen" while the children, John and Ruth, still carried the Morstad name. Daughter Mary had died in 1929. Nils died in October, 1931 in Minneapolis under the name Morstad.

Johannes Slaatland Halvorsen Melom

published August 2006   *Form 892*   *Jan Heusinkveld*

The author is the granddaughter of Johannes Melom. Her mother is Beata Melom.

Johannes was born December 30, 1830 in Jevnaker, Norway on the Haagenstad farm to Halvor Olsen and Barbara Hansdatter Melaas. Johannes was baptized January 2, 1831 in the Lunner Church. He married Johanne Hansdatter in 1852 in the Lunner Church. They had two children, Halvor Slaatland Johannessen, born December 15, 1853; Bertha Johannesdatter, born September 15, 1859 on the Stokogaard Farm. Johanne Hansdatter died July 16, 1866 and is buried in the Lunner Church Cemetery.

Johannes' second wife was Marie Iversdatter. They married November 28, 1867 in the Lunner Church. Marie was born November 20, 1847 on the Hytta farm to Iver Pedersen and Siri Pedersdatter. Their first child was a daughter, Johanne Sophie, born December 8, 1868 in Lunner, Norway.

Johannes and Marie left Oslo, Norway June 9, 1870 going to Hull, England. From there they took the train to Liverpool, England where they then took the ship *SS Holland* that arrived in New York on July 7, 1870. They

Johannes Halvorsen Melom about 1880

had registered in Jevnaker their destination to be McGregor, Iowa. Shortly after they arrived in Iowa, two of their children died, Johanne Sophie and Halvor Slaatland. We have not been able to locate the burial sites of these two children, but they are believed to be in Winneshiek County, Iowa. Also there was a son born in Winneshiek County on August 31, 1870. That is Joseph Simon Halvorsen. The family spent some time with the Halvor Bakken family after their arrival in America.

Their next home was at Fort Ridgely, Renville County, Minnesota. The army had vacated the Fort after the Civil War and there were log cabins that families could occupy. While living here there were four more children, Johan Fillip, born September 7, 1872; Carl Marcus, born June 26, 1874; August Herman, born May 27, 1876; and Jonette Marie, born May 13, 1878. Johannes was a circuit rider (evangelist) with the Hauge Synod in this area. There is a story that is recorded in Marie's obituary. Johannes was often away on long journeys and on one of those

occasions in 1878, there was a severe blizzard. Marie struggled to save the children and herself from freezing to death. She managed to keep the children warm and on the fourth day Johannes reached home.

Later that year they moved to Sacred Heart, Minnesota where Rev. Halvorson served a call to the Hoff Lutheran Church (First English Lutheran). Rev Halvorson Melom served this church from 1878-1892. While in Sacred Heart three more children were born, Mathew Halvor, born November 12, 1882; Halvor H., born February 25, 1885; and Idan Obed, born July 14, 1889. Rev Johannes Halvorson Melom died November 11, 1892, age 62, and is buried in the Riverside Cemetery, Dawson, Minnesota.

Johan and August Melom in their dormitory at Red Wing Seminary

Marie had homesteaded a farm in 1892 one and a half miles north of Dawson, Minnesota. This is where she raised her family. All of the children attended the Red Wing Seminary in Red Wing, Minnesota and they became pastors or teachers. Marie died August 2, 1926, age 78, and is buried next to Johannes in Riverside Cemetery, Dawson, Minnesota.

Bertha was married to Olaf Hendrickson January 15, 1879 in Sacred Heart by her father. She died October 27, 1925 in Homer, ND. Both Bertha and Olaf are buried in the Oslo Cemetery, Marshall Co., Minnesota.

Joseph Simon Halvorson (he was the only one in the family that did not change his name to Melom) was ordained in 1896 and served congregations in Pierpont, SD; Spicer, MN; Buxton, ND; Hillsboro, ND; and Gary, MN. He married Nettie Gurine Johnson in 1902. To this union there were nine children Ester, Ruben, Kenneth, Ruth, Manford, Nora, Milton, Ida and Pearl. Joseph died October 25, 1962, age 92.

Johan Erickson and Anna Erickson wedding, November 14, 1907. Idan Melom was Best Man and Josepha Thornby was Maid of Honor.

Johan Fillip Melom, who was the oldest son still living at home, helped his mother with the farm so that the other children could attend school in Red Wing. Johan was ordained May 1907 and served congregations in Wallace, SD; Newman Grove, NB; Dalton, MN; Pierpont, SD; Grand Forks, ND; and Elmore, MN. Johan married Anna Irene Erikson November 14, 1907 in Dawson MN. They had four children, Manfred, Hjalmer, Beata, and Ora. Johan died November 8, 1919 and is buried in Elmore, Minn.

Carl Marcus Melom graduated from the University of Minnesota in 1901 and married in 1904. Carl taught in the language department of the University of Minnesota from 1904 to 1913; then was a Berkeley in California for a year. Dr. Carl Melom was head of the language department at Fresno State Teachers College from 1914 until his death. Carl and Jennie had three children, Halvor, Carl and Helen. Carl died Dec. 20, 1921, age 47, from a reaction to a bee sting and is buried in Fresno, Calif.

August Herman Melom was ordained May 30, 1907 and served congregations in Fronteue, Saskatchewan, Canada; Norwich, ND; Velva, ND; Ruso, ND; and Veblen, ND. In his retiring years he worked at Augsburg Publishing. He married Emma Geline Haslerud June 25, 2907 in Lanesboro, Minnesota. To this union were born seven children, Joseph, Myrtle, Esther, Ruben, Olive, Arnold, and Ruth. August died Nov. 24, 1952, age 76, in Minneapolis, MN and is buried in Sunset Memorial Cemetery, Minneapolis.

Jonetta Marie Melom married Alfred Estwick in 1903 in Pierpont, SD. To this union were born four children, Selma, Olga, Adolph, and Manfred. They lived in Spicer, MN. Jonette died October 13, 1943 and is buried in Spicer, MN.

Mathew Halvor Melom lived and farmed on the home place in Dawson. He also taught in some of the schools in that area. He married Karen Kristine Storvik Gunderson in 1918 in Dawson. She had

The Halvorson Melom family home in Dawson, Minnesota.

246

two young sons, Carl and Marshall, and to their union they had five children, Mildred, Harold, Olive, Audrey, and Barbara. Mathew died November 14, 1965 and is buried next to his parents in Riverside Cemetery, Dawson, MN.

Halvor H. Melom lived on the farm also. The farm land was split between Mathew and Halvor and he built a new house and barn on his half. He also taught in the area schools. On January 2, 1909 he married Hannah Erickson in Willmar, Minnesota and to this union were born six children, Hattie, Naomi, Millard, Truman, Verna and Doris. Halvor died December 1, 1940 and is also buried in Riverside Cemetery, Dawson, MN.

Idan Obed Melom was ordained in 1912 and served the congregation in Roseau, MN; Elba, ND; and in Sacred Heart, MN. Idan was also an optometrist and had an office in Montevideo, MN. Idan was a paraplegic and had one of the first hand-operated cars. He married Hulda Thorson and to this union were born four children, Jessie, Miriam, Deborah, and Obed. Idan died March 1975 and is buried in Sacred Heart, MN.

Iver Christiansen Moen

published November 2006   *Form 168*   *Myron A. Gnadt*

I have been engaged in doing family research since 1971. Using Family Tree Maker, I have been able to add approximately 600 names to the branches of the family tree. This endeavor would have been impossible without the help of the Swedish Emigrant Institute, Vesterheim Genealogy Center, LDS libraries and cousins Lloyd Olsen, Per Hanshaugen and Kjell Wiker. Additionally, notes left by my mother, Mabel A. Moen, have proven to be priceless. Although I have been able to gather a plethora of valuable data, it continues to be an on-going process with new information added as it surfaces.

Iver Moen Family c. 1915
Standing: Carl, Mabel, Ellen, Theodore, Ida, Clarence
Seated: Iver, Alice, Mathilda, Alma

Iver Christiansen (Iver C. Moen) was born in Hadeland on Retrumseiet, 06 July 1866, the son of Kristian Iversen Retrumsmoen b. 02 March 1834 and Kirsti Andersdatter Djupdal b 25 March 1834 in Engen. He was the fifth child in a family of ten children. He received baptism and confirmation in Nes Kirke near Brandu. Iver grew up on the Retrumsmoen in a very spartan environment. The family lived on a farm where his father was the *husmann*. An ancient highway, *Gamle Kongesvei* (Old King's Highway), ran through the property – then a major thoroughfare from Oslo to Bergen and Trondheim. A brief visit to the farm still reveals evidence of the existence of this ancient road.

Iver's siblings who remained in Norway were Ingeborg, b. 12 October 1855; Siri, b. 07 May 1861; Ole, b. 25 December 1868; Kjersti, b. 28 June 1871; Marte, b. 12 January 1876; Kristine, b. 18 November 1876 and Karen, b. 17 May 1882. With the exception of Ingeborg, all the children were thought to have been born on Retrumsmoen.

Shortly after the death of his mother, Iver emigrated with his sister Kari, b. 02 May 1864 to Sacred Heart, Minnesota, arriving in the fall of 1884. They brought with them a handmade trunk with the entirety of their worldly possessions. This same trunk now resides with a cousin in Milan, Minnesota.

Four members of this family immigrated to America. Anders, b. 17 December 1856, was a tailor by trade in Norway, but made a rather unsuccessful attempt at farming in America. He later made plans to return to Norway, but his wife and children had already arrived in New York before his letter reached them. The youngest child, Karen, b. 17 May 1882, arrived with her father, Kristian, in 1899. Iver accompanied his father back to Norway to be present at the coronation of the new king in 1905. Kristian died in Hadeland in 1906 and is thought to be buried in Sokna.

After leaving Sacred Heart, Iver made his way to Lake Wilson, Minn., where an uncle Iver I. Moen (a.k.a. Uncle Ruen) had a farm. He worked for his uncle and ultimately met his future bride, Mathilda Oleson who was born in Decorah, Iowa of Swedish immigrants.

Bengt Olofsson and Marit Johnsson, the parents of Mathilda, emigrated from Offerdal in Jamtland, Sweden in April 1870. They left via the port of Trondheim aboard the ship, Norway, with their newborn son, Oluf.

The area of Jamtland was continuously under siege for many years from 1563 to 1677. During this time its citizens changed allegiance to the kings of Norway, Denmark and Sweden thirteen different times. Many Jamtlanders sought refuge in Norway to escape the constant war, plundering, murder and political turmoil.

In addition to the bloodshed during the various occupations, many Jamtlanders faced service in the Swedish army. In 1676, during the battle of Lund, a brigade of Jamtlanders was placed in the front lines to be slaughtered en masse.

During a period of relative peace in 1867, a severe famine migrated from northern Sweden to the southern wooded areas in 1868. In the winters of 1868-1869, there was a national epidemic of itinerant begging children. Religious persecution also forced many Swedes to leave for greener pastures.

Bengt and Marit were among the Jamtlanders who left their uncertain future behind and settled originally in Decorah, Iowa, where they purchased a small forty-acre farm. They lived and farmed in this area for approximately five years. Mathilda was born and baptized there in the Washington Prairie Lutheran Church.

In the spring of 1876, Bengt, family and meager possessions departed Decorah in a lumber wagon pulled by a team of horses for southwestern Minnesota. They had four cows tethered to the back of the wagon with the young calves following behind. Since there were no roads, the followed existing trails that crossed streams and rivers to the land of promise. The journey took over three months.

Mathilda's parents homesteaded a farm approximately one mile north of Lake Wilson, Minnesota. They were the first settlers in Chanarambie Township in Murray County.

Their first house consisted of a frame interwoven with slough grass. A severe Minnesota winter of epic proportions forced them to abandon the crude dwelling and live with friends until spring. Due to the early winter, many of their neighbors were unable to make the trek to the mill in New Ulm to have their wheat ground into flour. Consequently, Marit shared her flour with them until it ran out. They then ate corn meal mush and Johnnycakes made from corn ground in a coffee mill for the duration.

While in the barn doing chores, twelve-year old Mathilda spotted a muskrat. She killed it with a pitchfork, skinned it and walked thirteen miles roundtrip to sell the pelt for nine cents. I never found out what she did with the nine cents.

Iver & Mathilda on their 50th Wedding anniversary in 1939

When Bengt died, a neighbor constructed a pine box for a casket since the nearest mortician was ninety miles away in Mankato. Marit did not like its looks, so in Norwegian tradition, she painted it with a mixture of milk and soot. Both parents died early and left the homestead to their surviving minor daughters, Mathilda and Olena. Iver subsequently became the court appointed guardian for the two girls in 1886.

After Mathilda turned eighteen, she and Iver were married 27 January 1889 in Hadley, Minnesota during a typical prairie blizzard with a temperature of minus 32 degrees. The wedding party traveled to the ceremony in a horse drawn sleigh early in the morning. A heavy snow fell so that they could barely make out the horses pulling the sleigh. The wedding party was served a breakfast of chicken and *fattigman*.

This union produced eight children: Carl Bernhart Moen, b. 08 July 1889, d. 19 May 1961; Clarence Moen, b. 08 October 1891, d. 16 January 1973; Mabel Amelia Moen, b. 23 June 1894, d. 16 May 1996; Ida M. Moen, b. 12 December 1896, d. 13 December 1978; Ellen Moen, b. 21 October 1899, d. 09 June 1980; Theodore Roland Moen, b. 19 March 1903, d. 28 December 1987; Alice Beatrice Moen, b. 08 July 1908, d. January 2003; Alma Bernice Moen, b. 08 July 1908, d 06 June 1926.

All of the children were born on the homestead and lived there until their marriage or moved away. Five are buried in Minnesota, one in Wisconsin and two in California. These eight children produced fourteen grandchildren for Iver and Mathilda.

Many of the descendants have graduated from college and entered the ranks of teachers, college professors, nurses and engineers. Others have pursued careers in business and farming. Many served in the armed forces of the United States. All inherited the same work ethic that served their ancestors so well.

Iver and Mathilda lived and worked the homestead for over 50 years. The great depression of the early 1930s disrupted their first retirement. They lost their entire savings in a bank failure and had to go back to the farm for an additional ten years of hard labor.

Iver was not atypical for the Norwegian pioneers. A youth of hardship and deprivation tempered his character, enabling him to survive on the hostile Minnesota prairie. He grew up in Hadeland during difficult times and under meager circumstances. Their modest hone, which measured only three meters by four meters, had to be burned down after his mother died of typhus. Shortly thereafter, Iver and Kari immigrated to America. The remaining children relocated to live and work with families in the Hadeland area.

The early life of a farmer on the Minnesota prairie was not easy; and many immigrants found the hardships and loneliness unbearable, so they returned to their families in Norway. Those that remained contributed the work ethic, perseverance and genetic code that made for the greatest generation of Americans – the same Americans who helped to liberated Norway and the rest of Europe from the tyranny of Nazi Germany.

Iver and Mathilda were charter members of the Rosendahl Norwegian Lutheran Church, organized in 1903 in Lake Wilson, Minnesota. A number of the children received their baptism and confirmation in this sanctuary. Several were also married there.

Until 1926, all services were conducted in Norwegian. There are still four living descendants of the original charter members – three are Iver Christiansen's (Moen) grandchildren. My sister, Mardelle B. Arrant (Gnadt) living in Encinitas, California; brother, Arthur L. Gnadt living in Lake Wilson; and Myron A. Gnadt living in Vista, California are those three grandchildren.

After retirement, Iver spent his time visiting the local building projects around town or helping his son, Clarence on the homestead. On one occasion, a tractor accidentally ran over him, crushing his chest and separating several ribs. Despite the severity of his injuries and the advanced age of 76, he recovered and lived an additional thirteen years.

Iver and Mathilda are buried in the Hillside Cemetery in Lake Wilson, Minn., as well as are a number of children of this family.

With exception of Iver's daughter, who died while giving birth, all of the children enjoyed exceptional longevity. My mother, Mabel, became the only centenarian, however. She lacked just a few days of her 102nd birthday when she passed away. She holds the longevity record for this entire Norwegian/Swedish/American clan.

According to my cousin Lloyd Olsen, who has conducted extensive research into the Kristian Iversen Retrumsmoen descendants, there are over 700 now living in the USA. Lloyd lives in Milan, Minnesota where he wrote a book about the family. Of the four original immigrants, Anders, Kari and Iver remained in Minnesota. Karen moved to Louisville, Kentucky.

John and Kari Kroshus

published August 2007   *Form 876*   *Anne Sladky*

With thanks to many Kroshus cousins for information about and photographs of the extended Kroshus family.

My Mom was very proud of her pure Hadeland ancestry and my Dad was perhaps even more proud of his Telemark heritage. Growing up, I accepted the easy assumption that I was half Hadeland and half Telemark. The old pioneer settlement where I grew up was Teler in culture and character. My great-great-grandfather emigrated from Telemark, but as I researched the previously ignored heritage of the wives in the family, my Telemark roots quickly dwindled. My paternal great-great-grandmother hailed from Land, one great-grandmother's roots were in Krodsherad, Buskerud, Norway – and Great-Grandma Pauline was a proud product of Hadeland immigrants!

Tracing my great-grandmother Pauline's heritage was a challenge. No one seemed to know much more than that her parents had come from Norway. Her father had a gravestone that gave dates and a place to start, but his wife was more difficult to track. With a little help from Blaine Hedberg at NAGC in Madison, I was finally able to piece together the story of both of these great-great-grandparents.

John Anderson Kroshus was born on the Molstad farm on May 29 and baptized on June 8, 1823. His parents were *husmann* Anders Johnson and Oline Abrahamsdtr. John married Maria Andersdtr from Toten on January 25, 1846 in Gran. Their daughter Marthe was born later that year and died a few months later. A second daughter, Oline, was born while they were living on the Dvergsten farm in 1848. John, his wife, and their daughter registered their intent to emigrate in the parish *udflyttede* on February 21, 1850.

The two-masted brig *Vesta* left Christiania on June 25, 1850 and arrived in New York on September 3 with 86 passengers aboard, most from Hadeland, including John, Maria and Oline. They probably made their way west with other *Vesta* passengers and settled in Clinton Township, Rock County, Wisconsin.

Kari's father, Peder Helgersen, was the *gaardmand* on Gudmundshagen and married Berthe Joensdtr on December 14, 1812. (Descendants of their son Christen still live on the Snuggerud farm in Hadeland.) Kari was born on December 30, 1821 and was baptized on January 6, 1822. She married an older widower, Halvor Pedersen, in 1849. He was born in Hurdal and at the time of their marriage was a *husmann* on Dvergsten. Their daughter Randi was born a few months later. On April 19, 1851, the *udflyttede* records their intent to make the journey to America. Halvor, Kari and Randi sailed from Christiania on the sailing ship *Richard Combden* on May 22, 1851, and arrived in New York on August 2. They, too, made their way to Wisconsin and settled in Racine County.

252

Epidemics raged through the Norwegian settlements in Wisconsin in the 1840s and early 1850s. Cholera and typhoid fever claimed many lives. We can only surmise that both John and Kari's families were touched by this tragedy. John's wife Maria and both Kari's husband Halvor and infant daughter Randi died in 1851.

Kari and John Kroshus

John and Kari had probably known each other since childhood. They had both lived with their spouses and children on the Dvergsten farm before John's family left in 1850. They were married in Racine County, Wisconsin on March 13, 1852. They must have been intent on leaving all the sadness behind. In short order they moved to Houston County, Minnesota, and settled outside Spring Grove, where John is listed in a local history as one of the first settlers in the southern part of the township. It is in Spring Grove that they first used the Kroshus surname. Their first son, Halvor, was born on the farm on June 5, 1853. In keeping with tradition, he was named after Kari's first husband.

A good friend of John's from Hadeland, Andrew Pedersen, had been working at a sawmill in the Muskego settlement. In the fall of 1853 he walked the 275 miles from Muskego to Spring Grove and convinced John to sell him his 200-acre farm for $150. Andrew, in the old tradition of Norway, took the name of the farm (Kroshus) as his last name.

In 1854 John moved his family just across the border to Winnishiek County, Iowa. Five more children were born on the farm near Highlandsville in the Big Canoe settlement. Maria, named after John's first wife, was born October 11, 1856. Anna was born March 13, 1858. Peter, namesake of Kari's father, was born on March 24, 1860. My great-grandmother Pauline was born July 10, 1862, and Albert Julius was born December 22, 1864.

John's oldest daughter Oline (Ellen/Olive) (1848-1913) married Berge Olai Lee. Born in Voss, he served in Company H of the famed Scandinavian Regiment (the Wisconsin 15th) during the Civil War. They homesteaded a farm near Underwood ND, but would eventually join the migration from that area to Snohomish County, Washington.

Olina Kroshus Lee

253

Halvor Kroshus

Halvor (1853-1932) married a Hadeland girl named Christie Melbostad. They moved to Lee Township, Norman County, Minnesota in the late 1870s where he became one of the area's largest and most successful farmers. Halvor and Christie had 14 children. They and many of their descendants are buried in Bethania Lutheran Church Cemetery, rural Perley, Minnesota.

Maria/Mary Kroshus married Johannes (John) Olesen from Spring Grove, Minnesota. He was the son of Ole and Ingeborg Heggen.

John Anderson Kroshus died April 6, 1879, and is buried in Big Canoe Cemetery in Winnishiek County, Iowa. Mary's husband John/Johannes took over the Iowa farm and Mary and John adopted the farm name/surname Kroshus. Kari accompanied her son-in-law and daughter when they returned to Spring Grove in the late 1880s. Mary died on February 18, 1904. Many a cousin has been frustrated trying to connect themselves to members of Andrew Kroshus' and Johannes Kroshus' families in Spring Grove! Underscoring the general genealogical confusion that dates back to that time, Mary is listed as the daughter of *Ole* Kroshus in her obituary. It is believed that Kari continued to live with her son-in-law until her death on August 10, 1906.

Anna Kroshus followed her brother Halvor to Norman County. She married John Gaare, who had homesteaded in Clay County. They

John and Anna Kroshus Gaare

purchased an additional farm near Halvor in Lee Township, Norman County, and established their home there. John and Anna raised 10 children. She died July 7, 1908. John and Anna Gaare and many of their descendants are buried in Bethania Church Cemetery.

Little is known about Peter Kroshus, and he may have died as a child. He was born March 24, 1860.

Albert Kroshus was born December 22, 1864 and also settled in Norman County. He married Johanna Johnson on October 31, 1888. The couple had two children before Albert's untimely death on February 3, 1896.

My Great-Grandma Pauline (always pronounced in the Norwegian way: Paulina) was born July 10, 1862. She joined her

Albert and Johanne Kroshus

254

siblings in Norman County and took a job as a schoolteacher. She met Alexander Grover through friends and they were married on November 20, 1884. They had two children: Clarence (1886-1949) and my grandfather, Elmer (1889-1962). Elmer and his wife Alette Hegland had three children: Raymond Hegland (1915-1993), Gerald Alexander (1918-1989) and Wanda Pauline (1922-2006). My father Gerald married a 'purebred' Hadeland descendant, Ruby Alm.

Pauline was a woman way ahead of her time. She was intelligent, independent and headstrong. Teaching was her passion, and she was delighted when her husband took a lucrative year-round job working for a logging company in northern Minnesota. Logging camps were no place for a lady! It wasn't considered proper for a married woman to continue as a teacher, but with her husband gone Pauline played the "woman alone with two children to support" card (despite having income from their farm outside Perley *and* Alex's hefty salary from the logging company) and made her way back into the classroom. During his five-year absence she and her children spent some time living with Alex's parents. Pauline was exempt from household chores and could focus all of her attention on her students and the books she loved to read.

Great-Grandma Pauline

Tongues did wag, of course, both because of the marital separation and her job outside the home. It didn't stop when Alex returned from the north, but luckily gossip never bothered Pauline. She was a night owl who thought nothing of washing a floor by lamplight at midnight ("How can she see the dirt at that hour?") and then sleeping until 7 a.m. ("Practically noon, and she forces her husband to get his own and the poor children's breakfasts!")

Alex would set a time of departure but he soon learned that outside the schoolhouse, time was relative to Pauline. His sons loved to tell the story of how their dad would load them in the buggy and study his pocket watch until it was time to go. Alex would give the reins a snap and begin a slow meander down the driveway. Pauline would race from the house, petticoats flying and shoes untied, and leap into the slow moving vehicle. She finished with her buttons, her shoes and her hair en route to wherever they were going. Their parents might have a pleasant conversation in the buggy, but the subject of her tardiness and his solution for it was never discussed.

In the 1910s my grandfather Elmer brought Pauline to southern Minnesota to visit her family there. A bi-plane landed in a nearby field and all the neighbors gathered for an impromptu air show. One of her nephews recalled that Pauline had plenty of questions for the aviator and he offered her a ride – a dicey business in those early years. It took the combined will of a half dozen relatives to keep the 50+ year old Pauline out of the passenger seat. In her 70s she would sigh when a plane flew overhead and say that one of her great regrets was missing her one chance to "loop-de-loop."

Pauline's hair turned white before her 40th birthday. The gift of thick silver-white hair is one that her sons, grandchildren and great-grandchildren have been delighted to inherit (a little later in life).

One of her students went on to receive advanced degrees and had a noteworthy career in engineering. He paid her the ultimate compliment when, upon receiving an honory doctorate in Chicago, he allowed that everything he needed to know about basic mathematics he learned in a one-room country school in Minnesota from his brilliant teacher, Pauline.

She lived less than a year longer than the husband who understood her so well, and passed away on December 20, 1941. She is buried with Alex in the Grover family plot in Concordia Lutheran Church Cemetery, rural Glyndon, Minnesota.

Guthorm and Oline Mohagen

published November 2007   *Forms 135, 607*   *Doris Stark Morland*

Guthorm Mohagen

Oline Tingelstad Mohagen

Introduction

Ella Jorgine Mohagen Flom was the author of an article entitled "Mohagen Memories." She was born July 12, 1913 and died February 26, 2007. She was married to Torjus Flom of Grafton, ND. Ella was buried in St. Stephen's Cemetery, rural Milton ND. The information was recalled by her father, Robert Hans Mohagen. His wife, Nelsine Strom Mohagen was born July 11, 1878 in Nesna, Nordland. She died March 12, 1939 in Grafton.

Some of the information from that article was revised and additions were made as it was also of great importance to Doris Stark Morland. Her grandfather, Guthorm Hansen Mohagen, was Robert's brother. Doris' mother, Christine Nickoline Mohagen Stark was a daughter of Guthorm. In Norway, Guttorm's surname was spelled Mohagan. In America, the spelling was changed to Mohagen.

Norway

Late in the 18th Century, perhaps around 1780 or 1790, Reier Mohagen lived in Hadeland, Norway. One of his children, Guttorm, married Anne. This young peasant couple became the parents of three daughters, Randi, Kjersti, and Gudbjor; and two sons, Gulbrand and Hans.

Hans Guttormsen Mohagen (June 8, 1834-March 31, 1920) married Mari Hansdatter Heggen (January 8, 1836-March 8, 1879) on December 25, 1861. Hans was of special interest to the original author Ella

The Mohagen farm in Norway where Guthorm and Kjersti were born

257

Mohagen Flom and my mother Christine Mohagen Stark because he was their grandfather. Hans is buried in the Grafton Lutheran Cemetery.

Both Hans and Mari grew up in Hadeland. Hans learned the art of shoemaking. He worked for the landowner all week except for one day when he would care for his own small plot of land. The weeks preceding Christmas were the busiest as everyone had to have new shoes to wear on Christmas Day. The poor shoemaker worked until midnight for several weeks making shoes for Christmas. Hans and Mari's first three children were born in Norway. Guthorm Hansen Mohagen was born February 10, 1863 at the farm Almseiet in Gran, Hadeland, Norway; Kjersti was born October 14, 1864 and died in the US on January 2, 1927; and Anne was born September 1, 1867 and died in the U.S. on November 12, 1888.

On April 22, 1869, the young family emigrated to America, crossing the Atlantic on the sailship *Anna Delius.* My grandfather Guthorm was six years of age when the family left Norway in 1869. His sister Anne was only a year and a half at the time they sailed.

The voyage was a real hardship, as young "Fru" Mohagen was sick much of the time. Each family did tis own cooking and had a designated stove lid for its own use on board the ship. Hans did the cooking for his family while Mari was ill. When she felt strong enough, she went down to prepare the food and was politely informed by the other women that she was using the shoemaker's stove lid. The kindly women had never seen Mari, so they couldn't know that she was the shoemaker's wife!

America

The *Anne Delius* landed on June 14, 1869 at Quebec, Canada. After spending almost two months on ship, the passengers must have been thankful to be on land again. The almost penniless Mohagen family was able to borrow thirty dollars, which saw them to their destination in Fillmore County, Minnesota, where they lived for 11 years. Their occupation was farming. It was customary in those days, when a man borrowed one hundred dollars, he received only ninety, as he had to pay a bonus of ten percent.

Two sons, Hans (July 29, 1872-January 17, 1964) and Robert (May 2, 1875-August 6, 1970) were born near Preston, Minnesota, and are buried at the Grafton Lutheran Cemetery, Grafton ND.

Minnesota

In 1877 the family moved to Yellow Medicine County, Minnesota, but stayed there only one year. The grasshoppers took over and ate almost everything, including even some of the fence posts. This forced the family to move back to Fillmore County.

Sorrow soon came. Hans' wife Mari died on March 8, 1879. She was buried in North Prairie Norwegian Lutheran Cemetery, nine miles west of Rushford, Minnesota. The wooden cross which marked her grave is no longer there.

By now, the widowed Hans had heard about the rich Red River Valley of Dakota Territory, so he too decided to homestead there. One sister, Gudbjor, and her husband remained in Minnesota until 1882 when they moved to Dakota. The other family members all left together.

They left Minnesota in late spring, May 1880, because they had to wait until there was green grass for grazing the cattle along the way. There were five or six covered wagons in the train and all had horses except one wagon had oxen. The oxen were unable to keep up with the horses and were soon exhausted. This wagon, a huge chest and stove had to be shipped to Grand Forks, which was the end of the railroad. The huge chest is now in the home of Sandy (Mohagen) Stark and her husband Roger of Grafton ND. Grand Forks consisted of a few shacks and a post office. The smaller articles were loaded on other wagons and the family rode in the Hans Mohagen wagon. The Mohagen family didn't even know their exact destination, but headed northwest through Minnesota.

Minnesota to Dakota Territory

They would plod along all week and rest on Sundays. One day they were camped by a railroad track and trains didn't usually go on Sundays so they thought it was perfectly safe. However, that Sunday there was a train and it frightened the horses, who had been turned loose to graze. The horses took off, even the one that was hobbled, and ran for many miles before finally coming to a stop by a creek. Luckily one horse was staked so they didn't have to chase the horses on foot.

The Mohagen family could not make much headway with their covered wagons and quite often could see just a short distance back where they had camped the night before. Occasionally, the men had to take the wagons apart and carry each piece across the mud and slush. The men would go back and carry the women and children "piggy back" to the wagons. A child's chair, handmade in Norway in 1862, was set too close to the campfire and became charred. This chair is in a Stark home in Grafton.

The chair charred en route to Dakota Territory

The 17-year-old Guthorm and the other boys and girls herded the cattle as they moved along. Their faithful dog was very efficient at herding cattle so the young folks didn't mind their work. However when the party left Sauk Center MN, they missed their dog. Old Hans went back to look for the dog but was unsuccessful in his hunt. They had to continue on the way without their dog.

At Sauk Center they met a man who had been to Dakota Territory before. He acted as their guide for the rest of the way. Earlier on their trip they met an Englishman who guided them for some distance. Food was scarce so their main source of food was milk. They eagerly ate berries which they found along the way.

259

Dakota Territory

The Mohagen family settled in Walsh Center Township, Walsh County, near the town of Grafton. Five acres of the hard sod was broken up that first summer. This was done with a walking plow and four oxen. The prairie sod was very hard to break. About one acre could be broken in one day. Old Hans used his two oxen, Buck and Star, while a neighbor furnished the second yoke of oxen. After that the men of the new settlement went to older communities and worked in the harvest fields.

As there was not time for Hans to build a shack on his claim before leaving for the harvest fields, his four younger children stayed with their neighbors that summer. The house was a 14 by 16 foot sod house and just high enough for a man to stand erect inside. The walls were several feet thick.

The women had few housekeeping duties in a sod house. No washing or sweeping of the dirt floors was necessary. All cooking was done outside and on rainy days they lived on milk and bread. Some neighbors who lived a quarter of a mile west, owned a stone with an oven. They were good-hearted folks and allowed the Mohagen women to bring their loaves of bread and bake them in their oven.

Some of the women were in charge of the cows that grazed on the prairie. Sometimes in a rainstorm the women would be thoroughly drenched when they came home to the sod house. It was difficult to dry anything on rainy days. Huge logs had been hauled home from the woods for summer fuel. Those at home would whittle away at these logs for firewood but finally had to have the help of a neighbor who came and chopped the wood for them.

Their first summer in Dakota must have seemed very long – one day after another without change. You may be sure it was watched as far as the eye could see. During the summer the men worked on farms in Minnesota. Sometimes Hans, Guthorm's father, would send a small amount of money in the form of a check. Hans' sister would have to say that she was married to Hans in order to cash it.

When harvest was over the men returned with their yokes of oxen. That fall, with lumber purchased at Drayton, Hans built a frame house on his homestead. The roof was sod and the walls were also walled in with sod so that winter the house was cozy and warm. The one room was raised about four feet and improved in 1892 and was in use until the 1930s.

Roofs were leaky and not substantial on rainy days. One night it rained so hard that the Mohagens had to find other shelter. Hans and his oldest son Guthorm carried the two other little sons, Hans and Robert, over to Gulbrand Mohagen's home. They had a wooden house which was better than a sod house but it also leaked a little water from the ceiling. They set dishpans and kettles on the beds to keep the bedding dry. The young sleepers thought that the dripping rain made a pleasant sound.

No groves of trees and farm homes were in sight but only endless prairie met the horizon. Late summer brought an abundance of wild strawberries. Often the ground ahead of the plow was red with berries. The boys, Hans and Robert, ran ahead trying to eat them all before the plow came. Stomach aches from these strawberry days are still not forgotten.

Since the railroad didn't reach Grafton until New Years in 1881, supplies in town were scarce. After the snow came in the fall of 1880, Hans and three other neighbors went on skis to Acton, ND, to buy food. One of the men even mortgaged a yoke of oxen to buy groceries. In those days, if a man had a dollar he would gladly share it with others in need. They made the trip in a day but returned late, after dark. My grandfather Guthorm lit a lantern and put it on top of the house to guide them. They saw the light and went toward it knowing it must be someone's home. Happily, it turned out to be Hans Mohagen's own home.

The following spring, cottonwood trees were planted. A few of these trees are still alive. Sanitation in those pioneer times was very difficult. Flies in the early fall made even eating a difficulty. Screened windows were unheard of in sod houses.

In the fall Hans went to work in the harvest fields near Grand Forks ND. When work was completed he returned by train to Minto ND where the railroad ended. From there, he walked to his home , a distance of about 9 miles. Hans always brought gifts for his children.

The first school in the community and the second one in Walsh County (District #2) was conveniently located approximately one mile west of the homestead. My grandfather Guthorm attended school during the winter months and was also the janitor. This gave him a chance to correct his spelling on his slate and have a perfect mark every day. If the teacher suspected, she never told him. Many children of the neighbors of the Mohagens attended the same one-room school. A block of wood was kept under the teacher's desk for a footrest. After the block became dry it made fine kindling.

My brothers Gordon and Fred and I attended the same country school, District #2, for many of our elementary years. We continued our education in the Grafton Public School System, as our parents would move from the farm to town for the nine months of the school year. The country school, now a shed, is on the Wayne Lessard farm across from the original homestead.

The Mohagens always had a dog. A well-remembered one was a brown and curly-haired Fido. His shaggy hair almost covered his eyes. He was a wonderful watchdog and would hever let strangers touch anything when the Mohagens were away. Fido was a special guardian of young Hans, who had a crippled foot and couldn't run as fast as the other children.

Guthorm's sister, Kjersti married Kittel Strand and they moved to a home of their own. Anne died in 1926, leaving Hans alone with his sons. They managed quite well with young Robert doing the cooking, baking bread, churning butter, and making pancakes. When spring came, they hired a young woman to assist them in their home.

The winter of 1882-1883 was very severe and the three-day blizzards kept the family close to the fireside. The low barn was all but snowed under but it was necessary to reach it and care for the livestock. Whoever went to the barn tied the end of a twine to the door knob and then carried the ball of twine under his arm. In this way he made his way into the darkness of the storm and always found his way back to the house.

Summers brought storms. A bad hail storm was said to have broken every west side window of the Grafton Court House. Large branches broke off trees and corn and grain fields were also destroyed. Roads were almost nonexistent in those early days. The horse-drawn wagons made deep ruts in the ground. When the ruts became too deep, the next wagon would make a new track; the trail became very wide in places.

Guthorm married Oline Thingelstad in 1889 in Grafton ND. In Norway, Oline's maiden name was spelled Tingelstad. They lived a mile north of the original homestead and had five children:

- Marie, born January 20, 1890, married Henry Sather
- Manvel was born October 6, 1894 and died May 10, 1972
- Oscar, born January 21, 1899, died on November 23, 1918, during the influenza epidemic.
- Christine, born March 20, 1904, married Alfred John Stark on May 7, 1926. He was born September 13, 1898. Alfred died on November 22, 1968. Christine lived to the age of 82, and died on June 16, 1986.
- Olga was born October 30, 1905 and died before her second birthday on August 12, 1907.

All members of the family are buried in the Guthorm Mohagen family plot at the Grafton Lutheran Cemetery, Grafton, North Dakota.

Oline was only 44 years of age when she died on March 2, 1909. The widowed Guthorm lived on the homestead with his children for many years. He was very proud of his Hadeland heritage and was a member of the Hadeland Lag. He traveled by rain in 1925 to attend the Norwegian-American Centennial Celebration in St. Paul/Minneapolis. The special lapel medallion which he wore to the celebration, is among the special keepsakes in my home in Fargo, North Dakota.

My parents, Alfred and Christine Stark lived and died in Grafton. They had three children:

- Gordon Alfred Stark (November 16, 1926-December 26, 2003) is buried at the Grafton Lutheran Cemetery. He married Donna Margaret Erlendson (b. October 6, 1926) in Grafton, where Donna still lives. They had three children, and in 2007 had four grandchildren and two great-grandchildren.

262

- The author of this story, Doris Marilynn Stark Molland, was born on July 28, 1930. She was married to Robert T. Molland (1926-2012) and lives in Fargo ND. They had four children. As of 2007, they had four grandchildren and two great-grandchildren.
- Melfred Manvel (Fred) Stark was born February 7, 1932. He died October 19, 2009. He married Elizabeth Jean (Betty) Ebert in Grafton, North Dakota. She was born November 27, 1931. They made their home in Grafton and had two children. In 2007, they had six grandchildren.

Nels Christopherson Myrah

published February 2008   *Form 564*   *Andy Tweito*

Nels Christopherson Myrah

Of all the people who have lived through the ages, only a few actually "made history." Much like a movie, history is really made with a few "main" characters and a lot of extras. Although the extras far outnumber the stars, it is the stars who garner the accolades as the extras disappear into obscurity. The extras only notice comes as the credits roll and their names scroll down the screen for a moment and then disappear. So it is in history. The extras participate for their brief moments, then disappear into the forgotten parts of the past.

My great-great-grandfather Nels Christopherson Myrah was an "extra" in American history during the years 1854 to 1907. He got to be a part of some of the truly historical events as this country grew. He was never the star and he probably had no idea of the importance of the events he got to witness.

He was born on May 5, 1844 to Christopher Nilsen Myrah and Marthe Ellertsdatter in Hadeland. Nels' father died in 1850 from unknown causes. In 1854, at the age of 10, Nels and his grandfather, Nils Hansen Daelen Myrah (b. 1780), emigrated from Norway to the United States. The Myrah family traveled west in their "new" country and settled in Spring Grove, Minnesota along "Norwegian Ridge" just east of town on the Myrah farm. The stone for the first stone church built in Spring Grove was quarried from the Myrah farm and built by Nels' uncle, Hans Myrah.

Ten years after arriving in America, Nels joined the Union Army. On Sept. 2, 1864, under the name Nels Christopher, Nels became a private in the Union Army. Before leaving for Fort Snelling on Sept. 5, 1864, Nels married Kari Ellingsdatter Hellerud. Kari was born on Sept. 23, 1842 in Sigdal, Norway. Her family had come to America in 1861 and had also settled in Spring Grove. Nels had to pass a physical before he could report to Fort Snelling. In Rochester, Minnesota a doctor by the name of William Mayo gave Nels a physical, which he passed. Later Dr. Mayo helped found what is now the world-renowned Mayo Clinic.

Kari Ellingsdatter Hellerud

Thirteen days after he was married, on September 18, 1864, Nels and fifty-five other recruits from Fort Snelling joined the Second Light Minnesota Artillery

Battery at Fort Irwin, Tennessee, a part of the Chattanooga fortifications. Captain William A. Hotchkiss was in command of the Second Light. Under his direction the men were repairing the fort. According to Charles Eugene Flandrau, in his book *Minnesota in the Civil War and Indian Wars*, "December 1, 1864, obeying telegraphic orders from General George H. Thomas, Captain Hotchkiss organized a brigade of light batteries including the Second Light Minnesota and reported to General James Stedman. Confederate General John Hood's army had flanked Chattanooga and the Confederates were marching upon Nashville via Columbia, Tenn. and Franklin, Tenn. At midnight the combined artillery brigade reached Bridgeport, Tenn. By the middle of the forenoon of the next day the combined artillery brigade caught up with General Stedman at Cowan Station. The Battle of Franklin was being fought. In the evening of the next day the artillery brigade arrived in Nashville and was posted by Captain Hotchkiss on General Stedman's line between the river and the Murfreesboro turnpike road. When the Battle of Nashville began, this brigade of light artillery guns commenced the conflict. At the battle's conclusion Captain Hotchkiss and the Second Light Minnesota returned to Chattanooga where he remained in command until March 30, 1865. At that date the battery, under the command of its captains, proceeded to Philadelphia, Tenn. and served there as the garrison of the fort until the last week in July, 1865, when, pursuant to orders from the War Department, it started by railway for Fort Snelling, where it arrived without incident. On the sixteenth of August, 1865 the Second Light Minnesota was mustered out of service. 'Since the war,' said Captain Hotchkiss, 'most of the brave Second Light Minnesota Battery comrades have acquitted themselves honorably as citizens of the Union they helped to preserve – some of them have acquired fame in professions and in business, others have proved worthy in various other callings. If any of those who received an honorable discharge have proved unworthy it is not known to the writer hereof'."

Upon discharge from the army on September 4, 1865, Nels purchased 120 acres of wild land in Black Hammer Township, 5-6 miles northwest of Spring Grove. It was here that Nels and Kari had a son Elling Nelson Myrah (Tweito) born December 22, 1868. My great-uncle, Thomas Elmore Tweito – grandson of Nels, writes the following account in an old letter: "Grandpa farmed there for several years, but he decided to exercise his homesteading rights, since the Homesteading Act had been passed by the U.S. Congress in 1862." So he sold the Black Hammer farm.

Preparations for the westward move were minimal, since they had little to transport. Grandfather cut willow and hickory saplings and bent and tied them like arches over the wagon and covered them with canvas. The family packed all of its possessions in the covered wagon. Grandma's dishes, pots and pans, some bedding, clothes, potatoes, flour, wheat and other supplies were placed in the wagon box, as well as a plow, hand tools, ax and saw. Grandpa's gun, bullet pouch and powder horn were hung onto the wooden bows of the wagon. The wagon was "filled to the rafters."

They waited until the snow was gone and grass appeared, so the animals could forage along the way. Then, early one morning in April, they hooked a span of oxen to the wagon and pointed them westward toward "Sunset Land."

They followed a trail which was rather well marked to Rochester, thence to Mankato and New Ulm. Beyond that point, the trail had been less traveled and disappeared on the boundless prairies, which now merged into the Great Plains that swelled against the rim of a seemingly immense blue dome that was the sky.

Beyond Mankato and New Ulm they followed the Minnesota River Valley ever westward. This river had some sizeable tributaries that were not easily forded, so they were often delayed by high water. It was no easy matter to "gee" and "haw" the prodding oxen. Ten miles of travel a day was considered very good. But the pioneers crept onward into the mysterious silence of the great western plains.

They camped along the trail. Each night Grandpa would gather firewood and build a fire. He would also fetch water for cooking and drinking. A cow tied behind the wagon provided milk for the children and for cooking. Their livestock was tethered each night to graze.

After a month's journey, they reached Redwood County in the environs of present-day Walnut Grove. There they stopped, while Grandpa marked the quarter section he wished to claim. Then he went to the land office to file his claim. Many readers may be familiar with Laura Ingalls Wilder's books, *Little House on the Prairie* and *On the Banks of Plum Creek*. When my grandparents arrived there, no other house was within eyesight. While no claim is made that theirs was the "Little House on the Prairie," certainly their house was the prototype thereof. Moreover, the 12 by 16 foot cabin they built with logs cut from the walnut grove on their claim, was about twenty-five paces from Plum Creek. It was situated on the banks of that stream. Much of the original walnut grove was on their land, and in years ahead a village sprang up.

My grandparents lived on that claim for five years, but repeated grasshopper plagues, rivaling Biblical plagues, destroyed their crops annually. It is difficult to understand how they survived.

When the railroad was built, it crossed their claim. Jealousies arose because many people thought my grandparents would profit from the increased land value as a result of the railroad crossing their land. On one occasion Grandpa noticed a man with a gun in hand crouching in the tall grass to get near enough to shoot him. Grandpa got his own gun and ordered the man to get out or he would shoot. The stranger left amidst a stream of profanity.

My grandparents got a reasonably good offer for their claim. So, in view of jealousies, repeated crop failures, and the fact that Sioux Indians were constantly coming to ask my grandmother for her chickens or other food and taking what they wanted, they decided to sell and return to Spring Grove in 1874. They traveled in a covered wagon on their return trip, much like the one used to go westward to Walnut Grove.

In Spring Grove, they located a log cabin a few yards east of the road going south on Hospital Hill (*Smebakken*) where they lived during the next few months. My siblings and I remember that cabin very well. It was still standing the last time I visited Spring Grove.

Then my grandparents purchased a farm from *Staerke* Hans (Strong Hans) Tweito about a mile and a half south of Spring Grove. The place has been known as the "Old Tweito farm" since. However, my grandfather never used the Tweito name. He was Christopher Myrah's son and always called himself Nels Christopherson. That's the name that appears on his naturalization papers also. I have originals or duplicates of them.

The family enjoyed modest prosperity because of industriousness and the fertility of bottom fields of the farm that lay at the upper reaches of Pleasant Valley. Upon retirement, my grandparents bought a comfortable home in Spring Grove, where Grandma died in 1907. Grandpa died in Maddock, North Dakota, where a son and daughter lived and where the old pioneer was buried. He should have been buried in Spring Grove because he was an early settler and lived most of his life there, contributing to its early history.

When my grandparents sold their Walnut Grove farm, they did not get a cash settlement. Letters to the buyer brought no response. So in 1876 Grandpa went back to attempt to collect. He walked from Spring Grove to a point on, or near, the railroad between Winona and Rochester. He didn't know exactly where he was in the dark of the night. But he saw light flickering under a window shade in a building that looked like a hotel or tavern. He rapped on the door and was met by several men with pulled revolvers. He was dragged inside, and the weary traveler was submitted to a barrage of questions. He finally convinced them that he was a farmer and not a Pinkerton detective. They set him down in a chair, and he was guarded by one or more armed men all night.

At daybreak, they all mounted excellent steeds. Grandpa was put on a horse also in front of another rider. They rode ten or twelve miles into the wilderness. Then the men set their prisoner free with the admonition that if he said anything to anybody, they would hunt him down and kill him.

Grandpa didn't know where he was, but he wandered about until he got to the railroad. He caught a train to Walnut Grove, attended to his business, and then got on a train for the homeward journey. An extended stop was made in Mankato, where a large crowd of people had gathered. They were excitedly talking about the fact that a Northfield bank had been robbed, and the Jesse James-Cole Younger gang had been thwarted – some killed – in a hail of gunfire. Grandpa (Nels) was absolutely convinced, after viewing the caricatures on the wanted posters, that he had been prisoner of the James/Younger guard while they cased Minnesota towns for robbery.

Thinking about the parts of history my great, great grandfather was able to witness I hope he understood the significance of his experiences. He met Dr. William Mayo. He participated in the Civil War. He helped lay the foundations of Walnut Grove and some of the Laura Ingalls Wilder sagas, and he spent the night with Jesse James and the James gang. He came a long way from his boyhood in Hadeland. The whole story almost sounds like a dream. I guess it really was a dream – an American dream.

Ole and Kjersti Halvorson

published August 2008   *Form 448*   *Frank Evenson*

The Ole and Kjersti Halvorson family, probably taken in Colorado 1907-1908
Standing: Alfred, Clara, Nora Oscar, Ida and Mabel
Front: Ole, Clarence amd Kjersti

Ole Halvorson and Kjersti Larsdatter immigrated from Gran Parish, Hadeland, on Nov. 9, 1883. They informed their pastor of their intentions to leave Norway in November of 1883 and left Kristiania on the ship *SS Rollo*, a Wilson Line steamship. Accompanying them was Kjersti's mother Marthe Amundsdatter, son Louis (born in 1881) and daughter Berthe (born in 1883). Also on board was Kjersti's sister Kari, husband Hans Andersen Morstad and their 3 children.

Kjersti Larsdatter was born on the farm Morstad, Gran Parish, on May 10, 1859. Her father was Lars Eriksen, born on the farm Aschiem on April 15, 1804. Kjersti's mother was Marthe

269

Amundsdatter, born on the farm Wøyen on Oct. 12, 1814. Lars and Marthe were married on Oct. 11, 1837, Gran Parish. Marthe's parents were Amund Nilssen and Kirsti Olsdatter of the farm Wøyen.

Ole Halvorson was born to Berite Larsdatter on Feb. 20, 1853 on the farm Grua, Jevnaker Parish. Ole was baptized on March 28, 1853 and confirmed in 1869, while living on the farm Volstad Engen. His father was Halvor Olsen, born in 1829 on the farm Larmerud, owner of the farm Larshus, Jevnaker Parish, as shown in the 1865 and 1875 censuses. Berite Larsdatter was born on Dec. 3, 1833 on the farm Houer, Jevnaker Parish. The 1865 census shows Ole living with his mother on the farm Volstad Egen, where her occupation is shown to be a weaver. Berite's parents were Lars Larsen and Birtette Halvorsdatter of the farm Houer.

The 1865 census shows Lars Ericksen as the owner of the farm Grinimarken, Gran Parish. There are five children listed: Erik Larsen age 23, Anders Larsen age 12, Ole Larsen age 15, Mari Larsdatter age 17, and Kjersti Larsdatter age 7. It does not show daughter Kari who was married and living on the farm Morstad. Parish records show that Mari moved to Oslo in 1874 and Kjersti also moved to Oslo in 1879.

Ole started cutting wood while still living with his mother on the farm Volstad. He would take food with him and be gone for several weeks, using a horse and cart to haul the wood he had cut. Since military service was mandatory for all male youth, it is possible that Ole and Kjersti met in Oslo while he was in the service. Ole and Kjersti were married on June 8, 1880, in the Lunner Parish Church, Hadeland, Norway. When Lars Eriksen died in 1883, the farm Grinimarken was sold to Hans Larsen Haugerud.

Per Shager, an uncle by marriage of Anders (brother of Kjersti, now living in Minnesota) was making regular trips between America and Norway. Per was born January 1, 1819 and immigrated to America in 1846. According to the 1900 census of Minnesota he was living on a farm near Hartland, Minn. He helped immigrants who wanted to immigrate to America in exchange for free first-class passage. The passenger list shows Per Shager on the *SS Rollo*, which left Christiania every Friday, making the North Sea crossing in about 40 hours. The *SS Rollo* was 260 feet long and 32 feet wide, pretty small by today's standards. The following was written about the ship: the salon and sleeping berths are large and comfortable, mostly for two passengers in one stateroom; but there are also family cabins and ladies cabins, with every comfort and convenience. The accommodation is 42 first-class passengers and 30 second-class passengers. Upon reaching the port of Hull, England, they went through immigration and stayed in emigrant waiting rooms until leaving by rail. They may have traveled by Paragon Railroad to Glasgow, leaving about 11 a.m. on Monday, reaching Glasgow about 3 p.m. that same day. They left Glasgow on the steamship *SS State of Indiana* November 18 and reached New York November 30.

The *State of Indiana* was a new screw steamship built in 1874 for the State Line Steam-Ship Company, to be employed in the trade between Glasgow and New York. " The steerage

Mayflower Ranch, Hartland, Minnesota, October 7, 1934
Back row; left to right: Alfred, Oscar, Bertha, Ida, Louis, Clarence
Front row: Matilda, Hilda, Kjersti, Clara, Nora, Mabel

accommodation is unsurpassed. Separate compartments are provided for single men, for married couples and families and for single women – cleanliness and good ventilation prevails throughout; and in cold weather the entire ship is heated by steam."

They arrived in Hartland, Minn. in December of 1883 and stayed with Anders (brother of Kjersti) and his wife who lived on the Peter Johnson farm. The Myrebaken sod house, about a mile south of Anders' farm, was available so they lived there until spring. Ole and Kjersti worked on various farms around Hartland, Minn. while raising 11 children. Ole filed papers for "The Declaration of Intention" on Nov. 3, 1888 and final naturalization papers were signed on Dec. 14, 1896. Witnesses on his naturalization papers were Nels Jordahl and Andrew Nelson. There are no records that Ole and Kjersti bought any property while living in Minnesota.

In 1907 they moved near Genoa, Colorado, where they homesteaded a farm. It is believed they traveled by railroad while moving to Colorado. According to notes left by Mabel Halvorson Evenson, the train took five days to reach Genoa. They took cattle, horses and machinery on the train. When they reached the homestead, several men dug the cellar and put boards across the cellar with a chimney sticking out of the boards. Ole and Kjersti slept in the cellar, while the children stayed with Hilda (daughter of Ole and Kjersti) and Paul Simonson, who were already living in the area. There were wild horses and cattle running around the ranch house because there was no fence to keep them out. Because it was cool in the dirt cellar, they were able to keep the milk, cream and butter there. Son Oscar who was 18 years old dug the 58-foot-deep well for water. They put boards over the well, which Ole used to water the cattle by pail and chain. Ole and Kjersti lived on the farm near Genoa, Colo. until their death. Ole died on April 12, 1929 and Kjersti died on March 9, 1937.

The descendants of Ole and Kjersti celebrated the 50th anniversary of having a Halvorson reunion in 2008 at Rapid City, South Dakota. It is normally held either in Minnesota or Colorado where most of the descendants live.

Ben Hansen

"Hadeland Folkemuseum" published August 2008   *Form 899*   *Kari-Mette Avtjern*

Kaare Bakken from Brandbu has been eager to find out more about his family history. Kaare's grandfather had nine siblings and lived at Grinakereie in Brandbu. Both Kaare's grandfather's parents and six of his siblings immigrated from Brandbu to America. Kaare had some information and pictures of his relatives in America, but was searching for more.

One of Kaare's grandfather's brothers was named Bent Hansen. Bent immigrated to the USA in 1900 and visited his family in Brandbu in 1940. Bent sent some pictures of his American family, but that is all the information Kaare had about Bent. Some time ago, by luck, Kaare found "Wisconsin Telephone News" from November 1930 in his aunt belongings. There was no doubt why his aunt had kept this paper. An article in the paper tells about Bent, his life in Norway and in Wisconsin. Now we know what happened to Bent, or Ben as he called himself in America.

The article is an interesting story about a boy from Norway who ended up as city foreman and the early history of the telephone. Here is some of the article:

"Ben, being the champion bicycle rider of Norway in 1896 and 1897 decided that he wouldn't let Leif Erickson have anything on him so grabbed a boat for America, landing at Madison in 1900, with two suitcases, a package of dried beef and a small keg of smoked herring."

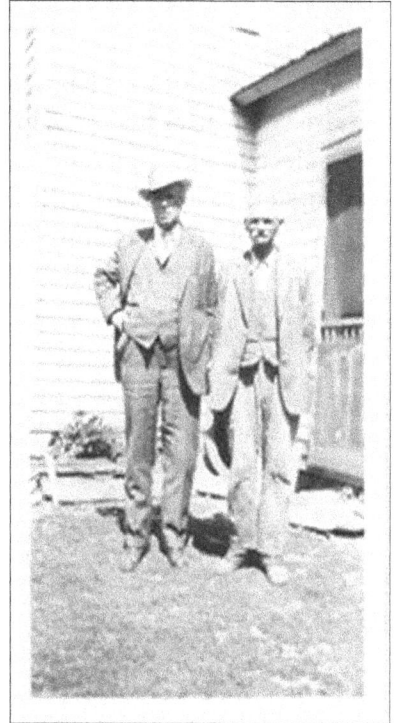

Ben Hansen and his brother Hans Hansen (1865-1944) on Hans' farm, probably in De Forest, WI

"In Norway, in the latter part of 1887, Ben Hansen started with what he has followed since, namely telephone work. Since those early days he has witnessed a complete change in the business. For instance, there were no common battery lines, all circuits being grounded, and transporting lines were unknown until a few years later. From 1887 to 1890 he worked as groundman, lineman, and was sent to the Electrical Bureau in Oslo to learn the manufacturing of telephones and switchboards. He also worked as troubleman in Oslo, working on instruments. In 1890 he was made foreman and in 1891 began construction of the first long line in southern Norway."

"In those days each man furnished his own groceries and meals made along the road. Barns

273

and farm houses furnished lodging – and there was no bath or running water either. Plenty of fish were caught by the men after work and more than once the shovel was scraped clean and used as a frying pan."

"In 1896 Mr Hansen began construction of a line from Kongsberg ... to Numedal. ... The farmers in those parts were sceptical about being able to talk over a wire from one town to another."

"In 1900 Mr. Hansen left Norway for the United States, his parents having previously located here. Soon after his arrival in Madison he was employed by the Fuller and Johnson Company as electrician. ... July 1902, at which time he was employed by the Wisconsin Telephone Company as lineman. In 1907 he was made sub-foreman ..., and in 1909 he was made foreman in the state construction department which position he held until July, 1930, when he was appointed to his present position, that of city foreman at Madison."

Ben Hansen sent this picture to his family in Brandbu and wrote: This is my boys." Are this Ben Hansens sons?

Hans Gulbrandsen Koller

published February 2009   Form 802   *Eddie Goplin*

My great-great-grandfather Hans Gulbrandsen Collier was born July 29, 1828 at the Koller farm in Gran, Hadeland, Norway.

The Koller house in Gran, Norway was built in 1629 and Lars Kristianson Koller, born 1939, is the owner of the farm today and lives in the original farmhouse. Lars is the great-grandson of Lars Koller, a brother of my great-great-grandfather Hans G. Koller. The farm today contains the 1629

Hans and Gudbjor Koller

farmhouse, a modern barn and other out buildings, with a herd of 50 cows, hogs and a couple of riding horses.

Hans took the name Hans G. Collier after immigrating to the United States in 1850. Hans and his sister Marthe departed from Christiania (Oslo) on May 5, 1850 on the brig *Incognito* and arrived in New York on July 17. After traveling through Albany and on the Erie Canal to Buffalo, they traveled through the Great Lakes arriving at Milwaukee on July 30, 1850. From Milwaukee they traveled to Koshkonong, Wisconsin, found work there, and later moved on to the Mineral Point, Wisconsin area where he found employment and remained until purchasing from the government (homesteaded) 120 acres of land in Richwood Township, Richland County, Wisconsin in 1856. Hans and Gudbjor spent their entire lives on this farm and had six children. Their children were Gilbert, Caroline, Thomas, Andrew, Maria, and Anna. Shane and Cherit Dilley and family reside on this farm today. Shane is the great-great-great-grandson of Hans Collier.

Hans G. Koller married Gudbjor Harstira (Berg) in 1855. After clearing land and building a log cabin and farm buildings, Hans and his wife Gudbjor spent their entire lives farming. Hans

275

organized and helped build one of the first Norwegian-Danish Methodist Congregation churches in southern Wisconsin. Construction on the first log church began in 1858, but the Civil War took many of the men so the building was not completed until 1866. The second church was built in 1895.

Hans G. Collier was a very religious man who attended a Church Conference on September 13, 1857, and was given the privilege of being the leader of the church as a layman. He was a leader in song and church meetings and also officiated at funerals. His wife Gudbjor died July 2, 1894 and Hans died in 1909. They are buried together in the Richland M. E. Cemetery, Richwood Township, Richland County, Wisconsin.

The Hans Koller house in Richwood Township. The oldest part was built of log in 1864. Additions and restoration work have been done through the years. The original house was built in 1855 and was located south of this house. Photo taken in 2008.

In an early letter written by their son Andrew, he mentions that "mother and her cousin left Norway together," and that "she did not come on the same ship as father." Information from relatives of Hans in Norway list Gudbjor's maiden name as Berg; however, Hans' obituary states that her maiden name was Harstira. Her death certificate does not include her maiden name.

In 1997 my wife Cheryie and I visited the Koller farm in Gran and were thrilled to stay with the present owner, Lars Koller and his family, in the same farmhouse where my great-great-grandfather was born and raised. While there, we were rewarded with two letters that Hans wrote back to Norway in 1850 and 1852 from Wisconsin, telling of his trip to the United States and advice to relatives planning to come to the U.S.

Following is one of those letters, dated November 26, 1850. It was published in the *Årbok for Hadeland* in 1977 (pages 67-70). It was translated into English by the Koller family of Gran:

> Dear Mother and Siblings,
>
> I would like, after my long absence, to write you a few lines and tell you how we are at present. I thank God for being healthy and I enjoy life and feel well at the present time. I cannot forget how difficult it was to say goodbye to Mother, sister, brothers and good friends; it is so difficult that nobody will believe it until they experience it themselves. Dear Mother, we are so grateful for everything you did for us, from when you rocked us in the cradle until the time we said goodbye to you. And to our dear sister and brothers we are also thankful

for all the kindness and honor they showed us. We are also grateful to our ear relatives and our good neighbors for what they gave us and for all assistance and honor. During the night in our sleep we dream that we are playing with our brothers and sister as usual. I say many thanks to all of you for every day we were together.

We left Christiania (presently Oslo) May 5, 1850 on the brig *Incognito*. On May 9 we had so much adverse wind that something on the ship broke and we had to sail into the harbor at Mandal where we stayed until the 15th. On the 17th, Norway's national holiday, the weather was nice; we played and danced and the Captain gave us all punch, so it was delightful and joyful because almost all of us were in good health. On the 18th we reached the English channel between England and France where I dislocated my left arm. We still had contrary wind so we did not get out of the channel until the 27th, 9 days to travel only 90 Norwegian miles (about 550 American miles). It was cold which made it airy and refreshing on board the vessel, but the continuous west wind allowed us little progress. We didn't have good wind for 10 days; the supply of water started running low, so for 7 days we were given only two quarts of water daily, but as a whole our health continued good. Only one or two of the passengers were ill; except when the wind and the sea were heavy, then quite a few were sick, but not for a long time. On July 2 a woman from Ruen at Hadeland died (*Editor's note: Her name was Anne Olsdatter Elvestuen, born at Gullerudseiet in Brandbu.*)

On July 12 we caught sight of land, and we were all very happy, as we had not seen land since we last saw England, seven weeks earlier. But suddenly our delight turned into fright; at 10:00 in the evening a loaded schooner crashed into us with a terrible bang so I thought both had been smashed because they were traveling about 14 miles an hour, but thank God it went better than it appeared.

On July 13 at 2:00 in the afternoon our pilot came on board and then we anchored in New York harbor in the afternoon. There was much to look at, primarily all the multitude of ships from many nations and secondly the beautiful surrounding countryside. We left New York on July 17 and arrived at Albany on the 18th on a big steamer with 300 passengers. We left there the same day and started for Buffalo on a canal boat pulled by two horses. This canal, where several hundred boats go back and forth, greatly facilitates the traffic through the countryside. It is 364 miles long and connects the Great Lakes with the ocean. We came to Buffalo eight days later on the 26th and left that same night on a steamer to Meelvake (Milwaukee) arriving thre July 30 in the evening. From Buffalo to Milwaukee it is 900 miles. From New York to Milwaukee the cost of the ticket for each was $4 with 100 pounds of luggage free, that is for those 1,400 miles, but it is better to pay $7 from New York to Milwaukee and then have all luggage free. In all the crossing cost me a total of about $40.

We left Milwaukee August 1 and came to Korskenang (Koshkonong) on the 3rd, meeting a man there from western Norway by the name of Niels Gravum. There I got work for $10 a month. We have met our good friends Peder Paulsen Schiager, Hans Eid and the Hvattum girls, and everybody was so happy that you would hardly believe it! We were together three weeks and had a big celebration. Marthe and the Hvattum girls went to *Minrialpeint* (Mineral Point) which is about 60 miles further west.

I am able to inform you that we have a Norwegian pastor here, also a Norwegian school and free religion. The modern Latin script is used here most of the time, and I advise those who wish to go to America to learn to read that script, to practice writing and to take pains to study an English language book in order to be acquainted with the language of this country.

I can also tell you that after a year a worker here in America may have earned enough so that after paying for food and clothes a man can save or have an additional $85, and a woman $55. As far as I can see, young women who go to America are successful. But men must certainly work, and if you work much you earn much. I can more easily earn 1 ½ *speciedaler* ($1.50) here than I can earn one *mark* (25 cents) in Norway, and the accommodations are very good, as you may have heard. A person can acquire more land for 150 *speciedaler* ($150) here than in Norway for 1,000 *speciedaler* ($1000). I need not mention more about the fertility of the land, as already expressed in letters from others, it is very good.

*Hans and Gudbjor
in later years*

For the benefit of those who might like to make the voyage I shall summarize what a person needs to bring: three pounds of meat, one pound butter, one pound pork, 4 pounds flour, 12 liters oatmeal, 12 liters peas, 20 quarts milk, 20 quarts beer, six quarts whey, 20 eggs five pounds coffee, five pounds brown sugar, ½ pound tea, ½ pound raisins and good herring – it is used as a refreshment at sea. Also bring well-baked bread, half from barley, half from herbs; also a well-constructed chest for one's clothes and a more simple chest for storing food. Asa regards clothes, they are almost like those in Norway, with the addition of a *bongsjoerer* or a cut-away coat, which is often used here. Everyone must have good undergarments, for instance underwear, good mittens and good stockings because it is usually colder here than in Norway. Once ready for the voyage the main task is to get a good captain and a good ship. I would advise every passenger who goes to America not to get drunk in the city of New York. He must be careful with his money because I have discovered there are those who take advantage of immigrants and a person must not trust anybody.

When you come to Albany and are going on a canal boat you must not be on deck during the night, because many have been injured by the low bridges over the canal. When you arrive in Milwaukee it is usually not easy to get transport to Koshkonong, but there are

278

Norwegian people living in Milwaukee where you can leave your luggage. When you get transportation you must take it to *Korskenangs prerie* (Koshkonong Prairie) Staaten Wiille (?) in Wisconsin where I and several Norwegians live. Nobody should be afraid of the sea, it is not dangerous. It is more difficult to travel inland here. Greet Anders Ausland and others and tell them that no falsehoods are being written about America.

 To Hvattum – Dear Fosterparents (probably from the Hvattum girls)

 I will again send you some lines and tell you how we are at present. We thank God for being in good health and we are living very well. God only knows how much we have experienced and seen since we left our dear home. It is impossible for you to imagine. We have now worked half a year in a town called Russin (probably Racine) where we earn $1 a week. There we have many friends. Dear father and siblings, it is our highest wish to see Ingeborg at our side and she must bring all her Norwegian clothes, except her hat, because hats are not worn here and with this I will finish my letter with best greetings from us always and to the end and wishing you well.

 Graavum, November 26, 1850, Hans Gulbrandsen Koller

Children of Hans and Gudbjor:

1. Gilbert Collier, born in 1856 in Richwood Township, Richland County, Wisconsin, married Annie Paulson. In 1880 they resided at LaCrosse, Wisconsin. In 1900 they lived in Duluth, Minnesota. Gilbert had a photography business located at 2005 West Superior Street in the 1890s and early 1900s. In the 1900 census of St. Louis County, Ward 6, Duluth, under the name Callier I find Gilbert Callier, 44; Annie, 42; Lille M., 17; Austin C., 15; Elton R., 13; Alma S.,11; Florence D., 8. I have not been able to find any information on this family' however, I recall a adaughter by the name of Senora, wife of Pete Hanson, visiting my grandparents in the 1940s. Thora Collier, daughter of Thomas, wrote to me years ago that Gilbert and Annie had sons George, Austin and daughters Flora and Senora and she, Thora, visited them years ago in St. Paul. I have not been able to find any further information.

2. Caroline Collier, born in 1857 in Richwood Township. The 1880 census of Richland County lists her as 22 years old, living at home. In December 1883 she married Olous Olson from Viroqua, Wisconsin and he died a few years later. Caroline then moved to Iowa and married Will Ward in the Clear Lake area and together they had a daughter Esther. Soon after, Caroline died and is buried in the Clear Lake area. Esther as a small baby was not being well cared for and her Aunt Maria and Uncle Charles Hanson traveled to Iowa and brought Esther back with them and adopted and raised her as their daughter. The date of Caroline's death is unknown.

3. Thomas Collier was born in 1859 in Richwood Township. The 1880 census of Richland County shows that he is living at home, age 20, and a laborer. Thomas found

Hans Koller Family
Top: Caroline
Standing: Anna, Charles, Thomas, Maria
Seated: Gilbert and Hans

found employment with the railroad and moved to the Clear Lake area in Iowa, where he met and married Anna Ward. They lived in Clear Lake and he and Anna had two daughters: Thora, who never married; and Leona, who married Cluet Searles. They lived in Postville, Iowa. Leona and Cluet had three children: Joan, who married Keith Irvin; Dr. James C. Searles of Iowa City; and Richard M. Searles.

4. Andrew Collier was born in Richwood Township in 1862. The 1880 census records of Richland County show Andrew living at home, 18 years old. Soon after this he moved to Iowa and worked on the railroad, farmed, and did logging work. He married Mayme Callahan and they had one son, Charles, who died at an early age, location unknown. It is told that Mayme left Clear Lake with a group of cowboys and Andrew lived along for the rest of his life. He spent his last years in a nursing home in Mason City, Iowa, and is buried in Clear Lake.

5. Maria Collier, my great-grandmother, was born in Richwood Township on January 17, 1866. The 1880 census shows Maria, age 14, living at home. She married Charles Hanson on March 4, 1890, and they lived on the original Collier homestead until retiring and living in Blue River, Wisconsin. Charles and Maria had one daughter, Ethel, born May 30, 1891. She married Edwin Goplin. Edwin and Ethel resided on the Collier farm until their son Jesse Goplin took over the farm in 1937. Charles and Maria raised their biological niece Esther (daughter of Caroline) as their daughter. Esther married Hillman Goplin. Charles and Maria are buried in the Richland M. E. Cemetery, Richwood Township, Richland County, Wisconsin. Charles died in 1931 and Maria in 1945.

6. Anna Collier was born September 20, 1867 in Richwood Township. The 1880 census shows Anna, age 12, living at home. Anna married LeRoy S. Chitwood and together they had one son, Lloyd Chitwood. They were active in the United Brethren Church. Anna died of a breast ailment on January 9, 1899, and Leroy died December 25, 1922. They are buried in the Sand Prairie Cemetery, Richwood Township, Richland County, Wisconsin.

Thorstein Koller

published May 2012   *written by Maren Koller*
submitted by Eddie Goplin

The author is a daughter of Lars Koller and still resides on the Koller farm in Gran. This branch of the family remained in Norway.

Storekeeper Thorstein Koller and his wife Anna Erikine, born Hultin

Thorstein Gulbrandsen Koller was born at the farm Koller in Gran, rural district in Hadeland on 26 December 1836. The farm had then been in this family's property for more than 200 years. According to the old church books, the following persons were earlier owners:

- Halvor Koller, owner from about 1630 to about 1645 (main building today is said to have been built in 1629)
- Gulbrand Halvorsen Koller was born about 1642-44 and died about 1690, was married to Anne Larsdatter (family name unknown)
- Lars Gulbrandsen Koller was born about 1672. He first married Mari Hansdatter Bjørge, then Berthe Lukasdatter

281

Romholdt, born about 1686 and mother of Hans Larsen Koller
- Hans Larsen Koller, born in 1720, married Margrethe Thorsdatter Sorum in 1752
- Lars Hansen Koller, born 1755, married Maren Larsdatter Skjervum
- Gulbrand Larsen Koller, born 1790, married Anne Olsdatter Hvaleby in 1821

The book says that Gulbrand, grandfather Koller's father, did not take care of the farm. He went bankrupt and the whole farm (almost) was sold to strangers. When Gulbrand died in 1842, the widow Anne Olsdatter took over the ownership of the farm and, later, the oldest son, Lars Gulbrandsen. Since then, there have been two Koller farms. Lars became a very respected man and also was the headmaster in the Gran rural district. This grandchild's grandchild, Lars Kristianson Koller, born in 1939, is the owner of the farm today. Even though there was a sale in 1842, the farm is still quite large and very well taken care of with 50 cows and calves.

Grandfather Thorstein Koller was the second to the youngest of his six children when his father died. The other brothers and sisters were Lars, Hans, Ole, Marthe and Maren. Hans emigrated in 1850 to the U.S., together with his sister Marthe. After two or three years he bought land and built up his own farm in Wisconsin where the descendants still are living. At the Koller farm, there are two original, very detailed letters from him, written in 1850 and 1852, with Gothic handwriting. They contain strong invitations to his brothers and sisters to come over and settle down in the U.S. The writer tells what they should bring on the trip for their stay there and how they would travel. Grandfather Koller was about 15 years old when these letters came, but they must have made a very strong impression on him, because a couple of years later he too decided to emigrate. He went, unfortunately, only as far as to England. There he decided to go back to Norway again. He went then to Denmark to get an education, probably as a storekeeper. After awhile he came back to Christiania (now Oslo), where he got a job with the Gunerius Petterson Company, which was quite new at that time. This company is still going strong. He lived in the same house as Gunerius Petterson.

After awhile, grandfather took his most important things in a bag and walked to Trondheim, which then was a thriving city. This must have been in the late 1850s. He slept at farms on his way and had probably nothing with which to pay. He has told that at one place on the road, he got not only free bed and food, but also a silver penny as a goodbye present. Some years later, when he became a respectable man, he went back to these friendly people with a specially made box, with the silver penny in the top of it.

Grandfather had luck. After a couple of years, he became an owner (together with some other people) in a smaller tobacco company. For a long time it went very well, but most of the customers were from stores from northern Norway, and during an economic down period, many of them wouldn't pay their bills so the tobacco factory went bankrupt. He then became a tobacco dealer on Kongensgata 12 in Trondheim. He bought a house when he married grandmother about 1870, and they lived in that house until their deaths: September 15, 1926 and March 19, 1937.

Grandmother Koller – Anna Erikine – was born in Denmark. Her father, Gregers Hultin, baptized in Aalborg on May 8, 1807, came to Trondheim and established himself there as a wholesale merchant. According to an old genealogical table, done by the *Personal Historisk Institut* in Copenhagen, the family in Aalborg can be traced back 20-30 generations to the old Danish kings, with Gorm the Old and his son Harald Bluetooth at the beginning of the family tree. Every generation contains both men and women.

Gregers Hultin had two children with his first wife Christine (Danish), a daughter Anna Erikine (Grandmother) and a son Sofus. Sofus went to Haugesund and he has probably some descendants there. After Christine's death in 1857, Gregers married her sister Emilie, who died in 1859 after having a baby, their daughter Kristine. Kristine's son Hermik Urbye, was an engineer and followed his uncle Thorvald Lind's footsteps as a leading engineer in Lillehammer.

Gregers Hultin was a hardware wholesale merchant in a building which he sold in 1879 to the bank of Trondheim. They were going to tear it down and rebuild a new building for a bank. The old building was called *Gamle Altona* and was built at the top of the ruins of the Gregorius Church. Grandmother Koller has said that she as a child used to play in the basement of the church, which her father used as a storage room for his goods. Many of the storekeepers in Trondheim at that time used to travel once a year to northern Norway with their goods. Grandmother Koller had many interesting stories to tell about these trips. Her father used to hire a bigger sailboat and fill it with goods and brought the whole family north and visited many places where they were always welcome.

Let me now tell you a bit about the Gregorius Church, which has a very interesting story. King Magnus the Good, Olav Haraldsson's son, built the Olavs Church about 1040. Close to the church he built himself a stone castle with a large hall. Harald Hårdråde, Olav Haraldsson's half-brother, became king together with and after Magnus from 1040 to 1066. He built his own castle and gave Magnus' castle to the clergy, who made it into a church and dedicated it to St. Gregorius. The Gregorius Church was used until the big city fire in the 16th century. It was in the cellar vault of that building where Grandmother Koller played as a child.

Grandfather and Grandmother Koller were married in 1871 or early in 1872. He was then 31 years old and she was 19 years old (born December 1852). Grandfather Koller, when young, was a very good cross-country skier and an avid outdoorsman. He was very interested in politics; he belonged to the liberal side and was very active against the conservative side. He was known personally and communicated with many politically liberal people.

When Grandmother Koller celebrated her 80th birthday in 1932 and also at the time of her death in 1937, there were long articles written about her in the newspapers in Trondheim. It says there that "smiling and friendly, Mrs. Koller wished the big family and their many, many friends welcome. They liked music and talked a lot about the political work at that time. Through her whole life, she was a beaming person and she loved everybody." Even though she was of Danish origin, she was very active in the use of the Norwegian language. She was even a special member in the local *Mållag* for those who wished a pure Norwegian language, not a language with Danish vocabulary and spelling. She was also a strict teetotaler.

Grandfather and Grandmother Koller had 10 children. Their names were: Kristine, Gudrun, Aagot, Einar, Reidar, Ottar, Thorleif, Erling, Hjørdis and Reidun.

Photo on the left shows Eddie and Cheryie Goplin in 1997, standing next to the tombstone of Thorstein and Anna Koller by the Nidaros Cathedral in Trondheim, Norway. Photo on the right is a detail of the tombstone inscription

Hans Lagesen

published May 2009　　　　　　*Form 452*　　　　　　*Harland Anderson*

Hans Lagesen (Henry Anderson) and Rasmine Christensen

Lage Iversen and Berte Hansdatter signed out of Jevnaker parish, Hadeland on April 8, 1854 to go to America. They were living as *husmand* folk on the farm Kingeie. Their children were

1. Marte, born Jan. 18, 1837, Haldum farm, Lunner, Jevnaker parish
2. Hans, born June 15, 1839, Haldum farm
3. Iver, born Dec. 25, 1842, Haldum farm
4. Gjertrud, born June 13, 1848, Tronderud farm, Jevnaker parish.

Lage Iversen was born on Halvorsrud farm and baptized Aug. 25, 1800, Jevnaker parish. His father was Iver Hansen, born in 1758, Jevnaker, Hadeland. His mother was Marte Andersdatter, born in 1763.

Lage was married on Dec. 27, 1834 to the maiden Berte Hansdatter, born Oct. 13, 1811 on Rya farm, Lunner. Her father was Hans Rolfsen, baptized June 3, 1759, born in Lunner,

Jevnaker parish. Her mother was Gjertrud Helgesdatter, born in 1776 in Lunner, Jevnaker parish. Lage and Berte were both living on the Balangrud farm, Lunner, Jevnaker parish, Hadeland.

The family of Iver Lagesen was found in La Fayette County, Wisconsin, farmers in the 1860 federal census. In the 1860 census in Fayette, La Fayette County the family was missing the eldest daughter Martha (Marte). She married a Mr. Wilkins from Scotland around 1874 and by 1880 was living in Norway township, Humboldt County, Iowa with her brother, Hans (Henry Anderson). She was a widow with two children born in Wisconsin: a boy born in 1875 and a girl born in 1878. Nothing more is known about Martha Wilkins or her children.

By 1861 the family became known as Andersons. Hans (Henry Anderson) enlisted in the army in Co. H, 3rd Regiment of Wisconsin at Darlington, La Fayette County, Wis. on June 2, 1861. Henry was discharged from the service July 10, 1862 by reason of an accidental gunshot wound to his hand. He was granted $10 a month invalid pension.

On Aug. 20, 1862, Iver (Edward Anderson) enlisted at Fayette, Wis., mustered on Oct. 9, 1862 in 31st Wisconsin infantry. He died of disease at Columbus, Kentucky on May 16, 1863. He is buried in Mound City National Cemetery, Grave 1553, Section C, Mound City, Ill. His original place of burial was Columbus, Kentucky.

Henry Anderson's father Lage Iversen died in 1865 in La Fayette County, Wis. age 65. Henry lived in La Fayette County, Wis. until 1869, then moved to Fort

Henry Anderson in the Civil War

Dodge, Iowa until 1875. After that he lived in Norway Township, Humboldt County, Iowa. His mother Berte Hansdatter went to Iowa with Henry Anderson. She was with him until her death in 1883.

By 1874 Gjertrud (Julia) married a widower, Martin Thompson. Martin Thompson (Torstensen) was born June 24, 1839 in Gjefseneiet, Gran, Hadeland, Norway. He married Birthe Olsdatter on Dec. 12, 1864. She was born June 16, 1841 in Braastadeiet, Lunner, Hadeland. They had two children, Maria, born Dec. 10, 1865 and Ole, born March 9, 1868.

Gjertrud (Julia) and Martin had eight children:

1. Lena, born 1875

2. Theodore, born 1877
3. Frederick, born 1879
4. Benjamin, born 1882
5. Mabel, born 1885
6. Jessie, born 1887
7. Arthur, born 1889
8. Clarence, born 1892

Martin was a stone mason and moved around. The first two children were born in Webster County, Iowa (probably in Fort Dodge near Henry Anderson and Berte Hansdatter), the next two in Minneapolis, Minnesota; the next two in Humboldt County, Iowa (same county as Henry Anderson); the last two in Wright County, Iowa, probably Eagle Grove (not far from Henry Anderson's farm near Goldfield, Iowa).

Julia died in 1898 and Martin Thompson later. They were buried in the Eagle Grove Cemetery.

On July 23, 1882 Henry Anderson married Rasmine Christensen, an immigrant from Denmark in Humboldt County, Iowa. Rasmine was born Oct. 7, 1858 in Humle, Langeland, Denmark.

On Jan. 23, 1883, Berte Hansdatter, Henry Anderson's mother, died. She was buried in the Ullensvang Cemetery, Thor, Iowa. Three of Henry and Rasmine's children who died in infancy were buried in the same cemetery plot.

Henry and Rasmine's children
Back: John Alfred and Karoline Emily
Front: Louise Kristine, Minnie Helena, Jenny Sorena

287

Henry and Rasmine had five children that lived to adulthood:
1. Louise Kristine, April 12, 1883-Oct. 7, 1977, was my grandmother
2. Jenny Sorena, Dec. 14, 1884-June 20, 1964
3. Karoline Emily, March 4, 1886-Oct. 28, 1968
4. John Alfred, Jan. 4, 1891-Dec. 3, 1972
5. Minnie Helena, Dec. 16, 1898-Jan. 6, 1985

Little Hilda Marie was born on April 23, 1895 and died on February 19, 1896. Three infants whose names are not known died: January 18, 1888, November 26, 1888, and December 13, 1889.

At about the same time Henry and Rasmine were married, Rasmine's widowed mother, Jensine Larsen, immigrant from Denmark, married Søren Madsen, a cousin of her first husband Christen Jørgensen who farmed near Thor, Humboldt County, Iowa. Henry and Rasmine lived near them and worked for Grandpa Madsen. In the spring of 1889 they moved to the Victor Gilbertson place. Then in the spring of 1890 they moved back to the little house by Grandpa Madsen. That spring Henry got his back Army pension which had been delayed because Henry had no proof of his age, forgot that they had changed their name to Anderson, so the Census records were of no help. With his back pay Henry bought an unimproved 80 acres from Henry Stoakes near Goldfield, Humboldt County, Iowa. They moved the little house from Grandpa Madsen's farm to the 80 acres. He was receiving $50 a month pension when he died in 1922.

When Rasmine died on Christmas Day 1898 (just nine days after the birth of Minnie Helena), my grandmother Louise Anderson's cousin, Juliane Martine Christensen Cody (Mattie), stayed with them for six weeks. She had three boys and while she was helping, all eight children got the measles. From then on Grandma Louise, who was only 16 years old, took over and did the best she could with the new baby.

Henry married again in February 1900. She was Knut Anderson's widow, Martha Peterson, with three of her own children, Peter, Herman and Ellen Anderson.

On May 7, 1901 Louise Anderson married Herman Anderson. Herman was at that time her step-brother, the son of Martha Peterson and Knut Anderson. Henry Anderson, my grandmother Louise's father, married my grandfather Herman Anderson's mother.

Henry Anderson died on Nov. 17, 1922. He was buried in Goldfield, Iowa.

Index by First Name

This index spans both volume one and volume two of the "Our Hadeland Ancestors" collection. Page numbers for volume two begin with 289.

Where only a first name appears in the text, if discernible an appropriate patronymic and/or surname has been added to the index to assist with identification.

Norwegian immigrants were unfamiliar with the idea of last name as family name. In Norway the third name was the name of the farm on which the individual resided; if residence changed, so did the 'last' name. This, coupled with a desire to Americanize both first and last names, meant that most immigrants tried out a variety of names and spellings before settling on a permanent moniker. Variations in spelling and alternative names that appear in the text are all included in this index.

This index is available to the public in the 'Resources' section of the Hadeland Lag website, www.hadelandlag.org

Fred W Wolf 365
Fred Wooldridge 401
Fred Yoss 376
Frederich J Schroater,Captain 416
Frederick Begert 339
Frederick Edward Inglett 527
Frederick Lafflin 97
Frederick Thompson 287
Frederick Tildman Erickson Korson
    564
Fredrick Foss 565
Fredrick Olson 408
Fredrick Raastad 103
Fredrick Sherva 408
Fredrik Larsen Nerengen 551
Fritjof Halbakken 196
G A Dahl 548
G O Brørby,Mrs 304
G Rostad 548
G T Hoff 486
Gabriel Gabrielson 104
Gabriel O Lee 443
Gabriel Oddsen 236
Gabriel Olsen 236
Gabriel Paulson Falla 548
Gail Baker 353
Gambler Thompson 401
Garfield Oluf Fjeld 565
Garfield Plomasen 180,181,184
Gary Jordheim 224
Gaulik Mona,Pastor 349
Gaylene Nelson 481
Gaylord Milo Swingen 448
Gea Johnson 201
Gena Hanson 294
Gena Josephine Wamstad 579
Gena Larson 507
Gena Pedersen 446
Gene Haugen,Mrs 292
General Grant 561
General Hood 566
General Jackson 561
General Price 566
General Sherman 561
Geneva Lillian Wahl 130
George Arlandson 364
George Bredesen 75
George Collier 279
George Dewey Davis 564
George Edwin Erickson 444
George Gilbert Gulbrand
    Gulbrandsen Vinger 569-570
George Gilbertson 417

George Gunderson 358
George H Thomas,Gen 265
George Håkenstad 92
George James Dean 455
George Krenos 384
George Martinson 577
George McAuliff 377,381,383
George Nikolai Harrison 339
George Olsen 535
George Pederson 578
George Petersen 85,86
George Rognstad 85,86
George Simmons,Mrs 241
George Swanson 481
George Tilberg 480,481
George Troe,Mrs 537
George Washington McAuliff 382
George Watkins 579
George Wilford Arlandson 364
Georgia Gunderson 359
Georgia Wamstad 464
Georgianna Gunderson 359
Gerald E Gilbertson 454
Gerald Alexander Grover 158,255
Gerald Julian Paulson 443
Geraldeen Haga Rude 406
Gertie Halbakken 47
Gertie Hanson 454
Gertie Johansdtr 369
Gertrud Weflen 86
Gertrude Stene 537
Ghorer Jensen 336
Giertrud Jonsdtr Svendsbratten 200
Gifford Palmer Paulson 443
Gil Bjone 425
Gilbert Anderson 40,547,563-564
Gilbert Bjone 424-426
Gilbert Blegen 174,547
Gilbert Brynsaas-Gilbertson 6
Gilbert Buraas 148
Gilbert Callier 279
Gilbert Collier 275,279
Gilbert Dihle 291
Gilbert Gilbertson 344,345,440,
    441,442,447,448,502,507
Gilbert Gilson 549
Gilbert Gribble 563
Gilbert Gundersen 422,505
Gilbert H Nass 549
Gilbert Haga 47
Gilbert Hilden 99,161
Gilbert Hilden,Mrs 153
Gilbert Holverson 456

Gilbert Hovland 17
Gilbert Jerve 488,507
Gilbert Jorve 505,506
Gilbert Kristofferson 547
Gilbert L Ostlie 149
Gilbert Lee 298,302
Gilbert Lia 399,401
Gilbert Monson 552
Gilbert Nelson 147
Gilbert Nelson,Mrs 537
Gilbert O Gilbertson 131
Gilbert O Melaas 552
Gilbert Ostlie 146
Gilbert Paulson 553
Gilbert Peterson 186
Gilbert Siebecker 235
Gilbert Thompson 451
Gilbert Thornason 444
Gilbert Ulrikson 144
Gilbert Vinger 549
Gilbrand Jerve 491
Gilfred Justus Lynne 487
Gillis Gulbrandson 465
Gilman Morstad 304,305,577
Gilman Topper 448
Gilman W Ruud 578
Gina B Paulson 442
Gina Beate Bredesen 75
Gina Bertina Paulson 443
Gina Brørby Stadum 310,311,312
Gina Gullheim 113
Gina Hansdtr 296
Gina Iversdtr Eggebratten 445
Gina Larson 384,386
Gina Otilda Brørby 308,309
Gjerdie Hagen Johnson 291
Gjertrud Hansen 285
Gjertrud Helgesdtr 285
Gjertrud Julsdtr Heggen 171
Gjertrud Olsdtr Toso 40
Gjertrud Olson 544
Gjertrud Thompson 286
Gjertrud Toso 125
Gjøri Bottoldsdtr Bygvik 485
Gjori Nelson 23
Gjori Torstenson 20
Gladys Florence Lee 444
Gladys Irene Gilbertson 131
Gladys Johnson 411
Gladys Marie Christianson 487
Gladys Marjory Wek 321
Gladys Opal Torgerson 369
Glen Ruel Anderson 183

Helge Hanson Stadum 578
Helge Johnson 183
Helger Iverson 151
Hellene Western 204
Helma Falla 491
Helma Hilden Nordstrom 567
Helmar Julias Lee 445
Helmar W Hoff 576
Helmer Fensand 514
Helmer Gilbertson 83
Helmer Halvorson 456
Helmer Hjermstad 47
Helmer Sundblad 130,289
Helvig Olsdtr Askimeie 79
Henrietta Peterson 363
Henrietta Wamstad 468
Henriette LeDuc 360,361
Henrik Larsen 511
Henry Adolph Jenson 513
Henry Anderson 286,287,288
Henry Augustin Anderson 545
Henry Bakken 134
Henry Blegen 174
Henry Brynsaas 7
Henry Daehlin 532
Henry Delano Hendrickson 454
Henry Edward Emberson 564
Henry Flaten 565
Henry Gilbert Western 203
Henry Gilbertson 342,343,345
Henry Grinaker 218,223
Henry Halvorson 456,457
Henry Halvorson,Mrs 304
Henry Hendrickson 452,454,512
Henry Iverson,Mrs 292
Henry Jackson 373,375
Henry Johnson 535
Henry Larson 507
Henry Leander Orstad 126
Henry Lia 401
Henry M Ulvick 579
Henry Melvin Harrison 340
Henry Melvin Wahl 130
Henry Olson 556,558
Henry Oscar Johnson 201
Henry Oscar Nelson 577
Henry Oschar Johnson 202
Henry P Hanson 293-297
Henry Paulsrud 154
Henry Pedersen Jackson 372
Henry Peterson Smerud 296
Henry Samuel Bakken 133,134
Henry Sather 262

Henry Shurtliff 121
Henry Stoakes 288
Henry Svaleson 481
Henry Wamstad 467
Herbert A Moe 577
Herbert Janson 481
Herby Wooldridge 400
Herman A Preus,Pastor 234
Herman Anderson 288
Herman Bang 164
Herman Gulbrandson 144
Herman Gulden 105
Herman H Buraas 148
Herman Hanson 374
Herman Heinz 138
Herman Johnson 576
Herman Klemesrud 470
Herman Knudsen Klemesrud 470
Herman Lund 118
Herman M Knudson 576
Herman M Ostlie 148
Herman Monte 375
Herman Ulrikson 144
Hermana Lund 118
Hermik Urbye 283
Hilda A Pederson 120
Hilda Aanes 146
Hilda Andrine Wahl 130
Hilda Grinaker 218,223
Hilda Halvorson 271,272
Hilda Hanson 144
Hilda Johanna Larson 126
Hilda Jorve 504
Hilda Larson 125
Hilda Marie Anderson 288
Hilda Marie Gilbertson 131
Hilda Ohe 46,47
Hilda Ostlie 139,146,149
Hilda Paulson Olson 478
Hilda Wahl 130
Hillman Goplin 280
Hilma Haakenstad 437
Hilma Haug 162
Hilmer Clifford Kjos 478
Hiram Butler Munger 120
Hjalmar Peder Oldin 240
Hjalmer Daehlen 66
Hjalmer Gulden 105
Hjalmer Johnson 535
Hjalmer Melom 246
Hjalmer Peter Thronson 446
Hjalmer Thoreson 394
Hjelmar Gulden 105

Hjelmer Jenson 513
Hjørdis Koller 284
Hjoren Olsdtr Haugen 15,17
Hoie Harrison 339
Hølje Stenersen 339
Holley Leonard Allerson 126
Horatio G Morse,Dr 121
Howard Ansel Paulson 443
Howard Christopherson 126
Howard Larson 507
Howard Lien 453
Howard M Hendrickson 575
Howard Orville Munger 120
Howard Thronson 446
Howard Wesley Wilson 545
Howard William Melbostad 446
Hugh Nelson,Dr 359
Hulda Thorson 247
I S Olson,Rev 188
Ida Amelia Kjos 475
Ida B Lowe Sorum 98,100
Ida Caroline Hovland Sommerness 24
Ida Foster 526
Ida Galene Gilbertson 131
Ida Halvorson 245,271
Ida Husby Wevik 191,194
Ida Johnson 202,534
Ida Joseph.Morstad Halvorson 304
Ida Kjos 474
Ida Laumb 514
Ida Louis Larson 174
Ida Lowe Sorum 96
Ida Lunder 31,434,435
Ida M Moen 249
Ida Manvella Scott 423
Ida Mathilda Bakken 134
Ida Mathison Haakenstad 437-439
Ida Matilda Bakken 133
Ida May Lund 447
Ida McCleary 452
Ida Melander 76
Ida Melia Pedersen 446
Ida Morstad Halvorson 305
Ida N Kjos 475
Ida Oe 44
Ida Ohe 48
Ida Pedersen 445
Ida Romsos 432
Ida Samuelson Self 290
Ida Stadum 309,310
Ida Thompson 449,450
Ida Victoria Johnson 545

I-17

Ivar Pederson 454
Ive Lutken 66
Iver Andersen Rokeneiet 473
Iver Arthur Thorson 579
Iver Bakken 549
Iver Brorby 45
Iver Brørby 308
Iver Christiansen Moen 248-251
Iver Egge 233
Iver Eggebraatten 445
Iver Fossen 131
Iver Gamme 3
Iver Grina 45
Iver Gundersen 505
Iver Guttormsen 549
Iver Haakenstad 431,432,437-439
Iver Halbakken 196,199
Iver Hallum 292
Iver Halvorsen Kanten 150-151,155
Iver Hansen 285
Iver Hansen Molden 132
Iver Herman Alm 157
Iver I Moen 249
Iver Iversen 151,171
Iver Iverson 151
Iver Jacobsen Sorlie 550
Iver Jacobsen-Røykeneie 171
Iver Jensen 530
Iver Johansen 551
Iver Johansen Morstad 238
Iver Johnson 48
Iver Jørgensen Brørby 47
Iver Kjos 472,478,481
Iver Lagesen 285,286
Iver Larsen 325
Iver Lyseneiet 233
Iver Martinus Thingelstad 50,148
Iver Molden 131,132
Iver Morstad 304
Iver O Grina 290
Iver Oleson 553
Iver Olsen 553
Iver Olsen Allergodt 233
Iver Olsen Drøvdalseiet 235
Iver Olsen Grina 47
Iver Pedersen 244,446
Iver Pederson 440,441
Iver Pederson Blegeneiet 445
Iver Pederson Lynsenseiet 233
Iver Peterson 85,86
Iver Ruden 292
Iver Steffansen 474
Iver Svingen 330

Iver Thingelstad 51,52
Iver Tingelstad 235
Iver Trondsen 504
J Andriasen 193
J H Nelson 297
J Hvattum 45
J K Hertsgaard 35
J Krohn,Pastor 521
Jack Hartley Sr 477
Jack Wooldridge 400
Jackie Grinaker Nichols 226
Jacob A Farmen 544
Jacob Brorby 408
Jacob E Milsten 478,479
Jacob Froiland 400
Jacob Grinager 69
Jacob Hans Ostlie 148
Jacob Ingebretsen Allergodt 235
Jacob Iversen 171
Jacob Jacobsen 551
Jacob Jensen 171
Jacob Larsen Noklebye 60
Jacob Laumb 491
Jacob Lofsvold 85
Jacob Lynne 374
Jacob Mathison 438
Jacob Milsten 475
Jacob Moldstadkvern 213
Jacob Nelson 568
Jacob Nielsen 568
Jacob Nielsen Nyhus 567-568
Jacob Nilsen Nyhus 552
Jacob Nokleby 488,491
Jacob Nøkleby 492
Jacob Olsen 60
Jacob Pedersen Grinager 70
Jacob Pederson 143
Jacob Rosholt,Rev 30
Jacob Steffensen 200
Jacqueline Fryhling 362
J'aime Brianna Schau 76
Jakob Bjerke 35
Jalmer Melvin Vane 544
James C Searles,Dr 280
James Campbell 235
James Carlin Dvergsten 574
James Edmond Franklin 544
James F Rasmussen 457
James Gilbertson 83,453
James H Campbell 235
James Ingram 121
James Johnson 104
James Jones 162

James Meyer 341
James Nelson 481
James Olson 557
James P Vane 544-546
James Ruden 292
James Skrove 158
James Sorenson 481
James Stedman,Gen 265
James Theodore Plomasen 183
Jan Olsen 2
Jane Ellen Plomasen 183
Jane Grinager Brown 67,70
Jane Kjos 477
Jane Lewis 381
Jane Lewissen 381
Jane Marie Pedersen 446
Jane McAuliff 377
Jane Plomasen 182
Janet Buness 481
Janet Buness Dreyer 481
Janet M Nelson 126
Janice Johnson 528
Janna Gilbertson 389
Janna Kjørven 319
Jarle Foss 318
Jason Geddes 121
Jay Gilbertson 83
Jean Francis Resvick 121
Jean Ronning 2
Jeanette Margaretta Bourdeaux
    Bowser 361
Jeanette Mellum 47
Jeanne Alm Jensen 157
Jeanne Cardinal Reiter 341
Jeanne Plomasen 180
Jeanne Thora Plomasen 178
Jeannetta Marie Pierce 485
Jed Gilbertson 83
Jennie Elvina Paulson 443
Jennie Mathilda Larson 125,126
Jennie Melom 246
Jennie Rekstad 159,162,164
Jenny Barber 76
Jenny Sorena Anderson 288
Jens Bale,Rev 34
Jens Ellingsen 509,513
Jens Gaardsrud 373
Jens Gilbertson 488,489,491
Jens Gulbrandsen 493
Jens Hoff 92
Jens Ingwell Finnerud 413-415
Jens Jackson 373
Jens Jensen 529,530

www.ingramcontent.com/pod-product-compliance
Lightning Source LLC
Chambersburg PA
CBHW080228270326
41926CB00020B/4182